International and Language Education for a Global Future

Fifty Years of U.S. Title VI and Fulbright-Hays Programs

David S. Wiley and Robert S. Glew, editors

Michigan State University Press

East Lansing

♾ The paper used in this publication meets the minimum requirements
of ANSI/NISO Z39.48–1992 (R 1997) (Permanence of Paper).

Publication of this volume was made possible by support from the U.S.
Department of Education, International Education Programs Service.

Michigan State University Press
East Lansing, Michigan 48823-5245

Printed and bound in the United States of America.

17 16 15 14 13 12 11 10   1 2 3 4 5 6 7 8 9 10

LIBRARY OF CONGRESS CATALOGING-IN-PUBLICATION DATA

International and language education for a global future : fifty years of U.S. Title VI and Fulbright-Hays programs / David
S. Wiley and Robert S. Glew, editors.
    p. cm.
  Includes bibliographical references and index.
  ISBN 978-0-87013-984-0 (alk. paper)
 1.   International education—United States. 2.   Languages, Modern—Study and teaching (Higher) 3.   Foreign
study—United States. 4.   Fulbright scholarships. 5.   Federal aid to higher education—United States. 6.   Education
and globalization. I. Wiley, David, 1935- II. Glew, Robert S.
  LC1090.I546 2010
  370.116—dc22

                                                                                      2010021398

Book and cover design by Sharp Des!gns, Inc., Lansing, MI

Michigan State University Press is a member of the Green Press Initiative and is committed
to developing and encouraging ecologically responsible publishing practices. For more information about the Green Press Initiative and the use of recycled paper in book publishing,
please visit www.greenpressinitiative.org.

Visit Michigan State University Press on the World Wide Web at www.msu.edu/msupress

Contents

PART 3. THE HISTORY AND SIGNIFICANCE OF THE PROGRAMS OF TITLE VI HIGHER EDUCATION ACT

PART 4. INTERNATIONALIZING HIGHER EDUCATION AND TITLE VI PROGRAMS

PART 5. GLOBAL COMPETITIVENESS

PART 6. ACCESSING, BENCHMARKING, AND ASSESSING TITLE VI

PART 7. FUTURE DIRECTIONS FOR TITLE VI AND FULBRIGHT-HAYS PROGRAMS

Acknowledgments

The editors acknowledge the many individuals who contributed to the success of the Title VI 50th Anniversary Conference and publication of this volume. We have appreciated the continued interest and support for Title VI programs from Lou Anna K. Simon, President of Michigan State University (MSU); Provost Kim Wilcox; and, Jeffrey Riedinger, Dean of International Studies and Programs. The support of senior administrators, at MSU as at universities across the country, is crucial to the internationalization of American higher education and institutional participation in the constellation of U.S. Department of Education international programs. The national advisory committee members for the conference provided critical input throughout the planning process, including development of the conference program and selection of the invited speakers for the conference. The invited speakers, most of whose essays are represented in this book, addressed key themes that formed the core of the conference program. We also acknowledge the significant contributions of the plenary panelists who stimulated lively conversations on current issues, future directions, and the advancement of international education. The planning team from Michigan State University's Center for Advanced Study of International Development and Center for International Business Education and Research provided invaluable assistance during all phases of planning for the Title VI 50th Anniversary Conference.

In addition, we received valuable suggestions on content for the conference from our colleagues at the U.S. Department of Education's International Education Programs Service, including the director, Richard LaPointe, as well as senior program staff Sylvia Crowder, Sam Eisen, Steve Pappas, and Karla Ver Bryck Block. We also appreciated the thoughtful feedback we received from program staff, including Peter Baker, Christine Corey, Cynthia Dudzinski, Susana Easton, Cheryl Gibbs, Tanyelle Richardson, and Amy Wilson.

The editors also express their gratitude to Marita Eibl, Breanne Grace, and Christine Root for assisting with final preparation of the manuscript, as well as to Stephen Backman and Christian Reed for assembling the data on the less commonly taught languages in Appendix E. Helen Farr and Kim Rector provided clerical support to the planning team. Finally, thank you to Miriam Kazanjian of the Coalition on International Education for providing data on the history of the appropriations for the Title VI programs.

Conference Organizers

Robert S. Glew, Michigan State University

Tomas Hult, Michigan State University

National Advisory Committee

Melissa Birch, University of Kansas

Craig Calhoun, Social Science Research Council, New York University

Darryl Crompton, Institute for International Public Policy

Gilbert W. Merkx, Duke University

Patrick O'Meara, Indiana University

Jeffrey Riedinger (convener), Michigan State University

Richard Schmidt, University of Hawaii

Sara Tully, University of Wisconsin-Milwaukee

Elizabeth Welles, The Council of American Overseas Research Centers (consultant)

Anand A. Yang, University of Washington

Karla Ver Bryck Block, ex officio, International Education Programs Service, U.S. Department of Education

Keynote Speaker

The Honorable Madeleine K. Albright

Plenary Panelists

Robert Berdhal, President, Association of American Universities

Gene Block, Chancellor, University of California, Los Angeles

Maureen Budetti, Director of Student Aid Policy, National Association of Independent Colleges and Universities

Craig Calhoun (moderator), President, Social Science Research Council and Professor, New York University

Constantine Curris, President, American Association of State Colleges and Universities

Mark Gearan, President, Hobart and William Smith Colleges

Madeleine Green, American Council on Education

Peter McPherson, President, Association of Public and Land-Grant Universities

Jeffrey Riedinger (moderator), Dean, International Studies and Programs, Michigan State University

Kim Wilcox, Provost and Vice President for Academic Affairs, Michigan State University

Conference Planning Team

Ronda Bunnell, Michigan State University

Marita Eibl, Michigan State University

Irem Kiyak, Michigan State University

Tunga Kiyak, Michigan State University

Lynn Lee, Michigan State University

Michael Reed, Michigan State University

Introduction: Seeking Global Competence through the Title VI and Fulbright-Hays Acts

David S. Wiley

The chapters in this volume result from the conference[1] in March 2009 to celebrate the fiftieth anniversary of the Title VI Programs of the Higher Education Opportunity Act[2] with the associated Fulbright-Hays programs. Congress and multiple administrations have continued support of these programs for half a century to maintain a remarkably stable focus on building more than 100 centers of excellence for modern foreign language and area studies education in more than fifty leading U.S. universities. To support that core effort, over the next three decades through the 1980s, Congress added several programs and expanded the mandates to include International Researach and Studies (IRS), Undergraduate International Studies and Foreign Language Program (UISFL), Language Resource Centers (LRCs), Business and International Education (BIE) and Centers for International Business Education (CIBEs), American Overseas Research Centers (AORCs), the Institute for International Public Policy (IIPP), and the Technological Innovation and Cooperation for Foreign Information Access (TICFIA) Program. (The purposes and work of each of these are described in Appendix A.)

In this introduction, we review some of the history of the Title VI programs, including the spirit of the moment of their founding during the Cold War and the twentieth-century context for their directions. Various essays in this volume

1

address the changing character of the programs and new directions to consider in light of new needs and the maturing of the programs.

Year after year, these centers, usually providing a 4:1 (sometimes 10:1) match of university to federal funds, have built the foundation of America's intellectual effort to comprehend the new global world of the twentieth and twenty-first centuries. They have conducted research on internationalizing the American university, built the corpus of language learning materials for use in college and government, improved language learning pedagogies, erected the most distinguished U.S. library holdings on foreign regions, supported indepth research abroad in virtually every nation, and created capacity to teach 200 less commonly taught languages (LCTLs). Elaine Tarone's chapter provides a broad overview of Title VI accomplishments in the LCTLs in the National Resource Centers (NRCs), LRCs, and Foreign Language and Area Studies (FLAS) programs, affecting a range of learners from K-12 students to PhD candidates.

In addition, these centers have brought new seriousness to the service or outreach mission of their agendas, offering language and area expertise to the K-12 and college communities, state and federal governments, businesses, and the media. To cope with the globalizing world, these centers do not teach insularly about customs of isolated peoples and cultures but rather teach about societies in a globalizing Africa, Asia, Latin America, and more cast in a context of global change in economics, politics, society, and communications.

The MA, PhD, LLB, MBA, and other graduates of these programs have provided the core of American faculties outside the Title VI centers that have the language capacities to work abroad in and teach expertly about China, Russia, Brazil, India, Pakistan, Japan, Syria, Hungary, Afghanistan, Iran, Ethiopia, Somalia, Mexico, Zimbabwe, and many other countries.

In 2009, the celebration of these programs was occasioned by a nearly unanimous and bipartisan agreement nationally, as voiced by Senators Richard G. Lugar and Christopher J. Dodd, that

> Title VI and the Fulbright-Hays programs have had a tremendous impact on our nation over the years by developing a strong foundation in international education, research and foreign language studies, especially in less-commonly taught languages that may be of U.S. strategic interest. These programs continue to be an integral part of our cultural diplomacy.[3]

Similarly, in March 2009, U.S. Secretary of State Clinton wrote that

> . . . In tandem, Title VI programs and their Fulbright-Hays overseas counterparts have proven essential tools for developing and maintaining international expertise among American students and educators. By combining opportunities for overseas study and

resarch with domestic programs aimed at foreign language instruction and area expertise, they have helped generations of Americans seize oppportunities and confront challenges on the ever-changing world stage. From the Cold War era to the current day, these programs have been essential for expanding the importance of international expertise to all aspects of modern life, from trade and technology, to healthcare delivery and national security.[4]

The full statements by Secretary Clinton and Senators Lugar and Dodd can be seen on the web site of the Coalition on International Education and the American Council on Education, Engaging the World: U.S. Global Competence for the 21st Century (www.usglobalcompetence.org).

Sputnik and Beyond

President Eisenhower, Congress, and indeed the American people were startled into a new consciousness of the globalizing world on October 4, 1957, as the 184-pound, beach ball-sized Soviet Sputnik glittered across the American night sky and beeped its radio signals to celebrate that International Geophysical Year.[5] The widely remembered "Sputnik Response" of accelerating the space race and the science and education races to compete with the Soviets and their Eastern bloc resulted in passing Title VI of the National Defense Education Act (NDEA). This was a broad act focusing on developing "highly trained individuals . . . to help America compete with the Soviet Union in scientific and technical fields, . . . including support for loans to college students, the improvement of science, mathematics, and foreign language instruction in elementary and secondary schools, graduate fellowships, foreign language and area studies, and vocational-technical training."[6]

To American leaders, Sputnik was an unambiguous signal from the Soviets of their intention to be a geopolitical leader in the postcolonial world. As self-determination and independence grew across the nations of the South, the European colonial powers were losing control and could not guarantee either access to the political power in the new nations (or votes in the United Nations) or to the strategic space-age minerals of the former colonies. The NDEA thus headlined a new U.S. commitment to give diplomatic and educational attention to the world beyond its borders.[7] That required teaching more of the uncommonly taught languages and then to learn much more about the politics, histories, societies, cultures, and economic systems of the Great Powers as well as of the rapidly multiplying "Third World" nations. As a result, the NDEA began with a plan to encourage study of less common foreign languages such as Russian, Chinese, Japanese, Arabic, Hindi-Urdu, and Portuguese. The international education portion of the NDEA began with focus on four areas by creating (1) language and area centers, (2) fellowships to students

3

for language study, (3) support for research and studies projects such as surveys of language teaching and pedagogy and development of language teaching materials, and (4) institutes to train language teachers and program administrators.

In September 1958, when President Dwight D. Eisenhower signed into law the NDEA, the precursor to today's International Higher Education Opportunity Act, little did he realize the long-term national and international impact it would have. In fact, in supporting the diverse goals of NDEA, including stimulating foreign language education, he was laying the foundation for what has become, fifty years later, the largest program in the world for international education in foreign language and area and international studies.

At the time, Eisenhower voiced his hopes that

> [t]his Act . . . will . . . do much to strengthen our American system of education so that it can meet the broad and increasing demands imposed upon it by considerations of basic national security. . . . Much remains to be done to bring American education to levels consistent with the needs of our society. The federal government having done its share, the people of the country, working through their local and State governments and through private agencies, must now redouble their efforts toward this end.[8]

Three years later, in his 1961 State of the Union address, Eisenhower was optimistic about the NDEA, which he said was

> already a milestone in the history of American education. It provides broad opportunities for the intellectual development of all children by strengthening courses of study in science, mathematics, and foreign languages.[9]

Then, in 1961, with momentum in Title VI toward communicating with the world in their own languages and studying and engaging the rest of the world, Congress also passed the Foreign Assistance Act of 1961, which sent technical specialists (including many based at U.S. universities) to Africa, Asia, and Latin America for development projects, especially in education, agriculture, and health. In her chapter, Nancy Ruther discusses the interplay of universities engaging in international studies with Title VI and development work with U.S. AID to 1988. Also in 1961, the Fulbright-Hays Act (the Mutual Educational and Cultural Exchange Act of 1961) became law. Reflecting both the Cold War competition for "hearts and minds" and the genuine desire for mutuality, the Act sought

> to enable the Government of the United States to increase mutual understanding between the people of the United States and the people of other countries by means of educational and cultural exchange; to strengthen the ties which unite us with other nations by demonstrating the educational and cultural interests, developments, and achievements of the people of the United States and other nations, and the

contributions being made toward a peaceful and more fruitful life for people through-out the world; to promote international cooperation for educational and cultural advancement; and thus to assist in the development of friendly, sympathetic, and peaceful relations between the United States and the other countries of the world.[10]

Finally, in 1961, the Peace Corps was established, first in March by Executive Order of President Kennedy and then in September by Congress:

to promote world peace and friendship through a Peace Corps, which shall make avail-able to interested countries and areas men and women of the United States qualified for service abroad and willing to serve, under conditions of hardship if necessary, to help the peoples of such countries and areas in meeting their needs for trained man-power, particularly in meeting the basic needs of those living in the poorest areas of such countries, and to help promote a better understanding of the American people on the part of the peoples served and a better understanding of other peoples on the part of the American people.[11]

Together, these new programs—Title VI, Fulbright-Hays, U.S. foreign aid, and the Peace Corps—moved beyond a simplistic Big Power Cold War competition to establish a more creative engagement with the people of the world. This included learning their languages and cultures; building mutual understanding across diff-fering cultures and religions through people-to-people exchange; developing part-nerships with foreign peoples (especially in their schools and universities and media); directly addressing problems of poverty, health, education, and building Western-style democracy; and sending bright Americans abroad to live with peo-ples in poorer nations, share and understand their lives, and help with local needs for education and services.

Over the years, the Peace Corps provided pivotal international experience to two U.S. governors, multiple U.S. senators and representatives, media executives at the Associated Press, NBC, and Time, Inc., as well as presidents and vice presidents of ExxonMobil, Levi Strauss, Citicorp, and Bank of America. As many Peace Corps alumni returned home with new African, Asian, and Latin American language skills, some came to the Title VI centers to seek graduate education in area studies, lan-guages and linguistics, and the sciences, becoming part of a new generation of fac-ulty with a depth of immersion abroad and sometimes a way to continue those links with their hosts abroad.

At the same time, intelligence and military engagements in the new nations often ran in a counterstream to fight the Cold War more aggressively, often seeking to shape the political futures of nations of the South away from allegiance to either the non-aligned movement[12] or the Eastern bloc. The United States supported dic-tators (e.g., Mobutu and Pinochet), minority regimes (e.g., South Africa and the

Portuguese colonies), and civil wars (e.g., Vietnam and Angola), and Western intelligence agencies mounted dirty tricks (e.g., assassination operations against leaders) in Africa, Asia, and Latin America. These policies often resulted in major cleavages between scholars, who had long histories and partnerships in those nations, and the intelligence agencies. In his chapter, Gilbert Merkx traces the complicated interplay of international centers and scholars with U.S. policy during wars and civil conflicts abroad. Mark Tessler delves more deeply into the role of Title VI centers and scholars in supporting and interrogating U.S. national security policy and actions.

Before Title VI, Fulbright-Hays, and the Peace Corps

These four programs, in fact, were not completely *de nouveau* developments, but represented the maturing of the U.S. engagement with the foreign world. From the trenches of France and the Treaty of Versailles in World War I; to the League of Nations in the 1920s and 1930s; the increasingly rapid expansion of U.S. corporations abroad; to World War II in Europe, Africa, and Asia and the Pacific; and finally in 1945, to the U.S. leadership in forming the United Nations—in all these, Americans were experiencing globalization, which was to change their world.

The early part of the twentieth century had seen a rapidly emerging global economic system and a drive for national self-determination. In 1900, there were only forty nations in the world, and many areas of Africa, Asia, Latin America, and the Middle East were under colonial rule. By 1920, sixty nations had emerged, and after the great movement of decolonization in 1948–1975, the U.S. State Department had to cope with 150 nations. In 2010, there are 192 member states in the United Nations.

During the first half of the twentieth century, American educators were pressed to understand global changes and to adjust their geographical and mental maps as well as their classroom lectures and teaching materials away from the stereotypes of "strange" foreign people and customs. But the notion of international education, and even coping with LCTLs, was not new to the university and foundation community or to the U.S. government. Already, by 1938, the Committee on Slavic Studies had been formed by the American Council of Learned Societies (ACLS) to supplement the normal classical higher education with modern language instruction, usually only in French and German. During World War II, the number of U.S. scholars studying foreign areas was small, as were foreign area studies programs in universities, other than Western European studies. By then, probably only about 400 PhDs in foreign area or international affairs had been completed in the United States, most concerning Europe and only a few on Asia and Latin America. Even after World War II and the advent of the UN, excepting Western European studies, there were only fourteen language and area studies programs on all U.S. campuses: six for Latin America, four for East and Southeast Asia, three for Eastern Europe, one for South Asia, and none for Africa or the Middle East.

In the 1940s, the universities and various U.S. government agencies began to develop special initiatives in language and area studies such as the Intensive Language Program (American Council of Learned Societies), the Foreign Language Program (Modern Language Association), and the Army Specialized Training Program. These and other programs became early prototypes of language training, models that would later become incorporated into the NDEA.

By the 1950s, however, there were twenty-five foreign area programs in U.S. universities, including the first African center, and the major private foundations were investing heavily in area studies in U.S. universities. Anne Betteridge, in her chapter, explores this important interplay of the foundations with the development of area and international studies. The United States began to assert global leadership, realizing that many of its security and economic interests were now abroad and that it needed to develop new policies and programs in support of these expanded interests, especially in the Cold War competition. By the early 1960s, the foreign policy experts of the State Department, the National Security Council, the Council on Foreign Relations, and other nongovernmental organizations (NGOs) lobbied for increased funding for foreign language and area knowledge. Under President John F. Kennedy, there was an urgent need to build a more consensual world order of détente and peaceful coexistence, continuing Eisenhower's opening the doors in 1958 to cultural exchange with the Soviets, the Eastern bloc, and the newly independent nations. With this bipartisan consensus to support mutual exchange and increased engagement, Title VI, Fulbright-Hays, and the Peace Corps made imminently good investments.

Adding the Fulbright-Hays Programs

Shortly after establishing the Title VI programs, the Department of Health, Education and Welfare, which administered the Title VI programs, agreed with the State Department and Senator Fulbright that the Title VI programs needed an overseas component—for field research for PhD dissertations, for renewing faculty experience abroad, and for group projects abroad, especially for college and secondary teachers. In 1964, these Fulbright overseas programs were established with Section 102(b)(6) and have remained a core component of Title VI student, faculty, and outreach activities since then. (See Appendix A for details.) In his chapter, Richard Lambert, one of the few Title VI directors to have been present at these early years, traces the beginnings of Title VI commitment to the LCTL languages, the frequently thin coverage of countries in foreign areas, and the broadening of the Title VI programs over their history.

In the 1980s, as détente continued and as the Berlin Wall came down in 1989, Title VI of the NDEA was redefined as Title VI of the Higher Education Act (HEA) of 1965. At the same time, the Title VI programs focused heavily on building language and international education in colleges and universities, strengthened by the creation in 1986 of the new LRCs to focus on language materials needs, teacher training, and pedagogy. By 1988, the NRCs were building strong programs to outreach to support the needs in K-12 education, media, and the private sector. Simultaneously, the new Centers for International Business Education were created in support of U.S. trade and business abroad. In their chapters, Melissa Birch and Michael Hitt describe the evolution of the BIE and CIBE programs.

National Security and Language

To cater to their particular and frequently intensive language training needs, the State Department, National Security Agency, and Department of Defense had long supported their specialized and richly funded language training institutes. After September 11, 2001, the alarm bell was sounded once again for developing greater U.S. government capacity in languages relevant to intelligence for national security, this time for the Global War on Terror. A series of federal initiatives for elementary, secondary, and tertiary language training were supported, and, across the language community, there was a new call for more languages, more intensively studied, begun earlier in school, and more richly funded to achieve far more highly proficient trainees and professionals. Simultaneously, Congress called for more evaluation of Title VI programs. The new efforts at assessment and evaluation of language proficiency and programs relevant to Title VI are described in more detail in the chapters by Catherine Doughty, Carl Falsgraf, and David Wiley. LaNitra Berger describes one assessment project supported by the IRSP program and the need to promote greater access to Title VI by historically black colleges and universities and other minority-serving institutions.

The Continuing and Unique Roles for the Title VI Programs

Although they are not well integrated with the new federal government security agency language programs nor funded at robust levels, Title VI centers continue to provide the foundational personnel, many experienced language teachers and area experts, intensive summer institutes in many languages, and language learning materials for many of these more recent federal initiatives. Ironically, the Title VI centers have been tasked with achieving excellence in language and area studies curriculum, building more robust faculties, supporting faculty travel and special seminars and conferences, enlarging their library holdings, linking with professional schools, and servicing educational institutions, media, government, and business—all carefully evaluated and assessed—with an average Title VI grant of about $230,000. (This is less in constant dollars than Title VI provided the centers in the 1960s.) A similar amount is provided annually to each center for around ten Title VI FLAS fellowships. (With four years of language trainng required for some proficiency and with all the investment of universities in these expensive LCTL programs, the average center completes only an average of 2.5 trained FLAS scholars per year.)

In fact, the appropriations for Title VI, although low relative to national and university needs, have increased significantly (38 percent) in the year after September 11, 2001.[13] However, despite these significant enhancements, Fulbright-Hays and several Title VI programs still remain below their 1967 funding high points in constant dollars. The fiscal year (FY) 2010 Fulbright-Hays funding level is 20 percent below its high point in FY 1967 in constant dollars; likewise, FY 2009 combined funding for three original Title VI programs that still exist today—NRCs, FLAS Fellowships, and International Research and Studies—was 30 percent below FY 1967 funding. In spite of the mounting national need, in FY 2009 the Department of Education awarded roughly 565 fewer FLAS fellowships (24 percent fewer) compared with the number in FY 1967. Shortfalls from historic highs in average program grants also have been occurring for many years, such as the NRCs (down 31 percent), the Centers for International Business Education (down 28 percent), and the LRCs in FY 2009 (down 45 percent).[14]

The Title VI centers, with their small staff and programs, cannot alone fulfill the increasing, almost universal, need for global knowledge on the part of the seventy federal agencies and offices that need employees with foreign language, international knowledge, and experience abroad. But Title VI graduates and faculty bring their depth of language and area studies education to five major and unique tasks.

First, Title VI programs are the unique repositories for the very costly instruction and pedagogical resources for the less commonly taught languages. A Department of Education study in 2000 found that Title VI-supported institutions:

> account for almost three-fifths (59 percent) of graduate enrollments in languages other than French, German, Spanish, and Italian. If one focuses on the least commonly taught languages, omitting the 10 languages with the highest enrollments (Arabic, Chinese, French, German, Hebrew, Italian, Japanese, Portuguese, Russian and Spanish), Title VI supported institutions account for *81 percent of graduate language enrollments nationwide.*[15]

Because of their very high cost, these languages likely would not be taught at universities in the United States were it not for Title VI funding and the interest of universities to provide large support to language programs and centers to compete for these prestigious awards and fellowships.

Second, Title VI faculty and graduate students often have been immersed in the foreign region for a long enough time that they build partnerships with scholars and universities that frequently endure for decades. They fulfill the original idea of the Fulbright programs of mutual exchange and mutual understanding and fulfill the new 2008 provision in the Title VI congressional legislation for centers to work "through linkages with overseas institutions."[16] These faculty and graduate students often are excellent ambassadors abroad, mirroring a respect for peoples, institutions, and cultures that may be quite alien to the American experience. At the same time, with their immersion in foreign language and cultures abroad, area studies faculty sometimes had complex and sometimes conflictful relationships with their home departments and their disciplines, which often were domestically focused. In their chapters, Craig Calhoun and Michael Kennedy explore those complexities and, from them, suggest some future directions for area and international studies in the contemporary U.S. university and how Title VI programs may need to adapt to new those realities.

Third, based on these cross-boundary partnerships, over time, Title VI faculty and graduates often are able to create new knowledge about the rapidly changing countries and global systems that should shape the perspectives of their students and colleagues, as well as policy makers in the administration, Congress, and NGOs. As Congress indicated in the Findings and Purposes of the Title VI legislation:

> The security, stability, and economic vitality of the United States in a complex global era depend upon American experts in and citizens knowledgeable about world regions, foreign languages, and international affairs, as well as upon a strong research base in these areas.

Because these new perspectives frequently undermine older orthodoxies about peoples, countries, and political systems, however, the perspectives of area specialists may not be congruent with current U.S. policy. A number of scholars in Title VI centers who had a long history and depth of understanding of particular countries have criticized U.S. policy on Vietnam and the Portuguese colonies, as well as support of minority governments in Chile, Nicaragua, Sudan, Somalia, Congo (Zaire), South Africa, and Uganda. In reaction to what is a healthy and open debate about U.S. policy, befitting a democratic society, some members of Congress worry about this scholarly debate and whether it is "balanced." As a result, congressional language reauthorizing the Title VI Act in 2008 mandated that the NRCs and programs must indicate how they "reflect diverse perspectives and a wide range of views and generate debate on world regions and international affairs, where applicable." (See the chapter by Gilbert Merkx on this issue.)

Fourth, faculty in Title VI centers and their students bring their language and area training to fill key roles in the U.S. government, media, business, and higher education. For example, recent graduates have served as advisors to the U.S. government on Bosnia and on the International War Crimes Tribunal; drafted United Nation policy on international drug trafficking; conducted research for World Bank on Russian banking; offered workshops with UNESCO for improving education in Bosnia; developed REESWEB, a comprehensive Slavic studies web site with 120,000 hits per month; directed "US-Japan Economic Agenda" parliamentary exchange program; conducted studies with Carnegie Corporation on U.S. humanitarian interventions around the world; organized a White House conference on "Aviation Safety and Security in the 21st Century"; provided workshops and scholarly exchange visits with South Africa and Botswana for business and economics faculty at historically black colleges and universities; consulted frequently with the State Department on U.S.–China relations; offered area studies courses at the Foreign Service Institute; worked as attaches and foreign service officers in Rwanda, Malawi, Tanzania, Cameroon, and Ethiopia; served as ambassadors to the Democratic Republic of the Congo and Ethiopia; assisted in establishing universities in Africa and South Asia; helped organize U.S. presidential summits in the Caribbean and Chile; created web-based resources about accurate reporting on Muslims and Islam; and conducted research on malaria, river blindness, filariasis, and schistosomiasis in Sudan, Tanzania, and Malawi.

Finally, the burgeoning outreach component of the Title VI centers has made them the incubators of many texts, reference grammars and dictionaries, curricular materials, and web sites for extending area, global, and language knowledge into the K-12 institutions, colleges, and universities across the land. Many Title VI faculty have been involved in developing curricula for K-12 and two- and four-year colleges, frequently providing resources free on their websites. The Technological Innovation and Cooperation for Foreign Information Access (TICFIA) program, begun in 1998, adds to this outreach by using new technologies to access, collect, organize, preserve, and widely disseminate foreign language and international education resources. (See Appendix A.) This enlivens the classroom experience and builds the cadre of international scholars in the next generation—and the media, businesses, and federal agencies are enriched by this extension of international knowledge.

At base, the Title VI and Fulbright-Hays programs are key to building the intellectual foundations, the international competence, and the language proficiency to cope with a competitive and turbulent world. The programs frequently need revision and renewal, and the national panel of the National Research Council at the National Academy of Science has made a number of proposals for change.[17] Former Title VI directors Patrick O'Meara and William Brustein also offer a number of proposals for new directions in their chapters.

Nevertheless, with these very ambitious goals and fifty years of results, after a lengthy assay in 2007, the National Research Council concluded that

> the Title VI/FH programs have served as a foundation for internationalization in higher education. Federal funding, sometimes through the priorities set by the ED for individual competitions, has served as a catalyst for language or area studies initiatives in higher education, with a frequent focus on advanced study of less commonly taught languages. Universities themselves have invested significant resources beyond those provided by the ED. The programs have built substantial capacity in the teaching of less commonly taught languages, with Title VI NRCs across the nation offering instruction in more than 250 less commonly taught languages. The programs have also developed instructional and other materials that are used by academia, K-12 education, and government.[18]

Notes

1 The Title VI 50th Anniversary Conference, Washington, D.C. was convened on March 19–21, 2009, by the U.S. Department of Education's International Education Programs Service (IEPS). Michigan State University made the arrangements for the conference with the IEPS. Details of the conference announcement and thematic organization can be viewed at http://titlevi50th.msu.edu/.

2 On August 14, 2008, The Higher Education Opportunity Act (HEOA) reauthorized all the Title VI programs previously authorized under the Higher Education Act. The conference report on the act can be found at http://help.senate.gov/Hearings/2008_07_29_E/KOS08400_xml.pdf. A review of the provisions of the new act concerning Title VI by Miriam Kazanjian of the Coalition on International Education can be found at http://www.naicu.edu/docLib/20081111_HEA101-CoalitInternatEd.pdf.

3 Letter from Senators Richard G. Lugar (R-IN) and Christopher J. Dodd (D-CT), March 12, 2009, www.usglobalcompetence.org/symposium/lugardodd.html# (accessed January 15, 2010).

4 Letter from the Honorable Hillary Rodham Clinton, March 17, 2009, www.usglobalcompetence.org/symposium/clinton.html#. (accessed December 15, 2009).

5 http://history.nasa.gov/sputnik/ (accessed December 15, 2009).

6 U.S. Department of Education, "The Federal Role in Education," www2. ed.gov/about/overview/fed/role.html (accessed January 29, 2010).

7 A fuller discussion of the emergence of the Title VI International Education Programs can be found in Wiley, David, "Forty Years of The Title VI and Fulbright-Hays International Education Programs: Building the Nation's International Expertise for a Global Future," in O'Meara, Patrick, Howard and Carolee Mehlinger, and Roxana Ma Newman, eds. *Changing Perspectives on International Education*, Bloomington: Indiana University Press, 2001, Ch. 3.

8 Eisenhower, Dwight D., Statement by the President upon Signing the National Defense Education Act, September 2, 1958, As enacted, H R.13247 is Public Law 85-864 (72 Stat.1580), released at the U.S. Naval Base, Newport, RI, Source: "The American Presidency Project," www.presidency.ucsb.edu/ws/index. php?pid=11211 (accessed January 28, 2010).

9 Eisenhower, Dwight David, State of the Union Address, January 12, 1961, www. infoplease.com/t/hist/state-of-the-union/173.html (accessed January 15, 2010).

10 U.S. Congress, Congressional statement of purpose, Mutual Educational and Cultural Exchange Act of 1961, USC 22: Chapter 33, Mutual Educational And Cultural Exchange Program, Sec. 2451. (Pub.L. 87-256, 75 Stat. 527), www2.ed.gov/about/offices/list/ope/iegps/fulbrighthaysact.pdf (accessed December 28, 2009).

11 The Peace Corps Act, Public Law 87-293 (September 22, 1961) (as amended), Sec. 2501. Congressional Declaration of Purpose, http://multimedia. peacecorps.gov/multimedia/pdf/policies/ms101.pdf (accessed December 15, 2009).

12 For the history of the non-aligned movement, beginning with twenty-five nations in 1961, see "The Non-Aligned Movement: Background Information: 1.1 History," at www.nam.gov.za/background/background.htm#1.1 percent20History (accessed October 24, 2009).

13 From FY 1990, when the Coalition on International Education was formed, to FY 2010, "Title VI funding increased roughly $76 million or 218 percent in current dollars, while Fulbright-Hays increased a little over $10 million or 203 percent. Put in constant dollars the increases are 92 percent and 83 percent, respectively. The largest resource enhancement in Title VI/FH history took place right after September 11, 2001 and the anthrax attacks in Congress. Fiscal Years 2002 and 2003 witnessed a combined increase of roughly $30 million or 38 percent in current dollars over FY 2001." Miriam Kazanjian, Coalition on International Education, e-mail message to author, January 28, 2010.

14 Ibid.

15 Brecht, Richard D. and William P. Rivers, 2000. *Language and National Security for the 21st Century: The Role of Title VI/Fulbright-Hays in Supporting National Language Capacity.* College Park: The National Foreign Language Center at the University of Maryland, 45ff., quoted in Kazanjian, Miriam. 2002. "Facing Historic Challenges in U.S. International Education: The Role of International Outreach," Keynote Speech to HEA-Title VI Outreach Coordinators, University of Wisconsin-Madison, May 2, 2002, www.wioc.wisc.edu/conference/speech. pdf (accessed January 28, 2009).

16 Title VI, "SEC. 601. FINDINGS; PURPOSES; CONSULTATION; SURVEY." Library of Congress, Thomas, http://thomas.loc.gov/cgi-bin/cpquery/?&sid= cp110okwwF&refer=&r_n=hr803.110&db_id=110&item=&sel=TOC_865185& (accessed January 28, 2009).

17 National Research Council (2007). *International Education and Foreign Languages: Keys to Securing America's Future*, Committee to Review the Title VI and Fulbright-Hays International Education Programs, M.E. O'Connell and J.L. Norwood, eds., Center for Education, Division of Behavioral and Social Sciences and Education. Washington, D.C.: The National Academies Press. Part III: Important Next Steps (209–210), 11 Monitoring, Evaluation, and Continuous Improvement (211–227), 12 Looking Toward the Future (228–248), www.nap. edu/openbook.php?record_id=11841&page=30 (accessed December 15, 2009).

18 Ibid. "Executive Summary," p. 10. (accessed December 15, 2009).

PART 1

The Role of Title VI Programs in National and Global Security

CHAPTER 2

Gulliver's Travels: The History and Consequences of Title VI

Gilbert W. Merkx

The original title of Jonathan Swift's 1726 classic was *Travels into Several Remote Regions of the World, In Four Parts, by Lemuel Gulliver*. The challenges of dealing with the unfamiliar, which made *Gulliver's Travels* so popular, have hardly abated. For the past fifty years, Title VI of the Higher Education Act (previously the National Defense Education Act) has been the U.S. government's primary mechanism for helping Americans acquire the cultural and linguistic competence needed to make the remote regions of the world seem more familiar. This chapter examines Title VI from three perspectives: first, in terms of the larger historical circumstances within which it has played a role; second, in terms of its own legislative history; and third, in terms of its impact on American institutions.

War, Knowledge, and History

The United States has been involved in wars and national security crises since it emerged as an international power in the 1890s. In chronological order, the more notable events include the Spanish-American War, World War I, the numerous U.S. interventions in the Caribbean Basin before 1930, World War II, the Berlin blockade, the Chinese Revolution, the Korean War, the Sputnik crisis, the Bay of Pigs Cuban intervention, the Cuban missile crisis, the war in Vietnam, the Central American

17

conflicts of the 1980s, the invasion of Grenada, the invasion of Panama, the Gulf War, the Somali intervention, the Balkan war, the September 11, 2001 attacks on the World Trade Center and the Pentagon, the war in Afghanistan, and the Iraq war.

Each of these wars or crises has been accompanied by a renewed appreciation of the importance of foreign military intelligence, of foreign language fluency, and of deep knowledge about the culture and politics of the areas involved, a combination that I will refer to as *foreign area competence*. Between wars and crises, however, the appreciation of foreign area competence erodes. There is a long tradition in American society of suspicion of foreign area competence, nicely reflected in the statement by President Charles Eliot of Harvard: "Prolonged residence abroad has a tendency to enfeeble the love of country and impair the foundations of public spirit in the individual."[1]

As the United States aspired to a role as a world power at the end of the nineteenth century, the need for foreign military intelligence became recognized. The Office of Naval Intelligence was founded in 1882, and the Army's Military Intelligence Division (MID) was established in 1885. The Spanish-American War and its bloody aftermath in the Philippines demonstrated the value of these intelligence units.

However, by 1908, the interest in foreign competence had waned. The MID was merged into the War College Division and, for all practical purposes, ceased to exist. In the run-up to World War I, the U.S. Army commander, Major General Hugh Scott, an expert on packsaddles and American Indian sign languages, vetoed efforts to reestablish a separate Army intelligence unit. When World War I began, the foreign intelligence deficit of the U.S. Army was appalling. In 1915, the War Department was called on to produce a preparedness plan. Captain Dennis E. Nolan of the War College Division, who was assigned to prepare the threat estimate, had to rely on data from open sources, basically, a 1914 almanac of the world's armies and a 1914 shipping register.

This early use of open source materials underscores another dimension of foreign area competence, that much of the information useful for intelligence is generated not by the military but by the press, academia, and other nongovernmental organizations (NGOs), such as religious missions and charities. Military intelligence has always benefited from information drawn from institutions. At the same time, the relationship between government and NGOs has often been problematic. In some cases, as in the Spanish-American War, the press has manipulated foreign or military policy through slanted news coverage. On other occasions, the government or the military have manipulated the press, enlisting correspondents as covert intelligence agents, planting propaganda stories, and limiting news coverage. News coverage has sometimes undercut official claims of military success.

Academic institutions are another source of foreign area competence, particularly with respect to foreign language expertise, deep knowledge of foreign cultures, and overseas contacts. Each war or crisis has led policy makers and national security institutions to recruit academic experts and draw on their knowledge. Sometimes the academy has responded with enthusiasm. But the academy, like the press, also can be the source of information and research that is highly critical of government policy.

Missionary work was an important source of foreign area competence in the nineteenth and early twentieth centuries. Many foreign area specialists of the mid-twentieth century in both academia and government were the children of missionaries. Following World War II, the overseas presence of U.S. corporations and nonreligious NGOs expanded rapidly, adding additional influences on government policy.

Whether the relationship between official policy and nonofficial sources of foreign area competence is positive or negative is largely a function of the specific war or crisis itself. Some wars and crises generate broad support from those with foreign area competence in the press, academia, corporations, and NGOs, whereas others generate opposition. The events that are broadly supported I will term, with intentional irony, "good" wars or crises, whereas the events that are widely opposed I will call "bad" wars or crises. Of course, opposition and support are absolutes, but they form a scale. Hence, some wars and crises can be considered "better" or "worse" than others. Support and opposition to a war also can shift over time, raising issues that will be considered elsewhere.

Running through the list of wars already mentioned, the fairly "good" wars and crises would include the Spanish-American War, World War I, the Berlin blockade, the Korean War, Sputnik, the Cuban missile crisis, the Gulf War, the Balkan war, September 11, 2001, and Afghanistan, all of which generated considerable support from those in the press and the academy with foreign area expertise. The fairly "bad" wars and crises would include the Caribbean interventions before 1930, the Chinese Revolution, the Bay of Pigs, the Central American conflicts of the 1980s (involving El Salvador, Nicaragua, Honduras, and Guatemala), Grenada, Panama, Somalia, and the Iraq war, all of which generated considerable criticism from academia, press, and NGOs. World War II stands out as a very good war that generated a high degree of support. The Vietnam War stands out as a very bad war that generated a high degree of opposition from Southeast Asian specialists in the press, academia, and NGOs.

The "good–bad" war or crisis scale has important consequences. A bad war can lead to retaliation against the critics who produce "open-source" intelligence with painful consequences for both the individuals involved and for overall national competence for dealing with the area in question. The triumph of Mao Zedong's

19

Chinese Communist Revolution of 1949 was followed by a witch hunt in the United States that targeted all the leading American experts in China, who had predicted that the U.S. policy of support for Chiang Kai-shek was doomed to fail. The most prominent academic victims included Owen Lattimore, John K. Fairbanks, and John DeFrancis. Press victims included correspondents Theodore White, Edgar Service, and Annabel Jacoby. The purge also reached into government, leading to the dismissal of many of the State Department's leading experts, including John Service, John Patton Davies, O. Edmund Clubb, and John Carter Vincent. The loss of these experts and the chilling effects of the hunt on press coverage and academic research created a deficit of intelligence on China that took decades to overcome. Press and academic criticisms of the Vietnam War, the Central American conflicts, and the Iraq war also led to negative, if less extreme, consequences for the critics.

In contrast, a good war can have highly positive effects on the relationship between government and other sources of foreign area expertise. World War II, in particular, led to new forms of intelligence collaboration that were to have long-lasting and beneficial effects for the nation. The surprise Japanese attack on Pearl Harbor in 1941 galvanized the American public and swept away opposition to joining the Allies. The War Department realized that it would have to fight a two-front war and that it lacked the foreign area competence to do so. The only way to obtain deep knowledge about countries in the two theaters of war was to draw on college and university faculty, and the only way to train the large numbers of officers needed to conduct operations in these fields was to send them to the nation's colleges and universities.

The Office of Strategic Services (OSS) recruited faculty members for their area expertise and put them to work as intelligence analysts. Studies of national character were commissioned for every country on both fronts. Some were later declassified and published after the war. Perhaps the most famous book to result was the anthropologist Ruth Benedict's study of Japanese national character, *The Chrysanthemum and the Sword*, which became both an anthropology classic and a best seller in Japan.

Very shortly after the United States entered the war in response to the Japanese attack on Pearl Harbor, the U.S. Army established the Army Specialized Training Program (ASTP), which sent officers to institutions of higher education for crash courses in needed skills, including foreign languages and foreign area studies. The total number of officers trained is not known, but at its high point the ASTP had 150,000 officers enrolled in colleges and universities. In 1943, the Navy set up a similar program, the V-12 Navy College Training Program, which enrolled more than 125,000 officers before it was terminated in 1946.

The ASTP and V-12 programs were hugely important in meeting the challenges of World War II. They also had significant long-term consequences. Most notably, these programs established a model of university–government collaboration for generating foreign competence that was to be the inspiration for Title VI of the National Defense Education Act (NDEA) of 1958. World War II also created a talented generation of internationally competent veterans who moved into positions of influence in government, foundations, and universities and collectively introduced the programs of collaboration between the government and academia through which America became more internationally engaged and internationally competent. These spin-offs of World War II include the Fulbright Act of 1946, the Marshall Plan of 1947, the Point Four Program of 1949, the NDEA in 1958, the Foreign Assistance Act of 1961, and the Title XII overseas agriculture assistance program of the Board for International Food and Agricultural Development (BIFAD), passed in 1975. World War I, in which preparedness was conceived in strictly military terms, had few effects on the U.S. government's international competence, although it did stimulate private efforts such as the founding of the Council on Foreign Relations. In contrast, World War II led to government institutions that transformed the nation's ability to function on the world stage.

The role of the World War II generation in shaping America's ability to meet international challenges has been little noted but should not be underestimated. The late Frederick Wakeman, who served as director of the East Asia Center at Berkeley and president of the Social Science Research Council, called attention to this generational effect in a talk given to the second Santa Fe conference of Title VI National Resource Center (NRC) directors in 1996. Wakeman argued that an interlocking directorate of internationally oriented veterans who knew one another and shared the same values moved back and forth among the major foundations, universities, and government agencies and used their influence to build America's international competence. A quintessential example was McGeorge Bundy, who worked in Army intelligence during World War II, served as an assistant to Secretary of War Henry Stimson, went to the Council on Foreign Relations, became a professor at Harvard and then dean of Harvard College, returned to government as chairman of John F. Kennedy's National Security Council, and finally became president of the Ford Foundation. But by the 1980s, the World War II generation was leaving the scene. The next generation of leaders was less internationally oriented, less networked, and less coherent.

Enter the Title VI Act

The stimulus for Title VI was, of course, a national security crisis. The Soviet Union's success in launching the first orbiting satellite, Sputnik, in 1957 led to a wave of public hysteria in the United States, comparable to the reactions to Pearl Harbor and the destruction of the World Trade Center towers on September 11, 2001. The Eisenhower administration was suddenly on the political defensive. The Soviets were seen as ahead in the newest frontiers of military technology and vastly superior in turning out scientists and engineers. This perception led the Eisenhower administration to propose federal support for science, engineering, language, and area studies in higher education. The point man for this legislation was the assistant secretary for education in the Department of Health, Education, and Welfare, World War II veteran Elliot Richardson. (Richardson later served as secretary of defense and attorney general under Richard Nixon, and was dismissed for refusing to fire the special prosecutor during the Watergate scandal that led to Nixon's resignation.)

The bill that resulted from Richardson's efforts was the NDEA, which was essentially an updated version of the ASTP that established a partnership between government and higher education. Although the administration was Republican, the Democrats in Congress were quick to recognize that the NDEA established a peacetime precedent for federal aid to higher education. The original bill, drafted by Richardson's staff, was sponsored in the Senate by Lister Hill and in the House by Carl Elliot, both Democrats. The bill was strongly contested by conservatives, who argued that the NDEA would open the floodgates of federal assistance to higher education. Senator Barry Goldwater declared it "the camel's nose under the tent," and Senator Strom Thurmond denounced the bill for its "unbelievable remoteness from national defense considerations" (Clowse 1981: 126). Nonetheless, the bill was passed in 1958 and signed by President Eisenhower.

In 1966, President Lyndon B. Johnson proposed to Congress the International Education Act, which called for broad-based programs to internationalize U.S. education in general and promote education exchanges with other nations. The act was passed but never funded, a victim of the rising cost of the Vietnam War and its political consequences. Nevertheless, its ideas were influential and, over time, led to an expansion of the Title VI mandate. The original Title VI mission of training specialists to meet national needs was retained, but new goals were added, such as outreach, citizen education, internationalizing the undergraduate curriculum, international business education, minority recruitment, language research, and support for overseas research centers (Scarfo 1998).

Because of the "good war–bad war" syndrome already mentioned, the appropriations history of Title VI became a roller coaster. The high point in Title VI appropriations, controlling for inflation, was reached early in the Johnson administration. But as academic criticism of the war in Vietnam grew, the White House became increasingly unhappy and the growth of Title VI funding stopped. The Nixon administration was even angrier about antiwar criticism from Southeast Asia experts, many of whom were in Title VI NRCs, and it decided to eliminate Title VI funding entirely. Although the funding was cut almost in half, Congress, controlled by Democrats, managed to continue the program. During the Carter administration, Title VI funding improved, although not to the highs of the early Johnson period. The Carter administration established a new cabinet-level Department of Education in 1980, and Title VI of the NDEA became Title VI of the Higher Education Act. In the same year, Jimmy Carter lost to Ronald Reagan. The Reagan administration pledged to eliminate the new department.

Because the Republicans never controlled both houses of Congress, the Reagan administration was unable to dismantle the Department of Education. Nonetheless, the first seven Reagan budgets called for the elimination of Title VI funding. Academic criticisms of the Reagan administration policies in Central America did little to endear Title VI to the White House. Nevertheless, the congressional defenders of Title VI were able to rescue it again and again from oblivion, with significant support from the defense and intelligence communities. Most notably, Secretary of Defense Caspar Weinberger, who during World War II served on General Douglas McArthur's intelligence staff, wrote personally to Secretary of Education Ted Bell, another World War II veteran, calling for continuation of Title VI funding.

The rescue efforts did not stem losses in the real value of Title VI appropriations, which continued to erode during the Reagan administration. The arrival of George H. W. Bush, who had promised to be an education president, seemed more promising. The Association of American Universities tried to rally support for international education by forming the Coalition for the Advancement of Foreign Languages and International Studies (CAFLIS), which was joined by more than 150 education associations. In 1989, after two years of work, CAFLIS presented its report calling for a new National Foundation for International Education, to be comparable to the National Science Foundation. Unfortunately, several of the associations refused to sign off on the report. With a divided community, it proved impossible to obtain support from Congress or the White House, and the proposal died.

The CAFLIS failure forced the international education community to recognize that it should stop trying for new legislation and focus its efforts on better funding for Title VI. The 1981 Rand Corporation report on Title VI had observed that for international education, "Title VI remained the only game in town" (McDonnell 1981: 11). That observation was still true in 1989 and it remains true in 2010. In any case, the CAFLIS fiasco led to a "bottom-up" effort to mobilize key Title VI constituents. The six higher education presidential associations at One Dupont Circle in Washington, D. C., joined with four international education associations in 1992 to establish the Coalition for International Education (CIE), which recruited Miriam Kazanjian to serve as its consultant. The coalition now includes more than thirty organizations that work in concert to support Title VI programs. Overall, Title VI appropriations have increased considerably since 1992, but funding for the original Title VI programs, such as NRCs and Foreign Language and Area Studies (FLAS) fellowships, remains at only about two-thirds of the mid-1960 levels.

The Consequences of Title VI

The consequences of Title VI over the past fifty years have been extraordinary, yet they are often overlooked and difficult to document. The original mandate of Title VI was to foster teaching and research on foreign areas and languages and to train foreign language and area specialists to meet national needs. The additions to this mission that were included in later authorizations focused on internationalizing education, including elementary and secondary education, the undergraduate curriculum, business schools, and the general public. These two different dimensions of the Title VI mission can be characterized as "broadening the base," which is the general education mission, and "sharpening the point," which is the expertise mission. The two missions are related in that success in broadening the base provides an improved flow of motivated people who can be recruited as foreign area specialists. Success in both missions creates a nation that is more internationally competent at both the popular and elite levels.

The General Education Mission: Broadening the Base

Since World War II, American higher education has become increasingly international in all its many dimensions. Two federal programs have been the drivers of this process: the Fulbright Act of 1946 (later replaced by the Fulbright-Hays Act of 1961) and Title VI of the NDEA. The initial Fulbright Act was conceived as a way of spending down lend-lease loans owed to the United States by World War II allies whose weak currencies could not be converted into dollars. This brilliant stroke of public diplomacy proved so popular that it was continued after the lend-lease funds were exhausted.

The Fulbright program had consequences for American higher education as well as for public diplomacy. By sending faculty and graduate students to foreign countries, and receiving faculty and students from those same countries, the Fulbright program established personal networks and stimulated interest in overseas research. It also familiarized Americans with foreign universities and foreigners with American universities. It was not long before foreign faculties began to use their U.S. connections to place their students in American universities. Foreign student enrollments in the United States had been virtually nonexistent before World

War II. After the passage of the Fulbright Act of 1946, enrollments of foreign students began to grow, first slowly and then exponentially. A second spin-off of the Fulbright program was that American faculty began to use their foreign connections to establish study-abroad programs for their own students. Study-abroad programs began to grow rapidly. These flows of students and faculty into and out of the United States are two of the distinctive international features of American higher education.

Title VI of the NDEA had an equally profound impact on American higher education. To qualify for grants as a National Resource Center for Foreign Language and Area Studies, and for the student FLAS fellowships that came bundled with the NRC grants, a college or university had to commit to offering language and disciplinary courses on a specific world region or area, which also meant hiring area specialists for its faculty, building a library collection, and supporting research overseas. Receiving a Title VI NRC grant conferred not only federal dollars but also prestige, which led to increasing competition for these prized grants. The original legislation anticipated that the government would pay half the cost of an NRC, but as universities competed against one another, government leverage increased. Today, universities pay more than 90 percent of the cost of their NRCs, a bargain for the federal government.

Title VI was not alone in providing support for language and area studies. Major foundations, such as the Ford, Mellon, and Rockefeller foundations, strongly supported the government effort with their own funds during the late 1950s and early 1960s. The large investments in international and area studies by the Ford Foundation alone during this period considerably exceeded federal appropriations for Title VI. These foundation investments trailed off in the 1970s and 1980s, but they left behind institutionalized and endowed programs on many campuses.

The increase in language and area studies course offerings and in foreign area specialists on the faculty allowed universities to capitalize on the interest generated by study abroad programs and Fulbright experiences. Enrollments in language and area courses grew substantially. Moreover, the existence of the area centers created intellectual communities that crossed disciplinary boundaries and reinforced faculty interest in foreign areas. On many campuses, the NRCs were the first successful interdisciplinary units, establishing a model that would later be useful for other intellectual purposes.

One of the spin-offs of these new intellectual communities was the establishment at the national level of foreign area studies associations. The Latin American Studies Association, for example, was established at a meeting of directors of Latin American NRCs. Likewise, the African Studies Association and the Association of African Studies Programs, the Middle East Studies Association, the

European Studies Association, and the American Association for the Advancement of Slavic Studies were all established as a consequence of Title VI. (The only area studies association to predate Title VI was the Association for Asian Studies.) By 1990, membership in these area studies associations totaled about 16,000 professionals.

The scholarly journals of these area studies associations were another consequence of Title VI. After these journals were established, interest in area studies grew further, leading to the establishment of additional journals. For example, the first interdisciplinary journal of Latin American studies was the *Latin American Research Review*, established in 1965. Today, the *Hispanic American Periodicals Index* references more than 600 journals that publish studies of Latin America. A similar proliferation of journals is found in the other area studies fields.

Another consequence of Title VI has been the development over the past half century of extensive foreign area research collections by institutions receiving Title VI funding. Given the chaotic conditions in many parts of the world, archives and research libraries in numerous areas are nonexistent. But because of Title VI incentives, U.S. academic libraries have built collections on other countries that have helped preserve the scholarly heritage of those countries.

The introduction of the Undergraduate International Studies and Foreign Languages (UISFL) program in 1976 had a significant effect on teaching institutions, much like that of the NRC program on research institutions. The UISFL program has made grants to more than 550 colleges and universities, providing significant assistance to the dramatic internationalization of teaching institutions over the past thirty years.[2] These institutions have recruited as faculty many of the PhDs produced by Title VI NRC and FLAS programs. The highest participation rates for undergraduate study abroad now are found in private colleges rather than in research universities.

In 1980, a new Part B was added to Title VI to authorize programs in business and international education (BIE). At that time the typical business school curriculum was almost entirely oriented to the U.S. economy. The first grants under the BIE program were made in 1983. In 1988, the Center for International Business Education (CIBE) program was authorized. The first awards under this program were made in 1989. Today, business schools are among the most internationalized of the professional schools found in American universities. The globalization of the world economy obviously provided a huge incentive for internationalizing the business curriculum, but the BIE and CIBE programs were in the right place at the right time to help lead this effort.

The part of the educational system on which Title VI has had the least impact is kindergarten through twelfth grade (K-12) education. Despite the valiant efforts of the educational outreach coordinators of each of the NRCs, the curriculum of the public schools of the United States is less international in 2009 than it was in 1958, when Title VI was first passed. Fewer schoolchildren are enrolled in foreign languages today than there were fifty years ago. The George W. Bush administration's "No Child Left Behind" legislation mandated testing in basic fields that did not include foreign languages, and the result was a further decline in foreign language offerings at K-12 levels. Title VI is, of course, part of the Higher Education Act, and therefore all it can do is to encourage colleges and universities to reach out to the public and private schools.

Overall, there can be no doubt that Title VI has been enormously transformative in helping to internationalize American higher education. The Fulbright and Fulbright-Hays programs generated the initial academic interest, the major foundations provided key initial investments, and Title VI provided the long-term source of continuing support for the institutional base of international, foreign area, and foreign language studies. No other country has achieved anything comparable. However, the decline of international education at the K-12 levels represents a serious national challenge. The nation needs a Title VI equivalent for K-12 education. The pending reauthorization of the Elementary and Secondary Education Act may offer an opportunity to do that.

The Expertise Mission: Sharpening the Point

The expertise mission of Title VI is to train people to be fluent in foreign languages, particularly the less commonly taught languages (LCTLs), and to have expertise, or deep knowledge, in foreign cultures and societies. The foreign mission has met with clear-cut success. In 2005, the Michigan State e-LCTL Initiative, led by David Wiley, released data showing that the 128 Title VI NRCs had the capacity to offer 226 LCTLs, excluding the "commonly taught" languages of French, Spanish, German, and Italian. In contrast, the Defense Language Institute (DLI) and the Foreign Service Institute (FSI) were able to offer only seventy-five LCTLs. In terms of enrollment in courses actually offered, the e-LCTL study found that during 2001–2002, more than 30,000 students enrolled in 128 LCTLs in the fifty-five universities with NRCs.

The number of LCTLs offered by NRCs and the overall enrollments in those LCTLs have no parallel in any other nation. This extraordinary accomplishment is due almost entirely to Title VI. A survey of NRCs conducted by the National Foreign Language Center in the late 1980s found that the NRCs supported their LCTL courses almost entirely with Title VI funds and that instruction in 80 percent of these languages would be dropped in the absence of Title VI funding.

It should also be noted that this linguistic achievement has been highly cost-effective. The expenditure on Title VI programs is only a fraction of the federal expenditures on in-house government language training programs, such as the Department of Defense's DLI, the National Security Agency's National Cryptologic School (NCS), and the Department of State's FSI. In fact, since September 11, 2001 the *increase* in the annual budget of the DLI alone has been greater than the total annual appropriation for all Title VI programs combined.

The production of expertise by universities with Title VI centers is equally impressive. The production of area specialist PhDs by Title VI NRCs was about 1,400 per year in the early 1990s, when Title VI funding was at its low point. The number was far higher in the 1960s and 1970s, when funding was at its peak. Beginning in 1993, there was a substantial increase in the number of universities receiving NRC or FLAS funding, leading to a jump in PhD production to about 1,900 language- and area-trained personnel (Schneider 1995b). Current numbers are not available, but because the number of NRCs has continued to show modest growth, can be estimated at well over 2,000 PhDs per year. The production of MA degrees by Title VI centers was far higher, reaching about 6,000 per year from 1991 to 1994 (Schneider 1995b), and it has certainly expanded since then. If we conservatively estimate that over the long term the median annual production of PhDs has been 2,000 and of MAs has been 6,000, and then multiply by the fifty years of Title VI history, the result is a total production of 100,000 PhD area specialists, and 300,000 area-trained MA graduates. No other nation, including the Soviet Union at its prime, has come close to this accomplishment.[3]

For a period in the early 1990s some critics attacked NRCs for offering area studies instead of disciplinary training, an argument based on a misrepresentation of what area centers actually do. Title VI NRCs are coordinating units that offer the LCTLs, whereas area-relevant courses and commonly taught languages are offered by disciplinary departments. The faculty who teach area-relevant courses must meet the standards of their own disciplines for tenure and promotion. Graduate degrees, especially PhDs, are also conferred in a discipline, not by area. Department of Education data for all graduate degrees produced by Title VI National Resource Centers in the 1991–1994 period, when the attacks on area studies were fashionable, show that 91.5 percent received disciplinary or professional degrees, whereas only 8.5 percent received areas studies degrees, and these were mostly MAs (Schneider 1995a, 9). Graduate students emerging from Title VI programs are not undereducated in disciplinary terms, but have added foreign language training, a technical skill required for overseas research. However, a foreign language can take years to acquire, which is why the Title VI FLAS fellowship program is necessary.

The Title VI model of government–university collaboration in establishing university-based centers for the purpose of generating international expertise is unique to the United States. In most nations with a tradition of foreign area research and training, as in the former Soviet Union, France, and China, the model used is the national academy, which is basically a government think tank. However, the national academy model has several features that make it less effective than the Title VI model. First, like military intelligence, the national academy is part of the government and therefore not likely to challenge official policy, however erroneous that policy might be. Second, the national academy is extremely expensive, because it does not leverage matching funds or create a national network of centers drawing on preexisting educational resources such as faculty, students, campuses, and libraries. As a result, the national academy tends to be a small, self-serving, and elite club. Third, the national academy is by definition not an educational institution. Therefore it consumes, but does not produce, new cohorts of foreign experts. Fourth, the national academy is a nondisciplinary institution, defined entirely by its area focus and not enriched by innovations in disciplinary theories and methods.

In contrast, Title VI produces experts who serve in the government, but who also populate higher education, businesses, and NGOs. The result is a substantial community of internationally competent professionals who not only carry out policy but also contribute to the kind of informed debate that characterizes a democratic policy process. Title VI has trained, and is training, far more people who speak LCTLs than the federal government can train in its own institutions, and it does so for far less money. Furthermore, Title VI creates and sustains new generations of foreign area experts and international educators. Finally, the work of Title VI centers is constantly enriched and renewed by theories and methods that reflect the state of the art in the academic disciplines.

Conclusion

Gulliver's world was marked by ignorance and miscommunication. In today's far more turbulent world, knowledge is preferable to ignorance, and communication is preferable to miscommunication. During World War II, the government and higher education were able to form partnerships to generate knowledge and enhance communication in the form of the OSS, the ASTP, and the V-12 programs. The Sputnik crisis led to the reinvention of that partnership through the mechanism of Title VI. Title VI served the nation well during the Cold War, and it has been equally important in helping the nation meet the challenges of the post-Cold War era and of the so-called War on Terror. If Title VI did not exist, we would have to invent it. Fortunately, that is not necessary.

Acknowledgments

I would like to dedicate this paper to Richard D. Lambert, whose many writings on Title VI have been a constant source of inspiration. I also would like to thank Francis X. Sutton and Craufurd Goodwin for their insightful observations on earlier drafts of the manuscript. The flaws, however, are entirely my own.

Notes

1 Citation from Stephen Mark Halpern, *The Institute of International Education: A History* (New York: Columbia University Press, 1969), as quoted by Hans de Wit, *Internationalization of Higher Education in the United States of America and Europe* (New York: Greenwood Press, 2002), p. 21.

2 Data provided by Christine Corey of the International Education Program Service of the U.S. Department of Education.

3 Unfortunately, because of changes in leadership and policy, frequent changes of office location, staff turnover, and other such circumstances, many of the administrative records of Title VI programs are in storage or have been misplaced. None have been properly archived. We do not know, for example, the names of the FLAS fellows of the first decade of Title VI history. I would like to add my voice to that of international education consultant Ann Schneider in urging that these records be given to the National Archive for proper cataloging and storage.

References

Barber, Elinore G., and Warren Ilchman. 1977. *International Studies Review* (New York: The Ford Foundation).

Berryman, Sue E., et al. 1979. *Foreign Language and International Studies Specialists: The Marketplace and National Policy* (Santa Monica, CA: The Rand Corporation, September).

Bigelow, Donald N., and Lyman H. Legters. 1964. "NDEA Language and Area Centers: A Report on the First Five Years," U.S. Department of Health, Education, and Welfare, Office of Education (Washington, D.C.: U.S. Government Printing Office).

Clowse, Barbara Barksdale. 1981. *Brainpower for the Cold War: The Sputnik Crisis and the National Defense Education Act of 1958* (Westport, CT: Greenwood Press).

"Defense Intelligence: Foreign Area/Language Needs and Academia," paper prepared for the Association of American Universities, SRI International, October 1983, p. 2.

Lambert, Richard D. 1973. *Language and Area Studies Review* (Philadelphia: The American Academy of Political and Social Science, Monograph 17, October).

Lambert, Richard D., et al. 1984. *Beyond Growth: The Next Stage in Language and Area Studies* (Washington, D.C.: Association of American Universities).

Lay, Stuart P. 1995. "Foreign Language and the Federal Government: Interagency Coordination and Policy," MA Thesis, University of Maryland, 1995.

McDonnell, Lorraine M., et al. 1981. *Federal Support for International Studies: The Role of NDEA Title VI* (Santa Monica, CA: The Rand Corporation).

Mildenberger, Kenneth W. 1966. "The Federal Government and the Universities," International Education: Past, Present, Problems and Prospects, prepared by the Task Force on International Education, John Brademas, Chairman, Committee on Education and Labor, House of Representatives (Washington, D.C.: U.S. Government Printing Office).

National Defense Education Act of 1958, as amended, as reproduced in Donald N. Bigelow and Lyman H. Legters. 1964. "NDEA Language and Area Centers: A Report on the First Five Years," U.S. Department of Health, Education, and Welfare, Office of Education (Washington, D.C.: U.S. Government Printing Office).

Prospects for Faculty in Area Studies, A Report of the National Council of Area Studies Associations (Stanford, CA: NCASA, 1991).

Rodamar, Jeffery, Office of Planning and Evaluation, U.S. Department of Education, personal communication, January 1997.

Ruchti, James R. 1979. "The U.S. Government Employment of Foreign Area and International Specialists," paper prepared for the President's Commission on Foreign Language and International Studies, July 12. Cited at length in Sue E. Berryman, et al., *Foreign Language and International Studies Specialists: The Marketplace and National Policy* (Santa Monica, CA: The Rand Corporation, September 1979).

Richard D. Scarfo. 1998. "The History of Title VI and Fulbright Hays," in John N. Hawkins, et al., *International Education in the New Global Era* (Los Angeles: UCLA, 1998), pp. 23–25.

Schneider, Ann Imlah. 1995a. "1991–94 Center Graduates: Their Disciplines and Career Choices," Memorandum to Directors of Title VI Centers and Fellowships Programs, September 26, Center for International Education, U.S. Department of Education.

Schneider, Ann Imlah. 1995b. "Title VI FLAS Fellowship Awards, 1991–1994," memorandum to Directors of Title VI Centers and Fellowships Programs, Center for International Education, U.S. Department of Education, September 15.

Shea, Christopher. 1997. "Political Scientists Clash Over Value of Area Studies," Chronicle of Higher Education, January 10, pp. A13–A14.

Wilkins, Earnest J., and M. Rex Arnett. 1976. *Languages for the World of Work* (Salt Lake City: Olympus Research Corporation, June).

CHAPTER 3

Title VI and National and Global Security: Current Status and Concerns Going Forward

Mark Tessler

In addressing the relationship between Title VI and national and global security, this chapter offers reflections on four interrelated topics. The first section discusses the importance for security-related concerns of global competence—defined as knowledge, understanding, and skills related to other countries and cultures and to world affairs more generally. It also calls attention to the contribution of Title VI programs in building global competence among ordinary citizens and in ensuring that the country has the foreign area expertise it needs.[1] The second section reinforces claims about the importance of global competence, and the programs that help to produce it, by reviewing instances in which policies and actions uninformed by knowledge of other countries and cultures have been detrimental to U.S. national security.

Although it is clear that security assessments and foreign policy decisions should be informed by knowledge of other countries and world regions, various constraints have limited the degree to which this occurs in practice. These constraints are discussed in the last two sections of this chapter in order to clarify the context within which Title VI programs operate and to focus attention on problems that must be addressed if these programs and the specialists they support are to contribute as fully as possible to advancing national and global security. The first of these sections reviews debates and disagreement among foreign area specialists in the United States and the normative considerations that make it difficult to translate indepth knowledge of other societies into unambiguous recommendations about the proper response to security challenges. The final section explores the complicated, and sometimes problematic, relationship between foreign area specialists and government agencies seeking to involve them in national security matters. Particular attention in this section is given to relations with the Defense Department and national security agencies.

Global Competence

Most of this chapter focuses on the connection between Title VI and the importance of the work it supports, on the one hand, and U.S. national security, with particular attention to American policies and actions relating to foreign affairs and defense, on the other. With the emphasis of Title VI on the production and dissemination of knowledge about other countries and cultures, and about global affairs more generally, this relatively specific focus reflects a desire to address what has been the central rationale for U.S. government support of Title VI programs and to examine the constraints and challenges, as well as the opportunities, that have marked the recent history of Title VI programs and define the context within which they will operate and make their contribution in the years ahead.

Although the topic is largely beyond the scope of this chapter, it must nevertheless be acknowledged and mentioned at least in passing that security involves much more than foreign affairs and defense, and also that the policies and actions of the United States are only one part of what is relevant for global security. Issues of economy, health, food, environment, migration, and much more all have national and global security implications. Moreover, the relevance of such considerations has contributed to broadening the way in which national and global security are understood, with the term "human security" often used to connote both an enlarged and more comprehensive perspective and the fact that security pertains to the safety and well-being of individuals as well as nations. In other words, security is defined by the rights and needs of all men and women, not just those of a state or the members of a particular population category. Many international and nongovernmental organizations (NGOs) therefore employ the term, and concept, of "human security" as a guide for their programs, formulating policies and taking actions that, as expressed by one analyst, respond to "the multidimensional realities of everyday existence" in an effort to "bridge the gap between theory and empiricism, analysis and applied policy research."[2]

In addition, although this is today something of a truism, the world's peoples and nations are increasingly interconnected, such that what one country—especially, though not only, the United States—does or experiences often has

34

significant security implications for others. The worldwide financial crisis of 2008–2009 is an example with particular significance at the time of this writing. Notwithstanding differing opinions about whether the United States bears primary responsibility or whether parallel developments in a number of countries brought on and intensified the crisis, it is clear that the impact is being felt in a large number of countries. Even as all countries are concerned mainly with their own security needs, this interconnectedness is evident in many areas, ranging from disease and natural disasters to migration, piracy, smuggling, drugs, and the availability and distribution of natural resources. With respect to issues of war and peace, which are the particular focus of this chapter, the World Bank offered an instructive description of the significant ripple effects associated with the events of September 11, 2001 and the U.S. response. According to the Bank, "the September 11 attacks on the U.S. in 2001 pushed millions of people in the developing world into poverty, and likely killed tens of thousands of under-five-year-olds—a far greater toll than the total number of deaths directly caused by the attack."[3]

Whether defined more broadly or with a focus on a particular set of issues and problems, such as foreign relations and defense, meaningful attention to national and global security requires what can be loosely described as "global competence." At its most basic level, this includes knowledge about other countries and cultures, including their histories, economies, patterns of social and political organization, and belief systems, and, ideally, the knowledge of one or more languages spoken elsewhere in the world. Knowledge of a foreign language, as has often been pointed out, not only gives the user a valuable skill, but also brings a deeper understanding of other cultures and, as one scholar recently wrote, it "makes students better problem solvers, unleashing their ability to identify problems, enriching the ways in which they search and process information, and making them aware of issues and perspectives that they would otherwise ignore."[4]

Producing and disseminating this combination of knowledge and skills, along with training the men and women who will do so in the future, are the goals that have led to continuing support of Title VI programs by the U.S. government, and today these objectives are more important than ever. These are tasks for the Title VI community, of course, because the knowledge and skill set possessed by any individual foreign area specialist will of necessity be limited. Indeed, many—and perhaps most—area experts rarely have indepth knowledge of more than a small number of the countries in the region in which they specialize, and perhaps only of certain issues, locations, or population categories in those countries. But taken together, the scholars, students, and others who are or have been affiliated with Title VI programs constitute a national resource. They collectively carry out the production, dissemination, education, and training functions that are the goals of Title

VI, and they collectively ensure the availability of the global knowledge that either already is or may in the future become important—indeed, critical—for national security purposes.

The connection between global competence and national and global security resides in a number of areas. One of these concerns is the importance of having citizens who are literate about international affairs and their country's place in the world. In addition to the tolerance and respect for diversity that comes with an awareness and appreciation of other cultures, it is important that ordinary men and women have at least basic factual knowledge, and a basic understanding, of the broader world community, if only so they can evaluate and respond in an informed manner to the proposals and arguments presented to them as voters.

The role played by foreign area specialists and the programs supported by Title VI in fostering global competence among American citizens is today more important than ever given the changing media environment in the United States and elsewhere. On the one hand, there has been a significant erosion of the role traditionally played by both print and broadcast journalism in keeping the American public informed about world affairs. Newspapers are reducing overseas coverage, if not closing entirely, and the foreign bureaus of most television networks have been diminished. Much of television "reporting" today looks more like entertainment than hard news, and on cable channels much of the time is devoted to partisan opinion, as it is on talk radio. On the other hand, advances in technology have created an entirely new information environment. New modes of disseminating information, ranging from blogs to wikis and social networking web sites, mean that people now have the ability to get news from multiple sources and to do so almost instantaneously. Although they are not without some welcome opportunities for global learning, these changes are at best an imperfect substitute for hard news and at worst a mechanism for disseminating misinformation and reinforcing prejudice. As Nicholas Kristof noted recently in a *New York Times* column, consumers are becoming their own gatekeepers, going online to select the kind of news and opinions they care about most.[5] All this makes it more important than ever for educators with foreign area and international expertise to give young men and women approaching adulthood a foundation of fact and understanding about the world—in other words, a measure of global competence—or at least an important start on the road to acquiring it, to guide them in evaluating and responding to the issues facing them and their country.

A second area of concern, and one more directly related to security considerations, is the need for the country to have available the knowledge, insights, and skills required to inform strategic assessments and policy making that pertain to international relations and world affairs. The importance of this kind of global competence has been emphasized not only by those within the Title VI community, whose objectivity might be questioned by some outside university circles, but also by those charged with ensuring U.S. national security. They stress in this connection that the country must have a strong corps of scholars and other specialists with indepth knowledge about other countries and world regions who can, when needed, advise leaders in government, business, and other fields as they discharge their responsibilities for ensuring the nation's well-being. Programs supported by Title VI play a leading role in building interest in foreign area and international studies and in training those who go on to become specialists.

The country's strategic analysts, policy makers, and political officials not only must be able to find and call on area and international specialists in academia and elsewhere when in need of information or advice, but they also must possess a reasonable level of global competence. Ideally, this should involve the knowledge and understanding that comes with meaningful overseas experience and proficiency in a foreign language. At the very least, this should involve a basic appreciation of cross-national and cross-cultural differences. It is in this context that former Secretary of State Madeleine Albright lamented in a speech at Wellesley College in June 2009 that there are members of Congress who have even "bragged about not having a passport."[6]

Albright has not been alone in stressing the importance of global competence, including knowledge of foreign languages, and in complaining about current limitations. She is one of eight former secretaries of state who recently issued a statement emphasizing that "national security is about more than bullets," that it also requires the projection of "soft power" through policies devoted to "diplomacy, development and democratic governance." Drawing on a recent report by the American Academy of Diplomacy prepared in cooperation with the Stimson Center,[7] as well as their own experience, the secretaries complained about the limited foreign language and area expertise of many people in the government agencies devoted to foreign relations. They pointed out, for example, that "nearly 30 percent of positions that require foreign language skills are filled by officers without them," and then stated that "sending diplomats abroad without language skills is like deploying soldiers without bullets." Focusing in particular on the State Department and the Agency for International Development, and calling for funds to permit expanded language training, they insisted that "providing the personnel and financial resources to manage our diplomacy and development policies is an urgent matter of national security." The secretaries also complained that "as regional and cultural conflicts have grown into issues of worldwide concern, our exchange programs for students and scholars have declined, along with the personnel to manage them."[8]

The concern is not limited to foreign language proficiency. Addressing the importance of global competence more generally, a former senior U.S. intelligence official opened his recent book about America's relations with the Muslim world by describing a conversation in Jordan that he considered highly instructive. "Talking to a bookseller in front of his stall in downtown Amman," he reported, the Jordanian told him, "If American leaders read half of these books, they would not be attacking Muslims all over the world. They would be speaking to us instead."[9]

Although knowledge of other countries and cultures is the foundation of global competence, both in general and as it relates to national security, this should not be understood as involving indepth and context-specific description, often described as "thick description," to the exclusion of the concern for explanation and broader analytical insight that is at the heart of the social sciences. On the contrary, global competence involves more than knowing the present-day and historical facts about particular societies. It also includes the skill set and perspective necessary to learn about the reasons things occur, to discover causal mechanisms and, in the language of social science, to account for variance, as opposed to merely knowing what is happening or has happened. Although somewhat artificial, this is frequently described as a distinction between "what" and "why," or between description and explanation. Further, it is also important to know when, or under what conditions, causal stories and explanations of variance do and do not apply. When dealing with different countries and cultures, none of this can be discerned without significant context-specific factual knowledge and understanding. But even though these remain essential, they are not sufficient for dealing with many of the concerns that occupy a prominent place on today's national and global security agenda.

There has sometimes been tension between the approaches to inquiry that characterize foreign area studies and theory-oriented social science. Increasingly, although not entirely, a thing of the past, there has been an "area studies debate" in which some scholars who favor one mode of inquiry have questioned the value, or at least the equivalent value, of the other. Against this background, the relationship between the two scholarly approaches was examined in detail in a 1999 collection of essays and research reports, *Area Studies and Social Science: Strategies for Understanding Middle East Politics*. Focusing on political science and offering examples from Middle East Studies, the contributors stressed the importance both of indepth and context-specific knowledge and of more generalizable explanatory insights. Even more important, they emphasized the interdependence of area studies and social science and demonstrated, through their contributions, the value of scholarship that draws on and integrates the two analytical perspectives. The following assessment, from the volume's introduction, applies to security-related concerns, as well as other concerns for which global competence is needed, and is as appropriate today as when written a decade ago.

> [Foreign area specialists insist] not only that their work is compatible with a concern for social science theory, but that the quest for theory cannot be pursued meaningfully without attention to the kind of contextual knowledge that area studies research provides. They note, for example, that theory construction often begins with observation, with the delineation of variance that hypotheses are then formulated to explain. Further, the hypotheses themselves will have explanatory power only to the extent that they are neither trivial nor obvious. Finally, hypotheses cannot be tested without the development of measures that are valid within the social and cultural context from which data are drawn. All of this, however, requires an ability to recognize, understand and evaluate the facts on the ground, which is precisely the kind of knowledge associated with area studies.[10]

There are many examples of studies informed by these scholarly values that address issues having national and global security implications. Some are the work of individual researchers and some are larger collections of projects sponsored by national and international agencies. Consider, for example, the problem of widespread illiteracy among rural women. Measuring and describing the facts on the ground are an obvious and necessary starting point. As a recent study in Morocco demonstrates, however, this does not by itself explain the reasons for the situation or suggest policies to remedy it. The study also shows that female illiteracy in rural Morocco cannot be understood wholly, or even primarily, by attributing the situation to Arab, Muslim, or Moroccan culture. Rather, given the absence of a modern water system in many impoverished Moroccan villages, "[w]omen and girls are usually responsible to carry the daily burden of transporting fresh water over large distances to their homes. This task is time and energy consuming. The result is often that girls fail to go to school and it impedes women to engage in other lucrative or cultural activities."[11] This example illustrates the need not only to focus on explanations and causal mechanisms but also, in so doing, to resist reifying culture when thinking about problems and solutions.

Another example, and one more focused on the concerns of foreign affairs and defense that preoccupy the remainder of this chapter, is the author's work on the attitudes toward international terrorism held by Arab and Muslim publics.[12] Employing data collected through original public opinion surveys, this research seeks to move beyond a description of levels of approval and disapproval of terrorist acts against Western targets and to identify the experiences and circumstances that account for this variance—those that lead to approval by some and those that lead to disapproval by others. Thus, again, descriptive information is the point of departure but it is not the final objective. In seeking to identify causes, the project

39

investigates the potential explanatory power of cultural, economic, political and other factors, and toward this end it draws on knowledge of the societies where surveys were conducted to formulate hypotheses. This research illustrates the utility of inquiry that takes seriously and makes use of the analytical perspectives of both area studies and social science and, as others have noted with respect to public opinion research in the Arab and Muslim world more generally, it demonstrates how the various components of global competence can come together and be employed to produce useful insights about matters with national and global security implications.[13]

The Consequences of Ignorance

Further illustrating the critical importance of global knowledge, including both factual knowledge of other societies and cultures and analytical knowledge about the dynamic processes shaping the behavior of peoples and nations, are the tragic consequences for U.S. and international security of important episodes in which such knowledge has either been unavailable or, more probably, deliberately ignored. Perhaps the most telling example in recent decades, and certainly one of the most disturbing, is the American adventure in Vietnam in the 1960s and early 1970s. With American foreign policy largely shaped by the ideology of the Cold War in general and, in particular, a "domino theory" that insisted that the establishment of a Communist regime in South Vietnam would threaten U.S. security by bringing Communist domination throughout Southeast Asia and beyond, U.S. policy makers saw no need to understand the facts on the ground in Vietnam or to ask the kind of questions about the country's history and politics that could not be answered without input from area specialists. The result, as we now know all too well, was a military and political defeat for the United States, which in fact did not lead to Communist domination in the region, as architects of the war had predicted, and the price of this disturbing and misguided adventure included the lives of 58,000 Americans and an estimated two to three million Vietnamese.

There were intense political debates in the United States during the Vietnam War. At the time, and to a certain extent even today, some would argue that the war was necessary for the defense of American security. Numerous others disagreed, however, calling into question official U.S. government assertions about the nature and causes of the conflict between North and South Vietnam and the administration's conclusion that the situation required an American military response. At the center of this debate were Robert McNamara and McGeorge Bundy, at the time, respectively, secretary of defense and special assistant to the president for national security. Both were extremely strong personalities, and both were considered to be brilliant. More than those of any others in the John F. Kennedy and Lyndon Johnson administrations, the convictions and judgments of these two "action intellectuals" shaped America's Vietnam policy. Brushing aside criticism and dissent, they neither sought nor accepted serious input from those who were knowledgeable about Vietnam. Reviewing a recent book about Bundy, Richard Holbrooke described his "detachment from the realities of Vietnam" and recounted a dinner with people who had lived in Vietnam and "knew things he [Bundy] did not" but who were consistently cut off or ignored by the presidential advisor.[14] The story of McNamara, who died at age 93 while this chapter was being written, may be even more disturbing. Eventually coming to realize that his elegant analyses were flawed, even as he continued for some years to defend the war in public, he later wrote that he had been "wrong, terribly wrong," and that of the various lessons he had learned "the greatest of these was to know one's enemy—and to empathize with him."[15] Given the exorbitant price paid for this insight, few were forgiving when McNamara, late in life, acknowledged his mistakes.

The 1983 bombing of the U.S. Marine barracks in Lebanon, which claimed the lives of 241 marines, also illustrates the importance of understanding the politics and culture of other societies. Although less well known, this episode is noteworthy because of the faulty assumptions that guided U.S. policy and led to this tragedy, and because some of these assumptions, particularly those pertaining to Islamic terrorism, still persist. In the aftermath of the Israeli invasion of Lebanon in June 1982, the administration of President Ronald Reagan sent troops to Lebanon, allegedly to serve as a neutral peacekeeping force. In fact, however, paying little attention to the country's internal political dynamics, which had been shaped by sectarian fighting for the better part of a decade, the Americans soon gave active support to the forces of the Christian government, firing from warships offshore to provide cover for attacks on rival Druze and Shiite units. In response, seeing the United States as a protagonist in the ongoing Lebanese civil conflict, Shiite extremists drove a truck laden with explosives into the Marine barracks at the Beirut airport. The U.S. administration described this as an act of terrorism, and in a sense it certainly was; but the episode cannot be divorced from America's own actions in Lebanon, which in turn were the result of ignoring the realities of the country and pursuing a policy that, as described by one scholar, was "blinded by ideological distortions."[16] In picking sides and intervening militarily, Reagan stated, in rhetoric reminiscent of America's Vietnam policy, "If Lebanon ends up under the tyranny of forces hostile to the West, not only will our strategic position in the Western Mediterranean be threatened, but also the stability of the entire Middle East."[17]

It is probably unnecessary to offer additional examples of the mistakes—indeed, the tragedies—that have resulted from efforts to advance American security   41 through policies uninformed by knowledge about the countries and cultures with which the United States is engaged. The recent American experience in Iraq must nonetheless be noted. There is a continuing debate about whether the American invasion and occupation of Iraq has enhanced or undermined U.S. security, and that of the Middle East more generally, with questions remaining to be answered about Iraq's political future, the growing regional influence of Iran, spillover effects on America's Arab allies, and the possibility that the war in Iraq has spurred the recruitment of terrorists. This has led some analysts, such as Marina Ottaway, director of Middle Eastern affairs at the Carnegie Endowment for International Peace, to state that "after all these years and the money we've spent, I'm not sure we're coming out in a stronger strategic position."[18] Less restrained is the judgment of Peter Galbraith, a former U.S. diplomat with knowledge of Iraq. Galbraith argues in a recent book that the U.S.-led war in Iraq has in fact weakened America's security position in the Middle East, doing the opposite of what was promised by the administration of George W. Bush.[19]

Not everyone agrees with these pessimistic assessments. But what seems beyond dispute is that the invasion was motivated by a combination of ideology and partisan calculations, that it was not informed by the knowledge and judgments of scholars familiar with Iraq, and that these factors contributed very significantly to the death, destruction, and chaos that marked the U.S. occupation. Indeed, apart from the cases for and against the war itself, the absence of knowledge about Iraq—and the absence of any sense that such knowledge might be needed—was reflected in the criteria used by the Bush administration to select the men and women to whom it entrusted the nonmilitary dimension of the occupation. Priority was given to those with conservative ideological and political commitments, and policies consistent with this orientation were pursued whether or not they fit the Iraqi reality. Even in instances in which U.S. officials sincerely sought to advance the welfare of the Iraqis, ideological blinders and a lack of local knowledge resulted in policy failures, chaos and corruption, and deepening anti-Americanism. This sad chapter in U.S. Middle East policy is recorded in detail in a number of penetrating studies. Among these are *Squandered Victory* by Larry Diamond, *Imperial Life in the Emerald City* by Rajiv Chandrasekaran, and *Losing Iraq* by David Philips.[20]

A final example—and one of a different kind, which raises additional questions—concerns the public diplomacy initiatives launched by the administration of George W. Bush. In the aftermath of the terrorist attacks of September 11, 2001, Washington began a public diplomacy effort with the goal of fostering a better understanding and appreciation of the United States.[21] The program was targeted at the Arab and Muslim world in particular, and behind it were two assumptions about the origins of the anti-Americanism that had become widespread in Muslim-majority countries in the Middle East and elsewhere. One assumption was that Arabs and Muslims dislike the civilization and values of America and the West. Whether presumed to be rooted in sincere distaste for Western norms and lifestyles or in some combination of ignorance and jealousy, this view supposes that Arab and Muslim antipathy reflects a profound misunderstanding of American society and, beyond that, a failure to appreciate all that the United States has done to assist Arab and Muslim peoples. The second assumption, which is related to the first, asserts that the origins of antipathy toward the West are to be found in Islam. According to this line of reasoning, Muslims possess and are attached to a civilization that is rich but whose core values are antithetical to the progressive and enlightened norms of the West, hence, the antipathy. The best known articulation of this view is probably Samuel Huntington's "clash of civilizations" thesis,[22] although Bernard Lewis used the same phrase earlier when describing tensions between Islam and the West.[23]

In line with these assumptions, the Bush administration appointed Charlotte Beers, an advertising executive recruited from Wall Street, to serve as undersecretary of state for public diplomacy and public affairs and charged her with developing a campaign to win the hearts and minds of people in the Arab and Muslim world. The team led by Beers designed a campaign around the theme of "shared values," the centerpiece of which was a series of videos showing the successful and productive integration of American Muslims into the mainstream of U.S. society. The goal was to demonstrate that America is an open society, welcoming to Muslims and others, and that there is no incompatibility between being Muslim and being American. The videos were of very high quality, and in the aftermath of September 11, 2001, with anti-Muslim sentiment on the rise in the United States, many felt that Americans themselves constituted the audience to which the videos should be directed. In the Arab and Muslim world, however, the campaign was a failure, as its architects themselves acknowledged, and it was terminated shortly after being introduced. It soon became clear, the campaign had not been informed by the knowledge or experience of those familiar with the Arab and Muslim world and, accordingly, it was based on flawed assumptions both about Islam and about the basis for anti-Americanism among Arabs and Muslims.

This episode provides another illustration of the need to draw on indepth knowledge of other countries and cultures when formulating policy, either diplomatic or military, designed to advance national security and enable the United States to advance its own interests while contributing to the welfare of others. In addition, however, the failure of the "shared values" campaign suggests a particular need for a deeper and more informed look at Islam. Public opinion research in

Muslim countries indicates that views about American society and culture are not especially negative, with anti-Americanism fueled by U.S. foreign policy, as it is or at least as it is perceived, rather than by antipathy toward American social, cultural, and political norms. Indeed, attitudes toward American education, technology, democracy, and even media are generally very positive.[24] But even though this and other research challenge the "clash of civilizations" thesis, helping to explain why the "shared values" campaign fell flat, many Americans continue to have a distorted view of Islam and believe that U.S. problems in the Arab and Muslim world flow primarily from the basic character of the religion. The rhetoric of some prominent Christian leaders and media personalities contributes to such thinking about Islam. For example, Rev. Pat Robertson declared on the news program of a major American television network that Islam is "violent at its core;" Rev. Franklin Graham, son of Billy Graham, and a well-known Christian evangelist in his own right, described Islam as "a very evil and wicked religion;" and Fox News Network talk show host Bill O'Reilly compared assigning a book on Islam to incoming freshmen, proposed by the University of North Carolina, to teaching *Mein Kampf* in 1941.[25]

This is not the place to take up questions about the true character of Islam. Muslims themselves, including knowledgeable and devout Muslims, do not fully agree about who is qualified to speak for Islam or about which of the competing interpretations advanced in the name of religion are most legitimate and authoritative.[26] Nor is it necessary here to ask about the motivations and reasoning of those who describe Islam as wicked or evil or inherently violent. But it *is* essential to replace misconceptions and stereotypes about Islam and Muslims with views informed by those possessing serious and relevant expertise. In part this is because the United States demands, quite properly, that others avoid stereotypes in their thinking about America. As expressed by *New York Times* columnist Nicholas Kristof, if we expect the leaders of other countries to confront the stereotypes and prejudices that exist in their own societies, we must confront those in our own.[27] In the context of this chapter, however, another reason is even more important. If we are to establish meaningful and productive relationships with Arab and Muslim societies, it is critical to have available, and to draw on, the specialized knowledge and insight of those with indepth experience in the Muslim world.

This assessment should not be controversial. The importance of producing, communicating, and drawing on regional and area expertise should be apparent. Indeed, this point has been made clearly and strongly in an important book by a recently retired senior intelligence officer of the CIA, Emile Nakhleh. Nakhleh left a career in university teaching to go to the CIA, and among his contributions there was the establishment of the Political Islam Strategic Analysis Program (PISAP), which has sought to incorporate the knowledge and independent insights of area specialists in academia into the agency's strategic and intelligence analyses. In the introduction to the book, *A Necessary Engagement: Reinventing America's Relations with the Muslim World*, Nakhleh recorded his suspicion that "our government lacks deep knowledge of the Islamic world and of the diverse ways that Muslims understand their faith, their relations with each other, and their vision of, and attitudes toward, the non-Muslim world." He later wrote that "winning the hearts and minds of Arabs and Muslims . . . requires a thorough knowledge of Arab and Muslim cultures and a long-term commitment in resources and personnel." Thus, as he concluded in terms consistent with the present discussion, the book makes a vigorous case for American diplomacy and international engagement "based on knowledge of the Muslim world."[28]

Nakhleh's assessment, like much of the present discussion, draws heavily on the difficulties that have plagued U.S. relations with the Arab and Muslim societies. These relationships have indeed been problematic in recent years, especially, though not only, in the wake of the September 11, 2001 attacks on the World Trade Center and Pentagon carried out by terrorists claiming to operate under the banner of Islam. It should nonetheless be apparent that U.S. engagement with all countries and world regions needs to be informed by indepth knowledge of the relevant peoples, cultures, and histories. Such knowledge should be produced and made available to those responsible for informing and making policy with national and global security implications, and those with these responsibilities must appreciate the need for this knowledge. Knowledge about other societies and cultures should also be disseminated more broadly so that U.S. citizens, as well as the citizens of other countries, can be properly informed about the world to which they are increasingly connected and can make informed choices about the positions and policies advanced by their leaders.

Politics and Values

Although the absence of indepth knowledge about other countries and world regions can lead, and has led, to flawed policies and actions relating to national and global security, including those that are not only unsuccessful but also counterproductive and costly, drawing on this knowledge does not necessarily, or by itself, produce satisfactory answers to international challenges or correct any unambiguous strategic assessments. This is not to say that such knowledge is unimportant after all; on the contrary, as the preceding section seeks to make clear, it is indispensible for effective policy making and informed citizenship. The point is rather to acknowledge that there is more to the story—that although it is easy and important to insist that knowledge of other countries and cultures must be produced and

45

made available, there remain unavoidable and less readily answered questions about what specific knowledge is most relevant in particular situations, about how this knowledge should be weighed and used, and about who decides these matters.

Two kinds of issues illustrate the challenges associated with the use of global knowledge to advance national and international security, both of which are normative in character. One set of issues flows from the fact that individuals who possess expertise about other societies and particular international problems often disagree, sometimes about the relevant facts and at least about the proper response to these facts, as they understand them. This leads inevitably to questions about the accuracy and objectivity of persons who purport to speak as "area specialists," including those with genuine expertise who deserve to be taken seriously, as well as questions about the politics that determine which of the various competing "informed assessments" gain currency and influence. The other set of issues flows from the fact that knowing the facts often raises, rather than answers, questions about costs and benefits, or even about right and wrong, and this poses choices that, however well informed, ultimately can only be made with reference to normative preferences and commitments. Both sets of issues are briefly discussed here to place the relationship between area expertise and national and global security in its proper political and normative context and to illustrate some of the challenges that face those who seek to produce and disseminate knowledge about other countries and world regions.

The first set of issues is illustrated particularly well by debates and disagreements relating to the Middle East, including both those about U.S. policy toward the region and those about political and cultural circumstances within the region itself. This plays out in Washington and has had implications for the way the United States sees its security interests with reference to Iraq, Iran, the Israeli–Palestinian conflict, and other regional actors and issues. It has also played out on U.S. university campuses, where, with implications for Title VI national resource centers, there have sometimes been efforts to prevent the expression of one or another point of view. Such concerns are not limited to the Middle East, and at various periods they have been particularly pronounced when the focus was on China, Russia, Nicaragua, South Africa, and elsewhere.[29] Debates and disagreements relating to the Middle East nonetheless provide a particularly instructive and illustrative case.

A classic illustration of the disagreement among Middle East "experts," well known in the field and not nearly as dated as it might at first appear, is the debate between Edward Said and Bernard Lewis at the 1986 annual meeting of the Middle East Studies Association (MESA).[30] Lewis, a senior scholar whose work on the Arab and Muslim world has been deservedly praised, has in recent years taken conservative political positions, adopted a strongly pro-Israeli stance on the

Israel–Palestine conflict, and argued that Islam bears significant responsibility for many of the Muslim world's problems. His 2002 book, *What Went Wrong*,[31] has been hailed by some as both incisive and courageous in telling the truth about Islam and Muslims, whereas others, such as University of Michigan History Professor Juan Cole, describe it as "a very bad book from a usually very good author." Cole criticizes Lewis's claim that Muslim societies lag behind the West in political, economic, and social development in large part because of their religious and cultural orientations.[32]

Said, who died in 2003, represents the other pole in the division in Middle East Studies. A passionate and articulate Palestinian–American scholar, Said's political commitments were on the left; he was strongly pro-Palestinian, even as he often issued scathing denunciations of inept or corrupt Palestinian leaders and other Arab officials; and he regarded the actions of the West, and in recent years those of the United States, as prime contributors to the problems of the Middle East. Although his most influential work of original scholarship is *Orientalism*, published in 1978, later works, most notably *Blaming the Victims: Spurious Scholarship* and *The Question of Palestine*, published in 1988 and 1992, respectively, set out his arguments with regard to the Israeli–Palestinian conflict and regional problems more generally. It is safe to say that a majority of those in MESA find Said's work, and especially his political analyses, much more congenial than those of Lewis. Yet, like Lewis, he has been strongly criticized by those with different intellectual and ideological commitments. According to Efraim Karsh, a professor at King's College at the University of London, for example, "Said's collected works demonstrate antipathy for integrity and scholarship" and often "pass off sweeping and groundless assertions as historical fact."[33]

The relevance of these descriptions for this chapter resides in two areas, one having to do with tensions and disruptions they pose for the academic community, and for Title VI national resource centers in particular, and the other in the questions they raise about which area specialists have, and which do not have, opportunities to play a role in shaping national policies toward the countries and regions about which they have expertise. With respect to the former, it is notable not only that both the "Lewis camp" and the "Said camp" have attracted scholars whose credentials are beyond dispute, as well as those whose attraction is purely partisan and political, but also that this division has had institutional implications within academia. Thus, joined by Fouad Ajami, another distinguished scholar, Lewis and others withdrew from MESA several years ago and formed the Association for the Study of the Middle East and Africa. Their charge was that MESA had abandoned genuine scholarship and become "politicized to a degree without precedent," adding that this "has affected not only the basic studies of language, literature and history, but also has affected other disciplines, notably economics, politics and social science."

Criticism of MESA—and, perhaps even more relevant, of the Title VI community—also comes from others who share this political orientation. Some have legitimate scholarly credentials regarding the Middle East and offer critiques that, though politically inspired, are informed by expertise. Others have only their partisan arguments to put forward. Prominent among those in one or the other of these two categories, who are active in the Middle East Studies wars within the academy, are Martin Kramer, Daniel Pipes, Stanley Kurtz, and David Horowitz. Kramer, for example, contends that Middle East studies in the U.S. are "deemed a national resource," subsidized by the federal government, "yet for the past twenty years, Middle Eastern studies in America have been factories of error. The academics, blinded by their own prejudices and enslaved to the fashions of the disciplines, have failed to anticipate or explain any of the major developments in the Middle East."[34] Kurtz told a congressional committee that Title VI and other Middle East studies programs at U.S. universities "tend to purvey extreme and one-sided criticisms of American foreign policy" and "discourage students from working for the government."[35] These criticisms, and strong verbal attacks by those with similar views, are also present on American university campuses. Groups such as Campus Watch monitor those they consider too critical of U.S. policies toward the Middle East, or of Israeli policies in the West Bank and Gaza, sometimes charging that they are anti-American and on occasion trying to pressure university administrators to ensure that students receive a more "balanced" perspective.[36]

These charges have, of course, been very forcefully rebutted. A particular target of Campus Watch and its supporters has been Rashid Khalidi, a prominent Palestinian–American historian who holds the Edward Said chair at Columbia University. Expressing views held by many in the Middle East studies community, Khalidi told an interviewer shortly after Campus Watch was established in 2002 that "it is a McCarthyite attempt to silence the very few voices that speak out about the Middle East, and to impose by fear a uniformity of view on the campus debate. . . . Most of what these people are saying is either false, cited completely out of context, or distorted. . . . This noxious campaign is intended to silence such perfectly legitimate criticism, by tarring it with the brush of anti-Semitism and anti-Americanism, truly loathsome charges."[37] Political scientist Lisa Anderson, a past MESA president, made similar charges in her 2003 presidential address. She denounced polemicists who "wish to dictate the range of respectable political conclusions [and accordingly] pose a serious threat to our scholarly integrity." Referring specifically to Campus Watch and other "self-appointed guardians of the academy," Anderson stated that their activities do not reflect a concern for accuracy and diversity, as they claim, but rather "the conviction of conservative political activists that the American university community is insufficiently patriotic, or perhaps simply insufficiently conservative."

Intolerance of opposing viewpoints is not found only among militant conservative and pro-Israeli activists, of course. Conservatives have long complained about feeling unwelcome at MESA and in at least some university-based Middle East studies programs. This is one of the factors that led Lewis and Ajami to form a rival scholarly association. A recent article by four political scientists who specialize in the Middle East, the present author among them, reviewed and denounced the efforts by some political conservatives to limit the expression and reduce the influence of views with which they disagree. The article also stated, however, that "in mobilizing to counter conservative watchdogs, many scholars and advocates seek to correct the record and promote tolerance, pluralism, and academic freedom, but some [others] commit the same violations as their opponents. In these cases, it is not the conservative viewpoints but the authors' right to advocate them that has been attacked."[38]

All this has been very disruptive to the field of Middle East studies, and it has often had a chilling effect on the kind of rigorous discussion and debate that is needed both to inform the country's foreign policy and to properly educate its students. In extreme cases, although their frequency should not be overstated, conservative organizations and scholars with no direct campus affiliation have sought to influence faculty hiring and promotion decisions, sometimes seeking to mobilize alumni, donors, regents, or others for this purpose. More generally, to be free of such battles, many universities have simply shied away from building Middle East studies programs or from hiring faculty who study the modern Middle East. This, too, should not be overstated; there are many strong Middle East programs and faculty members at U.S. universities. But those who teach and do research about the Middle East, and university administrators more generally, are fully aware that the field is marked by tension, controversy, and disagreements that are often expressed in ways that are at best unpleasant and at worst highly disruptive. This tends to chase away students who are not already aligned with one camp or the other and to reinforce rather than transcend the narrow partisanship with which other students approach the field. Thus, with university administrators sometimes walking on eggshells when it comes to the study of the Middle East on their campuses, all of this compromises, or at least makes it significantly more difficult to achieve, the goal of turning out students who possess a solid and balanced understanding of this region that has been, and is almost certain to remain, of critical importance to their country and its security.

Although discouraging, this situation might appear to have little connection to national security. In fact, that would not be correct. Title VI and other centers devoted to the Middle East, like those devoted to other world regions, are important not only for the production and dissemination of abstract scholarly   49 knowledge—basic science, as it were—but also to help ensure that the United States has a citizenry that is globally literate and able to make sound judgments about the proposals and arguments advanced by their leaders in the area of world affairs. These centers are also charged—and have been since the Title VI program was established—with ensuring that the country has a reasonable core of men and women with indepth knowledge of countries and regions that are critical to U.S. security, whether these individuals serve in government, business, as members of international organizations or NGOs, or simply as consultants and advisors from a base in academia. Disruptions and interventions that limit the degree to which universities and area studies programs can fulfill these educational and training missions are thus injurious to national security.

Beyond the on-campus challenges, however, this situation complicates the use of area expertise by the national analytical and policy-making communities. At its most basic level, even were there less partisanship and more respect for different points of view than is the case, at least with respect to the Middle East, the different judgments of specialists with indepth knowledge about other societies and its relevance for issues that have national or global security implications mean that analysts and policy makers seeking to benefit from such knowledge will be presented not with the information they need but rather with an array of competing and contested assessments, each made persuasive by the genuine "expertise" of those who provide it. In principle, and at least sometimes in practice, this is actually desirable, fostering exchanges that contribute to deeper reflection, the questioning of assumptions, and more thoroughly thinking through the implications of various courses of action. But even in these instances, this places into proper context the arguments made earlier about the relevance of knowledge of other countries and cultures. The claim that policy makers need to draw on the knowledge of area specialists, though correct, takes one only so far.

Of course, particularly with respect to the Middle East but also in dealing with other world regions and international issues, there frequently is too little tolerance and respect for different points of view. Rather, competition to have one's perspective prevail is intense in policy-making and strategic analysis circles, perhaps even more than on university campuses, and responsibility for this rests with the partisanship and ideological inclinations of those who make policy and carry out strategic assessments, as well as with those of men and women in the academic community.

This was evident, for example, in the run-up to the U.S. invasion in Iraq, which pitted State Department area specialists, often denounced by their critics as "Arabists," against the Defense Department and its Republican party allies. Similar and particularly intense contests are perennial in Washington with respect to U.S. policy toward the Israeli–Palestinian conflict. Indeed, this is often conflated with other national security issues, including the debate about whether or not to invade Iraq, as reflected in the preinvasion statement by Deputy Secretary of Defense Paul Wolfowitz that "the road to peace in the Middle East runs through Baghdad." The following description by Tony Karon, an editor and columnist for Time.com, gives a feel, admittedly from a partisan perspective, for the political in-fighting in Washington at the time of the Iraq invasion.

> The State Department "Arabists" have long been a favorite target of Washington neo-conservatives, precisely because their support for the hawkish Likud line in Israeli politics makes them hostile to any effort in Washington to balance U.S. foreign policy between support for Israel and recognition of Arab interests. [Former House of Representatives Speaker Newt] Gingrich and his pals in and around the Pentagon, like Richard Perle, Douglas Feith and Paul Wolfowitz, want to turn Iraq over to Ahmad Chalabi, the exiled banker (or swindler, according to the Jordanian courts) whom they have cultivated in their own image as a leader that would toe the U.S. line and embrace Israel.[39]

More recently, similar debates have emerged with respect to U.S. policy toward Iran, and specifically about whether engagement will advance U.S. security interests and contribute to stability in the Middle East. As noted by Jon Alterman, director of the Middle East Program at Washington's Center for Strategic and International Studies, "for advocates, engagement with real or potential adversaries is an elixir that softens hostility and builds common interests. For opponents, it is a sign of surrender to dark forces of violence and hatred."[40] In all these cases, not surprisingly, those with different positions attempt to buttress their arguments by calling on the academic area specialists who support their point of view.

The focus of this discussion, which may seem overly focused on the Middle East but seeks to make an important general point, is to place in context prior arguments about the relevance for national and global security of knowledge about other countries and world regions. Although important, and often critical, it is also necessary to consider the factors that determine whether and how this knowledge will be used. There is a normative dimension to this context as well as a political one. As stated earlier, knowing about other societies and cultures often raises questions about costs and benefits, or even about right and wrong, that can be addressed only with reference to normative preferences and commitments. Thus, once again, the production and dissemination of specialized area knowledge is only part of what must be considered when dealing with other societies for the purpose of advancing national and global security. This issue, too, deserves a brief discussion.

This issue is raised forcefully and provocatively in *Is Multiculturalism Bad for Women?* by Susan Okin.[41] Okin's central concern is whether there are universal values that should guide approaches to different cultures, as opposed to emphasizing what is locally practiced, historically validated, and thus culturally appropriate, in the name of respect for pluralism and tolerance of diversity. This might not seem relevant for national and global security, especially because Okin's focus is not entirely international and her principal concern is for the circumstances of women. But in fact she is raising the question of how knowledge of other societies and cultures *should* be used, just as the previous politically focused discussion asked what determines how such knowledge *will* be used.

Okin argues that most cultures are patriarchal, hence, detrimental to women, permitting—and, indeed, valuing—practices ranging from unequal legal rights and employment discrimination to seclusion, polygamy, and female genital mutilation. If equal rights, including equal rights for women, is a universal value, a view that Okin is hardly alone in holding, policies and actions seeking to advance security should not hesitate to confront local traditions and practices that contravene the universal standard of gender equality. On the contrary, the best policies would seem to be those that undermine traditions that, however authentic and locally valued, are ultimately unacceptable.

But others disagree, or at least argue that this is too simple a proposition to guide behavior and policy in the real world. The Okin volume contains insightful and instructive reflections by fifteen respondents, most of whom are women and many of whom are from other countries; although they do not all have the same views, as a group they raise questions about whether local customs are properly understood by outsiders who seek to judge them and, most important, whether outsiders, in the name of respect for a universal principle, should substitute their own judgment for that of millions of local women who claim to value the status quo.[42] This, in turn, brings the rejoinder that those who favor the status quo may in some cases be prevented from expressing their true opinions and, in any event, that they are insufficiently knowledgeable about alternative social and political models to make truly informed choices. A response to this is that traditional practices are defended by some, and perhaps many, non-Western women who are in fact familiar with Western or other alternative models; and so the conversation continues. The central question in all this is "Who should decide?"—how should the tension between respect for universal values and respect for cultural diversity be resolved in particular situations and, more specifically, when, if ever, is it proper in the name of universal values for those with one normative standard to pursue policies that seek to deny to others the choice of behaving according to a different normative standard?

The reason for introducing this challenging issue into the present discussion is to illustrate the normative questions that come with knowledge about other societies and cultures and that attend the incorporation of that knowledge into policy making. Adding to the complexity is the fact that almost all societies have multiple traditions, so that there are likely to be competing claims about what is authentic and culturally appropriate. Also, those who claim to be defending a particular standard are sometimes seeking to mask actions, whether to maintain the status quo or to promote "reform," that are in reality about something else—usually maintaining or acquiring power, status, or resources. In any event, it is impossible to escape normative questions about what knowledge of other societies and cultures is relevant and about how and for what ends that knowledge should be used.

Because fidelity to the principles espoused by the United States frequently does not align with America's national security interests, these tensions are often present in U.S. foreign policy and they are not reduced by area knowledge. The Middle East, and the Muslim world more generally, again, provide an instructive case, and one that is particularly salient in the post-September 11, 2001 era. On the one hand, the United States regularly puts aside its declared commitment to democracy and human rights, including women's rights, when forging international alliances and providing support to "friendly" regimes. America's relationship with Egypt and Saudi Arabia are clear-cut examples, although there are others in the Middle East and elsewhere. Both are repressive regimes that have resisted calls for reform, and Saudi Arabia in particular enforces the seclusion of women and other restrictions that deny to women the rights and opportunities available to men. The two countries are America's most important Arab allies, however, with Egypt receiving the second largest allocation of U.S. foreign aid. These relationships serve American security needs, at least as these have been defined by both Republican and Democratic administrations, and among these are oil, support in the "war on terror," and "moderation" toward Israel.[43] This is not the place to discuss the wisdom of U.S. policy toward Egypt and Saudi Arabia. The point is simply to note that what the United States does in the international arena in defense of its security interests, real or perceived, is often at variance with the principles to which the country proclaims allegiance;[44] and the United States is hardly unique in this respect. Specialized area knowledge can usually do little to resolve this tension, as it flows from issues that are political and/or normative.

On the other hand, there are instances in which U.S. action has been guided by the principles it espouses rather than by narrow and immediate security interests. For example, the United States pushed for free and fair elections in the Palestinian territories in 2006, even though there was a chance, which turned out to be the case, that these would be won by the Islamist Hamas party. Because Hamas refuses to recognize Israel and is allied with other countries and parties that seek to limit U.S. influence in the Middle East, many argued that American security interests precluded giving an opening to Hamas and the United States should therefore put aside its efforts to promote democracy in Palestine and elsewhere. The United States nonetheless did opt for democratization, and it is indicative that there continue to be debates about whether or not this was the right decision.

Space does not permit the development of additional examples, but these brief references should nonetheless be enough to illustrate the difficulty of doing the "right" thing when dealing with other countries, peoples, and cultures to advance national or global security, all the more so if human rights and equality of opportunity are understood as part of security. Questions about principles and priorities require normative judgments that can, and should, be informed by indepth knowledge about societies that are the focus of policy making. However, as this section of the chapter has sought to show, area knowledge does not by itself produce satisfactory answers to security challenges. Again, this is not to say that such knowledge is unimportant after all; it is rather to depict the political and normative context within which the contribution of area knowledge to national and global security is made. Thus, although it is easy and important to insist that knowledge of other countries and cultures be produced and made available to the fullest extent possible, there remain, as stated at the beginning of this discussion, unavoidable and less readily answered questions about what specific knowledge is most relevant in particular situations, about how this knowledge should be weighed and used, and about who decides these matters.

Motives and Trust

Another complication should be discussed: the relationship between area specialists in academia and the government officials and professionals, or at least some government officials and professionals, who have responsibility for U.S. national security and for America's contribution to global security. Cooperating and sharing information and insights with the government is only one of the reasons for producing and disseminating knowledge about other countries and world regions, of course. No less important, as noted earlier, are imparting this knowledge to young Americans, and to the public more generally, and training the next generation of area specialists. Moreover, as discussed earlier, these tasks are not without significant national and global security implications. Nevertheless, there is a reasonable and legitimate expectation that those in government with national security responsibility and those outside government with foreign area expertise will cooperate when this might be useful to their country and, perhaps, to the international system more generally.

In fact, however, there is a history of distrust between area specialists in academia and important elements of the U.S. government, particularly the Department of Defense and the national security agencies, and this has frequently led the former to refuse cooperation with the latter. As a result, at least some people in the government security community charge that many academics with expertise pertaining to other countries and cultures are either naïve about national security concerns or, more likely, embrace too rigidly the ideology of the political left, are therefore much too critical of U.S. foreign policy, and for these reasons are reluctant, and often unwilling, to participate in analytical activities involving cooperation with the Washington defense establishment. Contentions of this type were discussed earlier in connection with the denunciations of the Middle East Studies Association issued by conservative scholars who were disturbed by criticisms of American foreign policy and of Israeli actions in the West Bank and Gaza. This is not the view of all, and probably not even most, in the defense and intelligence communities. Indeed, as will be discussed, there have recently been new efforts to reach out to academia, based on a recognition that much of the basic research carried out by area specialists at American (and other) universities produces information and insight that are useful for the making of foreign and defense policy. Still, many university-based foreign area specialists, including many affiliated with Title VI National Resource Centers, have refused cooperation with the Defense Department and the national security agencies, and this has brought criticism of the judgment and political motivation, and sometimes the patriotism, of these scholars and of academia more generally.

Those in academia who have reservations about cooperation with government security agencies say there are good reasons for the positions they take. They assert that they would be, and have been, asked to gather intelligence information while concealing the purpose and sponsor of the research from their sources or to undertake analyses that inform policies and actions that violate human rights or are otherwise unethical. These scholars further argue not only that this kind of involvement with the government is unacceptable for ethical reasons, but also that it compromises their ability to work in other countries—to gain access for research and to collaborate and build relations of trust with local counterparts, and is thus counterproductive even from the perspective of the Washington defense establishment.

Resistance to cooperation with defense and security agencies extends beyond individual scholars. Although these concerns are not shared by all university-based foreign area specialists, and are more common among those who work in particular world regions—most notably, Africa, Latin America, and the Middle East—those who believe that scholars should not participate in defense and intelligence projects, and should not take funds from the relevant government agencies, have worked, to some extent successfully, to build a consensus for their point of view on many campuses. An important role in advancing this position has been played by the Association of Concerned Africa Scholars (ACAS), which was established in 1977–1978. Its leaders include directors and affiliates from some of the county's leading Title VI centers devoted to the study of Africa. One of these, David Wiley of Michigan State University, has written an informative account of the ACAS's history and position.[45] The following excerpts, published in February 2009, provide a useful summary:

> In 1982, several officers of the Defense Intelligence Agency (DIA) approached four Title VI African centers to explore their willingness to receive large annual budget supplements in exchange for being "on call" to develop unspecified reports and undefined services. The directors of the four centers, including several ACAS members, consulted and agreed to not accept the funding and that they should consult with the wider Africanist community about these policies. After that consultation, they concluded that it was not in U.S. interests to link with the DIA, which could compromise their partnership collaborations and linkages in Africa with African institutions and scholars, as well as potentially provide scholarly legitimacy to the broader CIA/DIA/DOD/NSA hostilities to progressive African governments. ACAS concurred with the decision and since then has opposed any mixing of military or intelligence funding with African studies.

Since the establishment of the ACAS, the organization and others, including the Association of African Studies Programs (AASP), an organization of more than fifty African Studies programs at U.S. universities and colleges, as well as the board of the African Studies Association, have reaffirmed this position and expressed their views in various resolutions.[46] In 2001, for example, under challenge from the political right in the aftermath of September 11, 2001, Title VI African center directors passed a resolution stating that they

> oppose the application for and acceptance of military and intelligence funding of area and language programs, projects, and research in African studies. . . . We believe that the long-term interests of the people of the United States are best served by this separation between academic and military and defense establishments. Indeed, in the climate of the post-Cold War years in Africa and the security concerns after September 11, 2001, we believe that it is a patriotic policy to make this separation.[47]

Contemporary history, as well as events during the preceding decades, shaped the thinking of Africanists and other scholars who were coming to distrust the architects of their country's foreign policy. At the time this included the Reagan administration's State Department, and of particular concern was U.S. policy toward South Africa. In the 1980s, American policy toward the apartheid regime was one of "constructive engagement," an orientation that purported to be gently and realistically encouraging change on the part of the regime in Pretoria but that apartheid's critics in the United States and elsewhere considered much too soft, if not indeed supportive of the status quo in South Africa. The policy was designed and championed by Chester Crocker, who taught at Georgetown University before joining the government and serving as assistant secretary of state from 1981 to 1987. Crocker argued that rhetorical denunciations of South Africa merely increased Pretoria's mistrust of Washington and made Pretoria more intransigent. Many Africanists found this misguided, if not disingenuous. As one critic explained at the time:

> The self-righteous and self-serving policy of constructive engagement has made the U.S. an accomplice to the South African counter-revolutionary rule, and to the torture and murders that South Africa has perpetuated in the past three years against the forces of change. Many of the worst atrocities of the apartheid policy are now either ignored or suppressed by the Reagan administration, and it boasts some of the most effective propagandists of apartheid. I am referring to people like W. Scott Thompson and Chester Crocker, the soft-sell ideologist who coined the phrase 'constructive engagement'.[48]

An earlier episode, Project Camelot, is probably the poster child for U.S. intelligence operations that have fostered distrust among scholars. Funded and carried out by the U.S. Army and the CIA in the mid-1960s, the project was concerned with the potential emergence of leftist regimes in Latin America, and particularly in Chile; as part of the project, researchers were sent to Chile and other Latin American countries to survey political attitudes. The sponsors said the purpose of the surveys was to gather data with which to assess the likelihood of "internal war," to identify actions a government might take to relieve conditions that give rise to such domestic conflicts, and to determine the characteristics of governments most likely to make use of this information. Although it might appear that the goal was to gather information to be used in addressing popular grievances, and in this way contribute to political reform, many social scientists, including but not limited to those in Latin American studies, understood that Project Camelot was part of an interventionist counterinsurgency effort. These critics insisted that the study was using social science research to assist in suppressing legitimate and popular revolutionary movements, which was unacceptable. They also complained that Army funding and CIA involvement, as well as the true goals of the project, had been concealed, and this, too, was unacceptable.[49] The project was widely denounced by Latin Americanists and many others after it was exposed by Norwegian sociologist Johan Galtung, who had been invited to participate in its design and implementation.[50] This led to congressional hearings, after which the project was canceled in 1965 by Secretary of Defense Robert McNamara.

Nearer to the present, there have been new and expanded government efforts, through the Defense Department and CIA, as well as the State Department's Bureau of Intelligence and Research and other agencies, to reach out to foreign area specialists and others at American universities. These involve making funds available to institutions, scholars, and students for research and training, for the study of foreign languages, and for the preparation and presentation of analytical papers. These efforts at cooperation with academia bear little resemblance to Project Camelot. Nor do they appear to be aimed at gaining support for a particular and controversial foreign policy agenda, the situation that led to the establishment of the ACAS. Rather, although there are differences among these initiatives, they include a concern for expanding foreign language instruction and increasing the number of undergraduate and graduate students with an education-abroad experience, goals that are certainly in line with those of the universities themselves; and many of the programs award funds on the basis of peer review. These initiatives also emphasize the value for security-related assessments of *basic* research about and in other countries that scholars carry out, thereby seeking to benefit from the knowledge and independent perspective of foreign area specialists rather than working for their support of, and perhaps help in designing, specific international policies or interventions.

Among these governmental initiatives are the National Security Education Program (NSEP), the National Flagship Language Initiative, and the Minerva Project, all supported and administered by the Department of Defense, and the CIA's PISAP. The sponsors of these programs insist that they are sincere support and outreach initiatives, designed to meet national needs and having no political agenda that could compromise the independence of individuals and institutions who receive funding. Nevertheless, they have been greeted with resistance, and occasionally determined opposition, in some academic circles.

The NSEP gives grants for international study and research to graduate and undergraduate students and makes awards to universities for program development. It was proposed by Senator David Boren of Oklahoma in 1991 and is often called the Boren Program. Recognizing that expertise in languages and cultures is critical to U.S. national security, Boren became concerned, following his daughter's graduation from the University of Oklahoma, about how few American students learn a foreign language or study in another country. But many in academia were disturbed that the program was placed in the DIA of the Department of Defense for both funding and staffing and that the governing board included the director of the CIA. There was also objection to the provision requiring grantees to work in the federal government "in a position with national security responsibilities" for a period equal to the duration of their grant. Even though the provision has been liberally interpreted and rarely enforced, critics of the program say that the Defense

Department and CIA connection may lead to suspicions that grantees, especially when working overseas, are doing intelligence work and that this could compromise their ability to do research or even put them in danger. Thus, as David Wiley writes:

> Most of the area studies and several scholarly associations, including the Social Science Research Council, immediately objected to this mixture of military and intelligence programs with academic area studies and urged that federal support for language and area studies be routed through the U.S. Department of Education and its Title VI Higher Education Act programs.

Wiley also reports that the ACAS "led a vigorous campaign to review and oppose the Boren funding, with articles, web announcements, leaflets, and panels at ASA." At the same time, Wiley's account, written in 2009, goes on to note that most scholars and institutions today accept Boren funding and that "Africanists, alone among area studies scholars, have continued to decline these fellowships."[51]

The story of the National Flagship Language Initiative is similar. Established in 2002 as a new program within the NSEP, the initiative invited universities to apply for grants to build programs that "are capable of dramatically increasing the number of U.S. students advancing to professional levels of competency" in any of the following languages: Arabic, including vernaculars; Hindi; Chinese (Mandarin); Japanese; Korean; Persian/Farsi; Russian; and Turkish. Soon after the program was announced, however, the MESA approved a statement urging members not to seek or accept funds under this program. The association declared, echoing complaints about the NSEP, that "a government-funded program that emphasizes cooperation between the U.S. academy and government agencies responsible for intelligence and defense will increase the difficulties and dangers of such academic activities, and may foster the already widespread impression that academic researchers from the United States are directly involved in government activities." Although this did not prevent the initiative from going forward, the *Chronicle of Higher Education* noted that when the first set of grants was announced, "some institutions well-known for their expertise in Arabic, such as Georgetown and Harvard Universities and the University of Michigan at Ann Arbor, were noticeably missing from the list of grant recipients." Michigan had in fact been encouraged to apply by officials of the program but, after considerable debate on the Ann Arbor campus, declined to do so. Near Eastern Studies Department chair, Alexander Knysh, told the *Chronicle* at the time that "the university's Arabists had some reservations about accepting funds from the program."[52] Again, however, as with the NSEP itself, opposition has diminished since the program was established, and the University of Michigan in fact applied for and received funding in 2008 to expand significantly its highly regarded Arabic program and become an Arabic Language Flagship Program.

The most recent Department of Defense program aimed at academics with expertise in international and foreign area studies is the Minerva Research Initiative. It offers support to scholarly teams at U.S. universities for programs of basic social science research that have national security implications. The stated goals of the initiative, launched by Secretary of Defense Robert Gates and for which $75 million over five years was allocated, are to "increase the Department's intellectual capital in the social sciences and improve its ability to address future challenges and build bridges between the Department and the social science community."[53] The first call for proposals, issued in 2008, designated five substantive areas in which applications were sought. These focused, respectively, on China, Iraq, Islam, terrorism, and "new approaches to understanding dimensions of national security, conflict, and cooperation." Many social scientists welcomed the emphasis on basic research and the explicit recognition of the value of such work, even as some considered the topics and languages deemed most relevant for national security to be too narrow; and indeed, a large number of proposals were submitted. Approximately 200 white papers were submitted in a preapplication round; of these, thirty-seven were invited to submit full proposals. Seven awards were subsequently made across the five substantive categories.

Although many scholars and institutions applied for Minerva funds, the initiative has had critics as well as supporters in academia, thus giving rise to some of the same debates and controversies that accompanied the NSEP and language flagship initiative. In the fall of 2008, the Social Science Research Council (SSRC) invited prominent scholars "to speak to the questions raised by Project Minerva and to address the controversy it sparked in academic quarters." These presentations have been posted on the SSRC web site and collectively offer a useful overview of the concerns expressed by critics. These include, as summarized by one scholar,

> a deep-seated reluctance to participate, intentionally or unintentionally, in the promotion of perceived U.S. imperial designs; the real potential for undermining academic freedoms and reducing formerly more autonomous scholarship and research agendas across the academy to questions of national interest and security; the recruitment of social scientists into clandestine research projects, where deliberate misrepresentation could irreparably damage the reputation of non-military field workers through a taint by association; and where an absence of open knowledge circulation would erode the academic public sphere; as well as the potential unethical application of social scientific knowledge production in pursuit of military objectives, including for the targeting of research populations in the form of intellectual "smart bombs."[54]

Anthropologists have been particularly vocal in expressing such concerns, not only about Minerva but also about other initiatives linking academic researchers and the U.S. military. In 2007, for example, the American Anthropological Association

(AAA) released a statement charging that DOD's Human Terrain System (HTS), which incorporates anthropologists and other social scientists into U.S. military teams in Iraq and Afghanistan, had violated the AAA Code of Ethics. The code mandates that anthropologists do no harm to their research subjects, and the statement expressed concern that some responsibilities assigned to the HTS anthropologists by military officials may conflict with their obligations to the persons they study or consult.[55]

The CIA's PISAP is somewhat different than the initiatives described above in that it does not solicit proposals and make grants but rather invites academic specialists with expertise on Islam to make presentations or participate in meetings and conferences organized for analysts from various intelligence agencies, including those from the State Department. Surprisingly, perhaps, given that the program is run by the CIA, there has not been much controversy associated with PISAP. It is impossible to know how many scholars have declined invitations because of the CIA connection, but a large and diverse array of scholars has participated in one or more of the events organized by PISAP. The program was established in 2004 and until recently was directed by Emile Nakhleh, an academic who was recruited by the agency. It built on and expanded the agency's academic outreach program that Nakhleh had already been directing for several years. According to the CIA web site, PISAP "relies on regional and functional expertise to promote, consolidate, and integrate multidisciplinary analysis on worldwide developments of interest to the US policy community."

Nakhleh's valuable 2009 book, *A Necessary Engagement: Reinventing America's Relations with the Muslim World*, discusses in detail what is the central premise of this chapter, as well as the one on which PISAP is built: Effective U.S. policy toward other countries and global challenges, and toward the Arab and Muslim world in this case, requires a thorough knowledge of local cultures, histories, and political circumstances; and further, complications and controversies associated with cooperation notwithstanding, much of this knowledge must of necessity come from area specialists outside the government. "Relations with the Arab Muslim world cannot be grounded mostly or exclusively in military and security policy," Nakhleh reminds his readers; yet, as he writes in his opening statement, "our government lacks deep knowledge of the Islamic world and of the diverse ways that Muslims understand their faith, their relations with each other, and their vision of, and attitudes toward, the non-Muslim world."[56]

Conclusion

Title VI centers and other programs at U.S. universities have been training young men and women who will work in government and provide some of the needed expertise, and more can and should be done in this connection. But there is an equally critical role for those in the academy with knowledge of other societies and international affairs. Given the value and relevance of the global knowledge and expertise that reside in the academic community, and the apparent recognition of this fact by many government officials with national security responsibility, it is important to identify and seek to resolve the obstacles and sources of mistrust that stand in the way of sharing of information and insight so the country can not only deal with its security challenges as intelligently as possible but can also do so in a manner that also respects the legitimate interests of others and contributes to global security more generally.

Even though there is not likely to be much disagreement with this principle, there is a legacy of distrust that must be overcome. Some in the Title VI community will continue to believe that any cooperation with military and intelligence agencies is unacceptable, that even care and good intentions cannot overcome the contradictions that are inherent in such relationships. This is a defensible position, and one that should not be dismissed as purely ideological or politically motivated. Further, even if contradictions are not inherent, they have been present and should be recognized. Accordingly, proposals that initiatives such as the NSEP, its National Language Flagship Initiative, and Minerva be administered by the Department of Education, rather than the Department of Defense, deserve serious consideration, and DOD's decision to have some Minerva proposals reviewed by the National Science Foundation is a welcome step that recognizes the need for independence and peer review in making awards. At the same time, scholars can respond to initiatives of the Defense Department and the CIA and other agencies that are part of the National Intelligence Council, as they increasingly appear to be doing, by taking a position that insists absolutely on established ethical standards in research and information sharing, as required by local institutional review boards, but that also assumes good faith on the part of government officials, at least until there is evidence to the contrary, and therefore not only accepts their responsibility to contribute what they can to strategic analyses and policy making concerned with national and global security but, in fact, welcomes the opportunity to have a voice in this important enterprise.

Acknowledgment

The author acknowledges with appreciation the valuable research and editorial assistance provided by Shannon Hill in the preparation of this essay.

Notes

1 For useful background, see Patrick O'Meara, Howard D. Mehlinger, and Roxana Ma Newman, *Changing Perspectives on International Education*. Bloomington: Indiana University Press, 2001.

2 Shahrbanou Tadjbakhsh, "Human Security in International Organizations: Blessing or Scourge?" *Human Security Journal* 4 (2007), p. 9.

3 *Human Security Report 2005.* Vancouver: Human Security Centre, Liu Institute for Global Issues, University of British Columbia, 2005, p. 6.

4 Mauro F. Guillén, "The Real Reasons to Support Language Study," *The Chronicle of Higher Education*, July 27, 2009.

5 Nicholas Kristof, "The Daily Me," *New York Times*, March 18, 2009.

6 For a summary, see Ben Terris, "In New Center, Albright Sees Promise for Diplomacy." Online at www.boston.com/yourtown/news/wellesley/2009/06/albright_returns.html

7 For access to the full report and supporting documentation, see the American Academy of Diplomacy, "Foreign Affairs Budget for the Future: Fixing a Hollow Service." Online at www.academyofdiplomacy.org/programs/fab_project.html.

8 The statement, dated June 25, 2009, was issued by former secretaries of state Henry Kissinger, George Shultz, James Baker, Lawrence Eagleburger, Warren Christopher, Madeleine Albright, Colin Powell, and Condoleezza Rice. It is available online at www.politico.com/news/stories/0609/24159.html.

9 Emile Nakhleh, *A Necessary Engagement: Reinventing America's Relations with the Muslim World.* Princeton, NJ: Princeton University Press, 2009, p. xi.

10 Mark Tessler with Jodi Nachtwey and Anne Banda, *Area Studies and Social Science: Strategies for Understanding Middle East Politics.* Bloomington: Indiana University Press, 1999, p. xii.

11 See Eco-Villages, "Water, Development and Literacy in Morocco." Online at www.eco-villages.org/pages/view/1053.

12 See Mark Tessler, "Public Opinion in the Arab and Muslim World: Informing U.S. Public Diplomacy." In Joseph McMillan, ed., *In the Same Light as Slavery: Strengthening International Norms against Terrorism.* Washington, D.C.: National Defense University Press, 2007.

13 For an insightful discussion, see Marc Lynch, "Public Diplomacy Practitioners, Policy Makers, and Public Opinion," in Report of the Public Diplomacy and World Public Opinion Forum, Washington, D.C., April 9–11, 2006.

14 Richard Holbrooke, "Review of *Lessons in Disaster: McGeorge Bundy and the Path to War in Vietnam* by Gordon M. Goldstein," *New York Times*, November 30, 2008.

15 See "The Fog of War: Eleven Lesson's from the Life of Robert S. McNamara," a documentary by Errol Morris (2003). See also George C. Herring, "The Wrong Kind of Loyalty: McNamara's Apology for Vietnam," *Foreign Affairs,* May/June 1995.

16 Michael Hudson, "The United States' Involvement in Lebanon." In Halim Barakat, ed., *Toward a Viable Lebanon.* London: Croom Helm, 1988, p. 229.

17 George Ball, *Error and Betrayal in Lebanon*. Washington, D.C.: Foundation for Middle East Peace, 1984, p. 76.

18 Steven Lee Myers, "America's Scorecard in Iraq," *New York Times*, February 8, 2009.

19 Peter Galbraith, *Unintended Consequences: How War in Iraq Strengthened America's Enemies*. New York: Simon & Schuster, 2008. For another valuable account that advances this thesis, see Seth G. Jones, *In the Graveyard of Empires: America's War in Afghanistan*. New York: W. W. Norton, 2009.

20 Larry Diamond, *Squandered Victory: The American Occupation and the Bungled Effort to Bring Democracy to Iraq*. New York: Henry Holt, 2006. Rajiv Chandrasekaran, *Imperial Life in the Emerald City: Inside Iraq's Green Zone*. New York: Vintage, 2007. David L. Phillips, *Losing Iraq: Inside the Postwar Reconstruction Fiasco*. New York: Basic Books, 2006.

21 For background information see "Changing Minds Winning Peace: A New Strategic Direction for U.S. Public Diplomacy on the Arab and Muslim World," Report of the Advisory Group on Public Diplomacy for the Arab and Muslim World, Submitted to the Committee on Appropriations of the U.S. House of Representatives, October 1, 2003; online at www.state.gov/documents/organization/24882.pdf.

22 Samuel Huntington, *The Clash of Civilizations and the Remaking of World Order*. New York: Simon and Schuster, 1997.

23 Bernard Lewis, "The Roots of Muslim Rage: Why So Many Muslim Deeply Resent the West and Why Their Bitterness Will Not Be Easily Mollified." *Atlantic Monthly* 266, September 1990.

24 See Tessler 2007, op. cit. See also Mark Tessler, "Arab and Muslim Political Attitudes: Stereotypes and evidence from survey research." *International studies Perspectives* 4 (May 2003), pp. 175–180.

25 Sources for these quotations, and others, are given in Tessler 2007, op. cit.

26 Many scholarly works examine the ideological and normative debates within Islam and the political context within which contesting interpretations are advanced and defended. A valuable book for those seeking further information on this subject, with special reference to Egypt, is Bruce Rutherford, *Egypt after Mubarak: Liberalism, Islam, and Democracy in the Arab World*. Princeton, NJ: Princeton University Press, 2008.

27 Nicholas Kristof, "Bigotry in Islam—And Here." *New York Times*, July 9, 2002.

28 Emile Nakhleh, op. cit., pp. xi, xiii, xv.

29 For complaints relating to Latin American Studies at an earlier period that echo the tensions that currently characterize Middle East Studies, see William Ratliff, "Latin American Studies: Up From Radicalism?" *Academic Questions* (Winter 1989-90), pp. 60–74.

30 See "The MESA Debate: The Scholars, the Media, and the Middle East," *Journal of Palestine Studies* 16: 2 (Winter 1987), pp. 85–104.

31 Bernard Lewis. *What Went Wrong: Western Impact and Middle Eastern Response.* New York: Oxford University Press, 2002.

32 Juan Cole, "Review of Bernard Lewis' *What Went Wrong: Western Impact and Middle Eastern Response*," *Global Dialogue*, 27 January 2003. Cole discusses Lewis's argument that in the modern era Muslims "could not consider science and philosophy the secret of success because they reduced philosophy to the handmaiden of theology."

33 Efraim Karsh and Rory Miller, "Did Edward Said Really Speak Truth to Power?" *Middle East Quarterly* (Winter 2008), pp. 13–21.

34 Martin Kramer, *Ivory Towers on Sand: The Failure of Middle Eastern Studies in America.* Washington, D.C.: Washington Institute for Near East Policy, 2001. See also David Horowitz, *The Professors: the 101 Most Dangerous Academics in America.* Washington, D.C.: Regerny Publishing, 2006. Horowitz's list contains a disproportionately large number of Middle East specialists, as well as those who are profiled because of their views relating to the Middle East.

35 Kurtz's testimony was delivered on June 19, 2003, at a hearing of the House Subcommittee on Select Education dealing with Title IV funding and area studies programs. Among his statements: "My concern is that Title VI-funded centers too seldom balance readings from Edward Said and his like-minded colleagues with readings from authors who support American foreign policy [such as] Bernard Lewis, Samuel P. Huntington, and Fouad Ajami."

36 For a fuller discussion, see Ellen Lust-Okar, Lisa Anderson, Steve Heydemann, and Mark Tessler, "Comparative Politics of the Middle East and Academic Freedom," *APSA-CP Newsletter* 18 (Winter 2007), pp. 12–15.

37 Nigel Perry, "Campus Watch: Interview with Prof. Rashid Khalidi," *The Electronic Intifada*, September 25, 2002.

38 Lust-Okar et al., op. cit., p. 14.

39 Tony Karon, "In Defense of State," *Time.com*, April 23, 2003. See also Stephen Glain, "Freeze-Out of the Arabists," *The Nation*, October 14, 2004. Glain complains that "America's most talented [State Department] Arab experts were until recently blocked from playing any meaningful role in the administration of postwar Iraq . . . [because] this administration doesn't like naysayers." For a more critical account of State Department and other Arabists, written a decade earlier, see Robert D. Kaplan, *The Arabists*. New York: Free Press, 1995. Kaplan contends, for example, that these Arabists promoted the appeasement of Iraqi dictator Saddam Hussein by U.S. President George H. W. Bush.

40 Jon B. Alterman, "Defining Engagement," *Middle East Notes and Comments*, Center for Strategic and International Studies (July/August 2009), p. 1.

41 Susan Moller Okin (with respondents), *Is Multiculturalism Bad for Women?* Princeton, NJ: Princeton University Press, 1999.

42 See, for example, Azizah Y. al-Hibri, "Is Western Patriarchal Feminism Good for Third World/Minority Women?" in Okin, op. cit.; and Bhikhu Parekh, "A Varied Moral World," in Okin, op. cit. Al-Hibri asserts that Okin "commits simple but significant factual errors in assessing other belief systems" (p. 42). Parekh states that "if others do not share the feminist view, it would be wrong to say they are victims . . . and in need of liberation by well-meaning outsiders" (p. 73).

43 A similar issue arises with the proposal by some that the United States seek to reach an accord with "moderate" Taliban elements in Afghanistan. Such an accord might be attainable, and if so it might reduce the violence and provide the United States with a viable exit strategy for its war in that country. At the same time, this raises the possibility that the Taliban, enabled by such an accord, would use their increased influence to impose on Afghan women the restrictions they enforced before the U.S. invasion that ousted them from power. For a discussion of the possibilities for reaching an accord with Taliban elements, see Fotini Christia and Michael Semple, "Flipping the Taliban: How to Win in Afghanistan," *Foreign Affairs* (July/August 2009): 34–45.

44 This double standard, or hypocrisy, also reduces the credibility of American foreign policy in instances in which the United States does genuinely seek to promote democratization. This point was made by Thomas Carothers of the Carnegie Endowment for International Peace in testimony before the Senate Foreign Relations Committee in June 2006. Discussing Eastern Europe and Central Asia, Carothers described a "glaring double-standard" and observed that the weak U.S. response to the manipulated 2005 elections in Kazakhstan and Azerbaijan undercut America's assertion of democratic principles in Belarus.

45 David Wiley, "Origins of the Association of Concerned Africa Scholars (ACAS) as a pro-Africa voice among American Scholars" (February 1, 2009). Available online at http://concernedafricascholars.org/origins-of-acas/.

46 See www.africanstudies.org/p/cm/ld/fid=107 for the full texts of the resolutions of the African Studies Association, the Association of African Studies Programs, and the Directors of the Title VI African National Resource Centers.

47 Wiley, op. cit.

48 Bernard Magubane, "Constructive Engagement or Disingenuous Support for Apartheid," *Issue: A Journal of Opinion* 12 (Autumn–Winter, 1982): 8–10. The journal was published by the African Studies Association. As stated by another

critic, "The Reagan administration's policy of constructive engagement would have done far more than merely transform the decolonization initiative and render it ineffective. It would also have permitted the South African government greater access to nuclear weapons to employ against the communist and procommunist states along its borders and possibly internally against elements of the South African black liberation movement." See Hanes Walton Jr., *African American Power and Politics: The Political Context Variable.* New York: Columbia University Press, 1997, p. 357. For a fuller account, see J. E. Davies, *Constructive Engagement: Chester Crocker and American Policy in South Africa, Namibia and Angola.* Oxford, OH: Ohio University Press, 2007.

49 Other aspects of Project Camelot involved using these and other attitude studies in an ad campaign intended to influence the outcome of Chilean elections. The CIA analyzed the data with a view toward identifying the fears and anxieties of individuals and groups sympathetic to leftist candidates and then recruited New York ad agencies to use this information. As reported by one scholar with experience in Chile, "The themes and images were outlined by the CIA, but were actually implemented by the ad agencies of McCann-Erickson and J. Walter Thompson. . . . Women were told that if [the leftist candidate] Allende were elected, their children would be sent to Cuba, and their husbands would be sent to concentration camps. On election day women voted as expected." See Fred Landis, "Psychological Warfare in Chile: The CIA Makes Headlines," *Liberation* 19 (March–April 1975), p. 22.

50 For a brief but useful summary, see Montgomery McFate, "Anthropology and Counterinsurgency: The Strange Story of their Curious Relationship," *Military Review* (March–April 2005). McFate also provides a useful summary of other episodes and problems involving attempts to involve American social scientists in U.S. counterinsurgency efforts. For a fuller and more contemporary account of Project Camelot, see Irving Louis Horowitz, ed., *The Rise and Fall of Project Camelot: Studies in the Relationship between Social Science and Practical Politics.* Boston: MIT Press, 1967.

51 Wiley, op. cit.

52 Anne Marie Borrego, "Scholars Revive Boycott of U.S. Grants to Promote Language Training: Do links to Pentagon tarnish the program, or are some professors posturing?" *The Chronicle of Higher Education*, August 16, 2002.

53 As explained by one Department of Defense official, it is important to leverage the intellectual resources of those with international and foreign area expertise in order "to help our government prevail in the face of challenges that are more complex, more interrelated, and potentially more deadly than any we have previously faced." Accordingly, he continued, "cultural knowledge and regional   67

expertise become critical enablers that we must add to our quiver of capabilities to help us deal with this rapidly changing world," and this includes fields like "history, anthropology, sociology and religious studies" that can "help in devising new approaches and unearthing innovative ideas to aid in solving the intertwined and complex challenges of the future." See Tom Mahnken, "Building Bridges and Communities," presentation on "The Minerva Controversy" made to the Social Science Research Council on December 30, 2008, and available online at http://essays.ssrc.org/minerva/category/all/. Seventeen other essays, most pertaining to Minerva but often considering academic–government relations more broadly, are posted on this SSRC web site.

54 Robert Albro, "Minerva and Critical Public Engagement," presentation on "The Minerva Controversy" made to the Social Science Research Council on November 14, 2008, and available online at http://essays.ssrc.org/minerva/category/all/.

55 See www.aaanet.org/issues/AAA-Opposes-Human-Terrain-System-Project.cfm, consulted 11/10/2009.

56 Emile Nakhleh, op. cit., pp. xi, xiii. For another example of the attempt to draw on scholars outside government when assessing foreign policy needs and options, see Joseph McMillan, *In the Same Light as Slavery: Strengthening International Norms against Terrorism*. Washington, D.C.: National Defense University Press, 2007. This volume brings together the papers of university-based scholars and others presented at a conference held at the National Defense University.

PART 2

Title VI Programs and the Less Commonly Taught Languages

CHAPTER 4

The Impact of Fifty Years of Title VI on Language Learning in the United States

Elaine E. Tarone

Why Americans Need to Learn Foreign Languages

Why is it important for Americans to learn foreign languages? In a nation that has been so resolutely English-speaking for more than 200 years, where U.S. citizens can apparently live their entire lives without ever needing to use any other language, why should they bother? Even for those interested in international travel and work, is it not enough just to learn about other areas of the world without having to learn the languages spoken there?

There are many good reasons, both individual and national, for Americans to learn foreign languages. At the individual level, bilingual mastery improves an individual's cognitive capacity as well as his or her employability in a range of professions. At the national level, more foreign language knowledge is essential if we are to effectively implement "soft diplomacy," avoid the impression of arrogance on the world stage, and build relational networks essential to our national security.

Individual Benefits of Multilingualism

For individuals, research has shown that a person's knowledge of a second or third language confers not only an aesthetic appreciation of other cultures but many cognitive benefits:

- Significantly higher levels of creativity and problem solving (Kessler and Quinn 1987)
- Improved cognitive flexibility (DeGroot and Kroll 1997)
- Earlier development of awareness of language (Bialystok 2001)
- Longer retention of fluid intelligence skills in aging (Bialystok et al. 2004)

In addition, Americans who are proficient in a second or third language have an undeniable competitive edge in job seeking and professional advancement compared with their monolingual competitors; the more advanced their proficiency in these languages, the more effectively they are able to use them in carrying out responsibilities in professions ranging from medicine to academic research to international business to intelligence gathering (American Council on Education 2009).

National Need for Foreign Language Ability

There is also a national-level rationale for improving the foreign language competence of U.S. citizens. There is a growing consensus among international advisors to the U.S. government that we need more use of "soft diplomacy" or "smart power" if we are to transform world opinion in ways that "hard power" cannot (Armitage and Nye 2008; Nye 2005, 2008). Where "hard power" is the use of force or military power, "soft power" is the ability to obtain the outcomes one wants through attraction and communication rather than payment, coercion, or military action. Central to the implementation of "soft diplomacy" is the ability to communicate across difference—and this does not just mean the ability to communicate in English. It is in fact arrogant to insist that all those we want to communicate with should switch to the only language we know. English is not the only world language—there are far more speakers of Chinese than English worldwide, and English is also rivaled by Spanish in terms of its central role in international communication. "Soft diplomacy" must include the ability to communicate with high levels of proficiency in other languages, including less commonly taught languages that are critical to the national interest (Gates 2009). Our country's overall diplomatic success[1] ultimately relies on person-to-person, private diplomacy, for which foreign language skills are essential (Heyman 2008).

The National Language Security Initiative (NSLI)—a collaboration at the highest levels of the departments of Defense, Education, and State with the National Intelligence Program—has made it clear that our security as a nation depends on our development of a cadre of citizens who can use critical foreign languages at superior levels of proficiency (Spellings and Oldham 2008). Each year, these federal divisions fund grant programs to support the learning of the same set of seldom-taught languages considered to be critical to the nation's security. The specific languages targeted can shift from one year to the next depending on economic and security conditions worldwide; as of this writing, these priority languages include Arabic, Chinese, Japanese, Korean, Russian, and languages in the Indic, Iranian, and Turkic language families.

The ability to communicate in other languages is considered to be an integral part of our national defense. Indeed, a major goal of the Department of Defense is to establish a cadre of language professionals with higher levels of proficiency in such critical languages:

> Conflict against enemies speaking less-commonly-taught languages and thus the need for foreign language capability will not abate. Robust foreign language and foreign area expertise are critical to sustaining coalitions, pursuing regional stability, and conducting multi-national missions especially in post-conflict and other than combat, security, humanitarian, nation-building and stability operations. *Language skill and regional expertise . . . are as important as critical weapon systems* (Department of Defense 2005: 3, author's emphasis).
>
> [Level 2] language skills[3] are insufficient to meet the requirements of the changed security environment. . . . A higher level of language skill and greater language capacity is needed to build the internal relationships required for coalition/multi-national operations, peacekeeping, and civil/military affairs (Department of Defense 2005: 10–11).

The level of proficiency needed is described in the memorable words of David S. C. Chu, Pentagon undersecretary for personnel: "This is not just figuring out how many tanks the enemy has. This is more nuanced work. This is tracking people who communicate with allusions, with metaphors" (Graham 2005).

Response of Local U.S. Educational Systems to National Foreign Language Need

This chapter assumes that, on the world stage, the ability to carry out "soft diplomacy" through advanced proficiency in foreign languages has become an increasingly important strategic tool for American security and diplomacy, and is needed for the economic well-being of the nation.

In spite of the demonstrable national need for large numbers of citizens who have high levels of proficiency in foreign languages, the historical response of our locally controlled educational system, both the public schools and the postsecondary colleges and universities, has (with only a few exceptions) been inadequate. In the absence of federal incentives and intervention, neither K-12 nor postsecondary institutions have been able to produce graduates with the levels of foreign language skills that are needed. As will be shown in this chapter, the

73

situation has worsened in the last decade. The failure is an institutional one, at local levels of both K-12 and postsecondary institutions; it is a failure that has necessitated the intervention of federal programs such as those in the U.S. Department of Education Title VI to encourage and support foreign language learning.

Foreign Languages in K-12 Schools

Research suggests that younger foreign language learners whose programs start early and provide uninterrupted continuity have the best long-term outcomes, so it is important to have strong, articulated foreign language learning opportunities beginning in the elementary schools and continuing through secondary schools. Over the past twenty-one years, the Center for Applied Linguistics (CAL) has used Title VI funds to conduct nationwide surveys every decade tracking the number of foreign language offerings in the public schools; the 2008 CAL survey results are reported in Rhodes and Pufahl (2010).

Table 4-1 shows that fewer U.S. elementary schools are teaching foreign languages today, than there were a decade ago: 25 percent in 2008 compared with 31 percent in 1997, with the most significant decrease of nine percentage points found among the public elementary schools.

Many teachers and school personnel surveyed believe that the No Child Left Behind legislation, which tests math and reading but not foreign language ability, has had a negative effect on efforts to offer foreign language classes in public elementary schools. The same downward trend has occurred in U.S. middle

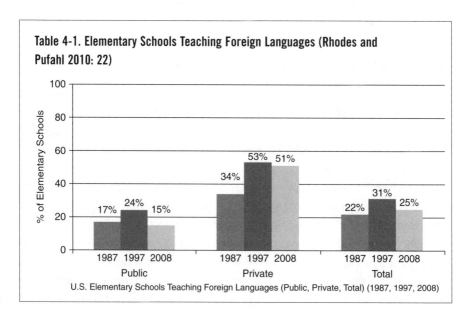

Table 4-1. Elementary Schools Teaching Foreign Languages (Rhodes and Pufahl 2010: 22)

U.S. Elementary Schools Teaching Foreign Languages (Public, Private, Total) (1987, 1997, 2008)

schools: Fifty-eight percent of middle schools offered foreign languages in 2008 compared with 75 percent in 1997. High school language offerings have remained level over the past decade at just over 90 percent. In the public elementary schools, there are pockets of excellence involving the use of intensive language immersion programming; in 2008, 14 percent of all public elementary school language instruction consisted of language immersion programs (Rhodes and Pufahl 2010: 38).

Table 4-2 shows trends over the past two decades in the languages the schools have chosen to teach.

Spanish has clearly continued to be the most favored language in both elementary and secondary schools and has even increased in its popularity over the past decade, whereas the two other favorites, French and German, have declined over the same period. There are more Mandarin and Arabic classes offered in elementary schools than there were a decade ago, with Chinese offerings now outstripping German at that level. Since the most recent CAL survey was conducted, of course, the nation has moved into a deep recession, and this is clearly taking an additional toll on foreign language programming in the public schools. Alarming cuts are clearly being made to foreign language offerings nationwide (Zehr 2009).

To sum up, the Rhodes and Pufahl (2010) CAL survey and more recent news reports provide us with sobering information about the degree to which locally

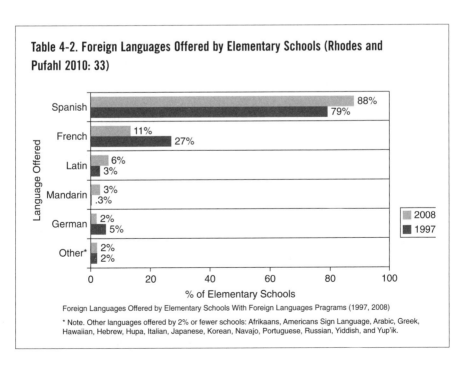

Table 4-2. Foreign Languages Offered by Elementary Schools (Rhodes and Pufahl 2010: 33)

Foreign Languages Offered by Elementary Schools With Foreign Languages Programs (1997, 2008)

* Note. Other languages offered by 2% or fewer schools: Afrikaans, Americans Sign Language, Arabic, Greek, Hawaiian, Hebrew, Hupa, Italian, Japanese, Korean, Navajo, Portuguese, Russian, Yiddish, and Yup'ik.

controlled K-12 schools have been able to respond to the national need for dramatically greater foreign language proficiency on the part of U.S. citizens. Although there have been pockets of excellence in the schools, the overall picture is not encouraging. Funding is needed for positions for K-12 language teachers across the nation. Federal initiatives such as Foreign Language Assistance Program grants and Language Flagship models have expanded K-12 language offerings in targeted locations, and Title VI grants have supported K-12 educational programs primarily through language teacher education resources and opportunities, but these programs cannot solve the primary problem of dwindling commitment at the local level to provide salaried positions for K-12 language teachers.

Foreign Languages in Postsecondary Education

U.S. colleges and universities also have struggled to find ways to offer a wide range of foreign languages at advanced and superior levels, and generally have been unsuccessful without access to substantial federal support such as that provided by U.S. Department of Education Title VI programs.

One obstacle is clearly financial and has to do with very low student demand for particular languages: postsecondary foreign language classes must attract enough students—and their tuition payments—to support instructor salaries. This has always been the case, but it is particularly important in the current recession and given our current national security needs. There is simply more student interest in some languages than in others. The "more commonly taught languages" (MCTLs), such as Spanish, French, and German, have historically been able to attract enough students to support classes financially at the first, second, third, and sometimes even the fourth year levels. In recent years, in college, just as in the public schools, more students enroll in Spanish and fewer in French and German. But the national need outlined in the first section above requires that a substantial number of students learn languages other than the MCTLs with priority given to the list of critical languages considered by the government to be priorities. Then there are the less commonly taught but not critical languages (such as Italian, Norwegian, or Greek) and the least commonly taught languages (LCTLs) such as Czech, Swahili, Vietnamese, and dozens of languages in South and Southeast Asia and Africa. Unless there is strong student demand for one of these LCTLs—as, for example, when it is a heritage language of the local community, such as Hmong or Somali in Minneapolis—postsecondary institutions typically cannot afford to offer an LCTL, even with distance education technologies, without external federal funding such as that provided by Title VI. To put it plainly, if the nation needs an LCTL to be taught in postsecondary institutions, then federal funding must be provided to help particular institutions and consortia of institutions offer that LCTL.

An additional barrier to the learning of all foreign languages, no matter how strong the student demand, is the traditional structure of foreign language departments in American universities. A major report issued in 2006 by the Modern Language Association (MLA) Ad Hoc Committee on Foreign Languages describes the unnecessarily limiting "two-tiered" structure of postsecondary foreign language departments and recommends that this structure be changed to provide students with the advanced and superior levels of proficiency they need for use in a wide range of professional and academic contexts:

> The standard configuration of university foreign language curricula, in which a two- or three-year language sequence feeds into a set of core courses primarily focused on canonical literature . . . represents a narrow model. This configuration defines both the curriculum and the governance structure of language departments and creates a division between the language curriculum and the literature curriculum and between tenure-track literature professors and language instructors in non-tenure-track positions. At doctorate-granting institutions, cooperation or even exchange between the two groups is usually minimal or nonexistent. . . . The two-tiered configuration has outlived its usefulness and needs to evolve. . . .
>
> In their individual scholarly pursuits and in their pedagogical practices, foreign language faculty members have been working in creative ways to cross disciplinary boundaries, incorporate the study of all kinds of material in addition to the strictly literary, and promote wide cultural understanding through research and teaching. It is time for all language programs in all institutions to reflect this transformation (MLA Ad Hoc Committee on Foreign Languages 2006).

It is unclear, at the time of this writing, whether postsecondary institutions have the will, on their own initiative, to make the sort of transformation envisioned in the 2006 MLA report. There is considerable inertia and a lack of incentive to make this kind of change within colleges and universities, particularly because the national organizations that rate language departments perpetuate the dominance of the study of literature over the study of language. It may be that even stronger external incentives from the federal government will be needed, but without the internal will of leaders in the colleges and universities to make this transformation, the outcome seems doubtful.

Fifty Years of Title VI Programs and their Impact on Language Learning

As other chapters in this book have established, the Department of Education Title VI programs are considered to have begun in 1958 with the passage of the National

Defense Education Act (NDEA), followed in short order in 1961 with the passage of the Fulbright-Hays Act. In 1980, the NDEA was replaced by the Higher Education Act, which was reauthorized in 1992 (Hines 2001). Each of these dates saw the addition of new programs, most of which provided some measure of support for foreign language learning. Over the past fifty years, by a conservative estimate, between 150 and 200 languages have been taught and/or supported by new materials, assessments, and pedagogical tools, using funding from a variety of Title VI programs. A review of the Foreign Language and Area Studies (FLAS) fellowship records on the U.S. Department of Education (USDE) International Resource and Information System (IRIS) web site shows that more than 75,000 such fellowships have been issued for individuals' study of a wide variety of languages.[3] The Title VI-supported National Resource Centers (NRCs) have funded instruction of a wide range of less commonly taught languages at universities that otherwise would not have offered them because of their prohibitive expense. Language Resource Centers (LRCs) and the Title VI International Research and Studies Program (IRSP) grants have funded the development of curriculum materials to teach the LCTLs, and offer teacher development workshops, conferences and summer institutes for those who teach them. In this section, I will review the impacts that just five of the twelve Title VI programs—the FLAS fellowships, the NRCs, the Centers for International Business Education and Research (CIBERs), the IRSP, and the LRCs—have had on the teaching and learning of foreign languages.

FLAS Fellowships

During a recent period of just three years between 2005 and 2007, 5,927 FLAS fellowships have supported university students' study of 125 different languages, either through academic year-long classes, or in intensive summer institutes (IRIS 2009). (See Appendix E of this volume for language enrollments and FLAS fellowships awarded in each world region.) Table 4-3 displays the top twenty languages studied over the last fifty years using FLAS Fellowships.

Table 4-3 shows the top twenty languages supported by FLAS Fellowships since the beginning of the program. Of the more than 75,000 FLAS fellowships awarded since the program began, more than 10,000 have supported the study of Chinese, 10,000 funded the study of Russian, and 8,000 supported Arabic study, followed in order by Japanese, Portuguese, Hindi, Spanish (advanced levels), Swahili, Indonesian, Turkish, Persian, Polish, Serbian, Tamil, Czech, Korean, French, German, Vietnamese, and Urdu. It is no coincidence that many of these languages include critical languages that are currently being prioritized by government agencies—and languages that would not otherwise have been offered by universities constrained by the financial contingencies outlined earlier in this chapter.

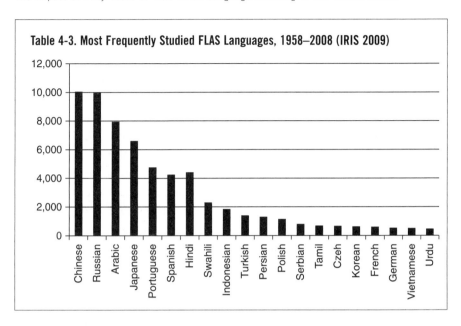

Table 4-3. Most Frequently Studied FLAS Languages, 1958–2008 (IRIS 2009)

National Resource Centers

There are currently 125 NRCs located on fifty university campuses in twenty-five states and the District of Columbia. In addition to educating college students and K-12 teachers about critical areas of the world, the NRCs dramatically expand their access to language instruction, funding on-campus courses in more than 150 different languages. These are typically less commonly and least commonly taught languages, ones that universities cannot afford to offer because they do not attract enough students to offset the cost of offering these classes. Wiley points out that these "much less commonly taught languages, such as Xhosa, Kazakh, and Maya, are not offered in any government institute but only at Title VI centers and their summer intensive language institutes" (Wiley 2001: 20). Without the subsidy by NRCs, these classes would not be offered. Of course, as the classes grow and attract more robust enrollments, then the university can afford to offer them on its own budget—for example, Chinese has increased in popularity at many universities to the point at which it can be offered without Title VI support. Thus, it can be argued that through the NRCs, Title VI funds leverage the investment by universities of their own resources, enabling them to teach a wider range of foreign languages than would otherwise be offered. With the help of the NRCs, the universities can offer low-enrollment LCTL courses and then take them over when enrollments grow to meet minimum self-sustaining levels.

To show in detail the impact that NRCs can have on foreign language learning, we will describe the three NRCs at the University of Minnesota (UMN), focusing on

79

Western Europe, Asia, and International (Global Studies). In 2008, these NRCs offer less commonly taught languages in intensive summer classes in Chinese, Dutch, Hindi, Hmong, Icelandic, Japanese, Korean, Russian, and Vietnamese. During the academic year, the NRCs support Foreign Language Across the Curriculum options for advanced-level language students in Spanish, French, and German; offer supplementary funds to provide teaching materials for LCTL teachers; and have a standing arrangement with the college to support third-year LCTL classes (on a sliding dollar scale) if their actual enrollment is so low that they would otherwise be cancelled (van Der Sanden 2009). In addition, FLAS fellowships to support individuals' study of LCTLs are administered through the NRCs. Over the past four years, twenty-six fellowships have been awarded to Minnesota students, more than half of them for foreign language study abroad, to support achievement of higher levels of language proficiency than would be possible on campus. When students do study languages abroad, the UMN Learning Abroad Center in the Office of International Programs makes sure they can earn credit toward graduation. Although we are happy to tell Minnesota's story, we would never claim that story is unique; each of the fifty universities that currently house NRCs can document similar levels of impact on language learning directly attributable to Title VI funding.

Table 4-4. Enrollments in African, Southeast Asian, and Central Asian/East European Languages at Title VI and non-Title VI U.S. Colleges and Universities in 1995 (Janus 1998: 168)

Language	Enrollment at Title VI Institution	Enrollment at Non-Title VI Institution	Percent of Students Registered at Title VI Institutions
Hausa	52	0	100
Swahili	478	707	40
Yoruba	62	46	57
Zulu	52	9	85
Total African	**644**	**762**	**46**
Indonesian	204	54	79
Tagalog	196	352	38
Thai	171	55	76
Vietnamese	202	808	20
Total Southeast Asian	**773**	**1,269**	**38**
Kazakh	5	0	100
Serbian/Croatian	230	153	69
Ukrainian	34	46	43
Uzbek	12	0	100
Total Central Asian and East European	**281**	**199**	**59**
Total All 12	**1,698**	**2,230**	**43**

Viewed from a national perspective, the impact of Title VI NRC funding has been complex historically. In 1995, Table 4-4 shows the number of students in 1995 who were taking a sample of twelve less commonly taught languages at colleges and universities housing National Resource Centers in comparison with enrollments in those same languages at non-Title VI institutions.

In 2009, this same comparison of the twelve LCTLs in Title VI and non-Title VI colleges and universities was repeated (Higgins 2009). Table 4-5 displays these enrollments for the year 2006.[4]

A comparison of the data in these two tables shows first, and hearteningly, that between 1995 and 2006 there was an overall rise in enrollments in these LCTLs, in both Title VI and non-Title VI schools. Second, there was an overall drop in the percentage of the enrollments in these twelve LCTLs in Title VI as compared with non-Title VI institutions. Perhaps non-Title VI schools may be beginning to take on the responsibility of financing the offering of these LCTLs on their own, without such heavy reliance on Title VI to support the majority of such offerings. Third, there are different patterns of change over the last decade in enrollments in LCTLs depending on world region and sometimes on individual language. For example, in 2006, there were more enrollments in the African and the Southeast Asian languages

Table 4-5. Enrollments in African, Southeast Asian, and Centtral Asian/East European Languages at Title VI and non-Title VI Colleges and Universities, 2006 (Higgins 2009)

Language	Enrollment at Title VI Institution	Enrollment at Non-Title VI Institution	Percent of Students Registered at Title VI Institutions
Hausa	54	3	95
Swahili	588	1,575	27
Yoruba	87	178	33
Zulu	85	47	64
Total African	**814**	**1,803**	**30**
Indonesian	236	65	78
Tagalog	289	655	30
Thai	222	85	72
Vietnamese	517	1,968	21
Total Southeast Asian	**1,264**	**2,773**	**31**
Kazakh	8	0	100
Serbian/Croatian	224	79	74
Ukrainian	48	55	47
Uzbek	23	22	51
Total Central Asian and East European	**303**	**156**	**66**
Total All 12	**2,381**	**4,732**	**33**

overall, and also higher percentages of these in non-Title VI schools compared with Title VI schools. However, we see the opposite trend in the Central Asian and East European languages that had marginally fewer enrollments in 2006 than they had in 1995, with a higher percentage in the Title VI than in the non-Title VI schools. These trends suggest that Title VI may be having a salutary but complex impact on language enrollments in postsecondary institutions. One possibility is that Title VI may be important in supporting the least commonly taught, overall least enrolled, languages in academia when they are financially unsustainable on their own, but that as particular LCTLs become more popular, postsecondary institutions may then be willing to offer them in non-Title VI settings where enrollments can be self-sustaining. More data are needed to determine whether this pattern holds for more LCTLs over time.

Centers for International Business Education and Research

In doing business in an internationally connected marketplace, Americans must dramatically improve their cultural understanding and language knowledge. Without this knowledge, their access to key players and marketplaces will be severely diminished and they will find themselves without a place at the "economic table." At the time of this writing, there are thirty-one CIBERs located in business schools on university campuses around the country, functioning to prepare students to do business in contexts where they must know the culture and language to be competitive. On these thirty-one university campuses, the CIBERs fund the teaching of less commonly taught business languages, including Arabic, Catalan, Chinese, Farsi, Filipino, Hebrew, Hindi, Indonesian, Italian, Japanese, Korean, Mandarin, Polish, Portuguese, Russian, Swahili, Swedish, Thai, Turkish, Vietnamese, and Wolof. The number of students provided with instruction in the uses of these languages for business purposes has steadily increased since the CIBER program began in 1989, from some 16,000 in 1995 to more than 181,000 in 2006.

Improving the Effectiveness of Language Instruction: International Research and Studies Program and the Language Resource Centers

But how good is the language instruction provided by means of FLAS fellowships, NRCs, and CIBERs? Money spent for poorly taught, ineffective classes would be money poured down the drain, as it would cause students to have great difficulty learning the language. Applied linguists seeking funding through the Title VI IRS and LRC programs are focused on improving effectiveness in language instruction and learning. They ask such questions as: Are language teaching materials designed to take advantage of what we know about second language acquisition by this population? Are the language teachers well prepared? Can they tell when the materials are not appropriate for the learning stage of their students, and can they adapt their teaching to fill in those gaps and write their own lessons to maximize their students' language learning? For example: It is easy to say you are going to teach a language via distance learning. It is not so easy to do distance teaching *effectively*. The effectiveness of any language course depends on the quality of its teaching materials and assessments and the quality of the teaching methods used by its instructor. Both the IRS and the LRC programs are focused primarily on improving the *effectiveness* of language instruction in the United States.

International Research and Studies Program

Since 1959, IRSP has funded the development of language and area studies teaching materials as well as projects focused on the development of language assessment measures, surveys, and research studies. The casual researcher browsing the IRS program grants on the U.S. Department of Education's IRIS web site will find 305 grant-funded projects just in the past twenty years, of which at least half have focused on the development of better-quality, more effective language curricula, language assessment measures, and language teaching approaches for the LCTLs. A sampling of some LCTL-focused IRSP grant titles includes Standards and Guidelines for Competency-Based Turkish, Intermediate Level Yoruba, Improving Listening Comprehension in Russian, Standardized Polish Language Proficiency Test, Proficiency-based Business Arabic, Iraqi Arabic, and Azerbaijani Languages.

Many useful surveys and research studies have been funded by IRSP. IRSP has also supported research on such topics as the role of LCTLs in historically black colleges and universities, the literacy needs at different grade levels of children learning noncognate second languages, and a study of innovations in elementary school foreign language teaching. Tables 4-1 and 4-2 are the outcome of IRSP-funded surveys carried out in 1995 and 2006 by the Center for Applied Linguistics.

Language Resource Centers

The LRC program was established in 1990 when three centers were funded, each located on the campus of a major research university. Specifically, the mission of the LRC program was to improve the nation's capacity to teach and learn languages effectively. That is, the LRCs were charged to focus on language and on improving the effectiveness of language learning and teaching processes. They were to do this not only by producing materials and language tests but also by expanding the quality and level of resources and support for the nation's language teachers. As new LRCs were added in each round of funding, some had a "general" focus similar to that of the first three centers and some were focused specifically on the languages of particular

83

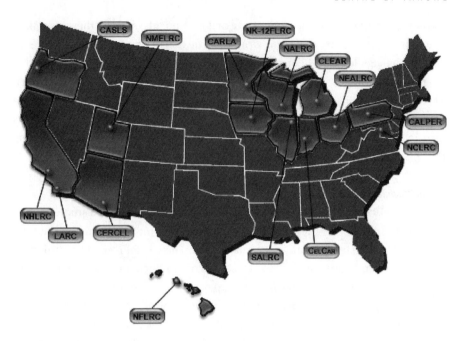

FIGURE 4-1
Locations of the Title VI Language Resource Centers (CALPER 2008)

world regions (one is focused on African languages, another on the languages of the Middle East, another on South Asian languages, and so on). Today, there are fifteen LRCs, located on research university campuses across the country (Figure 4-1).

Led by nationally and internationally recognized language professionals, LRCs create language learning and teaching materials, offer professional development opportunities for teachers and instructors, and conduct research on foreign language learning. Although some centers concentrate on specific language areas and others on foreign languages in general, all share the common goal to develop resources that can be used broadly to improve foreign language education in the United States (Language Resource Centers Coordinating Council 2008: 1).

Today, the LRC network carries out research, produces high-quality teaching materials; creates assessment tools and trains teachers to develop and interpret them; supports initiatives for the teaching of LCTLs; and disseminates these resources through summer institutes, conferences, and workshops for those language teachers (both university-level and K-12) whose expertise sustains the effectiveness of the language classes offered by the nation's K-16 system. LRC support is especially important for teachers of the LCTLs, because in many cases such teachers are not trained in pedagogy but rather have been hired to teach because they know the language. But knowing a language does not necessarily make someone a good language teacher. The LRCs also disseminate resources and information to language teacher educators, program administrators, and language policy makers who can find these materials and teacher education opportunities on the searchable common web site of the LRCs (http://nflrc.msu.edu) and in an informative booklet, *Language Resource Centers: Bringing Worlds Together*, written by the Language Resource Centers Coordinating Council (2008). Each LRC has its own web site to disseminate the product of its work, and some of these web sites receive more than one million hits a year.

The LRCs have produced a plethora of much-needed teaching materials for specific languages, such as:

- Handbooks for students of Middle Eastern languages such as Arabic, Hebrew, Turkish, and Persian (NMELRC at Brigham Young University);
- Learners' reference grammars for African languages such as Swahili, Amharic, Shona, Zulu, Asante-Twi, Kikongo, Somali, Akan, Hausa, Sesotho (NALRC at the University of Madison);
- Intermediate reading and listening modules and podcasts for Mongolian, Pashto, Tajiki, Uygur, and Uzbek (CelCAR at Indiana University); and
- Digital media archives including audio, video, and activities for teaching Arabic, Chinese, Farsi, German, Hindi, Italian, Japanese, Korean, Mayan, Portuguese, and Spanish (LARC at San Diego State University).

LRC projects also provide teacher support and resources that cut across languages, including:

- More than fifteen online peer-reviewed journals and newsletters for language teachers, such as the *American Council for Immersion Education* newsletter and the referred journal *Language Learning through Technology*;
- National conferences, intensive summer institutes and year-round workshops offered by the LRCs for language teachers on a wide range of current, cutting-edge topics in language pedagogy;
- Online tools to create language teaching materials with programs for recording, uploading, mixing, and interacting (CLEAR at Michigan State University);
- An online guide to the essential principles and methods of foreign language instruction (NCLRC at Georgetown University, George Washington University, and CAL);
- An online teacher guide specifically for K-12 language teachers (National K-12 FLRC at Iowa State University);
- A corpus portal providing easy access to corpus-based language teaching materials (CALPER at Penn State University);

- Online resources and lesson plans for content-based proficiency-oriented language instruction using technology (CARLA at the University of Minnesota);
- Content-based lessons in the social sciences in French, Japanese, and Spanish (CASLS at the University of Oregon);
- A database showing where LCTLs are taught in North America, with more than 12,500 listings for more than 300 languages (CARLA at the University of Minnesota); and
- An online catalog of language-focused study abroad opportunities in East Asia (NEALRC at Ohio State University).

The vast majority of the excellent resources produced by the LRCs are disseminated free of charge through the centers' web sites; the rest are distributed at very low cost. Through the common LRC web site at http://nflrc.msu.edu/ users can conduct specific searches for resources and activities offered on any topic related to language learning and teaching in the United States that are offered by the fifteen LRCs.

Conclusion

Title VI programs, including FLAS fellowships, NRCs, CIBERS, IRSP, and LRCs, have been fostering expertise in foreign languages in the nation's schools and universities, K-16, since 1959. Efficient use has been made of a relatively small amount of funding. But Title VI programs must be expanded if they are to have more widespread impact on the nation's foreign language expertise, building on its capacity in the K-16 school system. Programs such as Title VI need more funding and support if they are to truly address the nation's need for foreign language expertise in the twenty-first century. As the Department of Defense (2005) stated in its White Paper:

> This is the Call to Action to create that consensus, establish national level leadership, and move the Nation forward. Proficiency in foreign languages and cultural understanding must become strengths of our public and private sectors and pillars of our education system.

Acknowledgments

The author was asked to review the history of the impact of Title VI on language learning in the United States. However, the chapters in this volume authored by O'Meara, Wiley, and Merkx provide an extremely comprehensive review of the history of language and area studies in U.S. education, both before and after the establishment of Title VI programs in 1958. For this reason, this chapter offers a specialist perspective on the more recent history of language learning and Title VI, from the point of view of an applied linguist who has spent four decades in universities researching the process of second language acquisition and educating advanced level language teachers. She is grateful to Karin Larson, CARLA Coordinator, for able input in the preparation of this chapter.

Notes

1 Called "total diplomacy" by Heymann (2008).
2 The author refers to level 2 on the 5-level ILR proficiency scale: www.govtilr. org/Skills/ILRscale2.htm (accessed February 6, 2010).
3 These records on the IRIS web site are known to be incomplete, as the records of the earliest FLAS fellowship recipients are still being entered there. Thus, 75,000 fellowships is clearly a very conservative estimate, on the low side.
4 Higgins began with a list of 2006–2009 NRC awards (www2.ed.gov/programs/ iegpsnrc/awards.html) (reaccessed February 6, 2010) and checked which NRC schools offered which languages. Enrollment statistics came from the 2006 MLA enrollment survey for all the relevant languages: www.mla.org/all_other_ lang_pdf (reaccessed February 6, 2010).

REFERENCES

American Council on Education. 2009. Engaging the World: U.S. Global Competence for the 21st Century, Celebrating Five Decades of HEA-Title VI and Fulbright-Hays. Video produced by Richfield Productions, Inc., Washington, D.C..

Armitage, Richard, and Joseph Nye. 2008. Implementing smart power: Setting an agenda for national security reform. Statement before the Senate Foreign Relations Committee. Center for Strategic and International Studies (CSIS), April 24.

Bialystok, Ellen. 2001. *Bilingualism in Development: Language, Literacy and Cognition.* New York: Cambridge University Press.

Bialystok, Ellen, Fergus I. M. Craik, Raymond Klein, and Mythill Viswanathan. 2004. Bilingualism, aging and cognitive control: Evidence from the Simon task. *Psychology and Aging* 19:290–303.

Center for Advanced Language Proficiency Education and Research (CALPER). 2009. Unpublished map. University Park, PA: Pennsylvania State University.

DeGroot, Annette M. B., and Judith Kroll. 1997. *Tutorials in Bilingualism: Psycholinguistic perspectives.* Mahwah, NJ: Lawrence Erlbaum Associates.

Department of Defense. 2005. A call to action for national foreign language capabilities. *ERIC Document ED 48911*, www.eric.ed.gov (accessed February 6, 2010).

———. 2005. Defense language transformation roadmap. The Official Home of the Department of Defense. www.defenselink.mil/news/Mar2005/d20050330roadmap.pdf (accessed February 6, 2010).

Gates, Robert. 2009. Interview. In Engaging the World: U.S. Global Competence for the 21st Century, Celebrating Five Decades of HEA-Title VI and Fulbright-Hays. Video produced by Richfield Productions, Inc., Washington D.C..

Graham, Bradley. 2005. Pentagon to stress foreign languages. *Washington Post*, April 8, p. A4.

Heyman, David. 2008. Restoring American influence and security through service, education, and exchange. Center for Strategic and International Studies csis.org/files/media/csis/pubs/081201_american_influence_report.pdf (accessed February 6, 2010).

Higgins, Grace. 2009. Enrollments in 12 LCTLs in Title VI and non-Title VI colleges and universities. Minneapolis: CARLA (unpublished work).

Hines, Ralph. 2001. An overview of Title VI. In *Changing Perspectives on International Education*, ed. Patrick O'Meara, Howard and Carolee Mehlinger, and Roxana Ma Newman. Bloomington: Indiana University Press, pp. 6–10.

International Resource Information System (IRIS), International Education Programs Service, U.S. Department of Education, 2009. www.ieps-iris.org/iris/ieps/search.cfm (accessed February 6, 2010).

Kessler, Carolyn, and Mary Ellen Quinn. 1987. Language minority children's linguistic and cognitive creativity. *Journal of Multilingual and Multicultural Development* 8:173–186.

Language Resource Centers Coordinating Council. 2008. *Language Resource Centers: Bringing Worlds Together.* http://nflrc.msu.edu/ (accessed February 6, 2010).

MLA Ad Hoc Committee on Foreign Languages. 2006. Foreign languages and higher education: New structures for a changed world. www.mla.org/flreport (accessed February 6, 2010).

Nye, Joseph. 2005. *Soft Power: The Means to Success in World Politics.* Cambridge: Perseus Books Group.

———. 2008. *The Powers to Lead.* Oxford: Oxford University Press.

Rhodes, Nancy and Ingrid Pufahl. 2010. *Foreign Language Teaching in U.S. Schools.* Washington D.C.: Center for Applied Linguistics.

Spellings, Margaret and Cheryl A. Oldham. 2008. Enhancing Foreign Language Proficiency in the United States: Preliminary Results of the National Security Language Initiative. www2.ed.gov/about/inits/ed/competitiveness/nsli/index.html (accessed February 6, 2010).

Van Der Sanden, Klaas. 2009. Personal communication, University of Minnesota, Minneapolis, May 7, 2009.

Wiley, David. 2001. Forty Years of the Title VI and Fulbright-Hays International Education Programs: Building the Nation's International Expertise for a Global Future. In *Changing Perspectives on International Education*, ed. Patrick O'Meara, Howard and Carolee Mehlinger, and Roxana Ma Newman. Bloomington: Indiana University Press, pp. 11–29.

Zehr, Mary Ann. 2009. Elementary Foreign Language Instruction on Descent: Cutbacks Expected to Continue in Recession. *Education Week*, March 4, Issue 23, p. 8. www.edweek.org/ew/articles/2009/03/04/23language.h28.html (accessed February 6, 2010).

CHAPTER 5

The Growth of the Less Commonly Taught Languages in Title VI and Language Programs in the United States

David S. Wiley

> At this juncture in world affairs, it has become essential to our national welfare, perhaps even to our survival, that we understand the culture, the psychology, the aspirations of other peoples. Such understanding begins with a knowledge of foreign languages, and the competence of our citizens in the languages of other lands has become a national resource of great importance. It is essential that we develop this resource.
>
> —*Luther H. Evans, U.S. Librarian of Congress and Director General UNESCO, 1952*[1]

That the 130 Title VI National Resource Centers (NRCs) and Foreign Language and Area Studies (FLAS) universities have developed the capacity by 2006–2009 to offer approximately 195 less commonly taught languages (LCTLs) is an astonishing accomplishment made possible by a modest amount for funding from the U.S. Department of Education over the past fifty years.[2] Each competitively selected NRC receives only approximately $230,000 annually for all aspects of language and area studies training and a roughly equal amount for six to ten FLAS fellowships for academic year language instruction.[3] The small size of Title VI grants and limited number of FLAS fellowships contrasts markedly with the much higher federal funding of language capacity in the Foreign Service Institute, Defense Language Institute, and the National Security Agency.[4]

This chapter reviews the character, strengths, and weaknesses of these Title VI and Fulbright-Hays (F-H) programs by briefly reviewing their history and their rationale. Then, it turns to the productivity of these language programs, followed by investigating how this language instruction in the universities articulates with recent federal government priorities for particular languages. The chapter concludes with a review of enrollments and FLAS fellowship allocations in each world area, drawing on the data tables in Appendix E.

The Coming of Language Priorities before Sputnik

Although the coming of modern LCTL studies is normally associated with the 1957 appearance of the Russian Sputnik, there are many precursors, even in the U.S. Office of Education (US/OE), as it was known in the years of the Great Depression. In 1932–1933, US/OE, in its *National Survey of Secondary Education*, had a special study of "Instruction in Foreign Languages" with a survey of 200 language courses in a dozen states. (Some of these courses were in the Scandinavian and other European languages found in the churches and schools of large immigrant communities.) By 1942, US/OE had created the Division of Inter-American Education Relations with thirty staff members to promote inter-American cooperation and solidarity, appointing three language consultants in Spanish, Portuguese, and English as a Foreign Language.

During the same period, the private foundations and the growing experience of globalization led to developing new university area studies centers. In 1933, Rockefeller, followed by Ford and Carnegie, with larger investments in the 1950s, were pushing "academic instruction organized on an area basis (with language instruction as well) . . . [with] efforts [that] were decisive in assisting the universities to surmount their previous neglect of the non-Western world."[5] By 1946, the Social Science Research Council (SSRC) already had found twenty-two universities offering forty-five instructional programs with language. By 1951, even when using fairly rigid criteria for an area program, the SSRC identified twenty-five integrated area studies programs with nineteen potential programs with sufficient or nearly sufficient language and area instruction capacity to become a center.[6] In 1953, the US/OE convened a conference on the role of foreign languages in American education and sought to revive the Foreign Languages in the Elementary Schools (FLES) initiative. In 1954, there were fifty-five identifiable area studies centers in the United States, according to a State Department report, a number that doubled in only two years to 108 programs. US/OE had a full-time staff member in the field of foreign language teaching by 1956 to meet the growing demands for foreign language information and services.[7] In 1957, before the rise of Sputnik, so many

U.S. government agencies were enmeshed in global affairs that the commissioner of the US/OE, Lawrence G. Derthick, "convened a conference of representatives of 20 U.S. government agencies which train or recruit personnel for overseas assignments." The conference's purpose, he said,

> was to discuss the government's need for persons with competency in foreign languages. As a result of that discussion we felt that it was a matter of extreme urgency to acquaint school people with the shortage of Americans qualified in languages in order to get something done at the Federal level to accelerate the training of teachers and the preparation of students in languages not now in the curriculum.[8]

Beginning in 1958, the US/OE used the funds from Title VI of NDEA to invest in the International Research and Studies (IRS) grants to develop many LCTL learning materials—dictionaries, texts, target reference grammars, training, and audiotapes. The awards to centers focused heavily on language program development, and the FLAS fellowships provided the support for graduate students to take time from their disciplinary and area studies to develop three or four years of language learning. From these early beginnings emerged the largest project on the globe for developing teaching capacity, materials, and uses of the LCTLs for research abroad, growing by the 2000s to the capacity to teach more than 100 LCTLs annually in the centers and to offer the availability of another 100. By 1962, as an increasing number of African, Asian, and Latin American countries became independent, there were 136 U.S. university area studies centers, with some supported by the new National Defense Education Act.[9]

In the early 1960s, U.S. Commissioner for Education and Assistant Secretary of Health, Education, and Welfare Francis Keppel indicated pride in the Title VI program providing languages for technical assistance and language learning development (with audiovisual materials, language laboratories, and technical innovation).[10]

Clearly, within only a short twenty-five years, the United States had moved from a strongly isolationist position to participating in the League of Nations (1919), the United Nations (with fifty-one members by 1946), the occupation in Europe and Japan, seeking broad and deep relations with the Group of 77 "developing nations" (by 1964), and was enmeshed in a transforming Cold War. American international consciousness was even deeper, deriving from the turbulence of the two World Wars, the long-term missionary links to the non-western nations, the surge of new nations emerging in the 1950s and 1960s, and the liberal goals of democracy and mutual development—all of which caught the attention of U.S. universities. The entire twentieth century was characterized by a rapidly emerging global economic system and a drive for national self-determination, realities that continually strained the creativity of U.S. university educators to comprehend the change and

to adjust not only their maps but also their pedagogical goals, teaching, and institutions. The Title VI and F-H programs crystallized a national response to these
emergent needs and trends with a broad harnessing of the creativity and energy of
the research universities of the United States and their language and area faculties.

Character and Accomplishments of the Title VI and Fulbright-Hays Programs

As of 2009, about 135 LCTLs were taught at fifty-three research universities with the
130 Title VI NRCs, including several university centers that receive only Title VI FLAS
fellowships. Their work in the LCTLs is supported by the ancillary programs of the
Title VI Language Resource Centers and the American Overseas Research Centers.
(See Appendices A and B.) In 2006, these universities reported having the capacity
to offer 191 LCTLs, approximately seventy-five to eighty of which may have no students in any given year because of low student demand and/or the lack of FLAS fellowships (usually, six to ten per year, per center). During the 2000–2007 period, these
centers provided the treasured FLAS fellowships in 168 languages, many of which
are the "much less commonly taught languages" (MLCTLs). However, MLCTLs may
have particular value as the only indigenous languages for particular countries or
peoples, making them crucial for particular academic or scientific research projects.

The long-lasting partnership of the Title VI and Fulbright-Hays programs of the
U.S. Department of Education with these U.S. universities has created an unparalleled capacity to teach both foreign languages and "area studies" about societies
around the world—covering all inhabited continents. Indeed, for the past decade,
one study estimates more than 80 percent of all instruction in LCTLs was at
universities with Title VI-supported centers, excluding the "commonly-taught"
languages of French, Spanish, German, and Italian.[11]

Title VI programs have created the foundations of U.S. LCTL training capacity,
the breadth of which is unrivaled across the globe. Many LCTLs would not be
taught at all without the Title VI programs and the language-learning texts,
pedagogies, and technologies created by the NRCs, LRCs, and the Title VI IRS
program.

NRCs and LRCs have trained most of the nation's graduate-level international
expert scholars and professionals in foreign area studies with language competence. With Title VI support, these centers also usually have been the founders in
the United States and abroad of most of the intensive summer institutes in the
LCTLs. NRC grants also have provided important support for university library
holdings in foreign languages and area studies that complement the holdings of the
Library of Congress and other national libraries.

Title VI Incentives for U.S. Language Priorities and Instruction

This ingenious collection of Title VI federal programs has accomplished so much with so little by creating a competitive system among universities. In seeking to build national capacity in foreign language and international studies, Congress and the Eisenhower and following administrations did not use the command-and-control model of creating and funding all aspects of the program. Instead, the US/OE provided incentive funding that rewarded public and private university initiatives to respond to the national needs by investing in their faculties and administrators, language programs, center activities, and libraries for foreign language and international studies. Indeed, the leading research universities were willing to invest heavily with university funds in the quest for the high academic prestige of designation as one of the few institutions nationally to have an NRC in foreign language and area studies (or international studies) for a particular world area. As a result, federal funds often are matched by the universities at a ratio of from 10:1 to 20:1 of university dollars for each federal grant dollar in order to support these costs. In addition, the U.S. Department of Education mandates that the indirect costs allocated for NRC and FLAS grants are held to the low level of eight percent. In periods of recession and university contraction, some university administrators argue that the high costs relative to the small annual Title VI grants is "not worth the candle." Repeatedly, however, faculty come back with the reply that the academic honor of having such grants, the membership in the "elite pool" of Title VI programs, the possibility of ancillary grants from foundations and other federal agencies, and the valuable FLAS fellowships for graduate students makes competing for the Title VI awards ultimately attractive. As a result, a broad array of programs was created with only a small investment where there was a clear consonance in university goals and national needs. In many of these universities, decisions were made to sacrifice other domestic and internal needs for faculty and academic programs in order to seek national standing with centers built around broad and deep national needs for language and international studies.[12]

Since the inception of Title VI, in order to encourage competition among universities, US/OE has made awards to centers and programs only through merit-based competitions with anonymous academic peer reviewers who make quality rankings using a dozen or more criteria of excellence—and these are repeated in triennial or quadrennial competitions. The result, after five decades of such competitions, is that a number of area studies faculties frequently have grown to more than 100 faculty members. A similar process of peer reviewing by select academic experts is used in selecting the Centers for International Business Education (CIBEs), LRCs, American Overseas Research Centers (AORCs), and Fulbright-Hays awards.

Why Do Scholars and the Federal Government Want "Rare" Languages?

The interest of the university researchers in these many languages results from their passions to follow issues, problems, and socioeconomic and scientific phenomena wherever they appear in the 195 nations of the world. The globalization of transportation, communications, and migration has only increased the interest of scholars to access peoples and data in diverse sites to gain the deeply contextualized knowledge of the foreign world that is appropriate to a nation seeking to be a world leader. This is measured by the seventy federal agencies and offices that report needing language and area knowledge.[13] The rapid onslaught of global change for all nations has transformed the world and drastically increased need in the United States for international knowledge and the ability to form mutuality beneficial international collaborations.

In seeking high-quality data and long-term partnerships with foreign collaborators, researchers have gone beyond engaging informants by using the colonial lingua franca (English, French, and Portuguese—and, earlier in the century, German and Italian) or even regional languages that alienate the research subjects (e.g., using Arabic spoken by the Sudanese government to question people in Darfur or southern Sudan). Researchers seek to hire expert informants in the first language of the communities while having sufficient personal knowledge to interpret the assistant's interviews. Often, research needs require instructional capacity in a language that universities cannot support with a tenure-track professor of that language. Offering such MLCTLs to a small number of students (sometimes, a single learner) is costly. Thus, some universities with NRCs have innovated to increase their capacity to offer these additional languages by maintaining adequate instructional materials (texts, audio or video files, dictionaries, and target reference grammars) as well as a first-language tutor and a faculty linguist supervisor.

Looking more broadly to national needs, foreign language and international knowledge are the core needed for coping with and building a collaborative future with the peoples of the globe who face the same myriad transformations that the United States struggles to contain. Older domestic perspectives and simplistic solutions to defining a productive role for our country in the global system no longer work and require new knowledge and new perspectives.

Simultaneously, these changes open the door to many new possibilities for improving qualities of life, sustainable development, and international collaboration in this competitive world system. For a host of challenges we face abroad, language and understanding are crucial for a global purview—for example, political and white collar corruption, democracy and human rights, sustainable energy use and development, crime and economic exploitation, terrorism, proliferation of the drug business and arms trade, sexual exploitation, nuclear proliferation, and the rise of religious fundamentalisms around the globe. In such a radically new context, it is appropriate that the U.S. Department of Education has turned to consulting with other federal agencies about what LCTLs are of higher priority—and that their consultations now include not only the State Department and DOD but also the departments of Agriculture, Commerce, Health and Human Services (HHS), Housing and Urban Development (HUD), Labor, Transportation, and Treasury.

The technological changes that are engulfing and empowering the United States, especially the knowledge technologies through the computer and the Internet, are facilitating an explosion of information for us and nations abroad—much not in English—from distant corners of the globe. Suddenly, glimpses of international communities appear in our homes, our workplaces, our schools, and our daily lives. No longer are the foreign areas that Title VI centers and programs study so distant, and the rapidity of change for us and those abroad has accelerated measurably. The result is that the Title VI centers and programs have new opportunities to communicate with the peoples and nations abroad that we study and to reach out with new information and understanding for the American public. To build the knowledge that we extend to our fellow Americans, language is the first step for understanding.

Explosion of Federal Interest in Security Languages after September 11, 2001

After September 11, 2001, the alarm bell was sounded once again for developing greater U.S. government capacity in languages relevant to intelligence for national security, this time for what the Bush administration termed the "Global War on Terror." Many of these needs were for LCTLs. The stark shortages of translators in key languages of the Middle East and central and southern Asia needed by the federal security agencies sparked the DOD's development of the Defense Language Transformation Roadmap.[14] Stated more directly than usual, the roadmap made the assumptions that:

- Conflict against enemies speaking less-commonly-taught languages and thus the need for foreign language capability will not abate. Robust foreign language and foreign area expertise are critical to sustaining coalitions, pursuing regional stability, and conducting multi-national missions especially in post-conflict and other than combat, security, humanitarian, nation-building, and stability operations. . . .
- Establishing a new "global footprint" for DoD, and transitioning to a more expeditionary force, will bring increased requirements for language and regional knowledge to work with new coalition partners in a wide variety of activities,

often with little or no notice. This new approach to warfighting in the twenty-first century will require forces that have foreign language capabilities beyond those generally available in today's force.[15]

Traditionally, the Foreign Service Institute (FSI), now known as the George P. Shultz National Foreign Affairs Training Center, has been the lead institution of the Department of State (DOS) language and international training for foreign service officers (FSOs) and U.S. embassy personnel. Currently, FSI offers 380 nonlanguage courses and seventy languages in its School of Language Studies, provided "to more than 50,000 enrollees a year from the State Department and more than 40 other government agencies and the military service branches."[16] However, because of the erosion in the total number of personnel in the DOS in the past decade and the difficulties in using extant language proficiency because of the frequent transfer of FSOs to different posts, the need to improve language capacity is striking. According to a Government Accountability Office (GAO) study, as of 2008, 3,600 FSOs (31 percent) in overseas language-designated positions did not meet speaking and reading proficiency requirements for their positions. In the Near East and South and Central Asia, the shortfall is 40 percent, and in Arabic and Chinese, designated "supercritical languages," 39 percent.[17] As a result, DOS hired 300 new language trainers in fiscal 2009 and is hiring 200 more in fiscal 2010.

In parallel, over many years, the DOD built its own Defense Language Institute Foreign Language Center (DLIFLC) with separate schools for Middle Eastern, Asian, European, and Latin American languages; a Multi Language School for Persian Farsi, Pashto, Dari, and Turkish; and an Emerging Languages Task Force for Kurdish dialects Kurmanji and Sorani, Hindi, Urdu, Uzbek, and Indonesian.[18] The DLI has been richly funded, with $270 million in 2008, more than four times the entire Title VI NRC, LRC, and FLAS budget. Nevertheless, the same GAO study reports, the DOD shortfalls are critical. These are not new needs, as the former dean of the DLIFLC noted in 1990:[19] Together, DLI and FSI offer approximately seventy-nine LCTLs for instruction in San Francisco and Washington, D.C.

In the war zones, the problem is much more pronounced. Thirty-three of forty-five officers in language-designated positions in Afghanistan, or 73 percent, did not meet the requirement. In Iraq, eight of fourteen officers, or 57 percent, lacked sufficient language skills. Forty-three percent of officers in Arabic language-designated positions did not meet the requirements of their positions, nor did 66 percent of officers in Dari positions, 50 percent in Urdu (two languages widely spoken in South Asia), or 38 percent in Farsi (which is spoken mostly in Iran).[20]

The National Security Agency, with its special needs in crytography and its secret budget, also has training capacity in its Language Department of the

National Cryptologic School, and it has collected more than 25,000 volumes in 500 languages of interest. A series of new programs that have been organized around the Defense Language Transformation Roadmap includes more "robust strategic language and cultural program" at all three service academies. In tandem is the National Security Education Flagship Language Program, which is aimed at developing professional levels of competency in languages deemed critical to national security (defined as Arabic, Hindi, Korean, Mandarin, Persian, Russian, and Urdu).[1] After 2001, the FBI developed its Language Services Translation Center with the Directorate of Intelligence to develop translation capacity in 100 languages, with a focus on Middle Eastern and North African languages. Its 1,470 employees focus on Arabic, Chinese, Farsi, French, Hindi, Japanese, Korean, Kurdish, Pashto, Russian, Somali, Spanish, Turkish, Urdu, and Vietnamese. Even before September 11, 2001, the Vice Chairman of the National Intelligence Council reported to the Senate that

> There is little doubt that most managers in the intelligence business wish that the foreign language capabilities of the workforce—in technical jobs, overseas positions, or analytic jobs—were more robust. At present, the CIA, DIA, State/INR, and various other agencies identify key shortfalls in Central Eurasian, East Asian, and Middle Eastern languages . . . [including] Russian, Ukrainian, Armenian, Serbo-Croatian, Korean, Thai, Japanese and Chinese, as well as Arabic, Hindu, and Farsi, the language spoken in Iran, Afghanistan, and parts of Central Asia.[21]

Much of the new federal mobilization on "critical languages" has been organized by the Departments of State, Defense, and Education, as well as the Director of National Intelligence Education under the National Security Language Initiative (NSLI), funded at $86 million in fiscal year 2008 to expand U.S. critical foreign language education. Programs in this project include the Foreign Language Teaching Assistants Program; Intensive Summer Language Institutes for Teachers in Arabic, Chinese, and Russian; the teachers of Critical Languages Program, bringing native-fluent teachers in Chinese and Arabic to U.S. elementary and secondary schools; high school summer language institutes; and language study abroad.[22] (For further information, see chapter 6 by Catherine Doughty in this volume.)

Developing New Language Priorities in the U.S. Government

The decade after September 11, 2001 has seen an explosion of calls for more capacity in LCTLs related to the U.S. security conflicts abroad and to the languages of nations with powerful new economies. As Gilbert Merkx notes in chapter 2 of this volume, in addition to the slow growth of globalization throughout our society that necessitates the needs for new languages of immigrants and of countries abroad, U.S.

security conflicts abroad are the incubators for calls for more language capacity, according to the particular crisis. Senator Paul Simon once noted, "In every national crisis from the Cold War through Vietnam, Desert Storm, Bosnia and Kosovo, our nation has lamented its foreign language shortfalls. But then the crisis 'goes away,' we return to business as usual. One of the messages of September 11 is that business as usual is no longer an acceptable option."[23] In the 1980s, U.S. companies and the National Science Foundation called for more engineers and engineers in training to master Japanese as the innovations of Canon, Honda, Toyota, Sony, Mitsubishi, and others invaded the American markets. As the conflicts with Iran have increased since the fall of Shah Mohammad Reza Pahlavi in 1979, the calls for more Pashto (Pushto) have increased.

Now, both the conflicts and alliances with parts of the Muslim world and the new economic powers of Asia have reshaped the priorities for LCTLs as articulated by various agencies of the U.S. government. What is most notable is how those priorities for particular LCTLs kept changing as global events evolved. The absence of both Somali and Swahili from any federal priority lists of critical languages in the 2000s was striking, even after the first terrorist bombings had struck U.S. embassies in Swahili-speaking Nairobi and Dar es Salaam and when political turbulence developed around a virtually stateless Somalia.[24]

A new consensus has emerged in 2008–2010 about the U.S. government's needs for languages for national security, focused primarily on languages of the Middle East, Russia, and Asia. Of all the consultations of the various agencies, especially through the NSLI and the development of the Flagship Language programs for advanced proficiency, we find a fairly consistent four-tier prioritization of languages, even though the criteria for choices are not publically defined.[25] Table 5-1 summarizes the priorities across federal agencies.

The highest priority category of priority derives from the seven languages targeted by the interagency NSLI initiative of the departments of Defense, State, Education, and the Director of National Intelligence (DNI) for developing flagship language programs in their seven highest-priority languages.

In spite of a consensus across the federal agencies for those seven, there are specific variations in the expressed needs of different U.S. agencies. DOD includes Dari, Hausa, Pashto, Swahili, and Yoruba in its top eleven languages. To its first priority seven languages, DOS adds the Inner and South Asian languages of Azeri, Bengali, Dari, Kazakh, Kurdish, Panjabi, Pashto, Tajik, Turkish, Turkmen, and Uzbek. Departments with a domestic focus that are dealing with U.S. immigration and hemispheric relations in negotiating economic, political, and drug trade issues (Commerce, HHS, HUD, Labor, and Treasury) include Spanish as a priority need. HHS includes German, Hausa, Portuguese, Tagalog, Thai, and Vietnamese in its top

---

Table 5-1. Approximations of Critical Language Priorities from Multiple U.S. Government Agencies, 2010

Highest Priority
Arabic
Chinese (Mandarin)
Farsi (Persian)
Hindi
Korean
Russian
Urdu

Second Priority
Bengali (Bangla)
Chinese (Cantonese)
Dari (sometimes with Farsi)
Japanese
Kazakh
Kyrgyz/Kirghiz
Panjabi/ Punjabi
Turkish

Third Priority
Azeri (Azerbaijani)
Indonesian
Swahili
Uzbek

Fourth Priority
Hausa
Malay (Bahasa Melayu or Malaysian)
Tagalog
Thai
Vietnamese
Yoruba

Fifth Priority Approximately 50 other languages on the list resulting from the U.S. Department of Education consultations with other federal agencies and with members of the Title VI NRC, LRC, and language education communities.
(See notes 24 and 35.)

---

seventeen choices. Commerce has French, German, Italian, Polish, and Portuguese in its top list.

The general concurrence across these agencies on the top two priority levels, however, is quite striking. Clearly, the emergence under the Bush administration of the Global War on Terror—or, as termed by the Obama administration, the "Overseas Contingency Operations"—with the overt goal of defeating Islamic militant fundamentalism was seen as needing a focus on these languages of the Middle East and Central and South Asia. In addition, the rise of the Chinese and Japanese

economic powerhouses after World War II created a need to achieve nuanced understandings with proficiency in these languages to make possible better trade and economic policy negotiations with their governments and businesses. These seven
highest priority languages identified by the NSLI initiative also have large populations constituting a critical mass of about 11 percent of the earth's population.

Language Priorities in Title VI and Fulbright-Hays Programs

Title VI programs have struggled throughout their history in choosing which languages should have the investment of scarce Title VI and university funds. Throughout the Cold War, there was a continuing stress on the languages of Russia, Eastern
Europe, and China. Choice of languages has been particularly stressful for centers
of South, Southeast, and Central Asia; Africa; and Russia and Eastern Europe studies, where the numbers of languages are large and the "student market" for most
languages is minuscule.[26] Arriving at priority choices among languages also is particularly difficult when the research climate in particular countries and in the
United States changes rapidly, when some societies become unstable and dangerous or inhospitable to researchers, and when U.S. political priorities shift.

Nevertheless, from their beginnings, the NRCs, in conversation with the Department of Education, have sought to make "rational choices" among languages to
serve better the broad national interests of U.S. users in education, business, media,
and government. As former South Asian NRC director Richard Lambert wrote,

> our eventual goal in foreign language planning should be the development of a com-
> prehensive, integrated public policy on foreign language instruction and use.... Surely,
> one of the first items in language planning in the United States should concern the
> development of a rational decision-making process as to which languages to teach and
> which languages particular kinds of students should learn.[27]

In 1959, the US/OE addressed the priorities issue for Title VI funding by targeting a highest priority category of six languages: "Arabic (in its chief dialects, and
with the modern written language stressed), Chinese (in its chief dialects, and with
Mandarin stressed), Hindu-stani (or Hindu-Urdu), Japanese, Portuguese, and Russian."[28] A second NDEA priority was for "(a) the remaining national or 'official' languages of sovereign nations, and (b) a small group (40–50) of unofficial languages
spoken by many millions of inhabitants of a nation or region." Specifically, the
"official languages" included eighteen languages of South, Inner, and Southeast
Asia, and Middle East, Africa (1), and Eastern Europe (2).[29] However, the NRCs and
other programs were not restricted from offering languages they chose and, over
most of its history, Title VI administrators and regulations did not mandate

particular languages, leaving it to the universities to set priorities they thought would serve all users well and for which there were adequate enrollments.

In 2002–2005, a major effort, labeled the e-LCTL Initiative,[30] was made by NRC directors of all world areas to meet to seek some consensus among the NRCs of each world region about what languages should have high priority for the nation and for their centers.

Several factors affect what languages are offered on a campus. First, some faculties and centers plan strategically for which languages to offer and seek to hire requisite instructors or faculty accordingly. Decisions from these campus planning meetings usually reflect the history of that university regarding which languages were offered in the past, what tenure-track language and linguistics faculty of the area have been hired, and, occasionally, with which nations and peoples the faculty has partnerships requiring a specific language. The "market" created by the particular needs and research plans of graduate students often determines which languages are taught in intensive summer LCTL institutes on campus and abroad. Choices frequently are driven by the students' personal history in the foreign area, such as in the Peace Corps or religious internships. Sometimes, their faculty advisors recommend specific nations or research sites that are most relevant to the student's research issue or topic. The Africanist community has been especially eager to deal with priorities because they face at least 750 relevant languages on the continent in fifty-four nations.

After discussion for more than a decade in the 1990s, the e-LCTL Initiative proposed several criteria for choosing what languages to offer on campus, in summer institutes, and, perhaps, in Department of Education priorities. The basic assumption of the approach was that there was no single criterion to follow and that there is a great diversity in the needs for different languages by a great variety of constituencies, including government, business, media, schools and colleges, scholars, service agencies, and heritage communities.

In 2000, after consultations among NRC and some LRC directors, the following major criteria were proposed for prioritizing and choosing among languages:[31] (1) What is the number of speakers, both first language and "additional language" speakers? (2) Is the language a "national language," a primary language, or lingua franca for a nation? This includes whether the language is the official language or, if not, whether it extends across national boundaries and is widely used as a trade language or broad multinational lingua franca. (3) Is the language used widely in educational and government institutions, broadcast and/or print media, and contemporary written and oral literatures of the peoples? (4) Is the language found in large amounts of archival materials important for various disciplines? Some languages whose use is declining may have important residual archives and literatures

101

for certain classes of scholars and users. (5) Is the language important because of its usage or significance politically, culturally, and socially? For example, although Amharic is a language of the minority Amhara community in Ethiopia, its dominant usage for many years by government has vested it with importance above the number of speakers. (6) Is the language important for U.S. national interests, such as by a number of government agencies, business, media, foreign diplomacy and development assistance, and other government programs? This includes concerns such as the need for foreign languages to support political or economic ties between a nation where those languages are spoken and the United States, political relations with the nation, the strategic location of the nation or language, and the cultural and technological exchange programs requiring language support.

With these criteria, directors of each Title VI world area caucused and completed reports on their consensus or disagreements on prioritizing languages of their area. The full results of their discussions and decisions for each world area are found online at http://elctl.msu.edu. In general, they came to some agreements supporting these criteria, added some new criteria, and, for most world regions, came to some decisions on priorities among languages. Appendix E provides a different view of NRC priorities by demonstrating for each world region (and international NRCs) what languages actually have been taught, what were the enrollments, which are available to be taught if there is demand, and for what languages FLAS fellowships have been allocated.

Languages for Each World Area

African NRC and some LRC directors and language coordinators had five meetings and arrived at a ranking among the 750 to 1,500 African languages in fifty-four nations. A large first-priority category consisted of thirty-four languages (many national or regional), a second-priority category an additional twenty-seven, and a third-priority list thirty-one, totaling ninety-two languages. (See the lists at http://elctl.msu.edu/regions/africaoverview.pdf.) In practice, in recent years, the African centers have been teaching about twenty-five languages each year and have the capacity to offer an additional nineteen languages. Enrollments at these universities in Swahili and Arabic dwarf those for all other languages, followed by healthy enrollments in Lingala, Yoruba, Wolof, Zulu, Akan/Twi, and Bamana/Bambara. Allocations of FLAS fellowships in 2000–2007 largely followed a similar pattern, with 451 in Swahili and 139 in Arabic, although they supported the study of thirty-eight other languages. These included 101 Akan/Twi, ninety-five Zulu, ninety-one Wolof, sixty-one Yoruba, fifty-two Bamana/Bambara, forty-six Hausa, thirty-nine Xhosa, and

thirty-nine for Algerian, Egyptian, Gulf, Moroccan, and Sudanese Arabic.

The East Asian directors added new criteria for the "historical and cultural importance of the language," the importance for heritage speakers, the need to rescue disappearing languages, whether resources are available for teaching the language, and the political or strategic importance of the language.[32] Their consensus was to focus offerings on Chinese, Japanese, and Korean to the advanced levels in all East Asian NRCs. Additional languages such as Manchu, Tibetan, and Mongolian were determined to be best taught in summer institutes or distance learning. (See further details at http://elctl.msu.edu/reportEAsia.pdf.) Over the years 2000 through 2007, among the sixteen languages being taught, 76 percent of East Asian FLAS fellowships (1,402) and a similar proportion of enrollments were in Chinese (Mandarin, Cantonese Yue, Classical, Gan Minh, Jinyu, Min Bei). (See Appendix E for details.) There were other enrollments for Japanese (33 percent) and Korean (20 percent) and very small enrollments in Tibetan and Uyghur.

The Southeast Asia and Pacific Islands caucus began by making the first priority for national languages, therefore giving highest priority to Bahasa Indonesia, Bahasa Melayu, Burmese, Filipino/Tagalog, Khmer, Lao, Tamil, Tetun, Thai, and Vietnamese. In addition, they identified eight languages for a second category and nine for a third. The directors also used their meetings to plan for what has become an annual Southeast Asian Studies Summer Institute (SEASSI) for intensive study of these languages.[33] (See the directors' report at http://elctl.msu.edu/regions/asiapacific.php.) Among the eleven languages being taught by these centers with 875 fellowships from 2000 through 2007, the largest enrollments and FLAS fellowships have been in Indonesian (239), Thai (218), Tagalog (110), and Vietnamese (146). Smaller enrollments are registered in Khmer, Burmese, Lao, and Hmong. For Pacific Island studies, with only thirty-two fellowships between 2000 and 2007, Samoan and Tahitian were the principal languages.

The South Asian NRCs met and also made plans to initiate an annual South Asian Summer Language Institute (SASLI).[34] The group struggled with the great diversity of languages, the use of some for written and others only for oral literatures, their national importance, and the politics of choices. Their report noted the widespread offering of Hindi and Persian (Farsi) across the United States and that the eleven NRCs at that time were regularly teaching seventeen of the highest priority twenty-five languages with five others available with demand. They identified twenty-seven languages as of second priority and twenty-four as third. (See the report at http://elctl.msu.edu/regions/southasia.php.) In practice, in these universities with 1,336 fellowships between 2000 and 2007, the largest number of FLAS fellowships were in Hindi (42 percent) and Urdu (15 percent) with healthy numbers in Tamil, Tibetan, and Nepali. Smaller numbers follow in Bengali and Nepali, and fewer yet in Pali, Persian/Farsi, Sanskrit, Malayalam, Panjabi, Sinhala, Gujarati, and Marathi.

The Middle Eastern NRCs urged a continuing priority focus on "the big four" languages: Arabic, modern Hebrew, Persian, and Turkish. Of pressing concern to these directors was the danger of diverting FLAS fellowships away from these four languages if their classroom instruction were to remain viable. They identified a series of crucial issues affecting the development of good teachers in the languages of the region. (Read the report at http://elctl.msu.edu/regions/mideast.php.) During the period 2000–2007, approximately half the total enrollments and 67 percent of the region's 2,058 FLAS fellowships were in Modern Standard and other Arabics, followed by smaller numbers for Persian/Farsi, Turkish, and Hebrew. Of the other twenty languages being offered in these NRCs, Armenian, Turkish, Uzbek, and Tajik had FLAS fellows.

The easiest consensus about priorities may have been for the Inner or Central Asia region, with only a single NRC at Indiana University. NRC director William Fierman noted the considerable difficulties in choosing which languages should be the focus, concluding that several languages in this difficult-to-define region were of highest priority, including Azerbaijani (Azeri), Uyghur, Turkmen, Kazakh, and Kyrgyz. (See http://elctl.msu.edu/regions/centralasia.php for details.) Offering fifteen languages with 187 fellowships between 2000 and 2007, the larger FLAS allocations were to Uzbek, Kazakh, Tajiki, Hungarian, Uyghur, and Tibetan.

Directors of the Russian and East European and Europe and Russia NRC areas indicated they were teaching thirty-two languages on a regular basis and eighteen others were available apparently without the need for further prioritization. (See their list and discussion at http://elctl.msu.edu/regions/eurasia.php.) From 2000 to 2007, 43 percent of the 2,681 FLAS fellowships and more than half the enrollments for these NRCs were in Russian, followed with fewer of both in Polish, Serbo-Croatian, Czech, Ukrainian, Uzbek, Hungarian, and Romanian, in descending numbers.

The Western European group of directors, who regularly offer twenty-three languages with the capacity available for twelve more, identified the national languages of the region plus Arabic as those of highest priority, including Danish, Dutch, Finnish, modern Greek, Icelandic, Italian, Norwegian, Portuguese, Swedish, and Turkish. Basque and Catalan were the only second-priority languages. (These are reported in detail at http://elctl.msu.edu/regions/westerneurope.php.) At these eleven NRCs, the largest numbers of university enrollments and FLAS allocations (55 percent) were in the more commonly taught French, German, Italian, and Spanish languages. Lower allocations were to Portuguese (6 percent), with smaller numbers of enrollments and fellowships in Dutch/Flemish, Swedish, Greek, Norwegian, Gaelic, Polish, and Russian.

The Latin America and Caribbean NRC directors and language coordinators met several times, and to the previous criteria they added the linguistic interest of the language, heritage preservation, opportunity for use and study, demands by business and government, and security needs of the United States. These directors used their meetings to identify two priority categories of the indigenous languages of Latin America plus Brazilian Portuguese and Haitian Creole. (See their categorizations of these thirty languages at http://elctl.msu.edu/regions/latinamerica.php.) From 2000 to 2007, these twenty-three NRCs invested 42 percent of their 1,838 FLAS fellowships in Brazilian Portuguese, followed by Maya (19 percent), several dialects of Quechua (13 percent), advanced Spanish (12 percent), and Haitian Creole (5 percent). In a change from previous decades, 42 percent of these NRC FLAS fellowships were awarded for the study of twenty-one indigenous languages of Latin America and the Caribbean.

The nine International Studies NRCs, which are not linked to any single world area, provided FLAS fellowships for the study of seventy-one languages. Arabic, followed by Portuguese, Swahili, Chinese (Mandarin), Turkish, advanced Spanish, Hindi, and Russian, received the largest number of fellowships.

In 2008 and 2009, in response to the calls of other federal agencies, especially DOS and DOD, for a Title VI focus on priority languages, the Department of Education's International Education Programs Service (IEPS) developed a series of consultations with ten federal agencies, as discussed previously. For several years, the directors of the NRCs had asked IEPS to revisit the very narrow list of IEPS language priorities. From these consultations, the Department of Education developed a new list of critical or priority languages for Title VI and Fulbright-Hays programs separate from the NSLI priorities. The IEPS published this list for comment in the Federal Register and now, in the 2009 and 2010 grant competitions, is using the list of seventy-eight languages. The law calls for periodically revisiting the federal needs and implementing those priorities in considering applications for grants for Title VI and F-H programs.[35]

Conclusion

Over the fifty years of the Title VI programs, a diverse and dispersed teaching of modern foreign languages, principally of the LCTLs, has emerged in the United States. As the NRC, LRC, CIBE, AORC, UISFL, TICFIA, and other Title VI and F-H programs have matured, they have developed many new initiatives to teach more languages more efficiently and to develop a variety of print and electronic teaching resources. In the past two decades, regular national summer institutes have developed for intensive study of the LCTLs of several world areas, informed by a consensus about what levels of proficiency should be accomplished. Increasingly, these are supplemented with distance and blended instruction using the resources of the internet to share instruction across a number of universities. Some of the

NRCs and their language faculties that face student need and demand for instruction in many LCTLs are offering some of the needed languages by using on-demand systems. These require adequate print and electronic learning materials, motivated learners, first-language tutors trained in new pedagogies, and language and linguistics faculty members providing regular supervision. Finally, partnerships with foreign faculty and universities have opened the doors for students to deepen and refine their language proficiency on the ground where the languages and their variants are used daily.

Clearly, this cost-effective Title VI system has continued to serve the diverse needs of many learners, beginning with the next generation of U.S. experts on foreign places—the graduate students preparing with language for immersion and research abroad. It is these faculty-in-training who are the buttress for our future hopes to achieve a greater depth of knowledge of foreign peoples, cultures, polities, and economies. At the same time, these core 130 NRC language programs serve those undergraduates who want to begin learning the LCTLs before graduate education. They also offer academic year, summer intensive, and study abroad in LCTLs to the businesspeople and professionals preparing for trade and commerce abroad, the NGOs offering service and development assistance abroad, the media seeking better reportage of realities abroad, and the U.S. government and security personnel seeking language learning materials, professionals, training institutes, and understanding of the new global and foreign peoples and cultures, including those newly emigrating to our communities from abroad. These Title VI institutions are broader and more focused on long-term research than the new initiative of the federal security agencies. They make more foundational contributions to the nation's language and international studies capacities. The federal agencies have a different mission based on their pressing priorities for the languages primarily of the Middle East and Asia and their goals for the intensive training required for rapid mastery of these languages by full-time learners. The federal agencies also have the budget needed for building intensive training as well as the special LCTL initiatives in the schools, funds the Title VI programs have never had.

For both the Title VI universities and the U.S. government agencies, however, there are new commitments to building sustainable language learning systems that will serve the well-being of both the nation and the entire global community. There is room for more conversation among those committed to language learning and the LCTLs about how to achieve all these ends more effectively with complementarity. We also need to build these programs in collaboration with our partners abroad. That was the vision of the framers of the Title VI Act, which has continued over the years with little change, as expressed in the 2008 reauthorization:

The security, stability, and economic vitality of the United States in a complex global era depend upon American experts in and citizens knowledgeable about world regions, foreign languages, and international affairs, as well as upon a strong research base in these areas. . . . Advances in communications technology and the growth of regional and global problems make knowledge of other countries and the ability to communicate in other languages more essential to the promotion of mutual understanding and cooperation among nations and their peoples.[36]

Acknowledgment

Christine E. Root assisted with many aspects of the data analysis and preparation of this chapter.

Notes

1 Parker, William R., The National Interest and Foreign Languages: A Discussion Guide and Work Paper. Washington, D.C.: Superintendent of Documents, USGPO, 1954, p. iv.

2 Unless otherwise indicated, the data about NRC and FLAS in this chapter are from the International Resource Information System (IRIS) database available online by the International Education Programs Service of the U.S. Department of Education at www.ieps-iris.org. Tables for each world area that are drawn from these data are found in Appendix E of this volume.

3   A modest number of FLAS fellowships also are allotted to each center for students to attend summer intensive language institutes such as the South Asia Summer Language (SASLI) and Southeast Asian Summer Studies (SEASSI) Institutes at University of Wisconsin-Madison, Summer Institute for Languages of the Muslim World (SILMW) at University of Illinois-UC, and the rotating Summer Cooperative African Language Institute (SCALI) currently at Michigan State University. On occasion, and with IEPS permission, FLAS fellowships may be used to seek instruction in the foreign field where the language is spoken.

4 Indeed, in 2008, the funding increase for the Defense Language Institute alone exceeded the total Title VI funding for all NRCs and associated FLAS fellowships nationwide.

5 Bigelow, Donald N. and Lyman H. Legters, "NDEA Language and Area Centers," in Task Force on International Education, *International Education: Past, Present, Problems, and Prospects*, House Committee on Education and Labor, October 1966, p. 194.

6 The criteria included "1) Official university recognition and support of the program; 2) Adequate library resources both for teaching and for research on the area; 3) Competent instruction in the principal languages of the area; 4) Offerings in at least 5 pertinent subjects in addition to language instruction; 5) Some specific mechanisms for integrating the area studies; 6) An area research program; and 7) Emphasis on the contemporary aspects of the area." Ibid., p. 192.

7 Derthick, Lawrence G. "The Purpose and Legislative History of the Foreign Language Titles in the National Defense Education Act, 1958." *PMLA*, Vol. 74, No. 2. (May 1959), 48–51. http://links.jstor.org/sici?sici=0030-8129%28195905%292974%3A2%3C48%3ATPALHO%3E2.0.CO%3B2-X, (accessed October 15, 2008).

8 Diekhoff, John S. "Priorities in Language Education." *PMLA* Vol. 80, No. 2 (May 1965): 24–28.

9 Bigelow, Donald N. and Lyman H. Legters, Op. Cit., October 1966, pp. 193–94.

10 Ruther, Nancy L., *Barely There, Powerfully Present: Thirty Years of U.S. Policy on International Higher Education*. London: Routledge, 2002, p. 68.

11 Brecht, Richard D. and William P. Rivers. *Language and National Security in the 21st Century: The Role of Title VI/Fulbright-Hays in Supporting National Language Capacity*. Dubuque, IA: Kendall/Hunt, 2000.

12 See more on this theme at Wiley, David, "Conference Rapporteur's Synthesis of the Findings of the National Policy Conference on Title VI of the Higher Education Act and Fulbright-Hays Programs." *Proceedings of a National Policy Conference on the Higher Education Act, Title VI, and Fulbright-Hays Programs*. Edited by Hawkins, John N., Carlos Manuel Haro, Miriam A. Kazanjian, Gilbert W. Merkx, and David Wiley. Los Angeles: University of California, International Studies and Overseas Programs, 1998.

13 With global migration, Title VI centers also called for translation of foreign languages being spoken in the U.S., for example, of patients in U.S. hospitals, witnesses in U.S. courts, and potential customers of U.S. companies. For instance, the 250,000 Nigerian (largely Igbo–speaking) population of Houston, the more than 60,000 Somalis in Minneapolis-St. Paul, and the 70,000 or more Ethiopians and Eritreans in the Washington, D.C. region create significant demand for African languages.

14 Defense Language Transformation Roadmap, January 2005. www.defense.gov/news/Mar2005/d20050330roadmap.pdf (accessed December 15, 2009).

15 Ibid., p 3.

16 Foreign Service Institute. www.state.gov/m/fsi/ (accessed December 15, 2009).

17 Rogin, Josh, "Exclusive: GAO Report Finds State Department Language Skills Dangerously Lacking." In *Foreign Policy*, September 22, 2009. http://thecable.foreignpolicy.com/posts/2009/09/22/exclusive_gao_report_finds_state_department_language_skills_dangerously_lacking (accessed December 15, 2009).

18 "Language Schools." Defense Language Institute Foreign Language Center. www.dliflc.edu/schools.html (accessed January 8, 2010).

19 Clifford, Ray T. and Donald C. Fischer, Jr. "Foreign Language Needs in the U. S. Government." *Annals of the American Academy of Political and Social Science* Vol. 511 (September 1990), pp. 109–121.

20 Rogin, op. cit.

21 Laipson, Ellen. "Foreign Language Requirements in the Intelligence Community." Testimony to the Senate Government Affairs Commmitte. September, 14, 2000. www.dni.gov/nic/testimony_foreignlanguage.html (accessed December 15, 2009). Laipson was vice chairman of the National Intelligence Council of the U.S. government.

22 "National Security Language Initiative (NSLI) – Budget Information," 2007. www2.ed.gov/about/inits/ed/competitiveness/nsli/funding.html (accessed December 15, 2009).

23 Simon, Paul, "Beef Up the Country's Foreign Language Skills." *The Washington Post*, October 23, 2001, p. A23.

24 In the mid 2000s, the U.S. Department of Education consulted with the secretaries of state and defense about what languages should be categorized as "critical." In spite of the fact that the DLI was desperate for Somali speakers and teachers as well as for other African language resources, neither agency recommended their inclusion in the list. As a result, for several years, projects proposed to the department by potential grantees using LCTLs lost points to competing critical languages if they proposed an African language. After much consulting with Department of Education IEPS staff and a major and repeated consultation with eight USG agencies, a critical list of seventy-eight languages has been created for all world areas, including twelve from Africa.

25 This is not an official listing but rather the author's attempt to combine the published priorities of a dozen or more U.S. agencies and offices, beginning with the DOS and DOD.

26 In India, for example, the 1961 census recognized 1,652 languages, and *Ethnologue* describes 415. Even for the language mainstream, the Indian census of 2001 found that twenty-nine languages are spoken by more than a million first-language speakers. Africa, with its more than 700 languages (some estimate 1,500) and fifty-four nations is peculiarly problematic for setting priorities for diverse students, researchers, faculty members, and other users.

27 Lambert, Richard D. 1994. "Problems and Processes in U.S. Foreign Language Planning." *The Annals of The American Academy of Political and Social Science* 532 (March 1994), pp. 48, 54.

28 Derthick, L.G., U.S. Commissioner of Education, Department of Health, Education, and Welfare, "A Statement of Policy: Language Development Program, Centers and Research and Studies," Bulletin 2, June 17, 1959, published in *NDEA Language and Area Centers: A Report on the First 5 Years,* edited by Donald N. Bigelow and Lyman H. Legters. Washington, D.C.: U.S. Department of Health, Education, and Welfare, Office of Education, U.S. Government Printing Office, 1964: 72.

29 Ibid. In 1962, these included Bengali, Burmese, Finnish, modern Hebrew, Hungarian, Indonesian-Malay, Khalkha, Korean, Marathi, Persian, Polish, Serbo-Croatian, Singhalese, Swahili, Tamil, Telegu, Thai, and Turkish.

30 See http://elctl.msu.edu/ for reports on enrollments and priorities for languages of each world area.

31 For more details and background, see Wiley, David S. "Collaborative Planning for Meeting National Needs in the Less Commonly Taught Languages: Defining Criteria for Priorities in the Languages of the World Regions." The e-LCTL Initiative: A National Project for US/ED Title VI Programs. http://elctl.msu.edu/wileypaper.pdf.

32 Lewis, Michael. "Creating Priorities for East Asian Languages: Continuing Dominance of the Big Three." 21 December 2004, http://elctl.msu.edu/reportEAsia.pdf.

33 See http://seassi.wisc.edu/.

34 See http://sasli.wisc.edu/.

35 The seventy-eight (78) languages deemed critical on the U.S. Department of Education's list of less commonly taught languages (LCTLs) are: Akan (Twi-Fante), Albanian, Amharic, Arabic (all dialects), Armenian, Azeri (Azerbaijani), Balochi, Bamanakan (Bamana, Bambara, Mandikan, Mandingo, Maninka, Dyula), Belarusian, Bengali (Bangla), Berber (all languages), Bosnian, Bulgarian, Burmese, Cebuano (Visayan), Chechen, Chinese (Cantonese), Chinese (Gan), Chinese (Mandarin), Chinese (Min), Chinese (Wu), Croatian, Dari, Dinka, Georgian, Gujarati, Hausa, Hebrew (Modern), Hindi, Igbo, Indonesian, Japanese, Javanese, Kannada, Kashmiri, Kazakh, Khmer (Cambodian), Kirghiz, Korean, Kurdish (Kurmanji), Kurdish (Sorani), Lao, Malay (Bahasa Melayu or Malaysian), Malayalam, Marathi, Mongolian, Nepali, Oromo, Panjabi, Pashto, Persian (Farsi), Polish, Portuguese (all varieties), Quechua, Romanian, Russian, Serbian, Sinhala (Sinhalese), Somali, Swahili, Tagalog, Tajik, Tamil, Telugu, Thai, Tibetan, Tigrigna, Turkish, Turkmen, Ukrainian, Urdu, Uyghur/Uigur, Uzbek, Vietnamese, Wolof, Xhosa, Yoruba, and Zulu. See http://ed.gov/legislation/FedRegister/announcements/2009-4/100509b.html.

36 "Findings and Purposes." Title VI—International Education Programs, SEC. 601. International and Foreign Language Studies, Part A of Title VI (20 U.S.C. 1121 et seq.).

CHAPTER 6

Language Competence—Performance, Proficiency, and Certification: Current Status and New Directions

Catherine J. Doughty

Introduction

Throughout the first fifty years of Title VI legislation, reauthorizations, and funding appropriations, the U.S. Congress has charged the Department of Education with establishing a national capacity in foreign languages, cultures, and international and area studies. The companion chapter in this section documents the extensive successes of Title VI in developing a widespread infrastructure which serves as the foundation for this national capacity. In her chapter, Professor Tarone identifies the essential building blocks of this infrastructure: the many centers (e.g., National Resource Centers, Language Resource Centers, and Centers for International Business Education), fellowships (e.g., Foreign Language and Area Studies), and materials grants (e.g., International Research and Studies Program) that collectively have significantly increased the number of languages, courses, and materials developed and made available; offered teacher training; and initiated dissemination networks such as web sites, blogs, and online, peer-reviewed journals. Furthermore, Title VI program status has attracted matching funds from universities that have continued teaching a wide range of previously unoffered languages beyond the initial Title VI funding period, firmly establishing less commonly taught languages (LCTLs) in the national infrastructure. Nevertheless, despite all these accomplishments, Professor Tarone's review of the history and impact of Title VI programs led her to conclude that too few Americans have been able to benefit from these programs, and that "at the national level, more foreign language knowledge is essential if we are to effectively implement 'soft diplomacy.'"

I join with Professor Tarone in commending the tremendous Title VI effort to date; however, although the infrastructure may now be firmly in place, the point of departure in this chapter, which assesses current status and looks to the future, must be the clear-sighted observation that there is still much more Title VI work to be accomplished. As we shall see, building successful language programs on the foundation of national infrastructure will require more time, sustained effort, increased resources, and better oversight. Moreover, meeting the increasingly more critical foreign language demands of these uncertain times cannot be accomplished efficiently and effectively without implementing the scientific advancements made over the past three decades in understanding how foreign languages are learned and systematically documenting foreign language learning outcomes.

Current Status of America's National Foreign Language Competence

Recently, Congress asked the National Research Council to "review the adequacy and effectiveness of the Title VI programs in addressing their statutory missions and in building the nation's foreign language expertise—particularly as needed for economic, foreign affairs, and national security purposes" (O'Connell and Norwood 2007, p. 24). The council convened a committee to conduct a formal evaluation of the Title VI and Fulbright-Hays International Education Programs.[1] In this section, I draw from the relevant findings of this National Research Council evaluation to assess the current status of foreign language competence[2] and, later on, extend the discussion to put forward new directions in which I believe Title VI must lead.

The overall finding of the National Research Council Committee (NRCC) was that the Department of Education "has not made foreign language and culture a priority, and its several programs appear to be fragmented" (ibid., pp. 3–4). The report also notes the larger context of a nation and its educational system that have "placed little value on speaking languages other than English or on understanding cultures other than one's own" (ibid., p. 1). Although a similar inward focus was the original catalyst for Title VI in 1959, during the most recent decade of Title VI funding, increased terrorism, a global economic crisis, and new health risks to the nation have only worsened the inward focus in some sectors. Clearly, the Title VI mission is more vital than ever before; thus, it is essential that we determine through an analysis of the current status how to prioritize foreign language competence successfully and ensure the production of more American foreign language knowledge at expert levels.

The NRCC, on its own and through commissioned research, made a concerted effort to uncover indicators of successful foreign language achievement by Title VI grant recipients and by students in language programs funded or supported in some way by Title VI. Although the committee found a proliferation both in number and type of foreign language programs and quantity of instructional materials, there was not sufficient documented evidence to evaluate foreign language competence outcomes in Title VI programs. However, it was reported anecdotally to the committee in verbal testimony and written submissions that Title VI program recipients did not have the necessary language competence to meet current business, government, and national security requirements. Moreover, the committee established unequivocally through various surveys and interviews that the demand for foreign language expertise still exists and has continually expanded. Thus, given the impressive potential of the building blocks of the national infrastructure described in the preceding chapter and the worrisome findings of this NRCC evaluation, our analysis of the current status of foreign language competence begs the question: Why has the potential to develop a national capacity in foreign languages not yet been fully realized, and what are the remediable weaknesses in Title VI and its funding in contributing to this capacity?

The NRCC report attributes the problems in Title VI largely to four elements: the expansiveness of the Title VI program aims; the inadequacy of the funding, juxtaposed with the large scale of the aims; a lack of accountability for program outcomes; and a lack of senior-level leadership in the administration of the programs in the U.S. Department of Education. As evident in the range of chapters in this volume, the current Title VI mission, indeed, has expanded steadily and vastly from its initial focus on developing international expertise to meet particular national security needs and develop specific language competence in the LTCLs of strategic interest. The unique role of the current Title VI program is "to address a broad set of needs for foreign language, international, and area expertise, rather that to respond to the current demand for government expertise" (ibid., p. 83) and to fund "the creation of a broad skill base and on building a deep pool of area and language expertise nationally, not only in the government, but also in the K-12 system, academia and business" (ibid., p. 29). Thus, the conceptualization of Title VI entails the development of a "broad base" as a "feeder program" to other entities such as the Foreign Service Institute or the Defense Language Institute Foreign Language Center for specialized language training. Although this may have been very well intentioned, an unanticipated result has been breadth at the expense of the hoped-for depth in language competence. In other words, although the number of foreign language offerings has grown, widening the base of the foreign language infrastructure, the level of language ability acquired by program beneficiaries reportedly is not sufficiently advanced to fully address national and international needs—that is to say, sufficient foreign language expertise is still lacking.

The breadth-but-not-depth problem is intertwined with an annually increasing dispersion of Title VI funding. Although the national foreign language infrastructure has expanded over the years, the total amount of funding for the current nine programs remains equivalent, adjusting for inflation, to the amount of funding provided for the three inaugural Title VI programs (ibid., p. 33). Thus, as stated in the report, "the ability of the Title VI/FH to accomplish its broad mandate is hampered by the limited availability of funds" (ibid., p. 81). Thus, to raise the level of foreign language competence to a level that can meet the pressing demands, Title VI needs much more funding. According to a recent report issued by Lewis-Burke Associates, budgets for the Title VI domestic and international foreign language programs have been increased about 5.5 percent for fiscal year (FY) 2010:

> Title VI programs will receive $125.8 million, an increase of $7 million (5.5 percent) over FY 2009 at the President's request. Within this amount, Title VI domestic programs, which include the National Resource Centers and the Centers for International Business Education (CIBE), will receive $108.4 million, an increase of $6 million (5.5 percent) over FY 2009 at the President's request. The $6 million will be used to increase the amount awarded to the National Resource Centers and increase the number of Foreign Language and Areas Studies (FLAS) fellowships. Title VI International programs, which include the Fulbright program, will receive $15.6 million, an increase of $880,000 (5.6 percent) over FY 2009 at the President's request" (Lewis-Burke Associates LLC 2009, p. 9).

Though somewhat encouraging, in absolute terms, a budget of $125.8 million divided among all the Title VI programs remains inadequate to address the wide range of program aims. Funding of foreign language programs must be given higher priority by Congress.

In addition to increased funding, increased accountability to taxpayers is required, particularly in light of the effects of the 2009 global recession. From this point forward, Title VI programs should be held more formally accountable in the objective ways recommended by the NRCC. Furthermore, objective documentation of success can provide the basis for requests for increased funding and determining proper allocations. Beyond following the NRCC recommendations for evidenced-based assessment (discussed later in this chapter), to ensure program success, it will be essential that individuals examining Title VI program foreign language competence aims and outcomes be experts in the science of language learning and objective language-learning outcomes assessment. Moreover, to realize the prioritization of Title VI foreign language missions and to facilitate effective over-sight, Congress and the administration should continue to pursue senior-level leadership. More specifically, the NRCC recommended the administration of all K-12 and higher education international and foreign language programs by an executive-level presidential appointee who reports to the secretary of education, provides strategic direction, and coordinates with other federal agencies. "Raising the status of the programs is vital to demonstrate clearly the importance of foreign languages and other area and international education to ED and put direction and oversight of the programs at a level more comparable to the level of oversight at other key agencies" (O'Connell and Norwood, p. 243).[3] Finally, in addition to rais-ing the status of Title VI oversight to the executive level, if developing national for-eign language capacity is truly to become a priority, it will be critical to follow the precedent set by President Obama's appointment of scientific experts with relevant research experience to address problems faced by the nation—for instance, the appointment of Dr. Steven Chu to the position of secretary of energy.

We now turn to a constructive discussion of the Title VI foreign language pro-grams "on the ground" as they operate now and could be improved in future. Set-ting the funding inadequacies and lack of oversight aside for the sake of this discussion, but keeping in mind that progress cannot be made unless those prob-lems are solved, I propose that the continuing lack of foreign language competence in the United States is due primarily to four interrelated factors: scarce foreign lan-guage needs analysis; setting the bar too low for foreign language competence required for national and international work; slowness to implement scientific advances to innovate in foreign language pedagogy; and lack of sequencing within and articulation among programs, resulting in insufficient "time on task" for lan-guage learning.[4] The following sections discuss each of these four factors—needs analysis, foreign language expertise, innovative pedagogy, and sufficient time for foreign language learning—in greater detail.

Foreign Language Needs Analysis

The NRCC report called for needs analysis at a global level to "develop and main-tain competencies to respond to future national security needs, to remain compet-itive in global markets, to retain a scientific and technological advantage, and to develop analytic competencies and a generally more globally aware citizenry" (ibid., p. 18). Brecht and Rivers (2005) discuss the research methodology that can be employed to determine foreign language needs at the societal level (e.g., surveys of language requirements in federal, state, and military job descriptions; analysis of shortfalls in meeting the language demands). It is incumbent on policy and 115 decision makers who fund programs to ensure that the U.S. national foreign language needs are understood at this level and prioritized, and, crucially, that such information be provided to language program developers who can, in turn, use prioritized global foreign language needs as a starting point for conducting a more specific second language (L2) needs analysis for particular groups of learners.

Although rarely a part of current operational foreign language programs, L2 needs analysis is necessary if language learning is to become more efficient and effective. The straightforward rationale for L2 needs analysis as the essential first step in the development of any language program is as follows:

> In an era of shrinking resources, there are growing demands for accountability in public life, including education. In foreign and second language teaching, one of several consequences is the increasing importance attached to careful studies of learner needs as a pre-requisite for effective course design. . . . The combination of target language varieties, skills, lexicons, genres, registers, etc. varies greatly . . . meaning that language teaching using generic programs and materials, not designed with particular groups in mind, will be inefficient, at the very least, and in all probability, grossly inadequate. . . . Every language course should be considered a course for specific purposes, varying only . . . in the precision with which learner needs can be specified (Long 2005, p. 1).

The Centers for International Business Education (CIBE) is a notable exception to the current lack of needs analyses in U.S. language programs. Moreover, CIBE is the one Title VI program that actively engages in needs analysis, at least at the global level. By legislation, U.S. business interests must be represented on the CIBE Board of Advisors. A finding of the needs analysis of the CIBEs was that U.S. businesses, not having been able to rely on the foreign language proficiency of Americans, have chosen to depend on foreign nationals for running their businesses in other nations, with a few U.S. supervisors overseeing them. Thus far, this has resulted in an emphasis on area and cultural studies in U.S. institutions, perhaps at the expense of developing language proficiency in the U.S. workforce.

However, an L2 needs analysis that would result in programs leading to greater workforce foreign language proficiency should be very manageable. The first step would be to ask: What are the language needs of the overseas U.S. managers who supervise the local workforce? Data would need to be collected from the managers themselves in situ (what language barriers do they perceive?); from participant observers (documenting the language needs objectively); from their foreign business partners (if feasible); and from the U.S.-based supervisors of the managers (to what extent is the overseas management model effective for the business purposes?). More broadly, if reliance on the local workforce is merely a coping strategy

in the face of inadequate language skills, it would obviously be more effective in the long run to develop a multilingual U.S. workforce to place American businesses on an equal par linguistically in the global workplace. According to the NRCC, the average number of languages spoken by U.S. business executives is 1.5, in comparison with European executives who speak four languages; Chinese business executives typically know English as well as other languages of commerce. The methodology for conducting the L2 needs analysis for a workforce that could engage with its counterparts abroad would involve similar methods of triangulated data collection to gain an understanding of the tasks that business executives need to be able to do in the foreign language (e.g., from their perspective, from their supervisors' perspective, and, as viewed by taking the perspective of their competitors). L2 needs analysis methods are usefully described by Long (1985a).

The National Flagship,[5] a program funded by the Department of Defense, like CIBE, also addresses the needs for foreign languages in business, in addition to several other disciplines of importance to national security. For instance, in the graduate program Language Flagships, students with basic language proficiency (Interagency Language Roundtable [ILR] Level 2[6]) are admitted to programs built around their disciplinary fields, such as international economics, politics, and law. Flagship students spend one academic year at the U.S. institution preparing for an overseas experience. The structure of the overseas experience is developed on the basis of an L2 needs analysis for professionals in the disciplinary areas and entails direct enrollment abroad in college-level courses in the discipline, an internship in a business, nongovernmental organization (NGO), or other organization central to the discipline as well as an intensive engagement with contemporary print and digital media. Thus, Flagship students are integrated into the group relevant to their discipline. The key point here is that, in order to develop the curriculum, Language Flagships work backward from the professional needs ultimately required. The overseas components draw on the professional requirements in the prospective fields to determine the content of the overseas flagship component, and they conduct needs analyses during the overseas experiences. The stateside flagship programs prepare students to be able to function in the overseas domains by developing curricula to meet the identified needs.

In this way, the foreign language that is acquired is relevant to Flagship students' future professional needs and becomes increasingly complex as the demands increase during both the U.S. and the overseas flagship program components. For example, to prepare students for direct enrollment in disciplinary courses at Korea University, the University of Hawaii (UH) uses a task-based approach (discussed later in this chapter) to meet identified needs. One important target task is listening to lectures in one's own specialized field while enrolled in a course taught to native speakers of Korean. At the time of entry to the UH Flagship, this task is too difficult for the learners, who are at ILR Level 2 (roughly, conversational proficiency). To work up to handling this target task, they begin by listening to lectures that have been specially prepared to aid their comprehension by including elaborated language input, a technique that enables learners to cope with complex language without sacrificing understanding (Long and Ross 2009; Yano, Long, and Ross 1994). Next, they listen to lectures given by native-speaking graduate students in the discipline, followed by lectures given by professors who are accomplished experts in the field. Because the lecturers are addressing nonnative speakers, they naturally adjust their language to be more comprehensible to their audiences. The ultimate target task is listening to lectures at the overseas university delivered by native-speaking expert professors who are addressing native-speaking student audiences. By the time Flagship students enroll in Korea University, they are nearly able to handle this task, with the last phase of learning occurring in situ. Without such systematic preparation, overseas students are limited to the more typical programs for nonnative speakers of Korean, which are at a much lower level than courses for native speakers.

Having outlined these two examples of successful needs analyses, we must address a commonly encountered response to the call for needs analysis in the primary and secondary domains and even in undergraduate programs, all sites for Title VI funded programs: the "excuse" that it is difficult, if not impossible, to know the future language needs of children or high school or undergraduate college students. This response should not be readily accepted if progress in U.S. foreign language education is to be made. Instead, efforts must be made to solve this problem. For instance, much lip service is paid to the notion of the need for the U.S. education system to develop global citizens with skills necessary to meet global challenges. An L2 needs analysis within this broader prioritized aim could be conducted along these lines. For instance, what does it take to become a global citizen? Among others, at the very least, the following needs could be targeted:

- Knowledge of the world map, as conceptualized and written by a culture in which the foreign language is taught.
- Skills using technology in a foreign language: word processing, e-mailing, Internet searching via Google™, cell phone use, and electronic media.
- Knowledge of contemporary culture as gleaned in online media and television news programs.

Someday primary or secondary students may switch to another language, but this is not an acceptable excuse either; time will not have been wasted given that empirical evidence shows that prior language learning experience is a good predictor of subsequent language learning success.

From Language Competence to Language Expertise

After national priorities for language study have been identified and L2 needs analyses conducted, the starting point for the necessary foreign language pedagogy paradigm shift leading to pedagogical innovations is the recognition that learning (of any kind) is more than acquiring a body of static knowledge. Rather, it entails instead the development of the capacity to think critically, accomplish complex tasks, and achieve goals, such as making an important discovery through systematic investigation, curing a patient by diagnosing and pinpointing the problem and prescribing an effective treatment, or completing a trade agreement by skillfully negotiating in the relevant language the business, cultural, and societal dimensions of the impact of the agreement on the people and economies of all the parties to the agreement. These kinds of significant accomplishments are achieved by people who have become experts—that is, by scientists, doctors, or bilingual diplomats. To catalyze the shift in foreign language education, I propose (1) that the conceptualization of foreign language competence be redefined as foreign language expertise, (2) that the focus of Title VI programs be the determination of what it takes to develop expertise in various domains of foreign language use identified by needs analyses, and (3) that pedagogical innovations enable experiential learning, or "learning by doing." This is analogous to recent changes in math, science, and medical education, now viewed not as merely acquiring an encyclopedic knowledge of facts, taxonomies, or illnesses and diseases, but rather emphasizing problem-based learning and successful modeling of systems or simulations of diagnosis and care. The conceptualization of foreign language proficiency as expertise could potentially be the first step in resolving the breadth-without-depth foreign language problem in the United States described above. In short, the language-learning bar must be set much higher, and the pedagogy must become more innovative.

Innovations in Foreign Language Pedagogy

More often than not, foreign languages are still taught using outmoded, grammar-based methods, despite the scientific studies that have demonstrated their inadequacy (for a review, see Doughty 2003). Hours, weeks, and even years are wasted by learners memorizing complex grammar rules that research shows cannot be used in spontaneous language comprehension or production. Moreover, grammar-based approaches to language instruction, again, uninformed by research findings, assume that linguistic complexity drives language acquisition in a linear fashion—for example, as shown by the black line on the schematic language learning curve shown in Figure 6-1—often resulting in learners being taught language structures

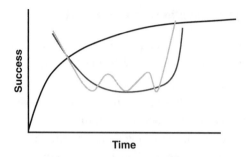

FIGURE 6-1
Schematic Foreign Language Learning Curve (success at foreign language learning over time)

they are not ready to acquire, and so, in turn, do not. Second language acquisition (SLA) research has discovered instead, that as in first language acquisition, progress is made in a U shape (i.e., chunked, targetlike performance followed by restructuring when language systems are acquired) or a W shape (i.e., ups and downs in performance, revealing the systematic progress of learners in analyzing language) (see Figure 6-1). The driving force is the learner's "internal syllabus," which is determined by the constraints and requirements of the developing new language system and the communicative pressures encountered by the learner. Put simply, it can no longer be assumed that what is taught is learned. Rather, the psycholinguistic needs of the learner should form the basis of the syllabus.

Moreover, these needs are best captured not in a priori linguistic descriptions, but rather in terms of goals for language use and means for enabling language expertise during experiential learning. To move beyond traditional, language-focused approaches, language teaching must guarantee conditions that engage language-learning processes. Figure 6-2 presents a brief historical overview of the advancements made in pedagogical approaches to language teaching, moving away from the ineffective traditional Option 1 (based on language forms and rules) to the more effective Option 2 (emphasizing communication) to the most effective and efficient Option 3 (marrying the two in a scientifically sound fashion). An example of an innovative Option 3 approach to language teaching that aims to meet these learning requirements is task-based language teaching (TBLT) (Long 1985). This method emphasizes the development of the expertise needed to accomplish real tasks in a foreign language and comprises an organized set of principles, which can serve as a checklist of necessary components for language teaching.[7] Some examples from the checklist are providing rich and varied language input; sequencing learning activities according to cognitive complexity, gradually approximating and ultimately accomplishing target tasks in the foreign language; and providing feedback on error (attention to language form) that is timed to be psycholinguistically

	Option 2	Option 3	Option 1
Language Learning	Analytic	Analytic	Synthetic
Language Focus	Meaning	Form	Forms
Syllabus Examples	•Natural Approach •Immersion •Content-based LT •Procedural Syllabus	•Task-based LT •Process Syllabus •Case-based •Project-based •Problem-based	•Grammar-translation •ALM •Structural •Lexical •Situational •Notional/Functional

FIGURE 6-2

Options in Foreign Language Teaching (from www.mhhe.com/socscience/foreignlang/conf/first.htm Adapted with permission from Long, *inter alia* and www.mhhe.com/socscience/foreignlang/top.htm.)

opportune and, hence, effective. (See Doughty and Long 2003a for the complete checklist.)

A perusal of many of the Title VI programs that provide online syllabi indicates that the pedagogy of LCTLs is very often still at the traditional Option 1 stage. Traditional syllabi typically list language features to be learned, and employ generic textbooks rather than analyze L2 needs that guide materials development. Some Title VI programs, however, are beginning to innovate. For instance, the 2007 South Asia Summer Language Institute (SASLI, University of Wisconsin-Madison), which is a formal educational collaboration of the eleven U.S. Department of Education-designated Title VI National Resource Centers (NRCs) for South Asia and the Association of Asian Studies, hosts a pedagogy corner[8] that introduces TBLT, blended learning approaches (technology plus classroom instruction), and heritage learning approaches. It is worth noting that the collaboration of NRCs and Language Resource Centers (LRCs), such as this, could provide the means for conducting needs analyses pertinent to both area studies and language expertise. Michigan State University's Title IV LRC, the Center for Language Education and Research (CLEAR) is innovating in the area of rich internet applications that support materials development.[9] Blended learning using such innovative tools is a promising area for Title VI programs to take a national lead.

Title VI also funded the LRC at the University of Hawaii to develop an innovative template for TBLT (in English) that was then applied to one language (Korean) and provides a manual describing how TBLT can be applied to any other language at any level. The project covered all six components in the design, implementation, and evaluation of an effective language program (a program-development checklist): needs analysis; syllabus design; materials development; methodology and pedagogy; assessment; and evaluation. Chaudron et al. (2005) describe the

121

task-based needs analysis carried out, how tasks were identified for materials development, how target discourse samples were gathered and analyzed to discover prototypical discourse features, the development of TBLT modules, and a discussion task complexity and sequencing.[10] For instance, a module for zero-beginners develops ability in following directions using different types of maps. The maps themselves become increasingly more complex, as do the requirements made of the learners. At first, learners listen to carefully grouped examples of target discourse while looking at a map that traces the route being described. Gradually, the task is made more complex. First, maps without traced routes are used, but the teacher checks step by step to ensure that learners comprehend and are not "lost." When learners are comfortable, the maps become more complex. Once they can follow directions, only then do they begin to give directions—production being more complex than comprehension—first in pairs, with feedback from teachers and, ultimately, on their own and unaided. During the production tasks, teachers provide feedback on error, which is the means for promoting accuracy according to the needs of the learner's developing language system. A suggested exit test for the module is a virtual reality map task in which learners must follow directions unaided.

A full implementation of TBLT was recently completed in 2007 for the U.S. Border Patrol Academy (BPA), which launched a task-based, residential Spanish program for its agents in training. This program could usefully serve as a model for future Title VI innovations at more advanced levels of expertise. The eight-week course includes eight hours per day of instruction organized around seven critical job tasks that were identified in a needs analysis—for instance, inspecting a vehicle, conducting an interview, or providing first aid.[11] The tasks are introduced to the class through audio and video recordings of experienced agents actually doing their jobs in Spanish. Class time is structured around tasks that students complete alone, in pairs, and in groups. These become increasingly complex throughout the course, beginning with simple activities in which students identify images associated with specific commands (e.g., "raise your hands," "drop your weapon") and ending with students identifying criminals from a "lineup"of images based on audio recordings of interviews with suspects. The course is conducted almost entirely in Spanish, including role-play work in the target tasks. There is no planned explicit grammar instruction; grammatical issues are dealt with when they arise; and the focus of the course is shifted briefly to language forms only when this becomes necessary for communication. At the end of each module, students are required to perform that module's target task in a performance-based assessment with native-speaking role-players; and, by the end of the course, students are expected to be able to perform all the critical tasks.

As described above, TBLT has also been successfully implemented at advanced levels of proficiency in the National Flagship Program, a centerpiece of the National Security Language Initiative (NSLI). The UH Korean Flagship and the University of Maryland Persian Flagship are two good examples. These programs typically are eighteen months in length, with nine months spent at a U.S. university in preparation for another nine months at a foreign university. The goal is to attain foreign language expertise in two or three skills at ILR Level 3 (i.e., professional proficiency), typically in a difficult language. The organizing principle in these Flagship programs is a needs analysis that feeds backward to inform course and materials development. The overarching idea is that Flagship students are beginning to develop expertise in a discipline (e.g., economics, political science, health care), and that they should do so in their foreign language.

These examples of TBLT illustrate how the paradigm shift in language instruction can be accomplished at all levels of proficiency in a very practical, if labor intensive, way. Although promising, until such principles are adopted more widely, national foreign language learning outcomes are likely to continue to be poor. Because the proper implementation of TBLT is both labor- and time-intensive, with adequate funding Title VI could play an important role in pushing TBLT successes (or any other research-based innovations; Long and Doughty 2009) further out into the national infrastructure, eventually accomplishing the goal of developing a deep pool of foreign language experts who can meet business, government, and national security requirements.

Time Required to Learn a Foreign Language

As should already be evident, acquiring foreign language expertise requires extensive time, effort, and opportunity to learn—far more than the few hundreds of hours in high school or several semesters at college. Moreover, unlike first language acquisition, the level of success in foreign language learning is quite variable and depends on the age of starting to learn and the quality of instruction and/or immersion opportunities (Hyltenstam and Abrahamsson 2003). The ultimate success of language learning is determined by the age of the first meaningful and extended exposure to language. Figure 6-3 provides a schematic representation of the effects of age on SLA revealing that the majority of people who begin acquiring a foreign language in late childhood or adulthood may not succeed to the levels required by current national and international needs. An early start, extensive time on task, and one more component—careful sequencing (articulation) of the K-16 curriculum—are three ways to mitigate the notorious difficulty of foreign language learning. An early start to language learning is essential because very young children learn languages 123

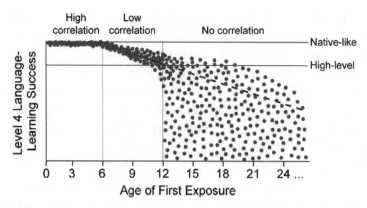

FIGURE 6-3
Language Learning Outcomes (from Doughty and Bowles 2009)

more readily and effectively than do adults, but this is true only if the conditions are conducive to child language-learning processes. Thus, even early-start programs must be carefully designed. Many schools currently offer programs aiming to interest children in foreign languages, such as by exposing each child to several different languages and cultures; however, although these programs may pique the interest of a child, valuable sustained time actually learning one particular language has been lost during the most opportune period. Other schools offer a foreign language for only ninety minutes to a few hours per week, which is woefully inadequate in terms of the time on task required. A concrete suggestion toward remedying this situation is that Title VI-funded primary programs could be evaluated in terms of adequacy of the time-on-task component. For instance, the number of hours spent actually engaged in foreign language learning could be measured against the number of hours in programs that are known to produce bilinguals, such as Canadian immersion programs (Cummins 2000; Johnson and Swain 1997) or English classes in Scandinavia or the Netherlands (see Program for International Student Assessment results).[12] Even better would be to measure actual language-learning outcomes, an important aim that will be addressed later.

Sequencing within a course and across programs is vital to future success in developing foreign language expertise, owing to the required time on task factor. Thus far, language program articulation across the K-16 instruction in the United States has been virtually nonexistent. For instance, the movement for immersion in elementary schools in the 1960s and 1970s met with a stark realization that immersion graduates had either no opportunity to continue with their foreign language in high school or were faced with traditional grammar-based courses not matched to the proficiency level of immersion students and, thus, demotivating. In 2006, the NSLI[13] was launched to coordinate federal foreign language efforts in

124

the departments of Defense, Education, and State and the Office of the Director of National Intelligence (ODNI) (Spellings and Oldham 2008). NSLI has only recently begun to function; however, the goal of synergy across all state and federal agencies and institutions toward a concerted national effort to significantly boost American foreign language competence is indeed promising. Many Title VI programs offering 220 LCTLs provide opportunities along this language-learning opportunity "continuum." It must be noted, however, that the new initiative suggests more articulation from one program to the next than actually exists. An approach that starts with the required foreign language expertise needs and builds backward along an articulated pathway of foreign language learning opportunities is required to enable sufficient time on task and a coherent language learning experience from primary education through professional training.

Sequencing within a foreign language syllabus is also important to the quality of language learning. Nearly all foreign language syllabi (in Title VI and other programs) are sequenced according to intuition. More often than not, the intuitions are based on materials' writers or teachers' perceptions of the difficulty of linguistic structures in a language, sometimes combined with notions of what might be most useful to learners. TBLT is the only methodological approach that formally proposes a sequencing approach that is empirical rather than intuitive. Cognitive task complexity is hypothesized as a psycholinguistic basis for syllabus sequencing. A discussion of this is beyond the scope of this chapter (but see the brief example above on following directions in Korean). For an introduction to sequencing issues, visit www.mhhe.com/socscience/foreignlang/conf/task1.htm. (For a more detailed discussion, see Robinson 2005, 2009; or see any of the web sites for TBLT conferences.[14])

Language Learning Outcomes Assessment

Thus far, I have argued that future Title VI programs should aim for language competence construed as language expertise, base curricula on needs analyses, innovate in pedagogy, and provide time needed to ensure the effectiveness of language learning opportunities made available through Title VI funding. After all these components are in place, it will be crucial to document success. In each of the eight areas of congressional inquiry into Title VI programs, the NRCC report found that there was not sufficient data to warrant any trustworthy conclusions about Title VI programs' effectiveness, including the language competence outcomes.[15] This is because all the programs studied had used only self-report outcomes measures, and the focus had been more on evaluation of programs than of individual learners. In perhaps its strongest recommendation, the NRCC report specifically stated that   125

Title VI programs should "stop doing self report and move toward more reliable and valid assessment" (p. 10).

There are several promising approaches to accurate assessment of language-learning outcomes with growing empirical support from the field of language testing. Three examples are evidence-based assessment, task-based assessment, and performance-based assessment. These assessment approaches all have in common that they aim to measure actual language use directly rather than rely on self-report, which is known to be unreliable, or indirect measures, such as discrete-point language measures (e.g., fill-in-the-blank, multiple choice, or constrained, constructed responses), which do not capture spontaneous language use. The general aim is to accumulate evidence of language ability across task performances. Ideally, the evidence gathered enables decisions to be made concerning whether the language learners have acquired the abilities identified during L2 needs analysis. To illustrate, we can return to the BPA Spanish language program discussed earlier. The final assessment is entirely performance-based, consisting of a series of tasks that encompass all the critical components of the course tasks. The assessments are criterion-scored, and there are no written language exams. This task-based approach is a complete departure from the BPA Spanish course it replaced, which was entirely based on grammar. Students in the previous course studied a different grammatical topic for each class meeting (conducted mainly in English) and had very little time to practice speaking Spanish. Many of the trainees failed the previous Spanish course and were required to repeat it. Nearly 100 percent of the BPA TBLT Spanish course students have completed it successfully.

Although Title VI programs do not seem to have an overarching plan for language assessment, many seem to rely on the national standards that have been established by the American Council of Teachers of Foreign Languages (ACTFL Standards for Foreign Language Learning) when making decisions such as selection and placement of students into levels. Unlike evidence-based approaches, standards do not start from empirical needs assessment to inform curriculum development and foreign language outcomes assessment:

> The standards are not a curriculum guide. While they suggest the types of curricular experiences needed to enable students to achieve the standards, and support the ideal of extended sequences of study that begin in the elementary grades and continue through high school and beyond, they do not describe specific course content, nor recommended sequence of study.[16]

As can be seen in Figure 6-4, the ACTFL standards are based on an Option 2-like communicative model of language learning. The assessment tool is the ACTFL Oral Proficiency Interview (OPI), in which trained raters probe learners' listening and

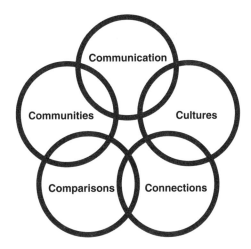

FIGURE 6-4
ACTFL Foreign Language Standards Domains (from www.actfl.org/files/public/StandardsforFLLexecsumm_rev.pdf.)

speaking and assign a proficiency rating such as Novice High or Advanced Low. Although it has been established that the OPI is a reliable instrument (when administered by properly trained raters), its validity has been questioned by language assessment researchers (Bachman 1988). Given that OPIs are time-consuming and expensive, in my view, the effort and money would be better spent in Title VI programs in L2 needs analyses and evidenced-based assessment of the ability to accomplish the identified tasks in the foreign language.

The National Language Flagship is the only federally funded foreign language program that has officially set an outcomes goal for its graduates. The aim is for learners to reach ILR Level 3 in at least two skills among listening, speaking, and reading. The assessment instruments are the Defense Language Proficiency Test (DLPT) and an OPI based on the ILR scale. Preliminary data[17] provided by the National Security Education Program, which oversees and funds the programs, indicate that the majority of learners reach ILR Level 3 in at least one skill, and more than half do so in two skills (see Table 6-1). Many others nearly meet the strict criterion for success, having passed or excelled on one test but not the other (i.e., 18 among the 25 in that group scored ILR 2.5 rather than 3 on the second test), also reflecting considerable success. In addition, three of the ten shown in the third row who exceeded one criterion but did not meet the second, for whatever reason, did not take the second test; and five of those ten scored 2.5 on the second test.

In addition to the summative proficiency results, some Language Flagships track the progress of learners using task-based assessments determined by needs

Table 6-1. Language Flagship Outcomes—Preliminary Data

Success on Criteria	103 Examinees	Percent Met		
Neither	11	45 percent (none or one)		
One met, one not met	25			
One not met, one exceeded	10			
One met, one exceeded	15	89 percent		
Both met	14	(at least	55 percent	
Both exceeded	28	one)	(both)	

analysis (e.g., the UH Korean Language Flagship, described above). An interesting future challenge for the Language Flagship and Title VI programs is to determine the relationship, if any, between proficiency scores and graduates' success in using foreign languages in their careers. The fundamental goal for all the programs should be to determine what is considered good evidence of success and how best to gather evidence to document success. Programs that have conducted needs analyses and based curricula on meeting these needs will be in a good position to document success. In this way, learners will be accountable to programs, which, in turn, will be accountable to funding agencies and taxpayers. In the case of Title VI, program administrators will have the evidence needed to convince Congress to continue to authorize funds.

Advances in Language Sciences

In this final section, we will examine how Title VI programs are implementing research advances in understanding how foreign languages are learning. Although there is always a certain amount of art and intuition in teaching, the science of language learning (the field of Second Language Acquisition) must inform teaching methodology and pedagogical practice, if they are to be effective and innovative. This understanding is readily available from the thirty years of empirical work, as discussed earlier in the section on innovations in pedagogy. An additional argument for a science-based approach to foreign language teaching can be made by considering the nature of materials development for the LCTLs. Visits to the web sites of LRCs and NRCs,[18] along with a review of abstracts of programs funded by the Title VI International Research and Studies Programs (IRSPs)[19] reveal an LCTL infrastructure transformed from an complete lack of materials in many of the LCTLs to a dizzying array of dictionaries, textbooks, teachers' guides, CDs, DVDs, or web-delivered materials, databases, repositories, web sites that collect or point to resources, blogs, distance and blended learning programs, and heritage language materials for the larger of the LCTLs. As impressive as this transformation has been, what is missing is a coherent approach to language teaching materials development and scientific procedures for assessing the effectiveness of the materials in the context of national and international foreign language needs. This is an area in which Title VI programs can take the lead, particularly with respect to blended learning, which can help address program articulation and time-on-task challenges.

Too often, scientific advances go unheeded, and foreign languages are still taught using Option methods (see Figure 6-2). This is perhaps because many language professionals are not properly trained in the new science of language learning. Indeed, one of the greatest obstacles throughout the broad expansion of foreign language offerings spearheaded by Title VI has been the shortage of qualified teachers. The LRC program was launched in 1990 to address this problem as well as the lack of foreign language materials in the LCTLs. The main strategy of the LRCs was to train native speakers of LCTLs in language pedagogy or to update the teaching skills of traditionally trained native-speaking teachers. Recent efforts encourage language teachers to collaborate with native-speaking content teachers. LRCs, some in concert with the NRCs, offer many varied "one-off" summer institutes and sponsor web sites for professional development of currently employed teachers—dealing with, for instance immersion,[20] pragmatics,[21] assessment,[22,23] materials development,[24] and technology and foreign language learning.[25,26] These Title VI efforts represent an excellent start. To guarantee that learners develop foreign language expertise, it will be essential that all prospective language teachers be properly trained and keep current with the science of language learning, for instance through obtaining a master's degree in Second Language Acquisition, instead of training in foreign language literature or linguistics, which have been default tracks to teaching credentials for lack of any other training opportunities,[27] or reading handbooks of relevant research (Doughty and Long 2003b; Long and Doughty 2009). A significant achievement of the LRCs has been to begin the professionalization of the teaching of LCTLs. Now, teachers can obtain certificates and master's degrees; several peer-reviewed journals have been launched (*South Asia Language Pedagogy and Technology*,[28] *Heritage Language Journal*[29]); organizations have been formed (National Council of Less Commonly Taught Languages and the Heritage Language Association); and, more recently, Title VI has encouraged communication and resource sharing among LRC, CIBE, and NRC grant recipients. The credentialing process can be further professionalized by ensuring the scientific training of new foreign language teachers.

Title VI LRC summer institutes should continue to advance the professionalization of all language teachers by enabling them to keep current on SLA research. Language teachers, like other professionals, should be required to keep their professional training up to date. In addition, the Title VI programs should support teachers and program developers to attend the major research conferences that focus on language learning issues—for instance, the Second Language Research Forum and the annual meetings of the American Association of Applied Linguistics and the European Second Language Acquisition Association. Teachers will need to make an effort to read leading journals that publish empirical studies of foreign language learning, such as *Language Learning Journal* or *Studies in Second Language Acquisition*. Ideally, Title VI should organize and oversee a coherent national agenda for implementing scientific advancements in SLA research in all the foreign language programs it funds and document the outcomes of these implementations.

Conclusion

This chapter has focused on the need, raised in the previous chapter, for more Americans with foreign language expertise. In brief, the current status of foreign language competence can be described as having a broad infrastructure built over the past fifty years largely by Title VI programs. However, a 2007 Title VI program evaluation, conducted by the National Research Council, concluded that the United States still has not made foreign language education a priority and that the foreign language needs of business, government, and national security are not being met. The NRCC report attributed this to four factors: the expansiveness of the Title VI program aims; the inadequacy of the funding juxtaposed with the large scale of the aims; a lack of accountability for program outcomes; and a lack of senior-level leadership in the administration of the programs in the U.S. Department of Education. We concluded that the funding and leadership issues urgently must be addressed in order to solve the "breadth but not depth" problem underlying the insufficiency of foreign language competence in the United States.

Beyond that, I proposed that foreign language pedagogy suffers from four additional problems: scarce foreign language needs analysis; setting the bar too low for foreign language competence required for national and international work; slowness to implement scientific advances to innovate in foreign language pedagogy; and lack of sequencing within and articulation among programs, resulting in insufficient "time on task" for language learning. I examined necessary improvements in foreign language teaching, proposed that a paradigm shift leading to pedagogical innovations is needed, and looked at some existing innovations that can serve as examples, some of which are from Title VI programs, and some from others. Next,

130

I noted that Title VI is leading the way in LCTL offerings and in the professionalization of teachers of these languages. Title VI is also poised to lead the way in pedagogical innovations, especially blended learning, which incorporates technology into language programs. Throughout the chapter, I discussed the need for accountability for success of Title VI programs, which can be established only through documentation of foreign language learning outcomes using evidence-based methods. This documentation would serve as a record of achievement and a basis for future funding requests.

It is evident that the mission of Title VI is more important now than ever before. The need for foreign language expertise increases and grows more pressing with each new political, economic, or health crisis. For many reasons, the United States is at risk of losing its capability to lead internationally, and insufficient foreign language expertise is a key aspect of this problem. Despite written policy and speeches by the past secretary of education, highlighting the importance of foreign languages in communicating and forming partnerships with citizens from other cultures and countries (Spellings 2006), the National Research Council was unable to identify any meaningful reference to foreign language study or international education in the Department of Education's strategic plan. Lack of senior leadership has been a serious problem, and the Bush administration was highly negligent, with the No Child Left Behind program diverting funding from arts, physical education, music, area studies, and foreign languages. If the United States is truly to make foreign language expertise a national priority, the Obama administration should provide high-level leadership and Congress should greatly increase Title VI funding. For their part, once adequately funded, Title VI programs will need to raise the bar for foreign language expertise, innovate in foreign language pedagogy, and collect objective evidence of successful foreign language outcomes.

Addendum 1: Key Areas for the Title VI Program Evaluation Identified by Congress (NRCC, p. 2)

1. Infusing a foreign language and area studies dimension throughout the education system and across relevant disciplines, including professional education.
2. Conducting public outreach/dissemination to K-12 and higher education, media, government, business, and the public.
3. Reducing shortages of foreign language and area experts.
4. Supporting research, education, and training in foreign languages and international studies, including opportunities for such research, education, and training overseas.
5. Producing relevant instructional materials that meet accepted scholarly standards.
6. Advancing uses of new technology in foreign language and international studies.
7. Addressing business needs for international knowledge and foreign language skills.
8. Increasing the numbers of underrepresented minorities in international service.

Notes

1 The expertise of the review committee encompassed members in international government relations, language assessment, policy studies, foreign diplomacy, international and public affairs, graduate education, world affairs and the global economy, educational psychology, and educational technology.

2 The report addresses eight key areas of interest to Congress, as shown in Addendum 1. The focus in this chapter is on the language competence dimension of the evaluation, which is an integral component of each of the eight key areas.

3 Miriam Kazanjian of the Coalition for International Education (personal communication) indicates that these efforts are under way, but not yet complete. She reports the following information: Rep. Rush Holt (D-NJ) sponsored a bill in the last Congress (H.R. 5179) to create an Assistant Secretary for International and Foreign Language Education in the U.S. Department of Education. Under H.R. 5179, the assistant secretary would be nominated by the president, confirmed by the Senate, and report to the Secretary. The provisions of H.R. 5179 passed the House as part of the Higher Education Act (HEA) reauthorization in 2008. However, the conference committee on HEA reauthorization instead adopted a provision to create a Deputy Assistant Secretary for International and Foreign Language Education, appointed by and reporting to the

Assistant Secretary for Postsecondary Education. This provision became law in 2008. The second position has been filled. As this outcome is not in keeping with the NRCC recommendation, Rep. Holt is still exploring the assistant secretary option. Much will depend on the new administration, especially the new secretary of education.

4 It is worth emphasizing that without ample funding and proper oversight, the proposals in the following discussion cannot get off the ground.

5 www.thelanguageflagship.org/ *The Language Flagship*. January 2010.

6 www.govtilr.org/ *Interagency Language Roundtable*. January 2009.

7 For an accessible discussion of the principles of task-based language teaching, see Catherine Doughty and Michael Long, "Optimal Psycholinguistic Environments for Distance Foreign Language Learning." *Language, Learning and Technology* 2003, vol. 7 no. 3, 50–80. http://llt.msu.edu/vol7num3/doughty/default.html.

8 http://sasli.wisc.edu/courses/pedagogy.htm. Hosted by University of Wisconsin System, 2008.

9 http://clear.msu.edu/clear/store/products.php?product_category=online. Center for Language Education and Research. 2005.

10 http://nflrc.hawaii.edu/publications/rn37/. Task-based language teaching: A demonstration module.

11 www.performtech.com/pt/features/SpanishAcademy.htm. Performtech. 2008.

12 http://nces.ed.gov/surveys/pisa/. National Center for Education Statistics. 2010.

13 www.ed.gov/about/inits/ed/competitiveness/nsli/nslibrochure.pdf. Archived Data. U.S. Department of Education. Accessed February 3, 2010.

14 TBLT 2005 (Leuven, Belgium): www.tblt.org; TBLT 2007 (Honolulu, Hawaii): www.hawaii.edu/tblt2007/; TBLT 2009 (Lancaster, UK) www.lancs.ac.uk/fass/events/tblt2009/index.htm.

15 The NRCC report does not discuss the validity of Title VI programs' foreign language pedagogy, which is a shortcoming of the evaluation.

16 www.actfl.org/files/public/StandardsforFLLexecsumm_rev.pdf. American Council on the Teaching of Foreign Languages. 2009.

17 The data reflect the 2005–2008 exit tests (DLPT 4 or 5 and OPI) from the graduate professional programs of 102 National Flagship Fellows learning Arabic (17), Chinese (23), Korean (38), Persian (1), and Russian (24)/

18 The portal to the all the LRCs is found at http://nflrc.msu.edu/.

19 Abstracts are posted at www.ed.gov/programs/iegpsirs/index.html. U.S. Department of Education, 2010.

20 www.carla.umn.edu/conferences/past/immersion2008/index.html. Hosted by Center for Advanced Research of Language Acquisition–University of Minnesota, 2009.

21 www.carla.umn.edu/speechacts/index.html. Hosted by Center for Advanced Research of Language Acquisition–University of Minnesota, 2009.

22 www.carla.umn.edu/institutes/index.html. Hosted by Center for Advanced Research of Language Acquisition–University of Minnesota, 2009.

23 http://casls.uoregon.edu/lfo.php. Hosted by Center for Applied Second Language Study–The University of Oregon, 2009.

24 www.carla.umn.edu/institutes. Hosted by Center for Advanced Research of Language Acquisition–University of Minnesota, 2009.

25 http://clear.msu.edu/clear/professionaldev/summerworkshops.php. Center for Language Education and Research. 2005.

26 A full list of LRC summer institutes and workshops appears at: http://nflrc.msu.edu/login/scripts/summer.php. Foreign Language Resource Centers, 2007.

27 It should be noted that a number of language departments offer tracks in SLA for students interested in becoming language teachers.

28 http://salpat.uchicago.edu. South Asia Language Resource Center, 2008.

29 http://international.ucla.edu/languages/nhlrc/journal.asp. Hosted by University of California, Los Angeles, 2009.

REFERENCES

Bachman, L. F. 1988. "Problems in examining the validity of the ACTFL Oral Proficiency Interview." *Studies in Second Language Acquisition* 10(2):149–161.

Brecht, R. and Rivers, W. 2005. "Language Needs Analysis at the Societal Level." In *Second Language Needs Analysis*, edited by Long, M. New York: Cambridge University Press, pp. 79–104.

Chaudron, C., Doughty, C. J, Kim, Y., Kong, D., Lee, J., Lee, Y., Long, M. H., Rivers, R., and Urano, K. 2005. "A Task-Based Needs Analysis of a Tertiary Korean as a Foreign Language Program." In *Second Language Needs Analysis*, edited by Long, M. New York: Cambridge University Press, pp. 225–261.

Cummins, J. 2000. *Immersion Education for the Millennium: What We Have Learned from 30 Years of Research on Second Language Immersion*. Ontario Institute for Studies in Education of the University of Toronto 2000. Accessed December 9, 2009 from www.iteachilearn.com/cummins/immersion2000.html.

Doughty, C. and Bowles, A. 2009. "A Talent for Language." *The Next Wave* 18(1):33–41.

Doughty, C. J. and Long, M. H. 2003a. "Optimal psycholinguistic environments for distance foreign language learning." *Language Learning Technologies* 7(3):50–80.

Doughty, C. and Long, M. (eds.) 2003b. *Handbook of Second Language Acquisition Research*. Malden, MA: Blackwell.

Hyltensam, K. and Abrahamsson, N. 2003. "Maturational Constraints in SLA." In Doughty, C. and Long, M. (eds.) *Handbook of Second Language Acquisition Research*. Malden, MA: Blackwell, pp. 539–588.

Johnson, R. K. and Swain, M. 1997. *Immersion Education: International Perspectives*. Cambridge: Cambridge University Press.

Lewis-Burke Associates LLC. 2009. *Summary and Analysis of the FY 2010 Consolidated Appropriations Bill: Federal Programs of Interest to Social Work Education and Research*. Washington, D.C..

Long, M. 2005a. *Second Language Needs Analysis*. New York: Cambridge University Press.

———. 2005b. "A rationale for needs analysis and needs analysis research." In Long, M., *Second Language Needs Analysis*. New York: Cambridge University Press, pp. 1–16.

———. and Doughty, C. (eds). 2009. *Handbook of Second Language Teaching*. Malden, MA: Wiley-Blackwell.

Long, M. H., and Ross, S. 2009. "Input elaboration: a viable alternative to 'authentic' and simplified texts." In *Feschrift for Yasukata Yano*. Tokyo: Kaitakusha.

O'Connell, M. E. and Norwood, J. L. 2007. *International Education and Foreign Languages: Keys to Securing America's Future*. Committee to Review the Title VI and Fulbright-Hays International Education Programs. Washington, D.C.: The National Academies Press.

Robinson, P. 2005. "Cognitive complexity and task sequencing: Studies in a componential framework for second language task design." *International Review of Applied Linguistics* 43, 1–32.

———.2009. "Syllabus design." In Long, M. and Doughty, C. (eds.). *The Handbook of Language Teaching*. Malden, MA: Wiley-Blackwell, pp. 294–310.

Spellings, M. 2006. "A Test of Leadership: Charting the Future of U.S. Higher Education A Report of the Commission Appointed by Secretary of Education." Washington, D.C.: U.S. Department of Education.

———. and Oldham, C. 2008. "Enhancing Foreign Language Proficiency in the United States: Preliminary Results of the National Security Language Initiative." Washington, D.C.: U.S. Department of Education.

Yano, Y., Long, M. and Ross, S. 1994. "The effects of simplified and elaborated texts on foreign language reading comprehension." *Language Learning* 44:189–219.

PART 3

The History and Significance of the Programs of Title VI Higher Education Act

CHAPTER 7

Title VI and Foundation Support for Area Studies: Its History and Impacts

Anne H. Betteridge

A review of Title VI support for area studies from the inception of the National Defense Education Act (NDEA) program in 1958 to the present has drawn my attention to three facts. The first is the enduring importance of Title VI programs as the mainstay of area and international studies in the United States. Second, area is not rigidly defined in Title VI legislation or for purposes of administration. Third, the continued existence of Title VI programs allows their partners in universities and private foundations to take area studies in new directions, secure in the knowledge that a solid infrastructure for the teaching of world languages and area studies already exists and is likely to continue to do so. Further, new initiatives often depend on the insights and scholarship of area studies specialists, many of whom received their advanced degrees from Title VI institutions.

The need for a federal program such as Title VI was noted in a 1950 Social Science Research Council (SSRC) postconference report, which commented, "The American educational structure is still almost as centered on Western Europe as it was when Cathay seemed almost as far away as the moon." The report cited one commentator's view that "the individual institution cannot do enough to give our education a world perspective. . . . 'Only a great Federal program can do it'" (cited in Wallerstein 1977: 206). Title VI programs continue to perform that vital function.

Indeed, Title VI programs make possible moves in important new intellectual directions, as other chapters in this volume reveal; these moves, in turn, strengthen the Title VI programs. Such innovative moves often have been encouraged by private foundations. The foundations and Title VI programs enjoy a synergistic relationship of great importance to the development of highly skilled scholars and practitioners and to progress in developing knowledge about a world in which intricate connections of many sorts affect cultural, economic, and political developments. In this chapter, I draw particular attention to the implicit, if not always stated, relationship between Title VI programs—in particular, the National Resource Centers (NRCs)—and private foundations.

The importance of global interconnections and the need for U.S. citizens to have "professional or technical training with knowledge of the languages, economies, politics, history, geography, people, customs, and religions of foreign countries" was highlighted in a 1943 SSRC Committee report on World Regions. The report observed that "our citizens must know other lands and appreciate their people, cultures, and institutions" and that "[r]esearch, graduate teaching, undergraduate instruction, and elementary education in world regions will be desirable as far as one can see into the future." The report concluded that "[c]oncentrations on regions may conceivably open the road to . . . a weakening of the rigid compartments that separate the disciplines" (Wallerstein 1977, pp. 196–197). At that time, a good deal of excitement surrounded area studies and their potential. Kenneth Prewitt built on this, writing at a time when area studies was firmly established, that "area studies holds area constant and invites the participation of multiple disciplines, in contrast to traditional comparative studies which held discipline constant and involved multiple areas. Area studies, consequently, has been the most successful, large-scale interdisciplinary project ever in the humanities and the social sciences" (Prewitt 2001: 78).

Formulations of Areas and Funding of Area Studies

Although the specificity of particular areas may appear to be constant in area studies because of continuity in terminology, the exact meaning of an area is not entirely fixed. Consequently, what might appear as a rigid system of classification is flexible in its implementation. For example, does Middle East extend west across North Africa and as far east as Afghanistan and Pakistan?[1] Many Middle East centers regard that full range of territory as well within their geographical purview. What of language affinities? If languages closely related to Persian and Turkish are spoken in Central Asia, might that not be a reason to broach the study of Central Asia within Middle Eastern studies? And if Islam is culturally salient in the Middle East and originated there, might not Islamic studies more broadly be a subject centers for Middle Eastern studies could reasonably claim, at least for comparative purposes? In fact, the premier journal of Middle East studies, the *International Journal of Middle East Studies*, stakes out just such broadly defined territory as its purview.[2] Institutions with Middle East NRCs include departments of Near Eastern studies, Middle East and North African studies, and Middle East and Islamic studies. In a number of cases, their names have changed over time to reflect more accurately the scope of their activities. And scholars associated with these centers may also study Middle Eastern populations in diaspora, although not with Title VI support. Attention to these populations in the form of heritage learners does, however, fit under the Title VI tent when it comes to issues of language instruction. The situation in all area studies regions is interestingly and productively complex and dynamic.

In practice, definitions of region need to respond to practical considerations. At a March 2009 conference organized by the Fares Center of Eastern Mediterranean Studies at Tufts University, General (Ret.) John P. Abizaid, former commander of the U.S. Department of Defense Central Command (CENTCOM) (2003–2007), delivered an address on "Security Challenges in the Middle East." He responded to a question about exactly this issue and was asked whether the definitions of region matter. He remarked that we need to synchronize boundaries for the twenty-first century and added that the boundaries are now synchronized for the Cold War. He agreed that it makes sense to bring India into CENTCOM (traditionally including the region from Egypt to Afghanistan and Pakistan) saying that "where things are linked, they should be linked"—for example, regarding India and Pakistan's categorization, with reference to Kashmir. The problem, of course, is that many things are linked—it is a matter of identifying the most important links for the purposes of analysis in any given situation, and the importance of those links can change over time. The names of regions, however, do not always alter to reflect changed conceptions and practices.

Specific regions are not singled out for attention in Title VI legislation even though a number of NRCs and FLAS fellowships weight certain world areas, nor is region defined in any specific way. The only firm boundary observed by Title VI programs is that Title VI funding may not support studies of the United States. Ralph Hines and the authors of *International Education and Foreign Language: Keys to Securing America's Future* (2007) proposed similar periodization of the development of Title VI programs.[3] For simplicity's sake, I draw on these to identify three periods in the development of Title VI programs—Foundation, Revision, and Extension.

In the Foundation period, Title VI legislation authorized centers for the teaching of crucial modern foreign languages and in "other fields needed to provide a full understanding of the areas, regions, or countries in which such language is commonly used" (PL 85-864-Sept. 2, 1958, Title VI, Part A, Sec. 601(a)). These fields included history, political science, linguistics, economics, sociology, geography, and anthropology. As Title VI programs developed and new needs became evident, new programs and emphases were introduced to strengthen the understanding of world areas. Fulbright-Hays educational and cultural exchanges were added in 1961. The period of Title VI extension and revision saw the establishment of Title VI in the Higher Education Act of 1965. In 1980 legislation, "area studies" was defined for the first time as "a program of comprehensive study of the aspects of a society or societies, including study of its history, culture, economy, politics, international relations and languages" (PL 96-374, Oct. 3, 1980, Title VI, Sec. 622(a)(1)). Legislation in 1986 authorized comprehensive language and area centers, "which would be national resources for teaching of any modern foreign language, for instruction in fields needed to provide full understanding of areas, regions, or countries in which such language is commonly used, for research and training in international studies, and in the international and foreign language aspects of professional and other fields of study, and for instruction and research on issues in world affairs which concern one or more countries" (PL 99-498-Oct. 17, 1986, Title VI, Sec. 602(a)(1)(B). The Higher Education Amendments of 1998 (PL 105-244) mentioned the need for government and the private sector to work together to generate and disseminate "information about world regions, foreign languages, and international affairs throughout education, government, business, civic, and nonprofit sectors." In the most recent Higher Education Amendments of 2008 (PL 110-315), the term "foreign area" was replaced by "area studies." At no time were exact regions specified; in fact, a broad definition allows scope for studies of multiple regions. Legislation consistently refers to areas, regions, countries, societies, world regions, and area studies in general terms.

Although regions are not specifically defined in Title VI legislation, a list of world areas is used to categorize the National Resource Centers (NRCs). The specific designation of these regions has changed over time in response to world events and to the ways in which scholars choose to study their regions of focus.

Grants funded in the first NDEA Title VI grant cycle supported attention to eight world areas: Africa, East Asia, Inner Asia, Latin America, Middle East, Russia/East Europe, South Asia, and Southeast Asia. Additional world areas were added in subsequent grant cycles: Western Europe in 1965; Canada, International Studies, and Pacific Islands in 1973; Caribbean and North America in 1997; and Europe, with seven centers, and Europe/Russia, in 2000. In all but two cases, one center was funded in each initial grant to a new area. The exceptions are for two Centers of International Studies in 1973–1976 and a remarkable seven to European studies centers in 2000–2004.[4]

World Area Selection sheets now included in Title VI proposals were added some three cycles ago when John Paul was chief of advanced training and research programs at the International Education Programs Service (IEPS). Applicants are asked to self-select the area in which they would like to have their proposals considered, so there would not be any misunderstanding. Few people mark "Other" and offer another world area designation than those provided. If they do, special panels are convened to make sure that the proposals relating to a new area have a fair reading. The list of world areas can be adjusted, based on new areas added under "Other."[5] Thus, allowance is made for flexibility in the definitions of NRC world areas.

Title VI support creates a continuing national resource of persons knowledgeable about all world areas and their languages so that capacity exists to respond to issues wherever and whenever they arise. Richard D. Lambert expressed a concern about the potentially skewed distribution of funding to support studies of all world areas during the Vietnam war years. He noted, "One of the endemic problems of area studies that is partially related to the availability of funding is its dependence on the swings in interest in particular countries or regions among the general public." He added:

> One of the major policy issues facing area studies in the future is how to determine and sustain the appropriate balance among area and country competencies among area specialists in the face of these short-term cycles of popular enthusiasm and differential external funding (Lambert 2001: 34).

Although Title VI NRC funding has given particular attention to certain regions in response to contemporary issues and concerns, fluctuations of funding amounts from one region to another have not been large or long-lived. This is independent of shifts in funding from private sources. Title VI programs have done a remarkable job of continuing to support area studies across the board. A look at funding emphases across Title VI NRC grant cycles demonstrates this point (see Table 7-1).

Shifts in regional and thematic emphases can best be understood by placing them in their temporal and legislative contexts. Immanuel Wallerstein noted the ascendance of the Soviet Union and China over Latin America and Japan as priority areas for U.S. interests following World War II (Wallerstein 1977: 201). The initial founding period of Title VI programs, 1959–1972, came at a time of national security concern over the launching of Sputnik by the USSR, which was the occasion for the subsequent enactment of the National Defense Education Act in 1958. The 1959–1973 NRC funding cycles reflected these priorities, relative to other grant cycles. Forty-three percent of NRC funding was devoted to East Asia, South Asia, and Southeast Asia centers. Russian and East European centers received 20.2 percent of

Table 7-1. Distribution of Title VI Funding to National Resource Centers, 1959–2009 (by percentage)[1]

World Area	1959–1973	1973–1981	1981–1983	1983–1985	1985–1988	1988–1991	1991–1994	1994–1996	1997–1999	2000–2002[2]	2003–2005	2006–2009[2]
Africa	9.4	11.0	10.3	10.4	11.2	10.1	10.8	12.5	11.2	10.0	7.3	8.9
North America	0.0	0.0	0.0	0.0	0.0	0.0	0.0	0.0	0.7	0.0	0.0	0.0
Canada	0.0	2.0	2.3	2.4	3.4	3.4	3.1	1.9	2.0	1.9	1.6	1.7
Caribbean	0.0	0.0	0.0	0.0	0.0	0.0	0.0	0.0	0.9	0.0	0.0	0.0
Latin America	12.9	10.8	12.1	13.1	12.7	14.0	14.1	12.4	13.5	16.6	12.8	14.6
Pacific Islands	0.0	1.4	1.1	1.0	1.0	1.0	1.0	0.8	1.8	0.9	0.8	0.8
Asia	0.0	0.0	0.0	0.0	0.0	0.0	0.0	0.0	0.0	0.9	0.8	2.4
East Asia[3]	see S.Asia	20.0	18.0	18.0	13.8	13.0	11.2	12.4	11.9	13.2	12.7	13.7
South Asia[3]	43.0	10.0	8.8	7.6	9.3	9.6	8.5	7.6	9.0	8.1	9.1	7.3
Southeast Asia[3]	see S.Asia	5.0	3.9	2.9	3.4	4.5	5.7	5.0	6.2	7.1	5.7	5.6
Sino-Soviet	0.5	0.0	0.0	0.0	0.0	0.0	0.0	0.0	0.0	0.0	0.0	0.0
Inner Asia[4]	0.8	1.5	1.1	1.0	1.0	1.0	0.9	0.9	1.0	0.9	1.1	0.8
Russia, E. Europe	20.2	16.6	14.0	15.1	13.8	15.1	14.0	14.3	13.5	13.1	13.0	12.9
Europe and Russia	0.0	0.0	0.0	0.0	0.0	0.0	0.0	0.0	0.0	0.9	2.5	2.4
Western Europe	0.5	2.0	3.5	3.5	4.5	5.1	6.3	7.3	6.6	3.4	8.8	8.0
Europe	0.0	0.0	0.0	0.0	0.0	0.0	0.0	0.0	0.0	3.7	0.0	0.0
Middle East	12.7	14.6	13.2	13.2	13.0	13.7	12.2	10.9	10.8	12.2	15.1	13.6
International	0.0	5.4	11.8	11.8	12.9	9.6	12.3	13.8	10.9	7.1	8.7	7.2
Total percentage[5]	100.0	100.3	100.1	100.0	100.0	100.1	100.1	99.8	100.0	100.0	99.9	100.0

[1] Information for the 1959–1973 through 1994–1996 grant cycles was drawn from a report table of the Center for International Education, U.S. Department of Education, provided by Ann I. Schneider. Information for later grant cycles is drawn from International Education Programs Service, U.S. Department of Education NRC and FLAS grantee lists and funding recommendations.

[2] Information for these cycles is for FY 2000 and FY 2006 funding only, not for the full grant cycle.

[3] East Asia, South Asia, and Southeast Asia were combined for the 1959–1973 funding periods in the table supplied by Ann I. Schneider.

[4] Funding for Central Asia was grouped with Russia and Eastern Europe for 1959–1973. In 1997–1999, one Central/Inner Asia Center was funded and is listed under Inner Asia.

[5] Not all totals sum to 100.0 because of rounding.

the funding, 12.9 percent went to Latin American studies, and Middle East studies centers were awarded 12.7 percent (see Table 7-1).

In the second period of Title VI program development, 1973–1991, a different set of concerns, including economic competitiveness, came to the fore. During this time, NRCs focusing on Canada, International Studies, and Pacific Islands were added. International studies centers were created to bridge the apparent divide between the studies of world regions. Two international studies centers were funded in 1973; fourteen were funded for the cycle that began in 1991. To clarify what was meant by "international studies," Ann I. Schneider, then a senior program officer for several U.S. Department of Education Title VI grant programs, wrote a paper titled "Defining International Studies (for purposes of Title VI)." The document was intended to define the category for the information of then-current and prospective grantees. She explained, "To compete effectively for National Resource Center funding, the 'international' studies center must provide not only instruction on the general topic, or topics, of interest in international affairs but must also provide the theoretical framework for their study—the basic courses in world politics, international economics, trade theory, and (or) others relevant to the orientation of the center" (Schneider 1991). The international studies category also allowed for flexibility in approaches to the study of world areas.

By the beginning of the third period of program development, priorities had shifted—the Cold War had ended, and the European Union was established. Following the fortieth anniversary celebration of Title VI, articles on international studies were replete with references to the end of the Cold War as a defining development (e.g., Collins et al., Hines, and Prewitt in O'Meara et al. 2001).

In the 1991–1994 cycle, a total of 25.4 percent of NRC funding was granted to the combination of East Asia, South Asia, and Southeast Asian studies; 14.1 percent to Latin American studies; 14 percent to Russia/East Europe centers; and 12.2 percent to Middle East studies. During this time, new categories of centers were added. In the 1997–1999 grant cycle, a new Caribbean studies center and a new North American studies center were added, although no centers were funded under these categories in subsequent cycles. Europe and Russia and Asia were added as categories with one center each in 2000–2002. Three Europe and Russia centers were funded in each of the following grant cycles. A single center for Europe was funded in 2000–2002, but not in later years. One Asia center was supported in 2003–2005, and three in 2006–2009.

Two factors have shaped the environment of the fiftieth anniversary of the act: first, the tragic events of September 11, 2001, with the consequently renewed appreciation of area studies expertise and fluency in foreign languages and, second, the global economic crisis. The changing sense of what underlies the importance of

Title VI is reflected in legislative language. Whereas the 1998 Higher Education Act noted, "Dramatic post-Cold War changes in the world's geopolitical and economic landscapes are creating needs for American expertise and knowledge about a greater diversity of less commonly taught foreign languages and nations of the world" (Title VI, Sec. 601, Part A, Sec. 601(a)(3)), the wording "post-Cold war" was deleted from subsection (a)(3) in the 2008 legislation.

In response to specific concerns, extraordinary funding has at times been awarded to certain world areas regarded as of particular significance. For example, in the spring of 2002, following the events of September 11, 2001, additional funding was allotted to centers for Central and South Asia, the Middle East, and Russia and Eastern Europe, with increased FLAS fellowship support for study of languages in these regions.[6] Relatively larger grants then were given to these world areas in the following grant cycle (FY 2003–2005). In the grant cycle that began in 2006, amounts awarded to centers focused on these world areas were adjusted downward to allow more even distribution of funding across world areas. In general, the relative stability in funding and continued support for studies of multiple regions over time is striking.

Histories of Title VI programs and their extended benefits often indicate the importance of federal government partnerships with institutions of higher education and other organizations. David Wiley, for example, commented on the fact that numerous core international programs "are made tenable only with matching funds from the universities and other recipients who provide 50 percent or more of the federal funding" (Wiley 2001: 19). In "An Overview of Title VI," Ralph Hines remarked on the excellent return on the federal investment that Title VI brings and the broad array of "courses, programs, institutions, and individuals" affected by Title VI programs. Further, he commented on the extent to which Title VI funds leverage additional institutional and private support, estimated at three times the federal investment by a Centers for International Business Education (CIBE) survey (Hines 2001: 10). Although it is difficult to assign an exact number to the scope of additional support generated by Title VI funds, it is well worth emphasizing their multiplier effect.[7] Although these relationships and their consequences are often conceived in terms of the strong partnership between institutions of higher education and the federal Title VI programs, private organizations also are important partners in supporting area studies. Title VI remains a fundamental source of support for area studies and foreign language education and research in the United States for which prestigious Research I universities actively compete. This role is especially important in times of constrained university budgets.

Private organization support also has been vitally important to advances in area studies,. David Wiley has pointed out that foundations were essential allies in creating the infrastructure for a "new U.S. spirit of internationalism, major foundations such as the Ford Foundation, as well as Rockefeller, Carnegie, and Mellon, joined in by providing additional specialized support" (Wiley in O'Meara et al. 2001: 14).

Foundation Support for Area Studies

Prior to the establishment of Title VI in the 1960s and through the years of its foundation and revision, private foundations devoted substantial attention and resources to area studies. Area studies had a productive newness about it, and attracted generous foundation support.

Foundations sponsored discussions that led to the establishment of area studies associations. Carnegie Corporation and the Ford Foundation supported African studies early on (National Council of Area Studies Associations [NCASA] 1991: 1). The Committee on Slavic Studies, formed by the American Council of Learned Societies (ACLS) in 1938, was important to the founding of the American Association for the Advancement of Slavic Studies (NCASA 1991: 19). ACLS, the Carnegie Endowment, and Rockefeller supported Asian studies, and in 1956 the Association for Asian Studies (AAS) was established. Support from the Ford Foundation was crucial to the expansion of AAS publications and member services (NCASA 1991: 37). The Latin American Studies Association and African Studies Association benefited from Ford Foundation support in the early 1960s (Pereyra ms., p. 1). The ACLS/SSRC Joint Committee on the Near and Middle East facilitated early discussions about Middle East studies in the United States, and the Ford Foundation provided important support in the Middle East Studies Association's formative years in the late 1960s and early 1970s (NCASA 1991: 53). Both the Andrew W. Mellon Foundation and the Ford Foundation contributed support to the National Council of Area Studies Associations in the late 1980s and early 1990s.

In the preface to *Crossing Borders: Revitalizing Area Studies* (1999), Susan Berresford, then president of the Ford Foundation, noted that from 1951 to 1966 the Ford Foundation was "the major philanthropic source behind the creation and institutionalization" of the new academic enterprise of area studies (Ford Foundation 1999: v). During these years, Ford contributed more than $270 million in grant funds to support the training of graduate students and to build centers of excellence at universities. Berresford commented that by the 1980s area studies was well established—a reference, I think, to the results of both Ford's investments in area studies and of Title VI support. Consequently, Ford chose to address what the foundation regarded as particular gaps in coverage in area studies education—for example, in liberal arts colleges and consortia of institutions of higher education, in less commonly taught anguages, and in "relatively resource-poor fields," such as Southeast Asian studies and African studies. At about this time Ford also funded ACLS and SSRC international studies endeavors, as well as a program to help predissertation graduate students develop competence in area studies. In the mid-1990s, Ford's concerns turned to strengthening of universities and area studies outside the United States. This was not an abandonment of area studies but a decision based on the assumption that a firm foundation now existed in the United States; the Ford Foundation felt obliged to use its resources to develop the field in relatively less well-funded areas.

A look at some assessments of area studies that appeared in the early 1990s suggests that, though criticized, area studies was not rejected entirely by foundations so much as deemed insufficient to address new concerns.

Decisions regarding future programmatic directions in four areas were presented in the 1993 president's report of the Andrew W. Mellon Foundation; among these was university studies of foreign areas and cultures. Mellon Foundation President William G. Bowen noted that staff members consulted with scholars with a broad array of area studies knowledge from a variety of disciplines, and staff members expressed dissatisfaction with "the traditional area studies approach, by which we mean studies that divide the world into geographic regions that are larger than a single country and more or less contiguous, and that focus on commonalities within the regions" (Andrew W. Mellon Foundation 1993: 4). They doubted the productivity of area studies approaches in part because of the increasing fragmentation within nations and areas, and the fact that "[c]ultural groupings—particularly those based on religion and ethnicity—cut across the sociopolitical territories and regions demarcated by most area studies programs." They commented on the lack of clarity in the geographical definitions of areas and the fact that area studies could not "offer a satisfactory approach to understanding some of the most striking phenomena of recent years such as the diffusion of values associated with contemporary Western culture and the spread of worldwide markets—or the profound implications of conflicting developments such as the increasing power of fundamentalism, desecularization, and traditionalism in many parts of the world." The report concluded that "work classified under the area studies rubric seems less likely than it once did to provide an optimal framework for many kinds of training and research." President Bowen noted increasing scholarly interest in comparative studies "and especially in those emphasizing the connections among culture, the economy, and society." As a result, Mellon established a new seminars program to address thematic issues important to multiple regions. Seminar themes included "nationalism and regional identities, religious conflict, ethnic rivalries, comparative urban cultures . . . and the roles played by violence in resolving (or exacerbating) disputes" (ibid.).

Interestingly, and characteristic of private foundation initiatives, the report emphasized that the new approach "would not create a new set of semipermanent institutional arrangements that require continued sustenance by hard-pressed universities; nor would it reinforce existing institutional arrangements which perhaps should be rethought in any case" (ibid.: 5). However, the report also noted, "While this program will replace much of the support the Foundation has provided for advanced training and research in area studies as traditionally defined, we expect to continue to make a few grants that are regionally oriented" in areas of special interest to the foundation (ibid.).

In spite of dissatisfaction with "traditional area studies," the Mellon report commended area studies education. "Serious scholarly training in many fields must be situated in the disciplines and also geographically and temporally. We agree with those scholars who wrote to us emphasizing the value of a serious grounding in the languages, history, and culture of a particular country or region. We are confident that the strongest area studies centers will continue to do good work, and to attract needed support" (ibid). This is, I think, a not too thinly veiled expression of confidence in continued support of Title VI NRCs by the U.S. Department of Education.

A critique similar to that of the Andrew W. Mellon Foundation was made a year later by Stanley J. Heginbotham, vice president of the SSRC. He felt that the end of the Cold War would have a decided influence on the organization and funding of international studies in U.S. universities. He thought that, whereas research on particular world areas would continue to be important, funding would shift to studies of broad global concerns and related problem solving. Further, he stressed that area studies programs would need to adjust to these new challenges and to engage with social science disciplines. At no point did he challenge the value of area studies knowledge, but he did advocate the application of area studies knowledge to broad global challenges (Heginbotham 1994a, 1994b). This raised the question of exactly what private foundations would choose to emphasize in their funding programs, especially as the SSRC discontinued several of its area studies committees.

Just a few years after the 1993 Mellon Foundation report and Heginbotham's articles on the need to shift the focus of area and international studies programs, the Ford Foundation in 1997 announced a new initiative, Crossing Borders: Revitalizing Area Studies. Crossing Borders did not constitute a rejection of area studies approaches; rather, it was an important effort to reenergize them. It was designed, first, to support intensive study of particular languages, cultures, and histories, building on the first half-century of work in area studies, and second, to foster innovative thinking and practices related to the field of area studies itself through a variety of partnerships, as well as disciplinary and other "border-crossings" (Ford Foundation 1999: vii). Crossing Borders funding encouraged area and international 149 studies scholars to think broadly and in many directions, not all of which were supported by Title VI funding.

Title VI and NRC programs are devoted solely to international studies. A sheet of "Tips for NRC Budgets" distributed at the IEPS February 2009 Technical Assistance Workshop included the general advice, "Do not request money for domestic or ethnic studies" and "Do not request money for languages indigenous to the United States." However, diaspora communities and their significant international connections are studied at institutions with NRCs though not with Title VI funding. Of the thirty projects profiled in the Ford Foundation's 1999 publication, *Crossing Borders: Revitalizing Area Studies*, five are listed under the category "Borders and Diasporas" (Ford Foundation 1999: 6–11). Descriptions of all the projects indicate that a full 60 percent had ethnic or diaspora studies components—topics that cannot be studied with Title VI support. Still, the relationship of the Crossing Borders projects to Title VI National Resource Centers is clear. Although fewer than half the institutions that received Crossing Borders grants for 1998–1999 had Title VI NRCs, the directors of a majority of the funded projects received their PhDs from universities with NRCs.[8] Title VI resources played an important, if indirect, role in nurturing Crossing Borders projects by providing indepth education about world areas and their languages, education that most other institutions are not in a position to offer.

It is important to place Title VI investment in international and area studies and in the teaching of less commonly taught languages into a financial context. Although that investment may not be large by federal standards, it is very substantial in relation to private foundation support for these areas. For example, the Ford Foundation's Crossing Borders initiative devoted $25 million to innovative projects in area studies fields over six years, beginning in 1998. During just one of those years, FY 2000, Title VI support for NRCs totaled $21,340,000 with an additional $15,090,000 in FLAS fellowships awarded in the same year, mostly to those NRCs. The Title VI NRC and FLAS investment is large and productive, and performs an essential function that other institutions often cannot assume, especially on a continuing basis. As the 1950 SSRC committee member cited at the outset of this paper commented, "Only a great federal program can do it."

Conclusion

David Wiley described Title VI as "one of the U.S. government's major endeavors for responding to the growing complexities of global politics and economics in the 20th century" (Wiley 2001: 11–12). This is as true in the twenty-first century. Title VI programs continue to develop and cross new disciplinary and professional borders in response to changing needs and interests, while supporting the core activities of teaching and learning LCTLs and the knowledge of regions where the languages are spoken. These programs provide a solid basis for new approaches to scholarship in area studies, international studies, and global studies on which those who encourage and facilitate new initiatives can rely.

Although it is now difficult for many U.S. scholars and students to study and conduct research in Iran, the study of Persian language and culture and of Iranian history and politics continues at many Title VI-funded institutions. They are able to provide continuity in understanding of Iran in a time of trade embargoes and restricted access. Some journalists are able to visit and report from Iran, but usually for relatively short stints, located only in Tehran, and not always having Persian language facility. Discussions at a diplomatic level have been few and far between in the years since Iran's 1979 Islamic Revolution. Scholarly pursuits, however, have continued, in part thanks to Title VI funding. Insights gained and connections made through scholarly research and networks can provide a basis for further understanding of and relations with Iran. Continuity in scholarship, scholarly relationships, and understanding in times of political discontinuity is an invaluable benefit of combined Title VI, foundation, and university support for area studies.

Notes

1 I use examples from Middle East studies as this is the field I know best. Similar examples could be drawn from other area studies regions.

2 The statement of Aims and Scope of the journal, printed in the inside cover of each issue, advises that the journal "publishes articles and reviews concerning the area encompassing the Arab world, Iran, Turkey, the Caucasus, Afghanistan, Israel, Transoxiana, and Muslim South Asia from the 7th century to the present. . . . Articles on communities or politics in other regions of the world that had or have strong Middle Eastern ties or contexts, or on relations between those regions and the Middle East, will also be considered."

3 In his "An Overview of Title VI," Ralph Hines divides the history of Title VI into three periods, the Beginning (1958–1971), the Middle Years (1972–1992), and 1993 on, a time of preparation for the coming century. The report of the National Research Council of the National Academies includes an appendix on legislative history, which demarcates significant time periods in Title VI as Laying the Foundations (1958–1972), Embedding and Revising (1973–1991), and Broadening the Scope (1992 Onward). For simplicity's sake, I represent the three eras as Foundation (1958–1972), Revision (1973–1991), and Extension (1992–present).

4   Figures for 1959–1973 through 1994–1996 are drawn from information provided by Ann I. Schneider and included in Table III, Distribution of Title VI Support to National Resource Centers, 1959–1995 by World Area that she prepared for the Center for International Education, U.S. Department of Education; numbers for later dates come from lists of NRC and FLAS award lists kept in the University of Arizona Center for Middle Eastern Studies files; a list of FY 2003–2005 grantees shared by Miriam Kazanjian, Coalition for International Education; and from lists of FY 1997–1999, FY 2000, and FY 2006 and FY 2007 NRC and FLAS grantees available on the IEGPS website at www2.ed.gov/programs/iegpsflasf/awards.html.

5   Personal communication from an IEPS NRC program officer, March 18, 2009.

6   Memorandum to NRC Directors and FLAS Coordinators from John Paul, Chief, Advanced Training and Research Programs, regarding FY 2002 NRC and FLAS Programs, March 19, 2002.

7   In fact, many universities contribute more than 90 percent of the costs of area studies faculty, teaching assistants, libraries, research, and even outreach programs, reflecting a very large cost match that is far larger than other federal grant programs (Communication with David Wiley, February 1, 2010).

8   Not counting consortia, 39 percent (11/28) of grantee institutions had NRCs at the time they received Ford funding. Of the twenty-one project directors for whom we could determine PhD.-granting institutions, twenty had received their PhD.s in the United States and eighteen (90 percent) of these received them from institutions with NRCs in their fields at the time their degrees were granted.

REFERENCES

Hawkins, John H. et al. 1998. *International Education in the New Global Era: Proceedings of a National Policy Conference on the Higher Education Act, Title VI, and Fulbright-Hays Programs*. Los Angeles, CA: University of California.

Heginbotham, Stanley J. 1994a. Shifting the Focus of International Programs. *Chronicle of Higher Education* (Oct. 19).

———. 1994b. Rethinking International Scholarship: The Challenge of Transition from the Cold War Era. *Items* 48(2–3): pp. 33–40.

Hines, Ralph. 2001. An Overview of TVI. In O'Meara, et al. *Changing Perspectives on International Education*. Bloomington: Indiana University Press.

O'Connell, M. and J. L. Norwood, eds. 2007. *International Education and Foreign Languages: Keys to Securing America's Future* (prepublication copy). National Research Council of the National Academies. Washington, D.C.: The National Academies Press.

Lambert, Richard D. 2001. Domains and Issues of International Studies, In O'Meara, et al. *Changing Perspectives on International Education*. Bloomington: Indiana University Press.

O'Meara, Patrick, H. Mehlinger, and R. Ma Newman. 2001. *Changing Perspectives on International Education.* Bloomington: Indiana University Press.

Prewitt, Kenneth. 2001. Redefining International Scholarship. In O'Meara, et al. *Changing Perspectives on International Education.* Bloomington: Indiana University Press.

Wallerstein, Immanuel. 1977. The Unintended Consequences of the Cold War on Area Studies. In Noam Chomsky, ed. *The Cold War and the University.* New York: New York Press, pp. 195–228.

Wiley, David. 2001. Forty Years of the Title VI and Fulbright-Hays International Education Programs. In O'Meara, Patrick, H. Mehlinger and R. Ma Newman, eds. *Changing Perspectives on International Education*, pp. 11–29. Bloomington: Indiana University Press.

Legislation

National Defense Education Act (Public Law 85-864), Sept. 2, 1958.

Mutual Educational and Cultural Exchange Act of 1961 (PL 87-256).

Educational Amendments of 1964 (PL 88-665).

International Education Act of 1966 (PL 89-698).

Educational Amendments of 1972 (PL 92-318).

Educational Amendments of 1976 (PL 94-482).

Educational Amendments of 1980 (incorporated Title VI into Higher Education Act of 1965; PL 96–372).

Higher Education Amendments of 1986 (PL 99-498).

Higher Education Amendments of 1992 (PL 102-325).

Higher Education Amendments of 1998 (PL 105-244).

Higher Education Extension of 2004 (PL 108-366).

Higher Education Extension of 2008 (PL 110-315).

Reports and White Papers

The Andrew W. Mellon Foundation. 1993. President's Report. William G. Bowen. www.mellon.org/news_publications?annual-reports-essays/presidents-reports/content1993. Accessed November 7, 2009.

Ford Foundation. 1999. *Crossing Borders: Revitalizing Area Studies.* New York: Ford Foundation.

O'Connell, M. and J. L. Norwood, eds. 2007. *International Education and Foreign Languages: Keys to Securing America's Future* (prepublication copy). National Research Council of the National Academies. Washington, D.C.: The National Academies Press.

Pereyra-Rojas, Milagros. 2004. NCASA Draft Report on the Latin American Studies Association. Pittsburgh, PA: Latin American Studies Association.

Prospects for Faculty in Area Studies: A Report from the National Council of Area Studies Associations. 1991. Stanford, CA.

Schneider, Ann Imlah. Defining International Studies (for purposes of Title VI), August 20, 1991.

CHAPTER 8

The Changing Form and Function of Title VI since Its Beginnings in the 1960s

Richard D. Lambert

It is immensely gratifying to contribute to the fiftieth anniversary celebration of Title VI, as I suspect that I am among the few survivors who participated in the founding and early operation of the program. My account will unavoidably be reminiscent, retrospective, and anecdotal because I have not been involved in area studies for some twenty-five years. Let me select a few issues that arose in the early days of Title VI, and those in the international studies field can judge whether they are still relevant today. For more organized and more detailed accounts of the early days of language and area studies, I direct you to three comprehensive surveys of the field that I conducted (see References).

In the brief space allocated, I will concentrate on problems in area studies that emerged again and again both in my surveys and my experience. I will discuss problems in (1) maintaining the funding levels in Title VI; (2) durable issues in the organization of area programs on campuses; (3) structural imbalances in providing language instruction; and (4) the need to foster relationships between academic area studies and external clienteles.

Funding Levels

It is especially gratifying for me to see in 2009 how robust and extensive Title VI programs are when in the early days its very existence was frequently in considerable jeopardy. I recall that in the early years of Title VI, a small cadre comprising Robert Ward, representing East Asian Studies at Stanford; Leon Twarog of East European Studies at Ohio State; and me in South Asian Studies at the University of Pennsylvania, along with two junior staff people at the American Council of Education, annually marched up Capitol Hill in Washington to meet with relevant congressional committee members. Our goal was to ensure a continuation of funding for Title VI, which in those days was by no means certain.

One particular occasion illustrated its fragility. In one of the early years, Representative Daniel Flood (D-PA), who at that time chaired the relevant congressional appropriation committee for Title VI, was traveling in Europe and was relaxing in a bar in Yugoslavia when he heard another American loudly denigrating American foreign policy and government. On inquiry, Dan Flood learned that the outspoken American was a faculty member of a Title VI center. As a result, he then vowed to eliminate congressional funds for the program. Hearing of this, our small lobbying committee contacted Holland Hunter of Haverford College in Dan Flood's Pennsylvania district, who spoke to him in the Serbo-Croatian dialect that was part of Flood's ethnic heritage. It would be the height of hubris to assume that our small ploy had any effect, but Title VI did not receive zero funding that year. It does indicate, however, how fragile we believed funding of Title VI was in those days.

A more serious threat came several years later when, during the Nixon administration, the Office of Management and Budget ordered that funding for Title VI be zeroed out in the Education budget. After a multiuniversity lobbying effort, we managed to have the secretaries of the departments of Defense and State to write unusual cross-department letters urging that Title VI not be dropped from Education's budget request, and it was not. These are just two examples of the vulnerability of Title VI in the early days. Every year we felt as though we were actors in "The Perils of Pauline," pulling Title VI from the railroad tracks. These life-and-death episodes no longer appear to haunt the field.

On-Campus Organization

In our many campus visits during our survey of campus-based area studies in the 1980s, we were repeatedly impressed with the way in which area studies faculty had built successful programs in a wide variety of academic settings. The organization of durable cross-school and cross-department programs is quite difficult to establish and to maintain, as I experienced at the University of Pennsylvania, where I was chairman of the South Asia Regional Studies (SARS) Department for more than fifteen years. We were fortunate in having an organizational environment that was quite favorable to maintaining a transdepartmental, trans-school organization. SARS was a full department with its own budget, support staff, and office space. Moreover, we could give B.A., MA, and PhD. degrees, and we could allocate fellowships and grants such as Title VI. In addition, as a department we could hire some faculty on our own, primarily native speaker "informants" in the language courses. Most members of the faculty, however, had primary appointments in disciplinary departments. While I was there, SARS had faculty members with home department appointments in anthropology, archaeology, art history, economics, linguistics, religious thought, geography, history, music, philosophy, political science, and sociology. Nevertheless, my negotiations each spring with departmental chairs for salaries and promotions for our jointly appointed faculty and for maintaining jointly sponsored courses were a bit of a nightmare. In many departments, accomplishments in area studies were given little weight. For instance, the fact that I and and one of my colleagues in SARS have been presidents of the Association of Asian Studies was of little importance in our disciplinary guilds. As I made dozens of visits to other campuses for the various surveys over the years, I found much ingenuity and fragility of arrangements for successful area studies programs on campus, as well as their organizational problems. On some campuses, the organization of area studies centers has become more systematized and more durable. Without that stability, the national cadre of area studies programs may well be in jeopardy.

Another issue faced Title VI programs individually and collectively. Under their broad geographic rubrics, in each of the world regions—African, South Asian, Latin American, Southeast Asian, East European, Middle Eastern, and East Asian studies—the coverage of member countries, languages, and disciplines was quite uneven. In South Asian studies, for instance, teaching and research tended to concentrate on India, mostly north India and not the south, where the Dravidian languages are spoken. Among all the South Asia studies centers throughout country, there was relatively less coverage of Pakistan, and even less of Bangladesh (after its creation) and Sri Lanka. In the early days, Afghanistan, which is now receiving a great deal of attention in our foreign and military policy, received almost no coverage in South Asian studies programs, either in substantive courses or in language instruction.

A similar patchy coverage can be found in other world areas. I recall being visited in my office at Penn by an Israeli consul general who asked me whether any of the Middle East centers taught Hebrew or gave courses about Israel. I told him that the inclusion of Israeli studies in Middle East programs was an unlikely prospect and it would be wise to help set up independent Israel studies centers on their own. In general, it would be useful to pay attention to the concentrations and gaps in regional coverage in Title VI area studies and language programs.

In addition, as more and more universities deliberately reduce the number of graduate students they admit, area studies programs will be facing a major organizational stress that was not felt in the past. This process may not only reduce their student clientele but the priority that disciplinary departments put on supporting both area studies students and faculty.

Language Instruction

One early case in 1973 illustrates the ambivalent position of language instruction in Title VI. I was working on the Social Science Research Council's first general review of Title VI. At that time I had been referring to the survey as a review of area studies. Early in the data collection process, the program's staff director in the U.S. Department of Education phoned to tell me that he had just had a visit from representatives of the Modern Language Association (MLA) who insisted that "language" be inserted first in the title of the study. Accordingly, the publication of the results was titled the *Language and Area Studies Review*.[1] The intercession of the MLA was a little ironic in that over the years it had been concerned primarily with the European languages, giving relatively little attention or representation in their programs and publications to the less commonly taught languages (LCTLs) that are the primary concern of Title VI programs.

Within Title VI programs themselves, the area studies curricula and faculty tend to receive more attention than the languages. In spite of the fact that the original impetus for the creation of Title VI was a national linguistic deficit, there was a perceived lack of awareness in the United States of events leading up to the launching of Sputnik, which became the precipitant in Congress for the Title VI legislation. This lack of awareness was attributed to the limited command of the Russian language in our school system, in the government, and in the public arena. The Sputnik language anxiety was generalized to include all the LCTLs. In spite of the importance of Sputnik in the origins of the program and the protestations of the officers of MLA, language instruction rarely played a dominant role in Title VI programs of the 1970s and 1980s. For instance, in those early days, relatively few center directors were language specialists. The entrepreneurs in the field were usually area specialists.

Within Title VI programs, the role of language instruction has varied considerably among the different area studies regional centers. Latin American studies programs, except for those that dealt with Brazil, could depend on having Spanish instruction provided in both high school and college-level arts and sciences curriculum to give a large number of students a moderate knowledge of Spanish. To a lesser extent, this was also true of Russian, Japanese, and Chinese, but area studies programs dealing with Southeast Asian, South Asian, and African studies had to maintain their own language instruction almost entirely within the program; moreover, their languages were taught almost entirely at the graduate level, where basic language instruction is not normally found. But in many of these area studies programs the role of language instruction rarely played a dominant part.

Nonetheless, language instruction did grow immensely within Title VI programs. After World War II, at first with private foundation support and later Title VI funding, university-based instruction in the non-European languages proliferated. In various national surveys, I have written at length about the achievements and problems in those language programs of the 1960s to the 1980s.

First, in world area centers such as Africa, South Asia, and Southeast Asia, the number of languages to be covered is large, and individual programs can manage to mount instruction in depth in only a limited number of them. Nevertheless, by the 2000s, the 125 Title VI centers have built experience and teaching materials so they have the capacity to offer as many as 220 LCTLs.[2] Second, because the learning of LCTLs must begin at the graduate level, time and curricular limitations mean that the proficiency level a student can achieve is low. The centers of Africa, South Asia, and Southeast Asia have added cooperative intensive summer language programs, with which some students can achieve four years equivalence of instruction in a dozen or more languages of these regions when continuing study on their home campus or abroad. A few collaborative supplemental programs for advanced language study in-country were developed and are funded with non-Title VI money. Many years ago, I conducted reviews of the programs in Cairo, Delhi, Taiwan, and Tokyo, but the number of students they served and the levels they could reach were both quite limited.

Third, foreign language skills tend to deteriorate over time when not used regularly. It is alarming how little is known about this process. Some years ago I initiated a number of projects to investigate what I called language skill attrition. Oddly, this research domain has proliferated in Europe but has received very little attention in the United States. Moreover, there are very few teaching facilities available for Title VI-trained specialists to upgrade and maintain their advanced skills. The Lang Net computer-based programs developed by the National Foreign Language Center are devoted to upper-level skill attainment and reinforcement in a few languages. However, the bulk of the users of these programs are employed in government agencies and not in academia. Fourth, until the founding several years ago of the Title VI Language Resource Centers (LRCs, discussed later), there were very few organizations in which Title VI language specialists could collectively develop teaching and testing materials for the various LCTL languages. As noted above, the principal foreign language professional associations such as the MLA or the American Council

159

on the Teaching of Foreign Languages (ACTFL) have tended to deal almost exclusively with the commonly taught languages. There is some opportunity for collective consideration of language issues within the area studies associations, but their primary focus is on area studies, not on languages. To help create centers in which the primary purpose would be to develop LCTL teaching and testing materials, in my 1984 review of area studies, we recommended the creation of a number of language resource centers. Their functions were to be:

> (1) to create a common metric against which individuals' language competencies can be rated; (2) to conduct the basic research and evaluation of various teaching styles that will help to maximize teaching strategies for various levels, students, and learning situations; (3) to train teachers in the administration and interpretation of proficiency tests, and in the most effective strategies for teaching their particular language; (4) to develop effective strategies for teaching in new formats and teaching styles for new and existing strategies both off and on campus; (5) to maintain summer and year-long intensive language instruction at the introductory and advanced levels for speaking and listening proficiency; (6) to serve as a site for periodic instruction in the least commonly taught languages; and (7) to relate the efforts of the academic teaching programs to those of the federal government.[3]

Shortly after the completion of the *Beyond Growth: The Next Stage in Language and Area Studies*[4] report, in part through the efforts of the staff of the Association of American Universities, the creation of the proposed new language centers was written into the Title VI legislation. Now, fifteen such centers serve a mix of functions in language learning research, language materials development, and specific focus on materials and training needs in Africa; Central, East, and South Asia; the Middle East; and even for K-12 LCTL learning.[5]

In addition to creating the LRCs, the *Beyond Growth* study defined a need within the language instructional community for creating a translanguage bridging mechanism, one that would assist the language teaching communities in the various world area studies groups to share the benefits of developments across language lines. Because this mission was not included in the new Title VI language centers, Richard Brecht and I facilitated creating a new professional organization, the National Council of the Teachers of the LCTLs,[6] which brings together representatives of the separate LCTL organizations to share developments in their associations and to work toward common goals.

Serving External Clienteles

Given its origins in the post-Sputnik era of the 1960s, it is clear that the creation of Title VI was intended to serve not only general educational needs, but also the needs of government and, later, of business. The intention of Title VI to serve these external clienteles was reflected in the 1980s with a congressionally mandated National Advisory Board on International Education Programs, which was established by the secretary of education to advise the department on the operation of its international education programs, particularly Title VI. Chaired first by James Holderman, then president of the University of South Carolina, and in its later years by me, this board included a variety of external clienteles. These included the departments of State, Treasury, Commerce, and Defense, plus the Export-Import Bank, the National Endowment for the Humanities, the Small Business Administration, the U.S. Information Agency, the Foreign Service Institute, the Defense Language Institute, and the International Development Cooperation Agency, along with various intelligence agencies. It also included a number of representatives of international businesses and administrators of secondary schools. The committee existed for only a few years and issued two reports: *Critical Needs in International Education* and *Recommendations for the Reauthorization of Title VI*. The very general recommendations in these reports largely concerned both the continued funding of Title VI, which was under imminent threat of abolition in Congress's reauthorization hearings, and the danger of Title VI being lost in the reorganization then under way in the Department of Education. The board did not recommend specific mechanisms to better serve the needs of external clienteles or some methods for a continuing measuring of the supply and demand for specialists on particular parts of the world and particular languages.

In the *Beyond Growth* survey, we attempted to assess the extent to which the publications of the faculty of Title VI centers addressed foreign policy issues in a manner that could be useful to government officers. First, for this first assessment, we tabulated the topics of 5,928 publications of members of the faculty between 1976 and 1981 as reported in their center applications. Of these publications, only 522 dealt with economic and social policy, 351 dealt with political or military policy, and only 81 dealt with U.S. policies directly.[7] In short, policy per se was not a primary concern of area studies faculty, as indicated by their publications.

In addition, we tried to measure the extent to which publications by the faculties of Title VI centers actually were used by officials in the internationally oriented government departments, especially the Department of State and the various intelligence agencies. William Bader, a former congressional staffer and later an employee of the Stanford Research Institute (SRI), interviewed employees of these agencies on the extent to which they used information in the materials published by the faculty of the Title VI centers. The SRI study presented "dramatic evidence of the limited day-to-day utilization of materials on other parts of the world produced by academics. The immediacy and high technical content of most Department of

Defense and intelligence requirements tend to push academic research, like much broad contextual information onto tomorrow's agenda."[8] Clearly, however, the Title VI faculty provided government officials and the general public primarily with background information on the non-European countries on which day-to-day policy rests. A reassessment is needed to see whether this situation of the 1970s and 1980s has changed.

Not all area studies linkages with government are only one-way. There are two domains in which academic area studies imported government practices. Area studies as organized on campuses mirrored prototype programs developed in the Army Specialized Training Programs (ASTPs) for educating army intelligence and military government personnel. One could see the influences in the Turkish language program in which I was a student at Indiana University. It was a typical area studies program, with a heavier emphasis on language learning than found in most academic area programs.

A second importation from a federal government model was the adoption from the government of a style of testing and a specification of skill levels in the LCTLs. Originally referred to as the Foreign Service Institute (FSI) oral testing and competency rating system, it was first imported into academic use by the ACTFL. Subsequently, it was adopted and widely used throughout the academic area studies community for characterizing competence in the LCTLs and is widely used in the Title VI language programs.

In addition to relationships between academic area studies and the U.S. government, we were equally interested in the contribution made by Title VI to the business community. Our *Beyond Growth* study was published just as the Title VI Centers for International Business Education were being created. Our studies indicated that in the 1970s and early 1980s, the business community had little appreciation of foreign language competence and international studies training. In 1984, we conducted three studies that revealed the situation. First, we researched the published output of area studies faculty to see how many of them were on topics that might be of direct or indirect interest to businesses. In our analysis of the 5,298 articles and books published by Title VI center faculty members in the period 1976–1981, fewer than 10 percent (522) concerned economic policy and almost none with business.

A second approach was to determine the demand for and evaluation of language competency by corporate personnel officers. We commissioned a study to interview the personnel directors in thirty-two companies that had substantial overseas operations.[9] We asked them about the importance placed by their company on foreign language competence. Generally, the personnel managers in companies that hired graduates of the international business programs ranked foreign language and international competence as having relatively low importance in their hiring practices.

Third, we were interested in the extent to which graduates of international business programs with a major language learning component actually used these school- and university-learned language skills in their jobs. We surveyed the recent graduates of three of the most highly reputed international business programs that had a substantial language learning component: the Joseph H. Lauder Institute of Management and International Studies at the Wharton School at the University of Pennsylvania, the Monterey Institute of International Studies, and the University of South Carolina's Master of International Studies. Each had a major foreign language component and provided a choice of instruction in a number of languages. The results of that survey on reported language use by the international business studies graduates is in the *Annals*, September 1990.[10] We found that 88.9 percent of the 496 graduates surveyed were stationed in the United States, and only 37.3 percent of them considered their business school-learned language to be important in their current job. An equal number considered it to be irrelevant. Of the international program graduates, 51.2 percent reported that their foreign language competency had diminished by the time of the survey. The use of learned foreign language among international business program graduates is likely to have increased greatly since 1990, as the overseas connections of American companies have expanded and more and more business schools have introduced an overseas residency experience into their degree programs. However, I suspect that foreign language use and the retention at a high level of competency still are problematic for graduates of international business programs.

In these comments on some aspects of Title VI in its early years I have concentrated on problems, not achievements. In closing, however, I want to offer my strong congratulations to my colleagues on creating, almost from scratch, the immense and successful enterprise of language and area studies over the past fifty years. We can look forward to the continued growth and maturation in the future of this largest, and perhaps most successful, foreign language and international studies program in the world.

Notes

1 Lambert, Richard D. *Language and Area Studies Review* (Philadelphia, PA: American Academy of Political and Social Science), 1973.

2 See the results of the national survey by the e-LCTL Intiative at Michigan State University at www.elctl.msu.edu/archive/summaries/PressRelease.pdf.

3 Lambert, Richard D., *Beyond Growth: the Next Stage in Language and Area Studies*. Washington, D.C.: Association of American Universities (1984): 87–88.

4 Ibid.

5 http://nflrc.msu.edu/index-1.php.

6 See www.councilnet.org/.

7 *Beyond Growth*: 166.

8 Ibid, 169–70.

9 Fixman, Carrol, "The Foreign Language Needs of U.S. Corporations." *The Annals of the American Academy of Political and Social Science* (1990): 25–46.

10 Lambert, Richard D., "Foreign Language Use among International Business Graduates," *The Annals of the American Academy of Political and Social Science* (September 1990): 47–89.

REFERENCES

Lambert, Richard D. 1973. *Language and Area Studies Review*. Philadelphia: Annals of the American Academy of Political and Social Science.

———. 1984. *Beyond Growth: The Next Stage in Language and Area Studies*. Washington, D.C.: The Association of American Universities.

———. 1989. *International Studies and the Undergraduate*. Washington, D.C.: American Council on Education.

CHAPTER 9

The Impact of Title VI Programs on the U.S. Higher Education System: Lessons from the First Thirty Years (1958–1988)

Nancy L. Ruther

From 1958 to 1988, federal policy was aimed at creating and sustaining capacity within the U.S. higher education system to provide international, regional, and language expertise and experts for the country. Title VI was forged into the core operational model of the federal international higher education policy arena, through the legislative and implementation trajectory of three programs: Title VI, U.S. Agency for International Development (USAID) university programs, and the never-funded International Education Act (IEA) of 1966.

The key question addressed in this chapter is: How did the history of the federal relationship with higher education, 1958–1988, affect the institutional capacity of the U.S. higher education system (approximately 3,000 institutions) to sustain and expand its international dimension, to internationalize? It also asks the diffusion question: How far and how deeply did the programs reach into the higher education system? The main focus is on Title VI of the National Defense Education Act (NDEA) of 1958, based in the domestic legislative stream and implemented by the Department of Education with universities. As a counterpoint, the chapter also considers Agency for International Development (AID) university programs, based in the foreign assistance legislative stream. To fully understand Title VI after 1966, it is important to grasp how the dynamic tensions between the domestic and foreign affairs policy streams were balanced and resolved, ultimately defining the bounds of the international higher education

165

policy arena. The AID university programs provide a proxy for the foreign affairs stream.

The International Education Act (IEA) of 1966, though never funded, was an ambitious attempt to merge domestic and foreign assistance streams into a single robust policy arena focusing federal resources into a combined program to build international capacity not only in the universities and colleges, but also throughout the entire education sector and for overseas humanitarian and education services. Through 1975, the IEA generated intense policy debate in Congress and the executive branch, in higher education and education sectors. In the end, the grand merger overstretched the legitimate bounds of a workable policy arena and was not funded. The IEA also committed a sin of omission in failing to address security and defense policy concerns as a key part of the international higher education arena. Despite its stillbirth, many of the aspirations of the IEA lived on, embedded in the domestic legislative stream through Title VI, whereas the foreign affairs stream with its AID university programs atrophied.

From the 1970s on, the international higher education policy arena became increasingly permanent and based largely in the domestic education realm. Higher education constituents' international interests were channeled through Title VI, and other education constituents' interests were addressed, if not fully answered, with outreach mandates added to the Title VI centers. The research universities continued with the original centers and fellowship programs of Title VI, in their current names of National Resource Centers (NRCs) and Foreign Language and Area Studies (FLAS) fellowships, along with the International Research and Studies Program (IRSP). Title VI added new programs reaching the two- and four-year colleges and comprehensive universities, enduring today as the Undergraduate International Studies and Foreign Languages (UISFL) and Business and International Education (BIE) programs.[1] From the end of the study period in 1988, the international higher education policy arena of the U.S. government expanded, responding to growing constituent urging. Title VI added programs based on the NRC model with the Centers for Business and International Education (CIBE) and later the Language Resource Centers (LRCs). Using the Fellowships model but under the Defense Department, not Education's Title VI, the National Security Education Act created the Boren fellowships to expand expertise in less commonly taught critical foreign languages and related area expertise.

The Higher Education Policy Arena

Conceptually, a public policy arena comprises an "iron triangle" of the executive, the legislature, and citizens–clients or constituents—that is, the universities themselves, in the case of higher education policy.[2] All sides of such a triangle recognize a stable core of policy issues as legitimate for national action to achieve a set of broad goals that are worthy of regular ongoing funding, albeit at varying levels. The U.S. higher education policy arena developed over the history of the republic, responding to both international and domestic policy needs. Six overarching substantive interests are generally agreed on as the legitimate sphere of federal higher education policy. By defining the overall policy arena, they provide the framework for the specific policy arena of international higher education, where Title VI is located. These six overarching national policy goals of the higher education policy are set out in Table 9-1.

These six broad goals can be traced through U.S. legislative history since the mid-1800s. Although they provided the foundation for the overall higher education policy arena in the United States, a more targeted international higher education policy arena developed after World War II. The Soviet launch of Sputnik was a key catalyst. The resultant National Defense Education Act of 1958 came to underpin the legitimate sphere of federal action in higher education.

The NDEA's Title VI became the seed at the core of the emergent international higher education policy arena. As we shall see, the new goals constituted a legitimate subset of the broader policy arena, adding an international dimension to goals that had been more domestic traditionally. This international focus also placed the emerging policy arena squarely and uncomfortably at the crossroads of domestic and foreign affairs legislative oversight and funding committees and their parallel executive branch agencies. This chapter argues that Title VI became the operational model at the core of this new international higher education policy arena. It was structured and solidified in this role through the crucible of legislative debate, executive implementation, and policy development of three programs: Title VI, AID's university programs, and the aspirations of the unfunded IEA.

Table 9-1. The Six Overarching Goals of the Federal Higher Education Policy Arena

1. Provide unique and high level knowledge and trained citizens, expertise broadly writ, in the economic, scientific, defense, and political spheres.
2. Provide leadership and meet national needs for national security and defense preparedness.
3. Provide leadership and help meet national needs for economic security and enhance competitiveness, both domestically and internationally.
4. Serve as a major source of social and economic mobility for U.S. citizens, as instrumental to major goals of national productivity and social justice.
5. Provide leadership and training to promote and support international understanding.
6. Serve as a major source for the creation of an informed, competent, and competitive citizenry.

Internationalization of the Higher Education System

We are concerned with internationalization of the overall higher education system, not of individual institutions. For systemwide internationalization, we begin with Henson's two-sided index of the degree of university internationalization with higher and lower levels, leaving the intermediate steps to the reader's imagination.[3] Table 9-2 is adapted from Henson and provides a tool for measuring the movement of institutions along the internationalization path. It considers a range of resources available to colleges and universities, helping put Title VI in context. To describe the system level, one must consider all five elements, both academic and institutional. The fifth element was added to acknowledge system-level needs for internationalization, such as communications and networks across institutions and individuals that are important to systemwide change. It added the system-linking variables such as membership and leadership in national associations for disciplinary and institutional groups of higher education.

Table 9-2. Internationalization Dynamics of the Higher Education System: Five Elements Indicating the Path to Internationalization, Contrasting High and Low Levels[5]

Lower Degree of Internationalization	Higher Degree of Internationalization
1. Leadership and Management	
• Leadership support nascent to some degree	• Leadership strong at all levels
• Resources do not match rhetoric, sporadic support to obtain external funding	• Resources match rhetoric, serious long-term commitment to international elements
• Little information or planning	• International as regular part of planning
• Disincentives in faculty policies for overseas work	• Neutral to supportive faculty policies for overseas work
• Few or weak links with national associations' international offices	• Strong or multiple links with national associations' international
2. Organization	
• Office of foreign students plus pressure from some other program units pro-international	• Multiple linked offices or strong central international office
• Weak links among interested parties	• Interested parties linked across campus
• Little support in organizational culture	• Supportive organizational culture
• Institutional member of NAFSA, other international associations limited to individual memberships on campus	• Institutional member of NAFSA and other internationally focused consortia, associations, and groups

Table 9-2. Internationalization Dynamics of the Higher Education System: Five Elements Indicating the Path to Internationalization, Contrasting High and Low Levels[4] (*continued*)

Lower Degree of Internationalization	Higher Degree of Internationalization

3. Program Activities
   - Some international and area courses in social science/humanities; minors maybe
   - Some foreign languages offered but not required; most common ones
   - Growing number of overseas students but few U.S. students involved in study abroad
   - Occasional faculty travel overseas but infrequent visiting scholars
   - Some development cooperation but not linked to other campus activity
   - Public service clientele hostile or disinterested to international programming

   - Variety of international degrees offered: B.A. to PhD.
   - Many foreign languages offered and/or required; enrollments rising
   - Regular movement of U.S. and overseas students including graduate research
   - Regular movement of faculty from and to overseas for teaching and research
   - Multidisciplinary research/teaching in area and global themes and languages
   - Development cooperation linked to other academic program activities
   - Public service clientele neutral to interested in international services

4. Resources
   - Administrators supportive, little flexibility
   - Faculty with international capacity limited, few with interest in international teaching/research
   - Funds limited for international activity
   - Few external grants beyond development cooperation
   - Library with few international books or journals, virtually all English materials

   - Administrators active, articulate, flexible
   - Faculty core internationally capable, many interested
   - Pro-international incentive funds available through internal competitions
   - Frequent external funds from many sources
   - Library collection with regional/themes focus and non-English materials

5. External Environment
   - Little demand from stakeholders and clients for international programs
   - Weak links between pro-international elements on and off campus
   - National association tepid or newly aware

   - Strong demand by stakeholders and key clients for international programs
   - Strong links between pro-international elements off and on campus
   - National institutional association active pro-internationalization

Variables for Analyzing Federal Effects on Internationalization of Higher Education

Pause to consider the analytic framework for understanding the effects of federal programs on the international capacity of higher education. Classic diffusion of innovation analysis holds that for an innovation to be successful, and not just a passing fad across the system, it must spread to and be sustained in a critical mass 169 of institutions. It must become part of the system's culture and operating assumptions. There are two critical variables, both of which are required: (1) *sustainability*, which is reflected in the institutionalization, persistence, and vitality of a federal program across different parts of the system; and (2) *diffusion*, which concerns the transmission, communication, acceptance, and participation in a federal program by universities across the system.

Both sustainability and diffusion have further conditions or indicators specific to higher education as Levine argued in his classic study of how to avoid failure in higher education change efforts.[5] For sustainability, Levine argued for compatibility and profitability as key indicators. Levine saw *compatibility* as a measure of the appropriateness of an innovation within existing organizational boundaries. Levine also described it as the degree to which an innovation is consistent with the norms, values and goals of a university. Compatibility is particularly key to the faculty elements of a university: Does it fit the standards of academic rigor and quality to which all faculty aspire? Is it sufficiently flexible and adaptive to fit within requirements of academic freedom and nurturing independent inquiry? Administrative or institutional "fit" is also important if universities are to integrate the innovation permanently.

Levine also saw *profitability* as a measure of satisfaction. It describes the degree to which institutions perceive the "value" of an innovation. It is not simply about cost but also about cost-effectiveness. It is about value for resources invested not simple financial returns. "Value" is especially important to acceptance by the administrative units but is also important to faculty or the academic side of the university.

Turning to the conditions for diffusion, drawing on the work of T. N. Clark, two mechanisms for promoting the transmission of innovation are important in the higher education system, that is emulation and the *traegerin* effects.[6] The *emulation effect* is the perceived quality and prestige of an innovation that leads other institutions to emulate it. The emergence of a perceived "gold standard" is often a key driver of emulation. Level of difficulty in attaining the innovation can enhance the emulation effect. National associations of universities and of faculty are potentially important for endorsing the target of emulation and sharing its innovation. The *traegerin* effect describes the phenomenon of young faculty and other "boundary spanners" carrying ideas and *modi operandi* as they move from university to university. Doctoral students are a particularly important vehicle for the carrying of new ideas to the universities at which they take up their teaching careers. More mature faculty moving to new institutions, especially when they move to take leadership roles, are also an important vehicle for transmitting and embedding new ideas.

To sum up, in analyzing the effect of federal programs on the international capacity of the higher education system, that is to internationalize, we are looking for evidence of both sustainability and diffusion. For each of these, we have identified two key mechanisms by which they operate. For sustainability, compatibility and profitability are crucial for both academic and administrative parts of universities to accept and embed the federal programs' innovations. For diffusion, both the emulation and *traegerin* effects are important to transmitting change across the higher education system. The study made three further assumptions to guide the analysis of the effects of Title VI and related federal programs on internationalizing the U.S. higher education system: (1) Stable participation in a federal program by good numbers of institutions over long periods of time reflects a program's sustainability as well as its profitability or value to the higher education system overall.[7] (2) The more categories of institutions participating in a federal program, the higher the level of diffusion across the system. The fullest possible range of engagement would include research and doctoral, comprehensive, four-year and two-year colleges from both public and private sectors of the higher education system.[8] (3) The higher the participation rate in a federal program of research and doctoral universities, the stronger the emulation and *traegerin* effects and, thus, the greater the impact on diffusion across the higher education system. By providing leadership if not the "gold standard" for the system, these universities' participation also supports the sustainability of the innovation.

Historical Development of the International Higher Education Policy Arena

How did the shifting educational and foreign affairs policy streams interact and affect the formation of the new hybrid, the international higher education policy arena? The notion of "stream" evokes the sense of forward movement within known but somewhat movable channels or boundaries. At critical junctures, streams may shift beds or converge for natural reasons or by overwhelming outside force. So, too, with policy streams. Between 1958 and 1964, the educational and foreign assistance policy streams ran in parallel with two separate policy arenas. There was little, if any, conversation between the legislative oversight committees, the executive agencies, or the constituents. They represented two different, largely disconnected, policy arenas. From 1964 intensely through 1967, and continuing with decreasing intensity through 1975, there was huge pressure to merge the two streams into a new policy arena for international higher education and overseas development. It was voiced through the development of the IEA of 1966. After serious setbacks in 1971 to both higher education and overseas development programs with Title VI and the AID university programs and the dimming prospects of the IEA, the two policy streams shrank back into their separate channels. The international higher education policy arena was channeled through the education legislative stream with Title VI as the main program vehicle with the executive agencies and university constituents.

Educational Policy Stream

In the 1955 election campaign, President Eisenhower and the Republican party, supported by many university presidents, had taken a strong position against federal involvement in education. Education was to be left to the states and higher education was either private or public, state-led.[9] The federal role would be very narrow, limited to running the military academies such as West Point, with no federal implementing or oversight function beyond statistics collection and analysis. In 1957, that stance was reversed with the Soviet launch of Sputnik and its implications for U.S. national security. The administration sent draft legislation to Congress which became the National Defense Education Act of 1958. The final version of the NDEA had eight substantive titles. The NDEA goals were to enhance national security with science and education as implementing pillars. Title VI, "Language Development," supported universities' nascent international programs.[10] Initially, Title VI consisted of three substantive sections: (1) Section 601(a) encouraged higher education institutions to establish centers for teaching languages and area studies; (2) Section 601(b) authorized fellowships for language training; and (3) Section 602 authorized research and studies to specify needs of language training and related fields. Centers, fellowships, and research and studies have been the operating core of Title VI from the outset.

To understand the operation of the Title VI program in this emerging policy arena, consider the triangle comprising Congress, the executive branch, and higher education institutions themselves. Thinking in these terms, we consider concrete areas of legislative objectives, implementation mechanisms, and campus priorities, respectively. The legislative objectives of the Title VI program, apparent since 1959, were threefold: (1) to create specialized knowledge and teaching in language and area studies; (2) to develop expertise for national needs in language and area studies; and (3) to diffuse expert knowledge in language and area studies. The Title VI legislative goals aligned well with a subset of the goals long considered legitimate within the broader higher education policy arena as described in Table 9-1.

The executive branch used three basic implementation mechanisms to channel Title VI funding to the higher education system, all highly compatible with higher education's academic norms and operating procedures: (1) competitive, peer-reviewed grants to institutions to create, sustain, and enhance institutional capacity for interdisciplinary language and area studies; (2) fellowships to institutions to support graduate students' training on the basis of merit rather than need (not only supporting graduate training but also crucially helping the institutions compete to attract the best students to international and foreign language fields);

and (3) competitive, peer-reviewed grants to individuals for research to generate new knowledge in language and area studies fields.

The U.S. Department of Education, under various names, has been the implementing agency for these programs. During the initial years, Title VI had very strong executive leadership and political support from the highest levels. Title VI was the "crown jewel" run at the highest levels of the department with the deputy secretary of education working closely with his or her opposite numbers, particularly in AID and the State Department. Over time, Title VI fell out of the crown and its direct administration was bumped down the ranks, moving farther and farther from the senior administration and political support levels. This weakening of the implementing agency was offset at least in part by increasing client and institutional advocacy from higher education and continuing if low level support from the legislative branch, particularly in the appropriations committees. Initially, in the legislature, key authorizing as well as appropriations committees in both the House and the Senate were strongly involved and supportive. Over time, this dwindled to a champion or two in one body or the other, usually with crucial support from an angel on the appropriations side. The clients or universities themselves, as the third side of the triangle, consistently competed for the Title VI grants and fellowships based on (1) institutional capacity, as demonstrated in depth of faculty, curriculum strength, the number and types of languages offered, strength of enrollments, library holdings, and the like; (2) institutional commitment, including among other items, the extent of financial "leverage," that is, the ratio of an institution's funds invested relative to the funding received from Title VI; and (3) the number of students trained and taking up jobs and careers working in the fields relevant to Title VI. In the early years, there were robust interactions, even revolving doors, between universities and the executive branch related to Title VI and AID programs. This disappeared over time, replaced by a small set of university leaders interacting with legislative champions around Title VI. The higher education associations took increasingly strong leadership on larger campus–federal concerns and gradually also took up advocacy for federal support for international higher education concerns.

Foreign Assistance Policy Stream

From 1949 onward, U.S. universities, especially land-grant universities, became engaged in technical assistance in developing countries. The Foreign Assistance Act (FAA) of 1961 provided a broad legislative framework for these federal–university relationships, which had been developing on an ad hoc basis in the early 1950s under the Truman administration's Point Four and similar programs under the Technical Cooperation Agency within the Department of State that engaged universities. The FAA of 1961 replaced the International Cooperation Agency with the USAID as a new agency in the State Department. The FAA's strength lay in an expansion in the level of foreign assistance provided to Africa and Latin America. Its role in supporting higher education's international capacity on the home front was narrow but robust initially. As with Title VI, it also began a downward slide over time. The collaboration of senior AID officials with the deputy secretary of education and high-level university representatives was extraordinary and provided a solid frame for the emerging policy arena around international higher education. Indeed, it produced a heady brew in the early years on campuses that won both AID and Title VI funding, usually with engagement of faculties of agriculture, education, engineering, and medicine. A well-known example was the University of Wisconsin-Madison with the AID-funded Land Tenure Center and several Title VI centers. Harvard's Institute for International Development and Title VI centers offer another example.[11]

In comparison with the NDEA Title VI funding, the FAA funding was much larger per university. On the negative side, the FAA focused on higher education as a direct instrument to meet its programmatic needs overseas rather than as a foundational, capacity-building partner. It worked with fewer universities and had less diversity in types of participating universities. Institutional capacity was only an implied goal in the legislation but was a high priority for the implementing officials in AID, at least in the early days. The FAA program supported direct research production for AID needs overseas. University priorities such as graduate training support and research support for the faculty focused on development subjects was a welcome by-product for the campus rather than the main goal of the AID university program. With the goal of capacity building of the universities dependent on the personal goodwill of AID leadership rather than on its legislative mandate, the FAA presented the universities with a lower "compatibility" profile than Education's NDEA Title VI. Despite higher funding, it also presented a lower "profitability" profile, as there was less prospect of long-term investment owing to the lack of a long-term rationale for university-based programs. The implementation mechanism of the FAA was AID contracting rather than peer-reviewed competitive grants as in NDEA Title VI in the early 1960s. That further deepened the compatibility gap with the research and teaching mission of universities. It also raised the cost side of the cost–value equation for university administrators because contracting required competing with noneducation actors, generally consulting firms, and creation of special administrative arrangements not typically found on campuses.

Attempt to Merge the Educational and Foreign Assistance Streams

Between 1965 and 1970, after having run in parallel until 1964, there was an attempt to merge the educational and foreign assistance streams into a single channel for the nascent international higher education policy arena. The policy direction was crystallized through three speeches by President Lyndon Johnson in 1965 and 1966. Two primary pledges emerged: (1) long-term commitment to American universities for international studies support; and (2) assisting the education effort of developing nations at all levels.

These commitments gave rise to the International Education Act (IEA) of 1966, which ultimately was signed by President Johnson on October 29, 1966. The "iron triangle" of the nascent policy arena seemed to be made of steel. It was so strong because of robust support of a powerful advocacy group in the universities, good supportive coalitions within Congress, and strong leadership and support in the executive branch, particularly in the Department of Education and the State Department. The three goals embodied in the IEA may be summarized as providing (1) international expertise for foreign affairs and education at all levels; (2) humanitarian assistance overseas including the education sector; and (3) citizen education to better understand and work with the rest of the world. U.S. higher education was the sector targeted for implementation of these ambitious goals, tapping the expertise and capabilities of both NDEA Title VI and AID-funded campuses and calling for expansion, adding new universities well beyond those participating in both programs in 1966.

The attempt to merge the educational and foreign assistance policy streams is clear in the IEA's combination of the goals of the Title VI program (international expertise) with the objectives of the AID programs (humanitarian and education assistance). The addition of citizen education implied broadening the IEA's reach to the entire society, at least to primary and secondary schools, rather than limiting the policy focus to the creation of experts and expertise through higher education. Indeed, the IEA attempted to expand the goals beyond those of the NDEA Title VI so the international higher education policy arena would encompass all six goals normally covered within the higher education arena (see Table 9-1) and would also reach out to add an international dimension for precollegiate education. For example, the promotion of "citizen education" fit the goal of creating an informed citizenry (objectives five and six of the higher education policy arena). The aim of humanitarian assistance overseas reflected the adoption of social justice (objective four) and foreign policy issues beyond security and defense (objective two) into the goal set of the policy arena seen in Table 9-1. The soaring height of the IEA's ambition was put in sharp relief compared with Title VI. The IEA's authorized funding levels were almost six times the level of Title VI authorizations in 1969, as shown in Figure 9-1.

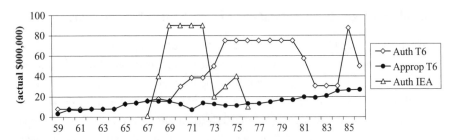

FIGURE 9-1
Authorizations versus Appropriations: NDEA/HEA Title VI and IEA (1959–86)[12]

Stillbirth of the IEA

In the November 1966 congressional elections, forty-seven new Republicans were elected to the House of Representatives. Because of the late passage of the IEA in the previous session, its appropriations were left to the incoming Congress. The new political context in which those appropriations were debated was crucial. Foreign aid budgets were slashed to the lowest level since 1958, partly a reflection of congressional disapproval over the Vietnam War policy and partly growing disenchantment with the progress of overseas development programs in general. Congressional and White House displeasure with general campus unrest and with specific protests against the Vietnam War, including by Asian studies faculty in Title VI centers, undercut support for higher education budgets. Tension around education policy in general was growing as a consequence of desegregation efforts. General inflation, growing costs of education budgets, and other expenses of the Great Society initiatives strained fiscal policy and sapped political will.

In the congressional session of the fall of 1968, the Johnson administration succeeded in securing passage of the Higher Education Amendments, extending authorizations until June 30, 1971. This included continuing the NDEA Title VI as well as IEA authorizations. Although authorized through 1975, the IEA was never actually funded by Congress. By 1976, the IEA was completely dead. This was the last year that an official from the Department of Education attempted to renew the authorization and secure an appropriation. After five years of intense policy work and another five years of continuing attempts to fund the IEA, the energy was completely spent, but its spirit was transported into Title VI. This transmogrification occurred through a series of programmatic additions to Title VI as we will see in a moment.

Begging the reader's patience, let me digress from the research trail and
explore a question that was raised at the Title VI fiftieth anniversary conference

in Washington, D.C. in March 2009 at the presentation of this research. What would the counterfactual scenario be? If the IEA had passed and been fully funded, would the U.S. higher and larger precollegiate education sectors be more deeply internationalized? Without a doubt! That line of inquiry is well beyond the scope of the author's research, but at the conference she was asked whether it would not be possible to fulfill all the objectives of the IEA today, if it was only a matter of funding. As will become clear in the rest of this chapter, the idealistic aspirations of the IEA were widely supported. The limiting constraint was more fundamental than funding. The first question was of the legitimate role of the federal government in fulfilling those aspirations and then the relative priorities for funding them. The IEA went well beyond the tolerances of up-to-then legitimate spheres of federal action in higher education and, perhaps, still today. Without a substantial increase in overall education funding, most likely provided by the Foreign Affairs legislative committees (or the even less likely creation of entirely new legislative oversight committees), the mechanics did not exist to fund the IEA. The operating structures within the executive branch were far from obvious for managing such a hybrid with clear foreign policy goals and resources while being based in the domestic education sphere of states and local governments and private universities. Other fundamental principles were also potentially in conflict, both of higher education and federal policy. They restrained the integrating of higher education and foreign policy, even when focused on the soft-power areas of humanitarian and education development policy. As the country moved into the 1970s, there were numerous other larger policy shifts in both foreign policy and higher education that worked against implementing the IEA, a bill born of 1960s ideals and activism. Take for example, the IEA's overseas development aspirations as they might be mapped onto today's university. Would higher education today be capable of or want to play the field-service role that nongovernmental organizations (NGOs) and consulting firms have assumed? Is higher education well situated to prepare students today with knowledge that enables them to work for and lead field operations in education, human rights, environmental, and disaster relief arenas, to name a few? In some ways, the lack of massive new funding from the IEA forced the higher education system back onto itself to develop its own international programs and institutional development strategies around faculty interests, student needs and institutional capacities. As higher education's goals became clearer internally and as common systemwide needs were acknowledged, higher education became a stronger constituent voice in shaping federal policy toward international higher education. With that in mind, we return to Title VI and how its development was affected by the demise of the IEA.

The Near Death of the Title VI Program

By 1971, Title VI also was under direct threat. It was affected by the same social, economic, and political pressures as the IEA. It also was part of the Department of Education that was targeted for elimination in the Republican presidential campaign platform along with severe reductions in many other social programs. Once in office, the Nixon administration attempted to "zero-out" funding for Title VI, along with many other federal programs. University and congressional supporters fought and preserved Title VI but at substantially lower funding levels. The price of preservation was for Title VI to be responsive to a range of new legislative, executive, and constituencies' interests. To survive, Title VI absorbed many of the programmatic innovations planned for the IEA, effectively adding new requirements while reducing overall and per-grant funding. Over time, champions in Congress continued attempts to rebuild and even grow the Title VI program. These developments are well illustrated by Figure 9-1, which shows the authorizations and appropriations for Title VI as well as the authorizations for the IEA.[13] Indeed, Figure 9-1 paints the high-flying aspirations in stark relief to the trudging reality on the ground of both IEA and Title VI.

The ambitious goals of the IEA are apparent from the scale of its authorizations in 1969, approximately six times the level of Title VI authorizations. The Nixon administration's attempt to zero-out Title VI is clear from the decrease in appropriations for the program in 1971. The scale of the funding cuts is underscored by the fact that the decrease in 1971 was more than one-third of the level of appropriations in 1970. In fact, if Figure 9-1 were redrawn on an inflation-adjusted basis, then the decline in Title VI appropriations would be even more dramatic.

As noted earlier, Congress continued its efforts to support international higher education, even though Title VI was the only legislative vehicle available. The Title VI authorization levels showed tremendous growth between 1969 and 1974, evidence of congressional support for the overall international higher education goals. Congressional support, however, was never sufficiently robust to secure similarly high appropriations, much less enough to offset the wasting effects of inflation on the nearly flat funding levels for Title VI. The continuation of high levels of Title VI authorizations into the early 1980s reflected the fact that the aspirations of the IEA lived well beyond its death in 1976, a theme to which we will return.

On the ground, the number of centers funded by Title VI dropped precipitously in the 1973–1975 cycle after the 1971 funding cut. The top line of Figure 9-2 shows the total number of Title VI centers funded between 1969 and 1988. The bottom three lines show the composition of the types of universities participating in Title VI centers and fellowship programs. All types of participating institutions of higher

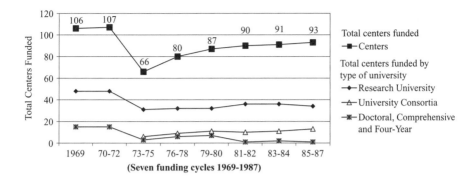

FIGURE 9-2

Impact of 1971 Title VI Funding Cuts on Number of Title VI Centers and Types of Universities Funded (1969–1988)[14]

education including research universities and doctoral, comprehensive, and four-year institutions decreased substantially between the 1970–1972 and 1973–1975 periods.[13] A few hearty campuses formed consortia to continue with shared funding—for example, the University of Massachusetts-Amherst, a research university, and four liberal arts colleges formed the Five Colleges Consortium for funding as an East Asian Studies Center. This was a defensive strategy to enable institutions to persist in the program. The number of centers rebounded slowly through the 1970s, albeit with many banding together in consortia. The number of research universities participating remained stable after 1975, but institutional diversity evaporated. The doctoral, comprehensive, and four-year institutions as solo grantees all but disappeared from the program. By the end of the decade, only one solo center remained outside the research university group—the center at San Diego State University, a comprehensive institution in the 1970s.

Aspirations of the IEA Lived on in the Rebirth of Title VI

Despite the lengthy demise of the IEA, finalized in 1976, many of its aspirations were carried into authorizations for Title VI and reborn as new programs within the Higher Education Act (HEA) Title VI. Figure 9-3 shows how Title VI funding was allocated across programs. Of the three original programs, the graph shows slow nominal growth of center awards after the severe drop in 1973–1975. At the same time, fellowships dropped to 1971 levels and then paralleled the funding pattern of centers. The funding for the IRSP program plummeted. In essence, the centers program was maintained at the expense of the other two original programs, confirming that the centers were the core of the operating model of the Title VI program. The other two original programs, fellowships and IRSP, were further reduced to make

179

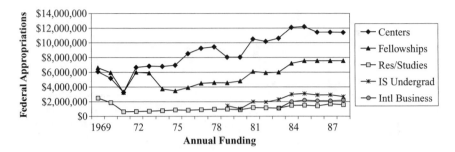

FIGURE 9-3

Title VI Funding by Program as New Programs Are Added (1969–1988)[15]

room for the new programs added in 1979. The per-center funding, though steady, was actually eroded by undertaking new mandates without additional funding and adding a new nonregional or international studies group of centers with the same program funds.

The new programs, mandates, and additions to Title VI embodied the aspirations of the IEA and went well beyond the original Title VI focus on graduate and area and foreign language training. The two new programs focused on four- and two-year colleges with short-term, generally nonrenewable, funding mechanisms designed to start up and spin off rather than provide ongoing federal support. The first was the Undergraduate International Studies program, aimed at creating capacity for citizen education by incubating new foreign language and area or international studies, which is known today as the Undergraduate International Studies and Foreign Language (UISFL) program. The second, with a similar *modus operandi*, was the Business and International Education (BIE) program, which responded to growing pressure to support constituent interest in internationalizing business education. For the centers, the addition was the International Studies/Graduate program, which focused on building professional schools' foreign language and international or area studies capacity. After a brief period of separate competitions, but without additional funding, it became a new non-area category for center funding in international studies. Eventually, both the traditional area and the newer international centers were also mandated to reach out to all types of professional schools on their campuses. Finally, outreach to schools was the new mandate for the centers to undertake with a portion of their grant funds, again without additional resources. This dilution of funding was preferable to the centers' constituents compared with the alternative of further diverting shrinking Title VI funds to create a separate program for precollegiate international education constituents. For the education constituents, the outreach mandate within the centers program

180   seemed the only alternative possible at the time.

By the 1980s, the absolute level of federal appropriations to the centers was higher than it had been in 1976 when the IEA died, at least in nominal funds not adjusted downward for rampant inflation. (See Figure 9-3.) However, this figure also makes clear the relative decrease in appropriations for centers that occurred in 1978–1979. This decrease reflected the broadening goals of Title VI and the addition of programs largely at the expense of centers and fellowships. Essentially, funding to create expertise was diverted into meeting the goals of citizen and other types of professional education. The research universities retained centers, but with lower grant levels and extra service requirements. With center funding, the grantees were now also required to add outreach to the broader K-12 and higher education systems, effectively reducing funding available within centers. The other new Title VI programs aimed to provide a vehicle for and resuscitate participation in Title VI of two- and four-year colleges and other types of campuses. Funding for centers, fellowships, and especially the IRSP held steady or dropped in order for Title VI to incorporate and meet new and broader constituent demands.

Put differently, the goals of the international higher education policy arena were expanding to encompass new goals, such as an informed citizenry and economic competitiveness. These existed within the broader higher education policy arena but had not previously been the focus within the international higher education arena. It helped to stabilize the new policy arena of international higher education. It provided new constituents and supporters for Title VI—but at what cost to overall goal achievement and program effectiveness? How did diversification and dilution of funding affect the ability of the Title VI program to build institutional capacity for international education throughout the U.S. higher education system overall?

Evaluating Sustainability and Diffusion Impact

Let us move now to evaluate the sustainability and diffusion impact of the Title VI and AID programs on higher education's overall international capacity in the United States, the original research question of the chapter. The basic evidence is positive, as seen in higher education data displayed and discussed below. Together, the programs reached a critical mass of approximately 14 percent of the 2,803 secular institutions eligible to participate between 1969 and 1988.[16] There was a fairly equitable distribution of programs and resources across the United States, both regionally and between the public and private universities. The institutional diversity was skewed toward the research and doctoral universities, which is conducive to emulation and *traegerin* effects supportive of diffusion. Their perseverance in the programs was an indicator of positive sustainability effects. Their reach across the system geographically and across types of universities, both public and private, was an indicator of positive diffusion effects.

Consider the geographic coverage of the two federal programs across the U.S. higher education system with roughly twice the number of participating universities in Education-Title VI as in the AID group from 1969 through 1988.[17] The regional location of participants was roughly balanced, with Title VI grantees most dense in the Northeast and Midwest, whereas the AID participants were most dense in the Southeast and West-Southwest states.[18] The differences in total funding awarded over the entire thirty-year period (1958–1988), were striking—AID had $2,073 million in funding and Title VI $327 million.[19] With many fewer grantees, it is clear that the per-university awards were much higher for AID than for Title VI. The expansion of smaller grant programs for Title VI also reinforced the gap in funding per institution. In geographic distribution, Title VI funding was heavily weighted toward the Northeast and Midwest, which had 65.5 percent of all funds, along with the densest cluster of grantees. For AID, 56.6 percent of its funding went to the Midwest and West-Southwest, with the highest proportion to the Midwest, its third densest area of coverage, perhaps owing to the concentration of land-grant universities there. Funding also seemed weighted more heavily to the regions of the oldest universities in the country earlier in the period, shifting later to the Southeast as universities expanded there later in the period.

The mix of public or private participating universities was less balanced but in keeping with the overall mix nationally, especially later in the study period. For Title VI, 54.6 percent of participants were public compared with 36.2 percent private, with the remainder under mixed governance, either consortia or particular hybrid governance systems, such as Cornell University. In contrast, AID programs focused more heavily on the public sector, with 63.9 percent public and 32.9 percent private. The skew of AID funding was even more pronounced, with the largest contracts going to the public or state universities and consortia of state universities.

Figure 9-4 compares the representation of categories of university participants of both the Title VI and AID programs with that of the overall higher education system. It supports a positive diffusion impact by showing how far across the higher education system the two programs reached. It is clear that every part of the higher education system participated. For example, in 1976, which is the base year for the classification used for the study, 19.2 percent of the 506 participating universities in the total study group were research universities, whereas these universities accounted for only 3.5 percent of the entire higher education system.[20] Participation of both research and the doctoral universities as the densest group and greater than their proportion of the overall system was positive for diffusion effects of the programs.

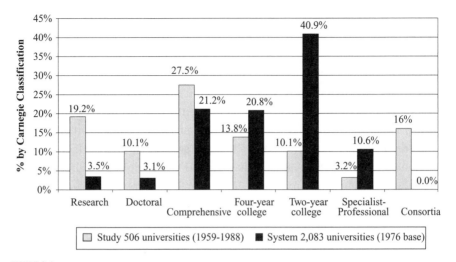

FIGURE 9-4

Representation of Types of University Participants in Both Federal Programs Relative to Their Share of the Overall Higher Education System (1959–1988)[21]

Consider the rest of the participating university groups in Figure 9-4. The relatively strong representation of the comprehensives (27.5 percent of the study group versus 21.2 percent of the system) suggested they used the federal international education resources as part of their institutional advancement efforts, possibly helping them to move into the doctoral tier. For the four-year colleges, being lower in the study group than in the overall system (13.8 percent versus 20.8 percent) reflected their inability to stay in the Title VI centers program after the 1971 funding cuts and also indicated the challenges of accessing the short-term support from the new Title VI programs such as UISFL. In the main, they also would not have been well suited to any of the AID program resources. Although the two-year colleges' representation was lower than that of the other types (10.1 percent study versus 40.9 percent system), their presence was a strong indicator of the community colleges' growing interest in international education. Most of them accessed Title VI funding through either UISFL or BIE programs. They also participated actively in AID participant training with international students on their campuses. Finally, 16 percent of the study group was consortia, which are not classified in the Carnegie classification system. As noted earlier, engaging in such collaborations despite the inherent difficulties suggested that the investment was worthwhile to secure federal resources for international programs.

In the discussion so far, the research universities dominated participation in both federal programs, garnering more than 85 percent of the funding available over the period. Such density of participation is a positive marker of the programs' 183 impact on sustainability at the top of the higher education system. As Title VI funding shrank and the barriers to participation in AID university programs increased, these were the universities in which the program model was most compatible with the international education strategies and programs of their campuses. The research universities found sufficient value in the programs to make the cost–value trade-off acceptable and implementation requirements feasible. It also meant that roughly 15 percent of the total program funds from Title VI and AID university programs reached the rest of the higher education system. For them, AID funding of $250 million was ten times greater than Title VI funding of $25 million over the period (1969–1988).[22] Not surprisingly, the doctoral, comprehensive, consortia, and four-year institutions received more funding from the AID program compared with Title VI by factors of 14.8, 10.6, 9.4, and 3.3, respectively. AID provided more funds to many fewer universities than Title VI, 125 versus 320.

Both Title VI and AID funded institutions in all categories. However, it appears that AID was absent in the two-year colleges, because most of these colleges' AID work was for participant training that did not appear in the program accounts, as did the other AID university programs. The consortia received the bulk of the funding after individual research universities. Although many of them included research universities, they most often included a mix of other categories, too, often with a healthy number of historically black colleges and universities. Many of the research universities used consortia as an explicit strategy for helping strengthen minority institutions or other parts of their state university systems, an active outreach strategy to the rest of the higher education system. The community colleges also had several consortia of their own that were very vibrant, with AID participant training and/or a mix of Title VI UISFL and BIE grant support.

The Paradox of Title VI Success

If AID provided so much more funding to a wide range of universities, how could the study conclude that Title VI was more successful in sustaining and diffusing international capacity across the U.S. higher education system? Returning to the theoretical framework at the beginning of the chapter, the AID counterpoint can help understand the often paradoxical reasons for Title VI's relative success. To be sure, both sets of resources helped reinforce the overall success of internationalization of the campuses. But it was the overall program model of Title VI that ensured success in capacity building. First, we will review the lessons of the AID programs and then move to the Title VI case.

Beginning with AID, a number of weaknesses can be identified that kept the AID universities program from having a greater impact on the internationalization of higher education. Although AID's high funding levels relative to Title VI would suggest strong profitability (in the sense that Levine intended—as the perceived "value" of an innovation), low compatibility in fact undercut profitability. The goals of the AID program focused narrowly and tightly on technical expertise and the operating mechanisms were aligned poorly with higher education. As a result, the AID programs were compatible with only a small range of institutions (or consortia that spread the high operational costs of special administrative arrangements across many partners). Furthermore, the AID grants and projects were oriented more toward faculty in the technical and applied fields of agriculture, education, and medicine, which had less focus on "internationalizing the curriculum" than faculties in the arts and sciences. The lack of peer-review selection methods for the AID projects, combined with the rigidity of the contracting and competitive process, was not well suited to campus governance and faculty decision making. Both were important to compatibility. With faculty, peer review has been a common, respected method for ensuring excellence and appropriateness of research. Contracting has been more suited to the business operations of the universities and difficult to mesh with substantive faculty research and training efforts required for successful work with AID programs. For the AID university programs, weak legislative oversight meant that operations were left largely to the discretion of implementing officials, increasing the potential for arbitrariness in contract specification and awards. When the personalities were supportive in the early years, it was a boon to international education on campus but in the later years, the lack of transparent systems and rules of the game undercut profitability in terms of longer-range returns. Would the relatively high investment needed to win and implement AID contracts be sustained long enough to justify the expense? The lack of peer review, combined with potential for arbitrary decisions, undercut the AID program's overall effectiveness in capacity building on most campuses across the system.

In contrast, Title VI had high effectiveness in both sustainability and diffusion vectors, despite its lower overall and per-university funding. Title VI fit the framework concepts in a number of ways. Scarcity value can be a contributor to creating a gold standard. Title VI became the only game in town. With the IEA gone after 1976 and the AID program narrowing and shrinking its funding for universities, the very fact that Title VI was available enhanced its perceived value to higher education institutions, thereby enhancing its profitability. The research universities were the largest group of grantees and also a protected group, albeit much diminished post-1971. This contributed to emulation effects. The limited funding for Title VI and the growing difficulty of securing center funding actually contributed to the sense of exclusivity of the core Title VI program. The combination of emulation and exclusivity factors around the top research universities and their unique leadership position in the higher education system helped to establish Title VI centers as the gold standard systemwide for international, area, and foreign language programs. With the fellowships normally coinciding with those universities that also competed for centers, the combination provided a way to underwrite graduate training while offsetting shrinking center funding by supplementing graduate support budgets. It was a perfect combination to serve both faculty compatibility and administrative profitability interests and help center universities maintain institutional competitiveness among peer institutions.

The Title VI program was highly compatible with higher education because of its reliance on peer review, flexible implementation methods, and a depth and breadth of resources acknowledged as legitimate within the participating universities. The current name of the center, National Resource Centers, confirmed this aspiration of special status and role within the higher education system and beyond. The continuity of funding, though perversely low, along with fairly stable implementation patterns provided institutions with a high degree of profitability, in the sense of known and relative value to the investment required. This was especially true because the competitive nature of the Title VI awards created a national prestige reference system, with losers as well as winners in each grant cycle. It benefited the reputations of universities that competed successfully to be designated as exemplars with a small group of the dozen or so centers for any given world region or in international studies. Similarly, this fostered emulation effects among other universities across the system.

The fellowships from the Title VI program supported the training of doctoral students which contributed to diffusion through the *traegerin* effect. Even when fellowships were cut, the centers continued to steward the fellowships program carefully, targeting them at PhD. training in an attempt to ensure sufficient replacement stocks of faculty for the burgeoning higher education system. With the fellowship resource, the faculty of the centers were able to sustain strong international, area, and foreign language programs in the universities and colleges in which their graduates would work. Many of those doctoral graduates would feed the growing postsecondary system, sometimes helping their new college homes to expand their international programs and sometimes securing Title VI funding. With the newer Title VI programs added and mandates absorbed by the centers from 1972 onward, emphasis was placed on outward diffusion and garnered new constituencies. The UISFL and BIE programs were particularly effective among the two- and four-year colleges, as well as the comprehensive universities.[23] These new programs, in turn, spawned more active members of the international higher education constituency, advocating for additional funding and further program innovations in Title VI with legislators and executive agencies alike to meet their growing international education needs.

We can find further evidence of the success of the Title VI model in the international higher education policy arena. Consider two significant structural shifts that occurred after 1988. The CIBE program was introduced into the Title VI umbrella through a legislative initiative sponsored and funded through legislation normally guiding and supporting the Department of Commerce. This was accomplished with strong advocacy from the national network of business schools. The fact that CIBE was introduced into the Title VI umbrella rather than spun off as a Department of Commerce program was a testament to the success of the "centers model" of Title VI. It also reflected a deepening of the Title VI beyond the tiny undergraduate Business and International Education Program to robustly incorporate the economic security and competitiveness goal fundamental to the overall higher education policy arena noted in Table 9-1. With CIBE, Title VI strengthened its core role in the international higher education policy arena, expanding its service to a significant professional education field and the related national business sector. Second, consider the National Security Education Program, known as the Boren Program, created in 1992. This program was intended to be under the Title VI umbrella, but it was based in the Defense Department because of a budgetary rule that prohibited shifting funds from the foreign affairs accounts to the domestic affairs accounts. This rule, which attempted to impose fiscal discipline and fend off increasing federal deficits, had the unintended consequence of establishing a competing program to Title VI and stretching the international higher education policy arena.[24] Even so, the Boren Program adopted a key element of the Title VI program, namely, the fellowships mechanism, to promote language and area studies expertise. Once again, this was a reflection of the extent to which Title VI had produced a workable program model and formed part of a stable policy arena. The Boren Program also was well aligned with Title VI in terms of the relatively high portion of Boren fellows who received their area training from Title VI campuses, especially those with centers.

Barely There, Powerfully Present

In sum, despite its low level of funding, the Title VI program came to anchor the international higher education policy arena in the United States. Its perseverance, flexibility, and comprehensiveness have allowed it to address, if not entirely fulfill, the high aspirations inherited from the IEA. The burst of support in the early years for AID and Title VI helped create a strong leadership base within the research universities. This, in turn, helped the overall higher education system develop robust international education programs, even as federal support shrank in real terms.

The chronic underfunding and hollowing out of executive leadership in the U.S. Department of Education meant that Title VI was barely there. In spite of this, it was also powerfully present. Title VI has played a powerful role in building, sustaining, and extending U.S. higher education's international capacity, institutionally and academically. Graduates of Title VI centers and fellowships programs have become the core internationalist faculty, teaching in and leading the higher education system. Many others from all Title VI campuses have become foreign service officers, teachers in schools, and trainers in the military, generators of language learning materials, librarians, organizers of programs in NGOs and the government, and generally anchored in indepth international studies across the nation. Title VI has provided both experts and expertise. It has helped to meet citizen education needs with outreach and growing undergraduate programs. It has become the core of a thriving, dynamic international higher education policy arena in the United States.

Acknowledgment

The chapter condenses the research and findings in the author's book, *Barely There, Powerfully Present: Thirty Years of U.S. Policy on International Higher Education* (New York: Routledge Press, 2002) and acknowledges the pitfalls and omissions inherent in the exercise. Whereas the author takes full responsibility for any errors or omissions, she gratefully acknowledges the skill and insight of John-Michael Arnold, a graduate student in International Relations at Yale, who helped to organize and synthesize the conference presentation and this post-conference chapter.

Notes

1 Many of the colleges and universities, especially the four-year liberal arts colleges, targeted by the "new" Title VI programs of UISFL and BIE had participated in the centers and fellowships programs of Title VI in the early years.

2 "University" is used as shorthand for all types of institutions of higher education, whether college or university in actual title.

3 Henson, James B. (ed.), *Internationalizing U.S. Universities: A Time for Leadership.* Conference in Spokane, Washington, June 5–7, 1990. Pullman,: International Program Office of Washington State University, 1990.

4 Ruther, Nancy. *Barely There, Powerfully Present: Thirty Years of U.S. Policy on International Higher Education.* New York: Routledge Press, 2002, p. 11.

5 Levine, Arthur. *Why Innovation Fails.* Albany: State University of New York Press, 1980. Levine's work argued that focusing on avoiding failure was actually more important than looking at how to promote change.

6 Clark, T.N. "Institutionalization of Innovations in Higher Education: Four Models." *Administrative Science Quarterly* 13, no. 1 (1968).

7 The author has not found a measurable indicator of "critical mass" in the higher education change literature.

8 Source: Ruther, 2002, pp. 205–222. See also The Carnegie Council on Policy Studies in Higher Education. *A Classification of Institutions of Higher Education.* Rev. ed. Berkeley, CA: Carnegie Foundation for the Advancement of Teaching, 1976. Ruther (2002) tapped classifications for 1973, 1976, and 1987, with 1976 as the base year for the study, including the total number of institutions of higher education (IHE) in the U.S. system over the study period. The denominator for systemwide analysis was 2,083 secular universities and colleges. The study adapted its categories using the following institutional types: (1) research universities, (2) doctorate-granting universities, (3) comprehensive universities/colleges, (4) four-year colleges, (5) two-year colleges, (6) combination of all of Carnegie's special/professional category, (7) consortia (horizontal groups) and state systems (vertical groups), (8) institutions not normally included in "higher education" per Carnegie's classification, and (9) religious training colleges. Groups 1 through 5 and 9 match the Carnegie classification directly. Groups 6 through 8 were derived for this study.

9 Private refers to nonprofit secular institutions, as there were virtually no for-profit universities during the study period. State-led refers to public institutions run by the states or other nonfederal government levels. In 1955, there were few two-year colleges and the community college system had not been created.

10 There are several excellent resources for those interested in the background actors who engineered Title VI into the NDEA. See especially Robert A. McCaughey, *International Studies and the Academic Enterprise*, New York: Columbia University Press, 1984, and Lorraine M. McDonnell, et al., *Federal Support for International Studies: The Role of the NDEA Title VI*, Santa Monica, CA: RAND Corporation, 1981. For the early days of AID's university programs, see Jordahl, Brian, and Vernon Ruttan, *Universities and AID: A History of Their Partnership in Technical Assistance for Developing Countries.* Paper no. PP 91–32. Department of Agricultural and Applied Economics, University of Minnesota. St. Paul, MN, 1991.

11 Fast-forward to 2010: Few of the AID-sponsored institutes of that era are still standing, at least in the private universities. The Harvard Institute for International Development has been absorbed into the Kennedy School. The Stanford Food Research Institute was also disbanded. The University of Wisconsin-Madison's Land Tenure Center still thrives as part of a larger 189

environmental institute. Its web site shows that it was founded in 1962: www. nelson.wisc.edu/ltc/about.html (accessed January 25, 2010).

12 Source: Ruther 2002, p. 165. For those not familiar with the U.S. legislative terms, *authorizations* describes "aspirational" funding levels—that is funding levels deemed necessary by the substantive committees to fulfill the law's goals. *Appropriations* reflects funding actually approved.

13 Source: Ruther 2002, pp. 205–207.

14 Source: Ruther 2002, p. 184.

15 Source: Ruther 2002, p. 167. The federal funding is not adjusted for inflation. Inflation-adjusted levels would show declining trends because there was very high inflation for much of the twenty-year period shown.

16 Source: Ruther 2002, pp. 205–207. The study total (N) = 506. Per-participant award data were not available for 1958–1968 but only for 1969–1988. Only secular institutions were eligible to participate.

17 Source: Ruther 2002, pp. 175, 205–207. The study total (N) = 506. Per-participant award data were not available for 1958–1968. The four regions were: WSW = West and Southwest (AZ, CA, CO, HA, ID, MT, NM, NV, OK, OR, TX, UT, WA, WY) SE = Southeast (AK, AL, FL, GA, KY, LA, MS, NC, PR, SC, TN, VA, WV); NE = Northeast (CT, DC, DE, MA, MD, ME, NH, NJ, NY, PA, RI, VT); and MW = Midwest (IA, IL, IN, KS, MI, MN, MO, ND, NE, OH, SD, WI). Five grantees were "national"—that is associations or nonprofit organizations funded mostly by IRSP for language materials or survey work.

18 "Grantee" is correct for Title VI participants, but most universities participating in AID programs were under contract rather than being awarded grants. The total value of AID funding is understated because they had separate reporting methods with full dollar value reports by university for grants and contracts but not for the universities that conducted participant training for AID. In those, they were given a no-cost contract and then paid per student trained. As a researcher, I could not find any mechanism for identifying actual funding received by universities for participant training.

19 Source: Ruther 2002, p. 176.

20 Source: Ruther 2002, pp. 205–207.

21 Source: Ruther, 2002, p. 180. Research universities as 18.5 percent in the book is corrected here to 19.2 percent.

22 Source: Ruther, 2002, p. 182.

23 Schneider, Ann Imlah and Barbara Burn, 1999, *Federal Funding for International Studies: Does It Help? Does It Matter?* The University of Massachusetts (Amherst, MA). This study of the UISFL program of Title VI showed that the

seed money strategy worked very well at building international capacity on a long-term basis among the participating universities and colleges.

24 Source: Ruther, 2002, p. 204. There were special budget agreements that precluded transferring funds from the foreign affairs accounts that had been tapped to fund the Boren Program. The decision to locate it in one of the three major foreign affairs agencies (State, Defense, or Intelligence) was hard fought within the executive branch and among university advocates. However, once the budget agreements lapsed, the program was not transferred to the Department of Education, and Senator Boren was no longer in the Senate. Later, Vice President Gore's task force report on government efficiency recommended that the Boren program be transferred to the Department of Education, but no action was taken. For full disclosure, the author was a member of a Boren Program Working Group in 1993 and 1994.

REFERENCES AND FURTHER READING

Becher, Tony, and Maurice Kogan. *Process and Structure of Higher Education.* London: Heineman, 1980.

Clark, Burton R. *The Higher Education System: Academic Organization in Cross-National Perspective.* Berkeley: University of California Press, 1983.

Clark, Terry N. "Institutionalization of Innovations in Higher Education: Four Models." *Administrative Science Quarterly* 13, no. 1 (1968). Reprinted in *Academic Governance: Research on Institutional Politics and Decision Making,* comp. and ed. Victor J. Baldridge. Berkeley, CA: McCutchan Publishing Co., 1971.

Finifter, David H., Roger G. Baldwin, and John R. Thelin, eds. *The Uneasy Public Policy Triangle in Higher Education: Quality, Diversity and Budgetary Efficiency.* New York: Macmillan and the American Council on Education, 1991.

Garvin, David A. *The Economics of University Behavior.* New York: Academic Press, 1980.

Gumperz, Eileen McDonald. *Internationalizing American Higher Education: Innovation and Structural Change.* Berkeley: Center for Research and Development in Higher Education, University of California, 1970.

Jordahl, Brian, and Vernon Ruttan. *Universities and AID: A History of Their Partnership in Technical Assistance for Developing Countries.* Paper no. P91-32. Department of Agricultural and Applied Economics, University of Minnesota. St. Paul, MN, 1991.

Levine, Arthur. *Why Innovation Fails.* Albany: State University of New York Press, 1980.

McCaughey, Robert A. *International Studies and Academic Enterprise.* New York: Columbia University Press, 1984.

McDonnell, Lorraine M., Sue E. Berryman, and Douglass Scott, with support of John Pincus and Abby Robyn. *Federal Support for International Studies: The Role of NDEA Title VI*. Santa Monica, CA: RAND Corporation, 1981.

Ruther, Nancy L. *Barely There, Powerfully Present: Thirty Years of U.S. Policy on International Higher Education*. New York: Routledge Press, 2002. This book provides the fuller study on which this chapter draws.

Ruther, Nancy L. "U.S. Government and Higher Education: Bridging the Gap in International Expertise". The MacMillan Center Working Papers, New Haven, CT, September 2006.

PART 4

Internationalizing Higher Education and Title VI Programs

Area Studies and Academic Disciplines across Universities: A Relational Analysis with Organizational and Public Implications

Michael D. Kennedy

How can we think about contemporary and historical relationships among disciplines and area studies in order to enhance the scholarly value of their encounters and their impact on the public good?

That is the broad question I pursue in a number of ways through other scholarship, but in this chapter I will focus on the contemporary, on how disciplines organize their area studies engagements, and on potential scholarly values in the reorganization of area studies. I also offer observations on some of the ways in which that scholarly reorganization can have public impact, how area studies differ across regions, and how history should inform our focus. But for the most part, I am contemporary, disciplined, and academic in my emphasis here.

Past Work and Disciplinary Influences

Of course there is much that precedes this effort (e.g., Ruther, O'Meara et al., Wallerstein, Mirsepassi et al.). Most of these contributions focus on broader intellectual currents, geopolitical histories, or institutional and policy worlds. Here, I focus on the cultural politics of area studies and disciplines within the academy by relying on the insights of those who lead this conjunction within universities. My analysis focuses on relationships—those between area studies and disciplines, and among them and their organizations and publics.

Beyond the particular method and orientation of my research, what may also distinguish this effort are my disciplinary roots. Like all good sociologists, and like Max Weber, an exemplar of disciplinary accomplishment who appreciated area studies, I believe it quite useful to begin with conceptual clarity. What are we talking about when we speak of disciplines and area studies?

According to Abbott (2001), disciplines are interactional fields based on portable abstract knowledge axes of cohesion organized through labor markets and education. Using that same framework, one might say that area studies are interactional fields based on contextual expertise and language reference organized around external funders, which in the United States over the past several decades has been most notably Title VI. Although labor markets and education might be pursued with reference to institutional logics, it is hard to approach area studies without offering a cultural political account, given the institutions that shape the knowledge practices of area studies.

I understand cultural politics to be the ways in which various actors influence and transform the meanings, identities, values, and representations accompanying the exercise of power and influence (Kennedy 2008). By itself, of course, cultural politics is not enough to understand everything—one needs to think about how those cultural politics are embedded in history, networks, institutions, and the distribution of resources to explain things from the energy security policies of nations to the academic missions of universities. I expect that this larger volume will address that broader array. For now, I am limiting my own analysis to exploring how cultural politics works in this relationship between area studies and disciplines across regions and disciplines.

I find such an analysis especially helpful when we are looking not only to understand these relationships for their own sake, but also to enhance their scholarly value and public good. Scholars may not control budgets or institutional priorities, but scholars can be more self-conscious about their own cultural politics and how they validate certain practices in research, teaching, and institutional leadership. That is evident even in the ways in which area studies is discussed substantively.

To be sure, area studies is in essence what Tansman (2004: 184) describes as "an enterprise seeking to know, analyze, and interpret foreign cultures through a multidisciplinary lens." Treated that way, the problem of translation is mainly a matter of hermeneutics. Of course it is also a matter of how one conducts social science. I appreciate especially Walder's (2004) elaboration: that translational capacity should be understood as variable. Not every area studies expert is fluent across languages, 196 knows relevant histories, understands contemporary and historical institutional arrays in the region, and, especially when there is national variety in that region, knows its full diversity. Sometimes, Walder notes, those inadequacies can be mitigated by collaborative work (see also Kennedy 2000).

One might also, following Dirks (2004), move beyond questions of translation to historicity and inquire into the degrees by which a knowledge culture comes to be aware of its historical formation and resists the ignorance of former (and ongoing) biases. Dirks (2004: 363) promotes a post-foundationalist history "in which attempts to grapple with the fundamental historicity of modernity in South Asia would necessarily be combined with critical attention to the historical formation of basic categories for the representation of South Asia." It is not only a matter of translation, one could say, but also one of reflexivity.

Of course, ideas such as those of Dirks inspired terrific debate within South Asian studies and some other postcolonial contexts. Such debates rarely cross all area studies fields, but Mitchell (2004: 75) may, in his own characterization of Middle East studies, find what is intellectually implicated in every area studies project. I paraphrase his characterizing questions: In what ways can area studies make a region seem knowable, yet not understandable with existing analytical tools and capacities, and how can investment in that knowledge produce good international policy and practice? A history of any area studies project could be organized around that very pair of questions. But that takes us directly to the question of what funders expect of area studies academics and practitioners.

To a considerable extent, most of the discussion about area studies and its funders functions at very general levels of history and theory. For example, Cumings (2002) moves seamlessly across decades of relationships between funders and area studies, making the cultural politics of area studies a reflection of much grander debates about the relationship between states and scholarship. Miyoshi and Harootunian (2002) remind us that other states also support area studies, helping us appreciate the significance of Asian, and especially Japanese, support for the development of how Japan is to be understood. Engerman's (2009) substantial account of Soviet studies also reveals much about governmental support for Soviet studies. But he also shows just how much variation there can be within those conditions, and of the significance of cultural politics not only between funders and practitioners, but among scholars and their organizations and institutions. History, economics, political science, literary studies, and sociology each had a very different encounter with the field, but these were not at all predetermined by disciplinary accents. Individuals and personal relationships, disciplinary ideas and their transformations, and institutional proclivities and commitments are all critical to understanding the actual mechanisms of Soviet studies' development.

This is, of course, more manageable when a field's formation is institutionally concentrated, as it was at Columbia and Harvard in Soviet studies' start. Indeed, this is not peculiar to that area study—University of Chicago was critical for South Asia (Dirks 2004) and Cornell critical to Southeast Asia (Bowen 2004). Bowen's very account of Cornell's place illustrates, once again, the importance of understanding the everyday practice of area studies and the value of understanding how institutions can take the lead in certain projects, and the implications of their success and the conditions and consequences of dispersal of area studies expertise across other institutions.

With that dispersal, the very careful history that Engerman (2009) exemplifies becomes much more difficult not only for the number of players, but also for the multiplication of relationships one must understand—disciplinary formations, local relations between departments and area studies and among area studies themselves, and their cumulation at the national and international level. For that reason, then, we need to find conceptual and methodological approaches that allow the everyday to enter, while simultaneously attending to broader structures and processes that can inspire new strategic action and effective cultural politics around area studies and disciplines.

Methodologies

One might analyze this relationship among disciplines and area studies from different vantage points, with a number of methods. For example, one might consider the conditions under which any particular world region becomes more or less important in a discipline. I know from my own discipline that Russian and East European studies and Chinese studies have taken off in part because of the ways in which the transition from socialism to capitalism have made these regions not only the interest of area studies scholars, but also more broadly in economic and political sociology as well as studies of inequality. In fact, however, it is more than dramatic change that inspires scholarly engagement; to understand this relationship effectively one should also consider scholarly networks and the place of a country in the discipline's previous and ongoing regional repertoire to explain why a particular place deserves focus (Kennedy 2004).

Alternatively, one might stabilize the discipline and consider the conditions under which different world regions become significant in a disciplinary imagination (Kennedy and Centeno 2007). In my past work, I have focused mainly on how publications reflect this engagement, but that is not the only way regions enter our scholarly worlds. There are many more subtle ways in which the cultural politics of scholarship works; one way to learn more about that is to examine the practices and words of the scholars themselves.

I have my own observations that have come from my experiences as an area studies director, a senior international officer at the University of Michigan, a director of an international studies research center, and someone who has reviewed many institutions for their own articulation of international studies, but in this chapter I rely principally on my colleagues to elaborate the relationship between area studies and disciplines. In fact, I base this method of electronic conversation on a prior effort's success (Kennedy and Centeno 2007).

For this project, I wrote to 173 scholars who are associated with area studies, first and foremost the current directors of Title VI centers, as well as those whom I have come to know in this field over the years. I received seventy-six substantive replies. Of those, a little more than half (39) have had major administrative experience in the oversight of area studies centers.

Most of my respondents (31) work in the area I know best—in Russian and East European studies. I also received a respectable number of replies from colleagues in East Asian, European, and Middle Eastern studies, followed by Latin American, African, and Southeast Asian studies. I received relatively few from those in South Asian, Canadian, and global studies (the last because I did not seek them out, focused as I was on area studies). Personal networks matter, as we know, but thanks to this method, I also have been able to move beyond my regions of greatest familiarity to other world regions.

Extending disciplinary range has been less difficult. Most of my respondents are not in my discipline—although I received the most responses from sociologists (16), historians (15) and political scientists (13) were almost as plentiful, followed by nine anthropologists, seven geographers, and seven scholars in literature or cultural studies. I received a smattering of replies from colleagues in economics or business, architecture, musicology, library, and law.

This survey is not meant to be representative, but it is intended to move beyond my familiar networks of colleagues to understand better the relationship between disciplines and area studies. Of course, I am best equipped to understand my own conjunctions, and the representation of respondents reinforces that capacity. But I look in these replies not for some notion of representative sampling, but for a way of combining insights that we typically do not pursue in our scholarly work. After all, we either work in our disciplines or in our area studies traditions—we do not have conferences or even journals that work across the disciplinary and regional range Title VI engages. That, our colleagues at the University of Washington suggested in a meeting I had there, ought to be remedied.

Following Abbott, disciplines seem to me to be the right starting point because they are the dominant organization of knowledge within higher learning, and the terrains on which certain scholarly practices become more and less legitimate. 199

My correspondence with these seventy-six scholars seems to reinforce that very point.

I followed an interview schedule that was adapted to how I knew the scholar previously and what I knew about his or her involvement in area studies centers. I asked about career and institutional experiences, specifically about my interlocutor's involvement with a Title VI center, the relationship between the Title VI mission and the center's broader mission, the identification of a scholar with a particular place more than others, and which disciplines have been most important to the success of that center. I also asked about exemplars in area studies and disciplinary practice: Who, for example, represents the best combination of discipline and area studies? In particular, which younger authors or more recent publications are exemplary? Finally, I inquired about the general relationship between area studies and disciplines, especially around how area studies reinforces or challenges disciplinary accomplishment.

I assured anonymity so that people would feel free to express their opinions, for good or ill. Indeed, as some of the commentaries will subsequently reveal, that anonymity is important to assure. In other cases, I am sure my colleagues would like to have their identities apparent, but for consistency's sake, I left out names and identifying affiliations even if that could be helpful in understanding the specificities of the relationships among area studies and disciplines. Those adjustments are not italicized in the following quotations.

Area Studies and Its Significance in Careers

Title VI has been directly responsible for the success of a number of respondents. Although many people might identify elements of a synergistic relationship with Title VI, this colleague stands out as having one of the most complete packages in the relationship between a discipline and area studies.

Title VI Centers have played a tremendously important role in attracting me into academics, assisting me in developing a research agenda as a young faculty member, advancing the development of my research network and in acquiring excellent graduate students. I still remember the pivotal role played by a FLAS [Foreign Language and Area Studies] *fellowship . . . in my decision to attend graduate school. My MA in area studies enabled me to gain regional and linguistic expertise, but more importantly offered a unique view into the possibilities of academic research. I never really thought of pursuing a PhD prior to my MA studies. The intellectual intensity, course offerings, visiting scholars, and events found at* [that area studies center] *drew me into an academic research career (for better or worse?). The programs and events held through* [that center] *provided an invaluable tie to the region, not readily available in my PhD program, which while rigorous, focused primarily on the American experience. The ability to meet visiting scholars from . . . was of irreplaceable importance to my dissertation fieldwork, and the shared knowledge of* [that place] *continues to serve as a valuable touchstone with researchers across* [the region]. *I also maintained close ties with* [that center] *throughout my PhD work , as did many PhD students. As a result, I have a wide inter-disciplinary network of "grad school classmates," who provide invaluable assistance when I need assistance with* [other regions'] *history, an inside line for State Department internships for my students or recommendations on the best current* [national] *fiction.*

My faculty position . . . was due, in part, to an institution grant to our Title VI center and the Department . . . to expand hires in underrepresented fields. The Center has pro-vided invaluable research support, access to research and teaching materials and regional periodicals and encouraged me to development courses integrating a regional studies focus with [my field]. *As an assistant professor, I both benefited from the resources and support from the center, and from speaking and conference invitations from other Title VI Centers. These trips increased my visibility as a scholar, sent positive signals to my departmental colleagues, and provided a unique opportunity to test out new ideas, methods, and theoretical approaches in a knowledgeable and supportive environment. Most importantly, contact with other centers enabled my integration into scholarly net-works focusing on the region.*

Access to travel grants, conference funds, and colloquia through Title VI centers has been critical in enabling my continued focus on the region. My "scholarly advance" within my discipline generally, and my department in specific, would be better served by focusing on secondary data analysis and more work focusing on the US (which, due to the relative concentration of research, tend to generate higher citation index scores). Continued engagement with the region, and extended fieldwork place added demands on tight personal and professional time. The scholarly support channeled through Title VI centers is vital in offsetting the "costs" of maintaining an area focused research agenda.

Of course, disciplines vary substantially in what they get from area studies cen-ters, and in the character of their association. As is evident from the preceding story, Title VI is most significant in an individual's career when the person is relatively iso-lated in his or her discipline and department, and has a particular regional focus that inflects methodological commitments that may differ from disciplinary convention.

Disciplinary Orbits around Area Studies

Although the modal disciplinary response to my letters was by sociologists, this reflects my network. It is not the norm in area studies. If we were to look at those who were listed as the principal faculty contacts in January 2009 for grants through 2010 listed on the International Resource Information System of the International Education Programs Service, we would find the pattern shown in Table 10-1.

Table 10-1. Leadership in Area Studies Centers by World Region and Discipline

World Region of National Resource Centers

Discipline of Center Leadership	Russia & Eastern Europe	Europe	Central Asia	East Asia	Asia	South Asia	Middle East & North Africa	Latin America & Caribbean	Southeast Asia	Africa	Canada	Pacific Islands	Total
History	5	2		5	1		5	4	3	1			26
Political Science	2	7		1			2	3	2	4			21
Language/Religion	7	3	1	8			3	2	1	2		1	28
Anthropology	2			1		4	4	3		1	1		16
Sociology	3					1		1		1			6
Economics/ Business									2	1			3
Geography								1			1	1	3
Music							1						1
Archaeology						1	1						2
Library						1							1
Art History						1		1					2
Total	**19**	**12**	**1**	**15**	**1**	**8**	**16**	**16**	**7**	**10**	**2**	**1**	**109**

It appears that those working in language and literature and other cultural studies departments, such as religion, are the dominant group among these faculty. In fact, there are twenty-eight scholars, more than one-fourth of the total, serving as principal faculty contacts who are working in such units. This is a deceptively broad category, however, as these scholars, more often than others, have their own area studies associations or indigenous cultural producers as their principal intellectual reference networks. Unless they attend the Modern Language Association meetings and treat comparative literature and other such global fields as their principal reference, they are not as coherent a group as other academic associations.

One should not underestimate the significance of this group in defining any particular area studies unit, however. In each unit, the modal category of faculty associate is typically those from the relevant language, literature, or philology units. In the future, it would be worth knowing how that distribution varies over time, by institution, and by region of study.

Despite the numerical significance of literary and cultural studies for area studies as a whole, there are other fields represented in the leadership positions defined by the U.S. Department of Education's International Education Programs Service

(IEPS). In this particular year, there were twenty-six historians serving as principal faculty contacts, twenty-one political scientists, sixteen anthropologists, six sociologists, three geographers, two economists, two architecture scholars, two art historians, one representative from musicology, and one from information science.

One imagines that for each of these faculty, the relevant area studies association along with their own discipline would be important reference groups for their work. One would further expect that the faculty working in the same conjuncture of discipline and region would know each other well and have very good mutual support networks. Here, the most powerful combinations beyond literary/cultural studies and philology include history in Russian and East European studies (REES), East Asian and Asian studies, Middle Eastern and North African studies (MENA), and Latin American and Caribbean studies (LACS). The political scientists are especially apparent only in European studies and to some extent in African and Latin American studies. The anthropologists are especially evident in South Asian, Middle Eastern, and Latin American studies, whereas the sociologists are concentrated in Russian and East European studies.

This distribution also allows us to compare how various area studies look in terms of their disciplinary leaderships, and that varies substantially. Latin American and Caribbean, Middle Eastern and North African, Russian and East European, and African studies each are quite diverse, even if their modalities differ somewhat. History is prominent in LACS, MENA, and REES and less prominent in African studies; political science is well represented across the board, especially in African studies; sociology is prominent only in REES, which also has a relatively large literary studies representation. Further research needs to establish how consistent these patterns of leadership are. Of course, this does not say anything about who the principal participants in area studies are; historians, even when they are not dominant in leadership positions, are typically prominent in area studies gatherings, as many of my interlocutors have emphasized.

Four other areas seem to have real disciplinary hegemonies within them, defined by having at least half of their leadership coming from one discipline—political scientists in European studies, literary scholars in East Asian studies, and anthropologists in South Asian studies. Historians in Southeast Asian studies are almost there. Again, a real hegemony would be evident if these patterns are consistent over time, but these distributions make sense given what we know of the disciplinary trends and the reasons for these trajectories.

For example, the significance of the European Union's search for unprecedented political organization and Europe's traditional place in the field of comparative politics in American universities clearly provide some explanation for the prominence of political science in European studies. As one of my respondents suggested: 203

In the field of European Studies, I think the disciplines and area studies have coexisted more easily than in some other world regions. Such coexistence is becoming more difficult, but I think it is still easier than in some other area studies centers. Given that political science as a discipline has favored the study of democracies as involving "real" political science, the fact that West Europe was democratic helped W. Europeanists be viewed as "real" political scientists by Americanists (the powerful within the disciplined) as opposed to, say, Africanists.

None of my other respondents offered explanations for why other disciplinary hegemonies existed in various area studies, although one could imagine the accounts—literary studies have been traditionally important in East Asia's study long before area studies was formally constituted (see also Tansman 2004); anthropologists have historically been involved in the colonial study of South Asia (Dirks 2004), even as they play a broader interdisciplinary role than in other world regions. Historians provide half the leadership in Southeast Asian studies, but I frankly would have expected that to be the norm across area studies itself. History, it seems, should enjoy the easiest fit with area studies as intellectual practice.

Disciplinary Discourses on Area Studies

In searching, then, for which discipline is simultaneously most coherent and most widely distributed in terms of providing area studies leadership, one could conclude that historians now play that role. But how do they understand it? At least one historian would define the value of area studies this way:

The importance and real contribution of area studies, as a framework for evaluation and funding, is to insist on specific knowledge of the particular area, however you draw its boundaries, as a counterweight to grand generalizations and also to very narrow ways of thinking. Across space and time.

Note that this is itself relational—primarily vis-à-vis other disciplines that are more generalizing in their ambitions. But, then, this also raises an intriguing question: Is not this also what history is? Another historian wrote that area studies and history are virtually identical, for

[i]n regard to history and ethnography, as virtually every respectable piece of work in these fields rests on a deep knowledge of the languages and cultures, politics, and geography of the region. Even as these fields have become more theory conscious (though rarely theory driven), no scholar can gain a hearing for his or her work unless it is solidly grounded in the empirics and languages of the region.

In fact, we might consider this to be one reason that historians often are central to area studies—there is little, if any, tension between the dominant discourses of their discipline and area studies. In fact, if we were to use other indicators, such as how prominent area studies journals are in disciplinary scholarly evaluation or how often historians serve as editors of these journals, we are likely to find further evidence for the simple affinity between the discipline and area studies. But is it so simple? After all, another historian wrote, "*My work doesn't exemplify an 'interdisciplinary area studies approach' to scholarship. I'm not sure what such scholarship would look like.*"

This historian raises an interesting question, one we should study more explicitly. Disciplines vary in how they work across disciplines. We know in France, for example, that some disciplines, such as economics, tend to be more international in their reference but very narrow in their disciplinary range; other disciplines, such as sociology, are exceptionally interdisciplinary, but they also are national in their scholarly reference (Heilbron 2009).

Although I have not seen similar research in the United States, I would propose that among our disciplines in this nation, geography is likely to be both quite interdisciplinary and international in its reference, and is likely to be core to area studies scholarship. As one geographer said:

> For geography, interdisciplinary study of a place reinforces both area studies and the discipline by creating new ways of thinking about both. This is also true for history. I was greatly inspired by the interdisciplinary study that came out in 2007, written by Jan Bender Shetler, called Imagining Serengeti. Shetler is an environmental historian. Her narrative depends on linguistics, archeology, archival research, oral history, literary studies, geographical information systems, and ecology. That is quite a range! I tell my students the average historian of, say, antebellum U.S. history, has nowhere near that skill-base or challenge.

This very example raised by a geographer, however, raises one of the issues we should consider in the relationship between area studies and disciplines: What happened to geography in the political economy of universities? In the late 1970s and early 1980s, several prominent universities, including the University of Michigan, the University of Chicago, Columbia, and Northwestern, closed their geography departments, to the detriment of area studies. Some believe that the spread of geographic information systems and other information technologies for the analysis of spatial structures could restore geography's place in universities, but this prospect seems to be little connected to area studies. Indeed, one geographer suggested that

> [g]eography has seen a real resurgence especially around the human-environment topic. Most large public universities have growing or at least thriving geography departments— even in this time of retrenchment. I do not believe that this will result in a re-engagement

205

of geographers with area studies because within the field topical/subject specialties are more critical to career development than regional ones.

That nexus might, however, deserve cultivation.

Anthropology, in contrast, has not struggled to find its place in universities, and its role in area studies is quite prominent and can be very comfortable. As one leading anthropologist said:

All anthropologists are expected to gain a sense of the languages, histories, and political-economic structures of the areas where they work. . . . ALL anthropologists are defined as area people. Because the connection with History has been especially strong for much of the 20th century and now as well, any good anthropologist is also learning the history of the region or space s/he will work in. Because anthropology includes the study of economic, political, social, and cultural systems, inter alia, whichever of these dimensions we happen to emphasize in our work leads us to read in the area-studies literature of the adjacent fields. (E.g., I do political anthropology, and I read political scientists.) Many anthropologists read the literature of their area and some use it in their work.

These most compatible disciplines—geography, and especially history and anthropology—differ radically from the professions.

It is very good, of course, that some scholars from professional schools have served as directors of area studies centers—architecture, law, and business have provided such faculty. In another work (Kennedy and Weiner 2003), I have discussed how different professions relate to area studies per se, noting that the contextual expertise of area studies has relatively great affinities for those in architecture and urban planning, but this stands in stark contrast to the globalizing interests of business schools. We should thus differentiate among professions when we speak of integrating the professions into area studies, but the experience of many from the professions does raise a critical issue: For some professions, and even a few disciplines in the liberal arts such as economics, area studies engagement does not contribute to scholarship; it is rather seen as a service obligation. One such scholar said:

My role as director did not contribute to my own work in my discipline. In fact, the opposite, as I had to interact with and be responsible for faculty and students in other disciplines. I consider this a "service" to the area studies community, and not to my discipline. . . . There is a much bigger divide between area and discipline now than there was 20 years ago in my area, even as more work is being done in both with respect to the area.

Another said:

I benefit from the center's reputation, I have good friends there, and tapping my colleagues' expertise is often quicker than going to the library—but I don't get much
more than that out of it.

In recent years, Title VI application guidelines have encouraged area studies collaboration with professional schools. I think that is important, and I have done it myself as a director. But I also think it is important to recognize that this very engagement can lead area studies to a kind of scholarly subordination to the professions. By this I do not mean to emphasize that these gracious directors from the professions experience area studies leadership only as a kind of burdening service. Rather, their disciplinary colleagues can treat area studies scholarship as supplementary to what they value in academic work, if they conceive it to be relevant at all. That is not good for area studies.

One might turn away from these fields entirely if there were not prospects for greater engagement. Economics is exemplary in this regard—once central to area studies, disciplinary developments turned the field away from contextual expertise. That potentially is changing, as one colleague suggested:

The relationship between mainstream economics and area studies has not been a good one, particularly since development economics went into decline in the 1980s and less developed countries became "data sets" rather than unique experiences to analyze and understand. There may be a resurgence of interest in field work/area studies under way, however, with the decline of the Washington Consensus, the rising discontent with globalization internationally, and the growing prominence in the field of institutionalist economics. Another bright spot is the growing prominence of LACEA, the Latin American and Caribbean Economics Association. It now has over 1,000 members, most US-trained Latin American economists. While generally following the mainstream paradigm, they tend to be more influenced by institutionalism—i.e., context matters. The down side is that along with the rise of LACEA there has been a decline in the number of economists participating in LASA, our main area studies association, and thus of economists interacting across the disciplines.

If we are interested in considering how area studies might contribute to scholarly advance, we might benefit more by focusing on the interactional fields in which there is potential value to be found, if hardly assured. Political scientists have written at length about this question (e.g., most recently, Beissinger 2009; Hanson 2009) but let me quote another of my political science interlocutors:

The old Bates-Chalmers debate between the discipline of political science and area studies was overblown, but it reflects the tensions between the two approaches to inquiry. It has also damaged, in my view, intellectual openness in political science. New graduate students and assistant professors assume they will not get a job if they pursue a more "area studies" focus. . . . Within (my region) the more interdisciplinary approaches have been replaced by "professionalization," meaning a more mainstream orientation. . . . I received several comments from those who wrote for my tenure file a few years ago that they were pleased that someone like me could still get tenure at a first rate University, meaning someone who used more interdisciplinary approaches and methods. That was a sad reflection on where the discipline of political science has gone, at least from my perspective . . . the political scientists hive themselves off in (area studies) conferences, without benefiting from the rich interdisciplinary dialogue that is happening around other broader questions of political memory, political action, political rhetoric, political performances, or politics more generally.

This debate is familiar to most of us in area studies, of course, but it is also interesting when we put it in broader context. First, this disciplinary debate is important for area studies because of how prominent political scientists are in the definition and leadership of area studies generally. Second, it does not appear to be that complicated for the political scientists who work in Europe, for there, they have managed to find a way to combine disciplinary and area studies interests. In that, they are more like historians in general, who tend to see a simple affinity between their discipline and area studies. Third, we might consider how political scientists in other world regions might find greater affinity with sociologists, especially those who have moved with the comparative and historical turn. One sociologist wrote this:

For sociology, it has been important to move away from a disciplinary approach that sought universal rules about societies, toward a more deeply contextualized understanding of how history, culture, and material practices shape and are shaped by social relations. Over the past thirty years, I think, sociology has been vastly improved by scholars who take context seriously—often, because they work outside the advanced industrial capitalist societies, and have been forced (by their area studies colleagues) to address more directly the way different historical, political, and economic contexts play out. . . . Sociology's classical theories were formed in early modern Europe, and there remains a tendency to assume that findings in Europe and North America will serve as the basis of theory-building. But in fact, many of the most interesting theoretical insights have come when scholars use material from outside those contexts to push at theoretical assumptions, to underscore the historical specificity and path dependence of patterns that were previously considered universal.

Another sociologist, from a different specialization and different world region, wrote:

Interdisciplinary study in Sociology is tremendously important for both theory development and empirical work in Sociology. A theory is not formulated in a vacuum. It is conceptualized with some assumptions about the kind of situations to which it is intended to apply, or in economics terms, with a set of initial conditions. Study of other world regions helps prevent Sociology from being identical with the study of American society, which limits the scope of thinking by theorists in Sociology and also limits the range of empirical work pursued by sociologists. This limited perspective in theory and empirical work then becomes mutually reinforcing. In addition, Sociologists who study other regions are compelled to justify the significance of their work in terms of general sociological or social scientific areas of concern. Those who study the United States too often neglect this larger argumentation of significance, because the importance for our country and its future can appear self-evident. Similarly study of regions helps promote cross-disciplinary contact and cross-fertilization. When you are studying a region other than your own, it becomes obvious that you need to know something (and preferably quite a lot) about that region's history, culture, and politics. This promotes contact between sociologists, historians, and anthropologists, and also often with political scientists and economists. The location of specialists from all disciplines who study a particular region in association with a regional area center facilitates and promotes this kind of interaction.

Here, rather than area studies being a challenge, it has become an asset in developing a core strength of sociology—the return to its classical traditions in comparative and historical sociology in the tradition of Max Weber and others. Whereas it is still true that publications in area studies journals are unlikely to be as valued as much as publications in the discipline's flagship journals, and although there are many in the discipline who work in such a way without affiliation with area studies at all, the place of area studies in sociology is relatively comfortable, especially in comparison with what we see in political science. That difference, of course, has to do less with area studies and more to do with the way in which sociology and political science are differently organized as disciplines.

Nevertheless, the critical point to be made here is that area studies knowledge becomes more valuable in sociology and presumably other social sciences to the extent that it is linked to abstract knowledge—that is, organized around method or theory. Area studies, as our first historian indicated, is not necessarily connected to such an ambition, and rather is designed to complicate those generalizing approaches. But complications can work in a variety of ways that are more and less connected to abstract knowledge. My key proposal is that area studies needs to be much more self-conscious about this methodological and theoretical ambition and diversity. Indeed, its own golden age suggests just such virtue.

Theoretical and Methodological Excursions

Modernization theory has been the object of a great deal of contemporary and even more subsequent theoretical and methodological critique, but, on a functional level, it also was a great boon to area studies' formation. It simultaneously provided a general theoretical and methodological approach that required some kind of area studies expertise as supplement and critic to generalizing theory (Gilman 2003; see Engerman 2009 for how important Parsonsian theory was for Soviet studies   209 development). As one colleague recruited in that era to sociology and area studies recalled:

> *I find it difficult to overstate the importance of area studies for disciplinary advancement. Through the 1950s it would not be much of an exaggeration to say that American Sociology was primarily American studies. The extent to which non-American societies informed our discipline was not very great. I think Sociology has benefited greatly from the opening of area studies and the strong place they have gained on leading American campuses.*

Of course, modernization theory is not generally useful any longer, for social science theory has at least explicitly moved beyond it. But in that movement we should not lose what it offered.

Too many write as if area studies practice is light on theory—Szanton (2004) is quite right to emphasize how wrong that is. But what modernization theory offered, and what contemporary theoretical engagements in area studies do not, is a theoretical and methodological approach that travels relatively well across regions while engaging questions that move beyond disciplinary preoccupations. Modernization approaches were useful because they had grand ambitions with theory and method built in. In addition, they had a terrific invocation of comparison, asking how universal processes might be reshaped by particular contexts. Is there a suitable approach today that might draw on modernization's strengths? Clearly, the answer must begin with discussing how comparisons ought to be developed.

Some have emphasized that the best comparative methodologies, ones that can truly reach macrocausal explanations, are those studies that hold most things constant while distinguishing key features. Here, then, comparing provinces within a narrow time frame and within a contiguous empire, such as the Ottoman or Russian, is likely to be more fruitful for identifying real causal mechanisms, in a careful methodological sense, than comparing across time and across the world (Sewell 1967). But our comparative ambitions are not only motivated by the search for more rigorous causal mechanisms. Sometimes, we also seek new and better questions. Indeed, one can develop better imaginations about social processes and how to communicate with those beyond one's particular geographical area of interest if one reads broadly. Too often, area studies scholarship is stuck in the region, as one colleague reflected:

> *I find area studies to be essential yet limiting, since the different area literatures are largely disconnected from each other. . . . Z was influential because we applied the insights of another area-studies literature to our own area problems; . . . I'm afraid that often, area studies scholars are as parochial as the Americanists, just tending different parishes. Yet, having said that, I am as demanding as any area specialist in regard to*

knowledge of my region; one of the flaws I find in so much of the stuff on region X is that it is written by people who know nothing at all about X, except that the region is "problematic."

This is a major issue to which we should devote substantial attention. Recall, however, that for certain disciplines, expertise in some regions requires expertise in others. I think that we often miss this accomplishment within area studies, and it should be highlighted.

Consider, for example, the musicologist working in a tradition beyond Europe and America. In order to get a job in a school of music in the West, that scholar must know the art music of the Western tradition in addition to that of one's own focus. This suggests the theoretical and methodological innovation possible in area studies by thinking about grounding and translation anew. I have pursued some of this work previously; in fact, the University of Michigan's Ford Foundation grant for rethinking area studies was organized around grounding, translation, and expertise, and thus I build on that (Cohen and Kennedy 2004). But my colleagues in these electronic conversations give me new ways to see this. One musicologist said:

[W]ithout the language skills, no one can understand [this tradition of] *music. The same goes for any music culture with a rich and documented history. Thus, only American schools with Title VI centers that can provide language classes/support, regular lectures and workshops that can sustain faculty and students learning cultures and musics outside Europe and North America. . . . Ethnomusicology students at XX, for example, are so limited by school and program rules which prioritize studying of European art music that they depend on the centers to learn the facts and issues about the cultures/regions that they study. A musicology student studying French music in the school will get a good education about French music within the school, but the same cannot be said about an ethnomusicology student studying* [another nation's] *music. They need that* [area studies center] *to supplement their quest for knowledge.*

In some ways, we might actually turn to another area, visual culture, to consider how this might work. As one colleague told me:

Analyzing films, TV, photography, painting, new media/satellite allows one to go beyond the inhibiting and obfuscating assumptions that are deeply ingrained in many of the disciplines . . . it allows one to examine notions of modernity in more historically compelling ways—giving a more empirically rich way to study the idea of "alternative modernities." Shiva Balaghi's and Nada Shabout's work show that the modern in Middle Eastern art was not simply a mimetic and later development in Arab and Iranian cultural history—but that the creative process of thinking about how to be modern and remain embedded in national paradigms was written into the birth of the modern in the Middle East—and that this is not a recent but rather a historical process.

Further:

[R]ecent coverage of the war in Gaza in the American media focused on the lack of accessibility of journalists to the conflict zone—the West raged against the authorities for not allowing journalists into Gaza while the IDF was conducting its operations. Images of Western journalists hovering on hilltops on the outskirts of Gaza stood in for the lack of access. In reality, Arab media covered the conflict in minute detail—Al-Jazeera, for example, had continual coverage of the conflict. The press can no longer simply be understood within the frame of traditional western media outlets.

In short, these examples in visual culture and musicology suggest that the relationship between knowledge production across locales cannot be simply read through the lenses supplied by the contexts in which one grows up or is educated. Area studies is about that kind of repositioning, thinking about how one comes to be grounded in other contexts, and how to translate that learning back into another knowledge culture. We should work more extensively to turn this implicit method practiced by area studies into something that is theoretically and methodologically explicit. This could draw in those social scientists potentially alienated by the equation of contextual expertise with language facility. Indeed, there is more to this than opportunity.

One of the dangers associated with Title VI priorities can be the elevation of certain disciplinary competencies above others. We might explore these limitations in a number of ways, but another colleague's experience seems critically important to recall, especially as we observe variations in area studies' practice across universities. After moving from one university to another, and valuing the area studies contribution in the former university, this social scientist

quickly became frustrated with the lack of opportunities for faculty affiliated with the center who did not work directly on foreign language issues . . . although it did attract some students in the MA program to my course, and in some instances helped to fund the dissertation research of my PhD advisees. . . . I began to work more with another center at the university.

Language expertise is clearly one vital element of area studies learning, but its place in a broader scholarly collaboration should be more clearly elaborated. Some of our interlocutors noted particular progress in this domain. One colleague reflected:

The importance of language expertise has also changed over time. Years ago, there was an extremely high language requirement imposed for any work on an area. This was often used as a way to "keep out" the interlopers in a non-constructive manner. Then, a more sensible approach mainly took hold, with the idea that for support of a project [by certain area studies organizations] *required whatever level of language proficiency that was necessary for the particular project.*

Not only does the elevation of theoretical and methodological training in area studies spell opportunity for enhancing social science participation in area studies, but it also might help us recognize more clearly the conditions under which language study is necessary, and the ways in which it is important when not otherwise apparent. Certainly, as this colleague observed, contextual expertise is less valuable when it is only a gatekeeper. It is more valuable when clearly tied to other accomplishments. How might we recognize those accomplishments?

Exemplars in Scholarship

One might devise a list of attributes toward which the aspiring exemplar might work and toward which we might teach, and against which we might review our colleagues and construct our associations' recognitions. One of my electronic interlocutors constructed such a list for colleagues in political science:

- *Theory-building in the discipline of political science, but with broader relevance to anthropology, history, sociology.*
- *Drawing on local knowledge, but with a strong comparative vision. Artful writing.*
- *An inspiration to new scholars to think outside the box, but to engage existing theoretical literature and approaches.*

Most of my respondents did not reply with such a theory of the exemplary but were rather moved to find examples, very often turning to recent winners of prizes. One colleague, for example, noted the example of David Schaberg:

> *With a PhD in comparative literature and East Asia Language and Civilization (with a focus on early China) from Harvard, Schaberg writes about and teaches literary, rhetorical, and intellectual traditions of early China with remarkable theoretical sophistication and philological soundness. His book,* A Patterned Past: Form and Thought in Early Chinese Historiography *(Harvard University Asia Center, 2001), won the Joseph R. Levenson Prize: Pre-1900 Category in 2003 awarded by the Association for Asian Studies....* [then referring to the citation for this award] *Schaberg shows us how intelligent individuals in early China strove to make sense of their historical experience. The book's main sources are the Zuo zhuan and the Guo yu, which jointly constitute pre-Imperial China's most important body of historical narrative. These texts portray members of a highly cultivated aristocratic social milieu manipulating language and shaping memory in a quest for the principles of ritually correct behavior. Schaberg shows masterfully how these protagonists formulated and presented their arguments in a competitive rhetorical arena. The book, like its source texts, touches upon the full richness of pre-Imperial Chinese culture. With its unique blend of historical, philological, and philosophical perspectives, it creates a new basis for understanding a crucial formative stage*

of Chinese intellectual history; and through its well-presented comparisons with Western traditions, above all, with ancient Greece, it opens up the world of the Zuo zhuan and the Guo yu to readers from the Humanities and Social Sciences at large.

Another colleague pointed to past winners of the "Melville J. Herskovits Award given by the African Studies Association to the best scholarly work (including translations) on Africa published in English in the previous year and distributed in the United States." That description, and the list of winners since 1965, is immediately available on Wikipedia (http://en.wikipedia.org/wiki/Herskovits_Prize) and from that list, one might deduce what it means to be exemplary. I would suspect that the general qualities making Schaberg's work exemplary, and those of the Herskovits award winners, would resemble one another. But very few, I would imagine, would read both him and the 2003 Herskovits award winner: Joseph Inikori's *Africans and the Industrial Revolution in England: A Study in International Trade and Economic Development.* (Cambridge: Cambridge University Press, 2002).

As it was, few individuals were mentioned as exemplars more than once, and when they were, they tended to be from within the same area studies tradition. There were a few exceptions—Barrington Moore and Clifford Geertz from one generation, and James Scott and Benedict Anderson from another. I suspect that were we to offer a more closed-ended questionnaire about exemplars, scholars such as these—who had contextual expertise but who also contributed more general theoretical arguments and were more explicitly involved in comparative studies in society and history—would find the most recognition.

Given the number of interlocutors who replied in Russian and East European studies, it is not surprising that if there were to be exemplars mentioned more than once within an area studies tradition, they would be there. Katherine Verdery was mentioned most often, with comments like this explaining why she is so important for area studies:

> *Katherine Verdery's brilliant work on Romania has simultaneously developed an indepth understanding of that particular society and anthropological theories of socialist and post-socialism, which are also of relevance to scholars in political science, sociology, history.*

Beyond this region's study, Ken Pomeranz is a name that was multiply mentioned. One colleague explained why Pomeranz might be so considered:

> *Ken Pomeranz's* The Great Divergence *(Princeton, NJ: Princeton University Press, 2000) stands out, as it is thoroughly grounded in China (couldn't have been done by someone who didn't read the language, etc.) but totally engaged with debates that are far from area studies-specific, and historical yet linked to debates in sociology, even economics. I like work that is up to the mark in disciplinary and area studies specific terms, yet is*

interdisciplinary and either comparative or has comparative pay-offs even if focused on one locale.

These two exemplars nonetheless illustrate some of the challenge for area studies and the disciplines. Verdery engages those interested in that world region and its systemic qualities, but not everyone worries about what was socialism and what came next. Even when she attends to property rights and burial rites, it is not always obvious that that those who study markets and dead bodies elsewhere will take note of how it works in Transylvania and its environs. And although it is hard to imagine scholars overlooking such fundamental questions in global history as the conditions for the rise of the West, the subordination of the rest, and the implications of that basic inequality for all scholarship, the structure of the academy can move us all toward ever more narrow fields of expertise to assure steadier careers, if more illusory grounding.

Bringing area studies into more explicit theoretical and methodological debate might be one way to bring contextual expertise to the heart of those disciplines for which history is past and context pales before the generalizeable rule. One of the exemplars for this very engagement comes in William Sewell's "postscript" to "Events as Transformations of Structures" in his book *Logics of History* (2005). He writes:

> [P]ractitioners of rational choice theory have only a minor interest in issues of cultural transformation . . . either as a residual . . . or as a framework within which calculations take place, but that is taken as given for the explanatory purpose at hand. . . . [Rational choice] need[s] to be joined to arguments about semiotic structures and their transformations and arguments about the socially generated emotional experiences that inspire invention and elaboration of new cultural meanings. (Sewell 2005: 268–69).

Clearly, area studies is essential for being able to read these semiotic structures and to understand the qualities of emotion that variably resonate with them. Indeed, one might even bring psychologists to this very endeavor—David Matsumoto researches facial expressions after athletic events in order to identify the biological foundations and social conditions that allow various measures of cultural influence to come through (Matsumoto and Willingham 2006). Americans, he found in this and other research, clearly smile more often than Russians.

I find this kind of work—exploring the relationship among cross-contextual and contextual processes—exceptionally challenging and potentially most rewarding for the conjunction of area studies and some disciplines not already identified with area studies. But it also is not the safest path for those who are not already well established within conventional forms of reference and their disciplines.

With the security that sometimes comes with years in rank, these more senior scholars have the chance to be exemplary in terms that go beyond prevailing 215 academic structures for reward and recognition. It is more difficult for those still working toward jobs and tenure, for here, the weight of convention and disciplinary authority in the labor market prevails. In some cases, this works directly against the power of the conjunction in area studies and disciplines, as one political science colleague reflected:

> *Younger scholars are almost compelled to develop generalizable models, most often imported from American politics or political economy, which gives short shrift to local intersubjectivities. There is a premium on cramming local realities into homogenized forms, rather than allowing local particularities teach us anything about that context, let alone about the world farther afield. Again, this is a sin of political science, in particular.*

For precisely these reasons, even though I explicitly asked for exemplars of their conjunction in the younger generation, many of my interlocutors were hard put to identify anyone. But once again, there were exceptions.

Alexei Yurczhak, Georgi Derluguian, and Genevieve Zubrzycki were mentioned more than once among scholars in REES. Their admirers went beyond disciplinary identity too, precisely because these scholars combined the ethnographic with the manifestly theoretical.

> *Alexei Yurchak's* Everything Was Forever Until It Was No More . . . *(Princeton, NJ: Princeton University Press, 2005) is concerned with understanding how power and subjectivity were formed during the Soviet era, whether we can apply the concept of "resistance," how informal spheres of practice, including art, culture, etc., reflected subjects' particular engagement with the state that has been heretofore glossed rather reductively as "resistance" or "complicity" by Western scholars. The innovative, impressive quality of Yurchak's study is that he takes on assumptions made by "Area Studies" scholars, from historians and political scientists to sociologists/anthropologists of the Soviet Union, and provides a critique and alternative view that simultaneously offers theoretically interesting insights to scholars who focus on other regions (from China and beyond).*

Anthropology, as I will discuss later, is especially dynamic in Russian and East European studies, but sociology is also being changed by its engagement with this region. Derluguian is an example, as one person wrote:

> *Georgi Derluguian's* Bourdieu's Secret Admirer in the Caucasus *(Chicago: University of Chicago, 2005) is one of my favorites, as it combines world systems theory with deep ethnographic familiarity with many post-Soviet regions.*

Derluguian's (2005) work is in some ways an even more radical combination, even within the world systems tradition, given its effort to combine biography with
the grandest of structures, processes, and comparisons in its effort to explain the

conditions of war and peace in the North Caucasus after the collapse of the Soviet Union. That kind of theoretical range is not always rewarded within disciplinary formations, of course. And that is especially true if you are engaging a world region that is hardly apparent in the discipline's canons.

Fortunately for Zubrzcycki, Poland is relatively prominent in the American sociological imagination, and one of the reasons for that prominence is in the vital Polish sociological community with which American scholars, regardless of interest in Poland per se, have a chance to work. Indeed, that very combination worked very effectively to help explain why it is that Zubrzcycki (2006) can become one of the young exemplars. Her first book was reviewed in quite powerful terms by Piotr Sztompka, one of Poland's leading sociologists and former president of the International Sociological Association, in the *American Journal of Sociology* (Sztompka 2007: 918–20):

> I do not know of any book by a Polish author that would analyze the relationship of Polish nationalism and Catholicism in such an insightful and revealing manner. But this should not be surprising. After all—*toutes proportiones gardée*—nobody analyzed American democracy better than the Frenchman Alexis de Tocqueville, and nobody understood the American racial dilemma better than the Swede Gunnar Myrdal. Like Zubrzycki, they were able to see things that the "natives" could not perceive.

Sztompka is able to do, in this review, what area studies practitioners cannot, but from which those interested in the conjunction of discipline and area studies can take something important. First, in a world of globalizing scholarship, we should be more explicit about what those who live elsewhere, but who have the facility to understand context, can do that indigenous scholars might not. Second, we should cultivate the ties with scholars elsewhere so that international collaboration and mutual recognition is as much a part of the area studies tradition as investing in learning languages and histories of distant places is.

These exemplars point toward ways in which we might codify the contributions area studies expertise makes to broader and more generalizing scholarship, and not only celebrate the ways in which area studies limits the generalizing ambitions of theorists. But it also helps us appreciate another important problem for area studies and globalizing knowledge cultures: What is the point of reference when we refer to the public good?

Exemplars in Public Engagement

Of course, area studies is funded not only to enhance scholarly excellence—it is designed first and foremost to contribute to the public good, and that happens through scholarship and especially teaching people to be better employees in   217 universities, government, and the private for-profit and not-for-profit sectors in a globalizing world. I propose, however, that those in area studies could do a better job in enhancing that contribution to that public good if area studies worked more explicitly on the ways in which publics are themselves constituted through scholarly work (Kennedy 2010).

For those within universities, our colleagues and students are the most immediate public. I especially appreciated one interlocutor who identified those who contribute to the basic infrastructure of those communities, and especially the capacities of those in the area studies with these examples:

> *Deborah Jakubs is one of the most important figures for area studies libraries and librarianship. Before becoming the Director of Duke's library, she was Duke's Latin American studies bibliographer (PhD from Stanford in Latin American history) and co-director of the Research Triangle's Latin America NRC. I also have enormous respect for Dan Hazen, currently the Associate Librarian of Harvard College, a Latin American scholar and previously bibliographer for Harvard's Latin America collection. Both have been exemplary practitioners of collection development. They have effectively collaborated with Latin Americanist colleagues in the States and abroad as well as across the boundaries of world regions. They have attracted foundation and other funding for their projects and programs. They have trained the next generation of bibliographers for area studies.*

Especially as one anticipates the digitalization of collections, and extending access to these resources to those beyond immediate publics, the value of such exemplary work as a global public good becomes even more apparent. Global media and transformations in information and communication technology offer remarkable ways in which to rethink the public impact of disciplines and area studies' engagements.

If our local colleagues and students are our most immediate public, those who have similar intellectual interests but are dispersed across the world are almost as proximate if new media are used effectively. Indeed, one of the greatest transformations in REES—the rapid growth and extension of anthropology—has in part to do with the exemplary work of those who did their fieldwork during the Cold War, but just as much with the self-organizing efforts of those younger scholars, those assistant and early associate and recently promoted full professors associated with an organization called Soyuz.

> *Soyuz is formally constituted as the Post-Communist Cultural Studies Interest Group of the American Anthropological Association (AAA) and is also recognized as an official unit of the American Association for the Advancement of Slavic Studies (AAASS). It is also more broadly conceived, first as a newsletter and now a web site, as an international congeries of anthropologists and other scholars working in postsocialist studies. We gather at AAA*

and AAASS meetings in North America, various conferences in Europe, and here on the web to distribute information on our projects (www.uvm.edu/~soyuz/frameset.html).

Not only has the group created new forms of community through the Internet, but it has also reached out across national traditions so that area studies is not just an American product but also a transnational public of scholars committed to thinking about postsocialist transformations in cultural terms. It has also had the positive by-product of making anthropology, not traditionally but now most certainly, among the most powerful elements of Russian, Eurasian, and East European studies (Rogers 2010).

Area studies' public engagement is, of course, designed to go beyond academic colleagues of the university. The most prominent example of this kind of outreach is in preuniversity education within the United States. There are many different kinds of outreach, as each area studies center must develop its own network. However, there are some units—for example, the Choices for the 21st Century Program at Brown University—that work across regions and directly in collaboration with policy makers to help clarify the ways in which contextual expertise could, and should, inform secondary education. Working with various experts, the program is dedicated to making complex issues understandable to high school students. Among its curricular units directly related to area studies traditions are packets concerning Mexico's identity and history from a Mexican perspective; the global impact of China's economic growth and societal transformation; the history of King Leopold's Congo Free State and the international debate about how to respond to it; Cuban history and especially the place of the Cuban missile crisis in the Cold War; the history of apartheid South Africa; Brazilian democratic transitions; and the partition of British India (www.choices.edu/about/index.php).

The media are another familiar partner for area studies' public engagement, and just as in secondary school outreach, there are many variations in approach. One exemplar for this kind of press outreach is Middle East Desk. It is distinctive among area studies networks for its work to connect journalists with experts from across the world on stories from the Middle East and North Africa. Not only does it help connect the press from various media to breaking stories, but it also works with the press to develop more substantial stories that go beyond the front pages. In addition, it provides powerful starting points for each country in the region—datebooks of newsworthy events, contact information for specialists, and a brief synopsis of the country's recent history and pressing issues (http://middleeastdesk.org/article. php?id=34).

In each of these cases, it is worth considering the conditions enabling such sustained engagement and originality. It is clear that individuals taking initiative and dedicating themselves beyond the conventions of careers make a difference, as do supporting networks within a university (such as Brown's Watson Institute for International Studies) or across places of employment and residence (such as the Middle East Research and Information Project). In both circumstances, consequential public engagement emerges from the sense that scholarship can improve not just policy expertise, but public discussion as well. One relatively new federal initiative brings both together in especially powerful fashion.

In the spring of 2008, Secretary of Defense Robert Gates announced a new initiative to identify and cultivate the kind of expertise needed in this era of national security. Invoking the National Defense Education Act of fifty years earlier, Gates recalled that

> *universities were vital centers of new research—often funded by the government—and also new ideas and even new fields of study such as game theory and Kremlinology.... As was the case at that time, the country is again trying to come to terms with new threats to national security. Rather than one, single entity—the Soviet Union—and one single animating ideology—communism—we are instead facing challenges from multiple sources: a new, more malignant form of terrorism inspired by jihadist extemism, ethnic strife, disease, poverty, climate change, failed and failing states, resurgent powers, and so on (www.defenselink.mil/speeches/speech.aspx?speechid=1228).*

Through what is now called the Minerva Research Initiative, the Department of Defense proposes to support social science research in a number of areas in which the nexus of area studies and disciplines resides. That, in turn, has spurred a substantial amount of discussion in a variety of academic settings. The American Anthropological Association has been especially prominent in the discussion, and the Social Science Research Council (SSRC) is trying to facilitate a more multidisciplinary discussion (http://essays.ssrc.org/minerva/).

Area studies, as a field, has steered relatively clear of that discussion, in part because of the relationship area studies has had to various federal government missions and the debates that have been scored around that. But the Minerva project is sufficiently complicated in intellectual, ethical, and political terms that it deserves more discussion. I am glad the SSRC has taken the lead on that interdisciplinary conversation, and that the American Anthropological Association has taken the disciplinary lead. Their conversations are ones that all area studies people should know and to which they might contribute more substantially. Indeed, by engaging publics as an object and partner in scholarship, area studies and disciplines might have even more fruitful collaborations. Minerva could even be the spark, but the more productive conversation could flow through an extension of Title VI.

Title VI funding has produced substantial benefits, both directly and indirectly, for policy makers and public understandings of various world regions. Each time applications for grant renewals are made, data are provided on the value of these investments. But unlike the debate around Minerva, these contributions remain out of sight, in part because they have become routine and taken for granted. One could be tempted to increase that visibility by asking for still more demonstrations of impact. One might, however, realize this in more effective fashion by implicating the question of Title VI value in larger discussions of the relationship between the academy and the public good.

One of the great changes in sociology—but not only for sociology—is for the discipline to rethink its relationship to various publics beyond the academy (Clawson et al. 2007). Anthropology has always been concerned about the ways in which knowledge travels, especially across national boundaries and through colonial and postcolonial networks; however, with the elevation of publics as an object of scholarship and partner in knowledge creation across broader parts of the disciplined academy, there might be opportunity for area studies to become newly tied with parts of scholarly communities not already embedded in these regions of interest. Developing a public social science of emerging democracies is one way to do that and is especially opportune for such area studies/international/discipline conversation (Kennedy, forthcoming). However, it can, and should be, complicated by questions of militarization.

Scholars including Cathy Lutz have already addressed the Minerva initiative in those very terms and examined how militarization itself could distort social science priorities and questions (http://essays.ssrc.org/minerva/2008/11/06/lutz). This work already is quite powerful in those regions where American military bases are long-standing (Lutz 2009); it would be additionally important to consider in places where American military engagement is presented as a bulwark against more recent and palpable threats. Certainly in Central and Eastern Europe, admission into NATO was cast in terms of enhancing democracy and security simultaneously, even if it was not universally understood as such among publics. Indeed, the relationship now between U.S. military support for Georgian independence and Georgian contributions to the war in Afghanistan suggest just how complex are the relationships among democracy, security, and independence—and why good area studies and good social science need to go together to develop an international public social science sufficiently grounded across contexts with public policy payoff.

Researching questions around militarization, democratization, and institution building is critical to good social science, area studies, and policy. It is even better if the debate focuses on the relationship among these trends unencumbered by questions of taint influenced by funding sources. Title VI has provided just such support for a long time, and could be extended again at this critical time.

Conclusions

As we rethink the relationship among area studies and disciplines, there is terrific value, I believe, to thinking relationally. In this chapter, I have managed to think only about variable relationships between disciplines and area studies in general. There are many more approaches we could and should consider, most especially in terms of how these relationships vary across universities and how the different organizational structures of universities afford different possibilities for local relationships among disciplines and area studies.

It is clear, however, that variations in disciplinary configurations are more prominent in defining the terms of the area studies–discipline relationships than are variations in area studies organization. Some disciplines are at home in area studies; some disciplinary and professional practitioners can treat area studies as data or service. Moreover, if the sense of area studies is compelling, some disciplinary practitioners can treat area studies as a powerful complement to what their discipline offers. To enhance the place of area studies, that contingent relationship ought to be addressed directly.

I have proposed that area studies practitioners could and should embrace, but also move beyond, the emphasis on language learning and historical sensitivity to make more explicit what theoretical and methodological expertise area studies brings to the global and comparative conversation. By making more explicit new forms of comparative study and kinds of data that defy simple translation, by highlighting the importance of interpreting semiotic structures and emotions, even those who are only interested in patterns across time and place might find value in the expertise brought by area studies.

But I am not only proposing supplementation. By taking the invitation to public engagement as something more than service and rather a central object and partner in scholarly work, area studies could be poised to reframe its place in the scholarly discussion. Publics are not only respondents to surveys or even occasional contributors to translated focus group transcripts. Publics are made by the issues that are brought to them, that they themselves inspire, and that together with scholars they can reframe. Indeed, I can imagine fewer more important discussions than the relationship among militarizations, publics, and democracy across the world and how transformations in global media might change those ties. Scholars are in the middle of that conversation—or at least they ought to be.

In the end, however, what is central to our common interests across area studies and disciplines is to rethink how the scholarly value of the encounter between area studies and the disciplines can be elevated. I have previously thought, but am now even more convinced, that area studies would benefit profoundly by more self-conscious reflection on theories and methodologies, especially those that could clarify the implicit claims of area studies to superior grounding and capacities for translation with new articulations of comparative studies and contextual expertise. This is not to say that area studies lacks theory or methods; what I do believe to be true is that our theoretical and methodological discussion rarely crosses disciplines and regions both. Both would be well served by that effort.

All these scholarly enhancements, however, are unlikely to be so productive for discussions of area studies vigor when disciplines control the terms of academic distinction and external funders define the conditions of organizational success. However, given the potentials for new relationships between knowledge production and publics, and the discussions taking place within disciplines and within universities and across them, not only within nations but across the world, we have new opportunities for foregrounding area studies in the elaboration of relationships among scholars and global publics. This extended reflection on disciplinary relationships to area studies is a small contribution, I hope, to that extended scholarly reflexivity in the public good.

Acknowledgments

This paper was previously presented at the [U.S. Department of Education] Title VI 50th Anniversary Conference, March 2009 and Yale University, MacMillan Center, February 2009. Thanks above all to David Wiley and Robert Grew for their leadership in this common project and their commentary on my paper; to those who discussed earlier versions of this paper at Yale and in Washington, D.C., as well as at the University of Washington–Seattle during a lunchtime roundtable discussion. I especially want to thank my live and e-mail interlocutors—Jeff Wasserstrom, James Nye, Michele Rivkin-Fish, Marcia Inhorn, Milada Vachudova, Richard Turits, Marilyn Booth, Megan Greene, Matti Zelin, Susan Brantly, Anne Betteridge, Ding Xiang Warner, Gail Kligman, Edith Clowes, Garth Myers, Michele Lamont, Neil Fligstein, Carmen Diana Deere, Genevieve Zubrzycki, Maria Todorova, Gil Eyal, Joanna Regulska, Mark Beissinger, Matt Sparke, Merilee Grindle, Doug Rogers, Richard Tempest, Beth Mitchneck, Sharon Hutchinson, Yuri Slezkine, Zsuzsa Gille, Sue Gal, Leigh Payne, Ted Hopf, Craig Calhoun, Charlie Kurzman, Amie Kreppel, Andreas Glaeser, Stephen Hanson, Gay Seidman, Alberta Spraggia, James Greene, Barbara Watson Andaya, Zsuzsa Gille, Andreas Glaeser, Gottfried Hagen, Cindy Buckley, Barbara Anderson, Gayl Ness, Laura Engelstein, Bob Hayden, Kate Weaver, Nezar AlSayyad, Mejgan Massoumi, Katherine Verdery, Jim McCann, Joseph Lam, Will Glover, Edna Andrews, Yana Hashamova, Mitchell Orenstein, David Ransel, Doug Northrop, Linda Lim, John Lie, John Micgiel, Katy Fleming, others who prefer to be anonymous, and especially Shiva Balaghi, who is my discussion partner every day, even around area studies and the disciplines.

REFERENCES

Abbott, Andrew. 2001. *The Chaos of Disciplines.* Chicago: University of Chicago Press.

Beissinger, Mark. 2009. "Political Science and the Future of Russian/Post-Soviet Studies," remarks given at the Davis Center's 60th Anniversary Celebration.

Clawson, Dan, Robert Zussman, Joya Misra, Naomi Gerstel, Randall Stokes, Douglas L. Anderston, and Michael Burawoy (eds.). 2007. *Public Sociology: Fifteen Eminent Sociologists Debate Politics and the Profession in the Twenty-First Century.* Berkeley: University of California Press.

Bowen, John. 2004. "The Development of Southeast Asian Studies in the United States," pp. 386–425 in David Szanton (ed.). *The Politics of Knowledge: Area Studies and the Disciplines.* Berkeley: University of California Press.

Cohen, David William and Michael D. Kennedy (eds.). 2004. *Responsibility in Crisis: Knowledge Politics and Global Publics.* Ann Arbor: University of Michigan Scholarly Publishing Office.

Cumings, Bruce. 2002. "Boundary Displacement: the State, the Foundations, and Area Studies during and after the Cold War," pp. 261–302 in Miyoshi, Masao and H. D. Harootunian (eds.). *Learning Places: The Afterlives of Area Studies.* Durham, NC: Duke University Press.

Derluguian, Georgi. 2005. *Bourdieu's Secret Admirer in the Caucasus: A World System Biography.* Chicago: University of Chicago Press.

Dirks, Nicholas B. 2004. "South Asian Studies: Futures Past," pp. 341–85 in David Szanton (ed.). *The Politics of Knowledge: Area Studies and the Disciplines.* Berkeley: University of California Press.

Engerman, David C. 2009. *Know Your Enemy: The Rise and Fall of America's Soviet Experts.* New York: Oxford University Press.

Gilman, Nils. 2003. *Mandarins of the Future: Modernization Theory in Cold War America.* Baltimore: Johns Hopkins Press.

Hanson, Stephen E. 2009. "The Contribution of Area Studies," pp. 159–74 in Todd Landman and Neil Robinson (eds.). *The Sage Handbook of Comparative Politics.* Los Angeles: Sage Publications.

Heilbron, Johan. 2009. "La sociologie européenne existe-t-elle?", pp. 347–58 in Gièle Sapiro (ed.), *L'espace intellectuel en Europe. De la formation des États-nations à la mondialisation XIXe-XXe siècles.* Paris: La Découverte.

Kennedy, Michael D. forthcoming. "A Public Sociology of Emerging Democracies: Revolution, Gender Inequalities and Energy Security," *Bulletin of University of Lviv: Sociological Series (Issue 3)* ("Вісник Львівського університету. Серія соціологічна". Випуск 3).

———. 2010. "Cultural Formations of the Public University: Globalization, Diversity, and the State at the University of Michigan," in Craig Calhoun and Diana Rhoten (eds.). *Knowledge Matters: The Public Mission of the Research University.* New York: Columbia University Press.

———. 2008, "From Transition to Hegemony: Extending the Cultural Politics of Military Alliances and Energy Security," in Mitchell Orenstein, Steven Bloom, and Nicole Lindstrom (eds.), *Transnational Actors in Central and East European Transitions.* Pittsburgh: University of Pittsburgh Press.

———. 2004. "Poland in the American Sociological Imagination," *Polish Sociological Review* 4(148):361–83.

———. 2000. "On Collaboration and Diversity," *Journal of the International Institute* 7(2):14–15.

———. and Miguel Centeno. 2007. "Internationalism and Global Transformations in American Sociology," pp. 666–712 in Craig Calhoun (ed.). *Sociology in America: A History.* Chicago: University of Chicago Press/An American Sociological Association Centennial Publication.

———. and Elaine Weiner. 2003. "The Articulation of International Expertise in the Professions," prepared for presentation at the conference on Global Challenges and U.S. Higher Education, Duke University, January. http://ducis.jhfc.duke.edu/archives/globalchallenges/pdf/kennedy-paper.pdf.

Lutz, Catherine (ed.). 2009. *The Bases of Empire: The Global Struggle against U.S. Military Posts.* New York: New York University Press.

Matsumoto, David and Bob Willingham. 2006. "The Thrill of Victory and the Agony of Defeat: Spontaneous Expressions of Medal Winners of the 2004 Athens Olympics Games," *Journal of Personality and Social Psychology* 91:568–91.

Mirsepassi, Ali, Amrita Basu, and Frederick Weaver (eds.). 2003. *Localizing Knowledge in a Globalizing World: Recasting the Area Studies Debate.* Syracuse, NY: Syracuse University Press.

Mitchell, Timothy. 2004. "The Middle East in the Past and Future of Social Sciences," pp. 74–118 in David Szanton (ed.). *The Politics of Knowledge: Area Studies and the Disciplines.* Berkeley: University of California Press.

Miyoshi, Masao and H. D. Harootunian (eds.). 2002. *Learning Places: The Afterlives of Area Studies.* Durham, NC: Duke University Press.

O'Meara, Patrick, Howard and Carolee Mehlinger, and Roxana Ma Newman. 2001. *Changing Perspectives on International Education.* Bloomington: Indiana University Press.

Rogers, Douglas. 2010. "Postsocialisms Unbound: Connections, Critiques, Comparisons," *Slavic Review,* 69:1–15.

Ruther, Nancy L. 2002. *Barely There, Powerfully Present: Thirty Years of U.S. Policy on International Higher Education.* New York: Routledge.

225

Sewell, William H. Jr. 1967. "Marc Bloch and the Logic of Comparative History," *History and Theory* 6(2):208–18.

———. 2005. *Logics of History: Social Theory and Social Transformation.* Chicago: University of Chicago Press.

Szanton, David. 2004. "The Origin, Nature, and Challenges of Area Studies in the United States," pp. 1–33 in David Szanton (ed.). *The Politics of Knowledge: Area Studies and the Disciplines.* Berkeley: University of California Press.

Sztompka, Piotr. 2007. "Review," *American Journal of Sociology*, 113(3): 918–920.

Tansman, Allan. 2004. "Japanese Studies: The Intangible Act of Translation," pp. 184–216 in David Szanton (ed.). *The Politics of Knowledge: Area Studies and the Disciplines.* Berkeley: University of California Press.

U.S. Department of Education, International Education Programs Service, International Resource Information System. http://iris.ed.gov/iris/ieps/.

Walder, Andrew G. 2004. "The Transformation of Contemporary China Studies, 1977–2002," pp. 314–40 in David Szanton (ed.). *The Politics of Knowledge: Area Studies and the Disciplines.* Berkeley: University of California Press.

Wallerstein, Immanuel. 1997. "The Unintended Consequences of Cold War Area Studies," pp. 195–232 in Andre Schiffrin (ed.). *The Cold War and the University: Toward an Intellectual History of the Postwar Years.* New York: New Press.

Yurczak, Alexei. 2006. *Everything Was Forever, Until It Was No More: The Last Soviet Generation.* Princeton, NJ: Princeton University Press.

Zubrzycki, Genevieve. 2006. *The Crosses of Auschwitz: Nationalism and Religion in Post-Communist Poland.* Chicago: University of Chicago Press.

CHAPTER 11

Renewing International Studies: Regional and Transregional Studies in a Changing Intellectual Field

Craig Calhoun

There are both public and scholarly reasons to wish for a renewal of international studies in American universities. Such a renewal would serve not only foreign policy but also private voluntary action, private business, and critical public awareness. Because U.S. universities have long been leaders in international studies, renewal—which the Title VI programs could lead—would be of global value. It would also make for intellectually exciting scholarship.

To be successful, renewal would mean not just more teaching and research on international topics, but also better connections across a several disciplines, interdisciplinary programs, and professional schools. Overcoming current fragmentation, international studies programs could better address the connections among local, national, regional, and global processes and deepen knowledge of the intertwined roles of culture, geography, politics, natural resources, markets, religions, and social solidarities.

Stronger international research and teaching would recognize not only the enduring importance of regions but also the ways regions are being reshaped by internal integration—in Asia as well as Europe; by shifting geopolitics that encourage new attention to previously neglected regions such as Central Asia; and by transregional connections, from media and migrations to world religions and world music. Understanding the changing terrain would require drawing on and renewing the expertise developed and taught within traditional area studies fields. But

227

traditional areas do not exhaust the relevant contexts. Cross-cutting connections from long-distance trading routes to zones of shared environmental concern require research that connects different areas as well as disciplines and professional fields.

Effective renewal thus cannot be a matter of restoration. It will not come simply by increasing resources for old institutional structures or intellectual perspectives; it will require both institutional and intellectual innovation. Many of the structures for international studies reflect the way international affairs looked to American leaders half a century ago. Renewal today means teaching different languages, approaching culture in terms of current creativity as well as historical civilizations, and analyzing politics in an increasingly multilateral world with new geopolitical issues.

Repairing the damage done by neglect of older area studies fields during the past thirty years is vital. However, it needs to be pursued in ways that encourage transregional research, attention to neglected areas, and participation in problem-focused inquiries. Area studies are vastly more important in a larger, collaborative field of international studies than by themselves. Indeed, much of the best area studies work has long been part of such broader inquiries. But to renew these strengths, area scholars need to overcome ambivalence toward both interdisciplinary international studies and professional schools—including not only schools of international affairs but also faculties of law, business, education, public health, medicine, and others.

This is a challenging prescription for area studies fields thrown on the defensive by neglect from funders, hostility from some social science disciplines, and a vogue for thinking of globalization in universal rather than contextual perspective. But many in area studies have already started.

To further the process, I propose in this chapter to reconsider the development of the tacit division of labor among area studies, disciplines, and professional schools and its transformation in recent years with shifting interests of funders and the rise of new interdisciplinary agendas. Although interest in area studies fields is currently being renewed, the future remains challenging. My hope is that all those interested in international studies may approach this future as collaborators more than rivals.

A Three-Way Division of Labor

In the wake of each of the two great World Wars of the twentieth century, intellectuals and public leaders argued that Americans paid too little attention to the international diversity of peoples, cultures, states, markets, media, and conflicts that shape the world. Universities responded with both curricular changes and new institutional structures for research and scholarship.

Three broad approaches emerged: disciplines, area studies fields, and professional schools. These can briefly be summarized as (1) the pursuit of innovation and cumulative knowledge based on analytic perspectives that disaggregate complex social phenomena into potential general variables, relationships, and causal mechanisms and usually minimize attention to context (a mainly disciplinary approach in the social sciences); (2) the attempt to gain a comprehensive view of social life in specific contexts, connections, and/or concrete complexity (especially in the area studies fields, though also, to some extent, in history and at least certain older styles of anthropology); and (3) the development of approaches to professional practice or public problems informed by knowledge from different disciplines and interdisciplinary fields.

Disciplinary departments were already gaining strength as the primary organizational units of American universities before World War I. This has continued, complemented but never really challenged by growth of interdisciplinary fields within the arts and sciences. The growth of professional schools has been a substantial development not always considered in discussions of academic international studies.

The founding of professional schools started after World War I. Georgetown's School of Foreign Service was founded in 1919, and its very name signals the emphasis on training for diplomatic service that dominated in this period. The University of Southern California followed in 1924, Princeton's Woodrow Wilson School in 1930, and the Fletcher School of Law and Diplomacy at Tufts in 1933. All had similar initial emphases. They were creatures of private universities engaged in training elites for public service, especially in diplomacy.[1]

Area studies took its modern form in the era after World War II. The University of Chicago was perhaps the most important early center for area studies, but several state universities, such as the University of Michigan, were also among the leaders. The development of area studies was closely shaped by foundation philanthropy and by the mediation of interdisciplinary committees organized through the Social Science Research Council (SSRC) and the American Council of Learned Societies (ACLS). At the same time, several academic disciplines strengthened their engagements in international research—from comparative politics to development economics.

The primary institutionalization of international studies in the postwar era was thus a tripartite division of labor. The parties to this division of labor were disciplines in the social sciences and humanities, the emergent area studies fields, and a growing number of professional schools. The terms of the division of labor were never clear, and relations among disciplines, area studies fields, and professional 229 schools have changed over time. Especially from the 1970s, many social science disciplines pursued different agendas at the expense of interdisciplinary area studies. Unlike the professional schools, the area studies programs seldom had control of autonomous faculty appointments.

By the 1950s, the basic structure of area studies fields and professional schools of international affairs that remains central today was in place. New fields were added and some fields were redefined—as, for example, studies of the U.S.S.R. grew prominent in programs previously structured as Slavic studies. Crises during the 1960s and 1970s brought more critical lines of analysis, not least in Southeast Asian studies. Calls for renewal in international studies after the Cold War shifted the balance away from area studies and brought in more studies of globalization as such. At the same time, interdisciplinary international studies emerged as a rapidly growing field of undergraduate study. Perhaps most important, area studies lost favor with many funders; the structure of centers and programs commonly remained in place, but with diminished resources. At the same time, professional schools of international affairs grew significantly and international studies in other professional schools such as business, law, and public health grew even more.

Area Studies

There is, of course, a prehistory to the development of area studies programs after World War II. European engagements with various definitions of "the Orient" stretch back centuries. The early twentieth century popularity of Orientalist inquiries led to the founding of Chicago's Oriental Institute and a range of other anticipations of area studies. However, these were for the most part structured with an emphasis on the ancient. Colonialism brought the formation of new kinds of knowledge focused on the contemporary lives of non-Western peoples.[2] Missionary work was another source of ethnological inquiry. The combination of humanistic and social science inquiry, however, was basic to the new area studies fields.

Together with the National Academy of Sciences, the SSRC (representing the social sciences) and ACLS (representing the humanities) launched an exploratory Committee on World Area Research at the end of World War II. This was the proximate source for the creation of a more or less comprehensive program of regionally focused committees to set agendas and sponsor training. Some of these had older roots; the SSRC had launched a Committee on Latin America in 1941 and run projects on China since the 1920s. The SSRC was active in the development of the modern fields of international relations and comparative politics. The SSRC and ACLS worked largely as mediators between the growing world of foundation-administered

philanthropy (and sometimes government programs) and academic researchers.

In 1950, the Ford Foundation began the Foreign Area Fellowship Program, but soon turned its administration over to the joint SSRC-ACLS committees on different world areas. Ford put nearly $300 million into this project, and in due course it was joined by other foundations and by the U.S. government, which made major investments in foreign language teaching and foreign area research. Today, many social scientists regard this as largely an investment in the humanities. Social scientists were, however, central to the area studies project. It is only in the past thirty-some years that area studies programs have tilted toward humanities fields. This is largely the result of secession by social scientists, not conquest by humanists.

The area studies fields differed from each other in the extent to which research and teaching focused on contemporary politics or civilizational history, and different disciplines accordingly figured more or less prominently. None escaped the influence of the Cold War, but this was, not surprisingly, most definitive for Russian and East European studies, including the demarcation of the region itself. South Asian studies certainly confronted political issues, but concentrated more on civilization and culture. In addition, there were other characteristic thematic foci in different area studies fields. Economic development was front and center for Latin American studies, thus, as were later questions about dictatorship and democracy. The formation of "new nations" was a key theme for African studies. Middle East studies could never escape the problems of Palestine and Israel, although questions about nationalism, political institutions, and religion appeared in other forms as well.

During the postwar period, despite their differences, all the area studies fields shared a broad intellectual orientation associated with the idea of modernization.[3] Economic development, political reform, and the creation of new national institutions, transformation of social institutions, expansion of literacy and consequent cultural production, and even change in psychological attitudes were all seen as parts of a common process. If modernization described what was shared in this process, different histories and cultures shaped distinctive patterns in each region. This connected work in the area studies fields to disciplinary agendas.

The connection, however, came unstuck. There was a fault line as old as the *methodenstreit* and the very distinction—always contested—between social sciences and humanities.[4] Leaders in many social science disciplines (not so much anthropology or history, which had strong humanistic sides) understood themselves to pursue generalizations. The area studies fields, in contrast, seemed to be particularizing, focused on the specifics of local conjunctures of history, culture, politics, and even environment. Social science knowledge was widely held to be nomothetic, abstracting from such specifics to establish more universal laws.

This was always a caricature of area studies research, and perhaps a misunderstanding of what social science disciplines themselves achieved. It is easy to mock 231 either side: the psychologist who thought human nature could be found in experiments involving only white, middle class, male American undergraduates; the anthropologist who responded to every assertion of a more general causal pattern with "well, it's not exactly so on the island I studied." There is a point of more basic significance, however.

The area studies projects, at their best, were not so much about idiographic particulars as about the various different ways to be human, to be social, to be political, and even to have markets—and therefore suggested that the pursuit of more general knowledge required working with attention to specific historical and cultural contexts and patterns. Such knowledge could be of broad application without being abstractly universal. Indeed, the area studies fields contributed to major analytic perspectives that far transcended their initial sites of development. Benedict Anderson's account of nationalism as a matter of imagined communities was informed by Southeast Asian studies, thus, but not contained by it.[5] The same is true of James Scott's effort to understand states, the ways state leaders saw societies, and projects of central planning.[6] Dependency theory, shaped by the UN's Economic Commission on Latin America, as well as work in Latin American universities, developed as an effort to understand specifically Latin American problems, as did Albert Hirschman's work on development assistance and unbalanced growth.[7] The "world systems theory" of Immanuel Wallerstein and colleagues was deeply shaped by African studies as well as by Braudelian global history and Marxist political economy and, indeed, the earlier Latin American dependency theories.[8]

Each of these examples became part of interdisciplinary discussions—of development and underdevelopment, class and power, power and knowledge, states and nations. Of these, only development studies really became an academic field of its own—and in the United States it developed relatively weakly, dominated by disciplinary economics and narrowed to questions about growth; it is institutionalized more substantially in Britain and some other settings. Marxism was for a time a vital interdisciplinary discussion, with strong social movement links, but never with strong academic institutionalization (outside the communist countries, where Marxism was itself an academic discipline). Wallerstein's Fernand Braudel Center at Binghamton was influential but not widely imitated. If political economy remains a topic or perspective that many social scientists would claim, its base of intellectual reproduction is not well established. Indeed, a renewal of interdisciplinary political economy that is neither sectarian nor narrowed simply to questions of growth may be one of the attractive prospects on the current agenda.[9]

This points to a more general challenge for interdisciplinary work. When it lacks institutional conditions of reproduction, it is at the mercy of disciplines that many either claim it or ignore it or—most often—incorporate some ideas from interdisciplinary projects without providing ways of sustaining the intellectual ferment that produced them.

The area studies fields demonstrate the force of this. In the 1950s and 1960s, the area studies fields were relatively well financed and often able to offer support to students not funded by their disciplinary departments. There was a new infusion of students—many drawn to their future areas of study by missionary, diplomatic, or Peace Corps service. More generally, while the university system expanded, there were jobs for the political scientists and sociologists with area studies emphases (without much taking away from opportunities for those engaged in disciplinary work that was de facto North American area studies).

Whereas a few universities set up autonomous departments of Latin American or East Asian studies, many more set up interdisciplinary committees or centers. These have had enough institutionalization—and enough external demands for the kinds of knowledge they produce and determination by committed scholars—to survive lengthy periods of disinterest or hostility from the core social science disciplines. Regional studies associations have been important. Despite the strong and influential work rooted in area studies in the later 1960s and 1970s, however, these fields never gained enduring capacity for autonomous reproduction. Area studies programs seldom ran the PhD programs in which future faculty were trained, and they needed the cooperation of disciplinary departments to make new hires and to award tenure.

Pivotal Change in the 1970s

Academic expansion slowed in the 1970s. A shortage of faculty jobs brought sharp tightening of tenure standards and disciplinary departments exercised discipline by rewarding intradisciplinary achievement. Graduate students felt new pressures to demonstrate disciplinary publications before entering the job market. These pressures were generally more acute higher in the academic pecking order, and in programs focused more on training future professors than producing applied researchers, but they were present throughout. In much of the social sciences, there was growing emphasis on quantification and the pursuit of context-independent knowledge.

Area studies programs saw their proportionate funding—and influence—decline, partly because of a structural shift. Area studies programs had long been an attractive source of funds for graduate students—few of whom had dependable financial assistance from their departments. When undergraduate enrollments began to grow faster than faculty recruitment, especially after the 1970s, teaching assistantships became increasingly important. These were administered mainly by 233 disciplinary departments. By the 1980s and 1990s, efforts to shrink cohorts and provide multiyear funding packages further consolidated disciplinary control.

Of course, other factors were at work during the same period. Many area studies programs suffered during the conflicts of the 1960s and early 1970s. There was high student interest, but a younger generation challenged older faculty members (including many associated with modernization theory). The Vietnam War was enormously influential, but the 1973 Yom Kippur War, the coups against democratic governments in Latin America, and the Iranian revolution also intensified disputes over different kinds of U.S. government engagements and funding. Senior area studies faculty members were attacked from the left for complicity with American counterinsurgency programs (that sometimes turned into counterdemocracy programs). They were attacked from the right for being too critical and for emphasizing too much the point of view of those they studied. Area studies programs remained sites of political controversy—sometimes intellectually productive, but commonly problematic for their capacity to maintain standing within universities. They nurtured critical intellectual perspectives, but their bases for academic reproduction were undercut. By the 1980s, business school enrollments were rising, there was a backlash against activist social science, and as the decade wore on disciplines turned away from engagements with context-specific knowledge as well as a variety of core political questions.

During the 1970s, the very idea of development—and especially development assistance and planned interventions in support of development—was increasingly challenged. Initially critiques came largely from the left, but by the 1980s, a neoliberal market alternative was clearly in the ascendancy. There was a critique of how much development funding was tied to support of domestic industries in donor states. There was a critique of the high cost of expatriate consultants. There was a critique of dependency, and not just the extent to which some developing countries became stuck in a dead-end economics of aid dependency but also the political problems created by close relationships with some developing country elites and international donors. There was a critique of the way notions of unilinear progress (following Western European or American trajectories) were smuggled into much thinking about development (and modernization). Perhaps most basically, there was the argument that the issues were structural, and that development assistance could not overcome the inequalities of the world system.

The recession of 1973–1975 played at least as big a role as arguments in political economy. Non-oil-producing developing countries felt the impact of OPEC's price increases directly.[10] But the recession also contributed to a backlash against foreign aid, and this dovetailed with growing hostility to a variety of government spending programs. This began an era in which there was an ironic confluence of left-wing and right-wing hostility to the state—anti-authoritarian 1960s rebels and Hayekian individualists were never allies, but were both suspicious of big government. So, when Margaret Thatcher pioneered what eventually became know as neoliberalism in Britain and Ronald Reagan followed suit in the United States, opposition was more muted and less coherent than it might have been.

In many social science disciplines, academic initiative turned away from theory (including more or less critical theory) and context-specific research (including small-N comparisons as well as case studies) and toward more or less formal methods.[11] Economics effectively seceded from the area studies interdisciplinary fields as it relied increasingly on mathematical models and on approaches (some lumped together as neoliberal) that stressed more or less universal microfoundations. Economists who retained strong area interests often wound up outside economics departments (and thus disciplinary reproduction). Many were based in interdisciplinary programs—not just area studies but also urban studies, policy analysis, development studies, and, indeed, business schools (which were interested in countries like China even when mainstream economics departments were not); others worked for the World Bank, the UN, or other nonacademic institutions. More unevenly, political science followed the lead of economics, increasingly emphasizing formal methods such as game theory and rational choice analysis and their application in context-independent ways (although, in principle, they could be combined with case-specific analysis). The pattern was less clear-cut in sociology, but it was influenced by the same trends.[12] During the same period, psychology moved more and more toward experimental research and toward closer links to biological and cognitive sciences. Even though they had perhaps never been at the core of area studies, cross-cultural research and research on psychological correlates of "modernization" had made for stronger connections in an earlier period, and these dwindled.[13]

The result was that social science engagement with area studies declined sharply during the last third of the twentieth century. Some political scientists and sociologists continued to do international field research, but their numbers dwindled. Anthropology was better represented in area studies, but also grew closer to the humanities and less connected to other social sciences. This is not a pattern limited to area studies; these fields are simply among those most deeply influenced by the rift between the humanities (and "soft" social sciences) and those social sciences that have conceived themselves as purveyors of hard, objective knowledge and more or less formal models. Connections between the humanities and social sciences peaked at the end of the 1970s, and already many in the humanities had begun a "cultural turn." This was often informed by poststructuralism, whereas many in the social sciences took a formalist, quantitative turn. History, which   235 straddled the division of social sciences from humanities, reasserted its humanistic identity after an era when "social science history" was ascendant.

Funding Issues

Along with other interdisciplinary fields, area studies have confronted recurrent funding challenges. Flourishing during a general expansion of academia does not guarantee staying power during a retrenchment. Interdisciplinary programs often offer intellectual stimulation and the excitement of innovation in flush times, but the tools of disciplinary control are strengthened by recession. This happened in the 1970s. In straitened circumstances, disciplines competed more effectively for scarce funds. Moreover, inside some disciplines—especially in the social sciences —there was a consolidation around "core" disciplinary agendas that reduced the space and support for area studies. Decline during the 1980s was mostly a matter of attrition (and the targeting of other fields) in tight job markets.

As the SSRC and ACLS had been pioneers of area studies, events at each epitomized the crisis.[14] Both the Ford and Mellon foundations withdrew their support for area studies committees. Neither abandoned international studies, however. Mellon, for example, continues to fund a large SSRC–ACLS fellowship program for international fieldwork. Ford gives international grants and runs offices around the world (although some have been closed in the wake of the 2008–2009 market crisis and amid shifting priorities). But academic area studies no longer seemed to most foundation funders to be an effective structure through which to encourage the international knowledge formation they wanted.[15]

With less drama and more complexity, and over a somewhat longer term, U.S. government funding also was reduced. Through the 1950s and 1960s, a range of programs had been founded that brought international students to study in the United States—programs that were central to the education of two generations of academics, professionals, and public leaders. Other programs supported U.S. academics in research abroad or helped to build linkages between American institutions and foreign counterparts. This work was focused especially on the developing countries. Much was organized through the United States Agency for International Development (USAID), although there were separate programs in a range of government departments and agencies, from Agriculture through Commerce and State as well as Education—and the Defense Department and intelligence agencies. A wide variety of universities participated, but especially important were the land-grant universities—Michigan State, Penn State, Iowa State, Wisconsin, Ohio State, Maryland—in which academic area studies programs could enjoy a synergy with professional schools and applied research programs, and where a disproportionate number of international graduate students received education.

Loss of the broad modernization-development consensus brought increasing quarrels within academic area studies fields and between them and more discipline-oriented social scientists. It also meant that there was no longer a tacit agreement between the academics and those who funded area studies, or between researchers and those engaged in practical action. The modernization-development framework may have been only loosely related to the work of many area studies scholars, but it provided a basis for congressional appropriations and foundation grants that was never replaced. The rhetoric of "internationalization" and "globalization" that has flourished for the past thirty years has never had a comparable theoretical underpinning, has never suggested as clear a relationship to improving human living conditions or, melioration of social problems, and has never been clear about the importance of context-specific knowledge as distinct from the global circulation of allegedly universalistic knowledge or best practices.

Some of the programs that started in the 1950s and 1960s survived all this and remain important. The Title VI program is a flagship among them. But some did not survive and many were diverted away from universities and away from the too-often critical humanities and social science faculties in universities. Think tanks and independent, nonacademic research organizations flourished, becoming something of a buffer between academic research communities and government and other policy makers. An organization such as the Center for Strategic and International Studies (CSIS) is indicative. Founded at the height of the Cold War in 1962, CSIS was initially based at Georgetown but became a free-standing organization in 1971. Over time, it incorporated the Pacific Forum and other organizations and hired a variety of specialists on different regions of the world as well as different policy issues. It continues to be organized with regional programs complementing programs on strategic issues and remains oriented to a combination of policy makers and diplomats. CSIS and many other nonacademic centers are reputable and serious; there are also a range of organizations more closely tied to government-funded applied research (and sometimes called "Beltway bandits"). But even the best such organizations have had the effect of reducing the synergies between government-funded applied research and academic area studies, reducing the extent to which universities are a resource for policy makers, diplomats, and others and reducing the extent to which critical voices and dissident perspectives are able to inform policy and public debates. At the same time, although there is more international work based in professional fields, the links to academic area studies are weak—and accordingly their practical concerns are often pursued without strong contextual knowledge.

237

Foundation support partially compensated for lost or redirected government funding for a time. Ford, Mellon, and others were major supporters of academic area studies during the 1970s and 1980s. But this concealed a vulnerability, for foundations as a group tend to dislike being long-term sustainers of fields and other projects: They seek to help launch new ventures, to be supporters of young and growing efforts, and then to withdraw as these projects become sustainable on other bases. The same goes for the SSRC, which supported area studies through the joint committees about three times as long as it ever supported any other program. Thus, when the foundations reduced their support and tried to orient it away from core funding to specific projects, this was devastating for the area studies fields. It changed the role of Title VI, which became much more often a primary source of funding instead of a complement to other resources. Behind this was the failure of universities to develop secure long-term bases and funding streams for academic area studies and the fraught relationship between these interdisciplinary programs and disciplinary departments.

I will not try to reproduce the whole story of either the 1990s crisis or changes in funding. But material conditions are important today as reasons for innovation rather than attempted restoration in international studies. Most foundations and most government funders focus mainly on trying to address practical problems in the world. Their support for the renewal of area studies will not come mainly from valuing them in themselves but rather from valuing their contributions to other, especially problem-focused, inquiries. Neither disciplinary pursuit of generalizations nor purely problem-focused inquiries can substitute for necessary context-specific knowledge, but neither will area studies be self-justifying.

As a broad pattern, foundation leaders have always sought to improve the human condition. They once believed that investing in social science generally, and area studies in particular, was a terrific way to do this. By the 1990s, few believed any more that this was efficient, even if they still thought social science or area studies to be good in themselves. Today, most prefer to try to work directly to pursue change, usually without any lengthy detour through attempts to improve knowledge. They prefer to work on specific problems—AIDS, women's education, small-business support—but not necessarily on the larger contexts in which those problems are embedded. Moreover, foundations' favored partners are not academics (who are seen as expensive, slow, and motivated by self-interest—every academic report ends by calling for more research, not enabling action). They are at least as often nongovernmental organizations (NGOs), service providers, and community organizations. This is especially true of newer foundations. Even among the old, though, the Mellon Foundation is distinctive for its continuing commitment to academic humanities scholarship and related work in the social sciences. In general, foundations want to be close to the action and they like the new, not the continuing. Each wave of new presidents and program directors brings calls for change and, indeed, grant renewals and the duration of grants have both declined.

Of course, many other issues—too many to cover here—also made for change in area studies. Shifts in the Peace Corps reduced what had been an important recruitment path.[16] Some other voluntary action programs remain important sources of student interests in other places, although increasingly this is channeled into professional or quasiprofessional programs, not area studies. At the same time, students from the various world regions who were native speakers of local languages came to figure more and more prominently in area studies. This enriched them with new connections to the different regions. Students spending less time studying languages often learned new methods and brought active theoretical engagements into area studies fields. At the same time, however, this shifted the context for those who needed language study.

Not least, there was the difficulty many in area studies fields had in coming up with a strong forward-looking account of the value of their fields when they were attacked. This was partly because the leaders in the 1980s and 1990s, were children of the 1960s. They had spent much of their careers attacking previous orthodoxies and power structures. As David Szanton remarked, when funders began to rethink their support, "Area Studies was under attack from scholars in several fields who in general argued that Area Studies had been an invention of the Cold War [and] reflected US political interests and Eurocentric prejudices."[17] These attacks often came from area studies scholars. In fact, the critiques themselves were part of a transformation of those fields, and when crisis came in the 1990s the Cold War heritage was much attenuated. But self-critique was not a persuasive sales pitch. More generally, after being thrown onto the defensive, area studies researchers found it difficult to articulate positive and proactive agendas. Many spent too much time restating the importance of the regions they studied, the scarcity of expertise, and the difficulty of the skills they had spent years acquiring (none of which countered the charge of particularism). All the points were sound, but they did not in themselves clarify to funders what area studies scholarship was good for. And, of course, under, members of different area studies communities often defended their particular regional concerns rather than making effective common cause.

With further irony, the end of the Cold War encouraged a dramatic expansion in international work conceived as directly global—that is, about what might in principle happen everywhere— rather than as context-specific. Attention to globalization came at the expense of attention to the specific regional and other contexts through which globalization was refracted and in which it took on different meanings. Professional schools of international and public affairs were beneficiaries not only of the focus on globalization but also of the desire of many young people to make a career of practical engagement with global issues—human rights, emergency relief, development, or working conditions, to name a few.

Professional Schools

Many discussions of international studies have been framed in terms of conflicts between disciplines and area studies fields. These conflicts have been real and remain important, but focusing only on them neglects two other significant phenomena: (1) the actual growth in universities (and much of the growth in international studies) has occurred largely outside arts and sciences departments—in professional schools and problem-focused research centers;[18] and (2) the ecology of academic fields has changed, making the places of both "disciplines" and "area studies" less clear. Differences in analytic approaches have opened divides among social science disciplines, between some social science disciplines and the humanities, and within some social science and humanities fields. New interdisciplinary clusters have also been created—notably around decisions and rationality, around formal modeling, and around neuroscience and cognition.

It is also noteworthy that during the same time period, university dominance of knowledge building and public discourse on international affairs first waxed and then, to some extent, waned. It waxed mainly as universities grew (and with them university presses and university-operated public television and radio stations). It waned, especially in and after the 1970s, not only as academic growth slowed but also as a whole field of think tanks and NGOs emerged and new communications media flourished. Relations to both journalism and policy makers shifted and the place of nonpartisan intellectual inquiry was challenged.

Inside the universities, the biggest change began earlier, during the era of expansion, but it became fully apparent only in the late twentieth century as growth in arts and sciences faculties slowed, whereas that in professional schools continued. Before World War II, arts and sciences faculties were dominant in almost every dimension of academic life. The late nineteenth and early twentieth century rise of the PhD and development of the corresponding undergraduate major took place within arts and sciences faculties (or, indeed, in many cases, as part of the creation of arts and sciences faculties). The main academic disciplines were those of the arts and sciences, and the interdisciplinary projects that tried to keep them connected to each other from the 1920s forward were also mainly arts and sciences projects. The mid-twentieth century flourishing of interdisciplinary area studies, and eventual tensions with disciplines, both took place inside arts and sciences faculties.

By the late twentieth century, however, the big growth in universities was in professional schools. These had been drawn into universities during the same late nineteenth and early twentieth century period when the arts and sciences fields were recast as research-based disciplines. More recently, though, professional schools had not only grown but also developed major research enterprises of their own. They also increasingly internalized intellectual and educational agendas once associated overwhelmingly with the liberal arts, from "critical thinking" to international studies.

A wide variety of professional fields began to embrace more international dimensions to both research and practice. In some cases, this meant merely international connections among professors in professional schools, as, for example, professors of various specialties in academic medicine might meet international counterparts. But in many cases, international studies flourished as a content area in professional training and in research. Public health schools, for example, became pioneering centers of international research, from epidemiology to health policy. Somewhat later, business and law schools followed suit. International business education grew especially large and active with strong connections to other fields, such as international finance and marketing, and to executive education. In some universities—such as Georgetown—this was closely connected to professional schools of international affairs; seldom was it closely integrated with area studies. Law schools did not match the scale but the field of international law, and international inquiries and partnerships more generally, both grew. Research about and training of professionals for rapidly growing fields such as human rights and transitional justice, for example, flourished in law schools. International or comparative education became a topic in at least the more research-oriented education schools. Whereas faculty for these ventures came initially from the arts and sciences disciplines, sometimes with area studies training, the professional schools increasingly began to train future faculty members in their own doctoral programs.

The growth of international research, education, and practice was important in nearly every field of professional study. Most relevant for present purposes, however, is the expansion of professional education directly in international affairs. After World War II, the older professional schools were joined by several new ones. Many added graduate programs, usually centered on politics and economics. The School of Advanced International Studies at Johns Hopkins (founded in 1943) and the School of International and Public Affairs at Columbia (founded in 1946) were graduate schools from the start. Princeton's Woodrow Wilson School added graduate programs in 1948. Many of these schools of international and public affairs included some level of area-specific training in their programs, and correspondingly they either ran area studies centers or employed faculty who participated in university-wide area centers. There was another wave of foundings in the late 1950s and 1960s, linked to the broader expansion of the university sector. American University's School of International Service (1957–1958) and Denver's School of International Studies (1964) were among the leaders. Still more have been added, and they have been joined in an Association of Professional Schools of International Affairs (APSIA).

Most of these schools offered undergraduate as well as graduate programs, often to large enrollments. But they specialized in professional master's programs (roughly analogous to MBA degrees). Like other professional schools, however, they employed faculty members with research agendas and they became increasingly engaged in training their own future faculty. This was especially important in the field of international relations (IR), which maintained a hybrid character between an arts and science discipline (or subdiscipline of political science) and a professional field oriented to informing foreign policy. IR was in fact a new quasidiscipline forged in the post–World War II era, shaped partly by German immigrants, and situated as one of the social sciences.[19] Oriented mostly to "realist" analysis of relations among nation-states, IR turned away from both diplomatic history and area studies.

Although some of the APSIA schools hosted area studies programs, there was in fact a growing division between the thematic content of area studies research and the intellectual projects of the "core" APSIA school faculty, which was composed mainly of international relations specialists and secondarily of other political scientists, economists, and, occasionally, sociologists. The heritage of realism lived on, even where debated by constructivists. It informed emphases on directly political and economic factors in international relations and security studies, and neglect of the mediating influence of culture. Although by the late twentieth century a growing proportion of students intended to pursue careers in the nonprofit sector, faculty research remained centered on state relations. Certain topics—perhaps, most prominently, religion—were neglected in the APSIA schools, and were seen as associated with humanities scholarship and area studies (as will be discussed later). This is only one of a number of lacunae in attention opened by a problematic disciplinary division of labor. Area studies scholarship is crucial to remedying such weaknesses in connection with both disciplines, but especially relating to other interdisciplinary ventures, such as professional programs.

Connections, not Containers

Important paths for the renewal of international studies today involve opening collaborations across regions and among different disciplinary and professional approaches. Think of the way study of global cities can combine the work of area specialists with political economists, network analysts, architects, and designers. Or, think of issues such as transitional justice that bring together questions of law, culture, and social change. Or, consider how culturally specific inquiries into ideas of moral obligation and the category of the human inform the study of human rights and humanitarian action. Creative new projects are indeed breaking some old molds. Younger scholars are willing to think outside some of the boxes and quarrels of their elders. There are strong desires to understand real-world phenomena that demand the knowledge created in different long-standing academic fields but that cannot be contained by any of them.

There is even (in some quarters, not everywhere) willingness to suspend debates over the right label for the enterprise so as not to derail its renewal. New intellectual agendas could be grouped together as international, interregional, transnational, transcultural, global, area, or comparative. "International" is convenient because the label is already commonplace and institutionally recognized. A moment's etymological and genealogical reflection, however, reveals its initial focus on relations among nations and, implicitly, nation-states. It is foundational to international relations as a field, but not as precisely apt for understanding, say, transnational religion or the circulation of musical styles or even markets (although we still collect statistics on international trade). Some such combination of limits can be raised for any of the other potential umbrella terms as well. A label is needed, but it is doubtful that a perfect one will be found.

This points to a more basic issue. We have trouble speaking about the domain under consideration here partly because it has been constructed negatively. The "international" has been approached as the "foreign." More precisely, most of the humanities and social sciences have been constructed on the basis of nation-states, with a primary focus on the "domestic." Thus, history has been primarily national histories (with each country most interested in its own). Literatures have been national literatures, although they are sometimes compared. Sociology constructs society first and foremost on the model of the nation-state. Political science is about politics within states—usually emphasizing one home state but also including comparisons of domestic politics. Economics has looked at national markets and economic policy tools and even tried to grasp the non-national on the basis of national statistics.

Not every field has been as centrally organized on national lines (not classics, for obvious reasons, although it has not been free of the national influence either). Many fields have long incorporated interests not only in what is "foreign" from any one vantage point but also in shared lineages (Romance languages and literature, for example, or English or Francophone literature as distinct from that of England 243 or France). To an impressive degree, however, the social sciences and humanities developed as fields implicitly defined by nations and national projects. Research and teaching were both oriented disproportionately to either the domestic affairs or national policies of individual states. The focus was sometimes explicit (for instance, American history or American politics) and sometimes implicit (for example, sociology or economics taught as general but taking most examples from the United States). This reinforced defining the rest of the world as the "other," so that even efforts to break out of the national container appeared as looking abroad, at the foreign. Moreover, the rest of the world was commonly approached as either (1) the study of similarly "internal" phenomena in other places (comparative politics, comparative literature), or (2) the study of the relationships among these national monads (international relations).

This is changing. Not only is there dramatically increased attention to world history, but there is also an exciting project of internationalizing American history.[20] Not only are Europeanists paying attention to the literatures or politics of former colonies, but they are also recognizing the extent to which Europe itself was shaped by its colonial projects and relations with people elsewhere. Not only are sociologists studying societies other than their own, but they are also trying to break down the assumption that societies are sharply bounded and internally coherent units modeled on the ideal type of nation-states, and therefore they are attempting to study the flows and connections across borders. None of this means that the national ceases to be important. Indeed, it may be the explicit object of study but thereby precisely not the tacit, taken-for-granted frame of study.

The intellectual shift is challenging. Take the struggle of international relations scholars who have recently, somewhat reluctantly, had to figure out how to take religion seriously. The problem arose because religion had been assigned to the "domestic" realm and ruled out of the international in an ideology dating back to the 1648 Peace of Westphalia. This was absorbed into the very constitution of the field of international relations.[21] It is changing only slowly and only in response to dramatic pressure after 2001. As Robert Keohane explains, "the attacks of September 11 reveal that all mainstream theories of world politics are relentlessly secular with respect to motivation. They ignore the impact of religion, despite the fact that world-shaking political movements have so often been fueled by religious fervor."[22] Researchers seeking to change this face problems not only with reigning theories but also with lack of knowledge and institutional and intellectual distance from those with more knowledge—often area studies specialists and researchers from the humanities and fields such as history that straddle humanities and social science. This, of course, also reminds us that the area studies fields are of value not

simply because of an abstract desire to "cover" world regions, but also because of real-world engagements with other contexts and configurations of social life and culture. Although the leaders of area studies often articulate the rationale of "coverage," the demand for area studies is more commonly focused on pressing social concerns. Part of the importance of area studies fields is realized only in better connections to other fields not defined by area.

Doing substantially better with international studies means more than simply increasing the amount of attention to the "other." It requires rethinking the very frames of reference of the humanities and social sciences. It is accordingly as much about the disciplines as about interdisciplinary programs. Diasporas and migrations offer a simple example. National borders are crossed, and national policies are clearly at issue as are national economic futures. However, the process is hardly contained by the national (as though immigration could be understood without attention to the rest of migration or to the societies and cultures from which migrants come and which, to some extent, they carry with them). Moreover, migration flows connect not only "sender" and "receiver" societies but also circuits of sites of diasporic settlement. Sikhs in Toronto are connected to Sikhs in London as well as those in the Punjab and, for that matter, Yuba City, California. Understanding Sikh communities and connections is thus not only a matter for South Asian studies any more than Islam is only a matter for Middle Eastern studies. However, trying to understand Sikh communities abroad without having a serious knowledge of Sikhism in South Asia is silly, as is trying to understand Muslims in Europe without paying attention to both Islam's historic roots and its long-standing transnational connections.

But do not let the example mislead. It is not just that there are some new phenomena that make national frames of reference problematic now. When was the United States not a migrant society? Was the Methodism central to the antislavery movement simply American Methodism? Was not the very transformation of the American university, led in the late nineteenth century by Johns Hopkins, Chicago, and Cornell, part of an international transformation of intellectual institutions? There may be more and stronger transnational connections now than in the nineteenth- and twentieth-century heyday of nation-state projects. But the social sciences and humanities internalized a great deal of that nineteenth- and twentieth-century orientation to a world structured by nation-states and international relations. Nations and states remain important in contemporary global structures, but making them intellectual presuppositions actually gets in the way of making them objects of analysis and studying contemporary social and cultural relations that cross national boundaries.

The opportunity in the present era lies not in simply changing the balance but in getting away from the idea of a Manichean division between the national and everything beyond, outside, or cross-cutting it. We can reduce the extent to which disciplines emphasize the first and relegate the second to interdisciplinary programs.

It is not only the implicit nation-centeredness of the humanities and social science disciplines that is problematic. It is also the extent to which efforts to complement this with area studies and other interdisciplinary programs produced partial mirror images. One of the problematic features of area studies programs was the extent to which many were constituted as collections of specialists on different nation-states within various areas. Few scholars in East Asian studies programs, for example, actually studied East Asia; most studied China, Japan, or Korea.

The prospect before us is to strengthen the ways in which we attend to contexts—not by reifying certain contexts as necessary, but by making a comparative and historical concern for context part of all knowledge-forming projects. When we do this, we see that the area studies fields are structures for organizing valuable resources, but not in and of themselves definitive of relevant contexts. This is made evident by (1) the many historical and contemporary patterns of connection across areas, not only at frontiers but also over long distances; (2) the prominence of certain regions that are omitted from or situated on the frontiers of area studies fields (most prominently, Central Asia); (3) the development of new (or renewed) transnational networks and fields associated with a range of activities and issues, from markets to environment and to religion; and (4) projects of integrating regions such as Eastern and Western Europe or greater Asia, or the Mediterranean or the Pacific.

Regions are thus as important as ever, but they are being redefined. This suggests both the limits of old containers for knowledge and the virtues of studying new connections. These inquiries depend on knowledge developed in area studies, but also on opening area studies fields to more cross-cutting inquiries and new forms of integration with other perspectives.

This is an important agenda for undergraduate education as well as research programs. Since the 1980s, undergraduate international studies programs that connect different disciplines, regions, and problem-oriented approaches have proved attractive and grown large. They frequently have good students; some restrict entry. Not surprisingly, these programs have often faced resistance, given the substantial enrollments at stake and internal competition in universities, especially in an era of slow growth. Area studies programs have often seen a tension with their own majors and their claims to autonomous curricular importance. Political science departments have sometimes tried, for example, to maintain that "international studies" was not a field in its own right and that student interests were better met by the study of international relations (perhaps combined with comparative politics). However, the effort to "hoard" majors may have been counterproductive even where it succeeded, because it was the interdisciplinary, integrative programs that were most attractive to undergraduates.

Interdisciplinary undergraduate programs provide an important base for area studies that is sometimes neglected in research-centered discussions. Student demand translates (albeit not perfectly) into a potential financial basis.

The biggest catch for area studies programs and for other interdisciplinary scholars is that there has not yet been a reorganization of doctoral teaching or research fields to match the breadth of the undergraduate interdisciplinary studies majors (or, indeed, professional master's programs). These majors have remained collaborations among people whose primary intellectual homes and academic jobs are elsewhere; they have commonly amounted to curricula composed of courses offered in separate departments and area programs. Yet, area studies faculty and, indeed, disciplinary faculty neglect such programs at their peril.

Over the past thirty-five years, growth in university finances has favored science, technology, and professional schools. The liberal arts—particularly the humanities and social sciences—subsist much more on tuition or on the enrollment-driven parts of state contributions. Current financial upheavals are only exacerbating this trend.[23] Student demand for context-specific teaching can support faculty positions, but this student support will be expressed less through area studies majors—which are tiny—than through courses that fit into other programs. Obsessing over competition between area studies and disciplines is a distraction. Disciplinary majors are also likely to shrink. The growth areas are professional and preprofessional studies and broad interdisciplinary fields, often focused on public issues. The latter include not only transregional international studies, but also environmental studies, development studies, communications studies, and policy studies, among others. These will be much less intellectually serious and practically useful if they neglect deep context-specific knowledge, but to thrive in connection with them, area studies fields need to open themselves to more transregional and problem-oriented teaching.

Prospects

Context-specific knowledge remains important—but which contexts matter most is shifting. The regions addressed by traditional area studies fields are more, not less, significant in contemporary global affairs—but so are other regions and connections across regions. Sustaining area studies depends on openness to new configurations.

Decades of intensifying globalization have made clear that growing global connections do not amount to a simple process of unification, let alone peaceful and 247 uniformly prosperous integration. Globalization has produced new security threats, demands for shifting structures of international cooperation, wars on several continents, and tensions among a cluster of regional powers that may foreshadow a new multilateral order replacing a brief era of unilateral U.S. dominance. It has produced electronic integration of financial markets that can both underpin a boom and speed a bust. It has produced divisions as well as connections between buyers and sellers of energy and natural resources. Global religions contribute to complex conflicts as well as advocacy for global peace. Think not only of Islam but also of the role of African and Latin American dioceses in the growing split within the Anglican Communion and the American Episcopal Church. Globalization has given impetus to a re-regionalization of global political economy with the European Union, with the North American Free Trade Agreement (NAFTA), and with pan-Asian integration. It has brought to the fore several regional powers, some intent on hegemony with regions they help to anchor. In some cases, such as Central Asia and Northwest China, tensions over regional hegemony have coincided with new alignments rooted in global religion.

At the same time, transnational cultural flows have hardly brought a simple global sameness. Some have indeed brought similarities within large-scale zones of circulation. Not only transnational religion but also transnational taste cultures are prominent. Some join people who are not at all spatially proximate, and thus are poorly grasped by notions of region or area even as they are far from globally universal. But transnational cultural flows are not necessarily encompassing of all or most people in the countries and regions they cross. Jazz, for example, is global even though it is a minority culture wherever it takes root. Opera is popular music in Italy and Argentina, but it attracts a narrow elite in the United States. Both jazz and opera have many fans, however, among a cosmopolitan cultural elite, they are plausible gambits for conversation in business class airline seats. The existence of a transnational elite culture is an aspect of globalization; it is sometimes support for the illusion among frequent flyers that globalization is more complete than it is; but it too is a minority culture even if far-flung.[24] The same is true of diasporic cultures that link (and sometimes change) countries that send migrants with centers in several host countries and each of these centers with each other in networks of cultural as well as marriage and economic exchange.

In short, much is missed by both the new wave of globalization studies, with its pursuit of knowledge of the world as a whole, and traditional area studies programs, with their divisions of the globe into seemingly separate regions. We need at once to see the differentiation within global interconnection and to see the ways in which each area is shaped by its connections to the rest of the world and offers distinctive vantage points on the processes and structures of globalization.

The global is misunderstood if it is approached with attention only to that which grows more similar. The regional and local are misunderstood if analysts expect all the crucial resources to be internal rather than reflections of their situation in larger contexts. Organization exists at many different scales.

Global integration produces an ecosystem in which there are subsystems with considerable capacity to maintain homeostasis and others with less of this capacity. Different regions and localities have both their distinctive patterns of internal organization and their distinctive relationships to the whole. Long-distance trading networks and diasporas each have an organization distinct from that of the regions through which they pass. The global looks different from different places, from different long-distance networks, and from positions of different resources and opportunities within each.

Thinking about the many different scales of organization and the way they interact opens up exciting intellectual possibilities. Paying attention to transregional connections and to the transformation of what seem to be regions can both reinvigorate area studies and connect regional knowledge in different ways to other projects.

Alas, this does not mean that renewal will be easy. Old grudges, resentments, and suspicions remain obstacles—not least sustaining the tensions among disciplinary, area studies, and professional school perspectives. There is a deficit to overcome, as neither government nor foundation support for international studies has kept pace with globalization over the past thirty years. Not only has the extent of global engagements and concerns outpaced the extent of international education and research in American universities, but the pattern of globalization has also created a need for studies of previously neglected regions such as Central Asia and reshaped relations across all regions. There are also practical and political questions, however, posed by certain sources of funds—such as whether scholars should embrace or resist military and Defense Department efforts to learn from social science and area studies.[25]

For fifty years, Title VI programs have played a basic role both in providing support for area studies and language teaching and in encouraging stronger public outreach and connections to professional schools. This is not and should not be episodic support tied to specific short-term agendas. It is a matter of sustaining investments that make it possible to bring knowledge to bear when new issues emerge.

The idea of national resource centers is instructive. Context-specific knowledge is a resource that can be crucial in new circumstances—when security challenges change, for example, or new environmental risks appear, or shifting migration patterns create new international connections. The needed knowledge cannot be created on a moment's notice; it must be nurtured. Continued Title VI support for the maintenance and renewal of core intellectual resources is vital.

Those who keep reminding decision makers of the continued importance of basic scholarship will risk looking conservative. However, if American universities are to rise to the challenge of providing the international knowledge that can inform policy, educate practitioners in a variety of fields, and help citizens understand our global pressures, engagements, and opportunities, then the core tasks do include basic scholarship as well as pursuit of new lines of research. We need both basic and advanced language teaching—which can be done in innovative ways. We need serious historical knowledge—which can transcend the national structures that usually organize it. We need understanding of cultural patterns—which include clashes and creativity as well as civilizational continuities.

Important as they are, however, national resource centers by themselves are not enough. Their vitality and their value depend on connections. First of all, they depend on much better connections to each other than most, in fact, achieve. The kind of knowledge sustained in Title VI centers flourishes when connections and comparisons across regions are pursued.

Universities should build on the resources sustained by Title VI to strengthen both undergraduate and professional curricula so students understand the ways specific regional contexts and transregional connections are shaping the world today. This will require investments from universities themselves, not least in creating faculty positions. But this is vital to make sure that students gain not only a smattering of facts about different places, but also an awareness of the importance of deeper and better integrated knowledge so they can seek it when they or organizations they work in need it.

Private philanthropies also have the opportunity to invest in ways that enhance the payoff of the resource centers Title VI programs sustain. Some will seek to support individual scholars or research groups in pursuing new intellectual agendas. We can only hope that many will directly value achievements of scholarship and their effective communication. Others, probably more, will seek to enlist those with deep context-specific knowledge in collaborating with practitioners working on major problems. But whether foundations back historians shedding new light on old connections between regions or sociologists trying to make AIDS treatment programs more effective, they depend on intellectual resources often rooted in area studies programs. But they also depend on area studies specialists to be open to projects not contained by traditional regional definitions or scholarly agendas.

Renewal of interest in international studies comes with new topics, challenges, intellectual agendas, and practical concerns. Most of these are potentially exciting, but they bring their own frustrations. Even if funding grows, in most cases, it is not likely to restore old budget lines. As often, what seems new and different will be favored. Some funders will be more interested in social problems than in cultural achievements. Africanists will worry that a continent rich in music, art, and religious innovation will appear only as a set of human security challenges. Sinologists will worry that an ancient and enormously complex civilization is reduced to an economic opportunity or threat. However, there is no realistic way to deal with these frustrations by resisting the idea that regional knowledge should be brought to bear on practical projects or asserting that it is simply an end in itself.

This is not merely an issue of resources. Established, even carefully cultivated knowledge needs frequently to be rethought in light of new practical problems and new intellectual perspectives. This is how it lives.

Notes

1 It is impressive to what extent the professional schools of international affairs were formed at private rather than public universities—an imbalance not matched in any other professional area. This is perhaps tied to recruitment of social elites into diplomacy. Even today, public universities are represented in the Association of Professional Schools of International Affairs (APSIA) mainly through schools of public policy focused primarily on domestic affairs. The School of International Relations and Pacific Studies at University of California, San Diego, and the Jackson School at the University of Washington are among the few exceptions.

2 See George Steinmetz, *The Devil's Handwriting* (Chicago: University of Chicago Press, 2007) on the development of ethnological and colonial expertise in Germany.

3 For an insightful look back at the project of modernization theory, see Nils Gilman, *Mandarins of the Future* (Baltimore: Johns Hopkins University Press, 2003).

4 See Craig Calhoun, "Explanation in Historical Sociology: Narrative, General Theory, and Historically Specific Theory," *American Journal of Sociology*, vol. 104, no. 3 (1998), pp. 846–71.

5 Benedict Anderson, *Imagined Communities* (London: Verso rev. ed. 1991, orig. 1983).

6 James Scott, *Seeing Like a State* (New Haven: Yale University Press, 1998).

7 Among many, see Raùl Prebisch, *The Economic Development of Latin America and its Principal Problems* (New York: United Nations, 1950); Andre Gunder Frank, *The Development of Underdevelopment* (New York: Monthly Review Press, 1966); Fernando Henrique Cardozo and Enzo Faletto, *Dependency and*

251

Development in Latin America (Berkeley: University of California Press, 1967); Albert O. Hirschman, *The Strategy of Economic Development* (New Haven: Yale University Press, 1958).

8 Immanuel Wallerstein, *The Modern World System* (New York: Academic Press, 1974) is the classic work. It is worth noting that nearly all the major protagonists of the first generation of world systems analysis—including Giovanni Arrighi, Terence Hopkins, and John Saul—were initially active in African studies, and many spent time teaching in African universities.

9 International political economy was previously strong in both political science and sociology. Its relative decline may reflect both the orientation of some area studies fields toward approaches rooted in the humanities and the failure of disciplinary departments to emphasize context-specific international research. See Rina Agarwala and Emmanuel Teitelbaum, "Trends in Funding for Dissertation Field Research: Why Do Political Science and Sociology Students Win so Few Awards?" *Political Science and Politics,* forthcoming.

10 Obviously, more was at stake in those fateful years than oil—the collapse of the Bretton Woods financial structure, the Yom Kippur War, struggles both for and against popular economic participation that helped produce Latin American dictatorships, generational struggles over the political direction of rich countries, and the impact of the Vietnam War. The 1970s crisis was not resolved, but deferred—largely through a dramatic increase in the use of credit and through attacks on state welfare spending commonly labeled neoliberalism. This contributed directly to the 2008–2009 crisis. This is relevant partly because the 1970s ushered in thirty years of shifts away from public funding of higher education, deep problems for scholars in many of the world's regions, and hard times as well for humanists and social scientists in the United States who sought to study other parts of the world.

11 See Craig Calhoun and Jonathan VanAntwerpen, "Orthodoxy, Heterodoxy and Hierarchy: 'Mainstream' Sociology and its Challengers," in C. Calhoun, ed., *Sociology in America* (Chicago: University of Chicago Press, 2007). Ironically, this happened at the same time that largely French-inspired theory became influential in literature departments and some other parts of the humanities.

12 See Michael Kennedy and Miguel A. Centeno, "Internationalism and Global Transformation in American Sociology," in Calhoun, ed., op cit.

13 While both economics and psychology reduced their ties to other social sciences, they forged new ties to each other (including ties in the interdisciplinary field of cognitive sciences, which economics entered through interest in decision making). Moreover, economics and psychology are different from the other social sciences in having much more substantially retained their

connections to nonacademic "practitioners" and applied researchers. An economist working for the World Bank or a psychologist running a testing program for a school district remain members of the discipline that granted their PhDs to a much greater degree than, say, sociologists or political scientists working in various branches of government, the UN, NGOs, or business.

14 For a broader context, see David Szanton, ed., *The Politics of Knowledge: Area Studies and the Disciplines* (Berkeley: University of California Press, 2004).

15 One important difference between the two was that Mellon remained focused mainly on American universities, though no longer area studies, whereas Ford turned its focus increasingly to direct funding of work in the global South and to nonacademic organizations.

16 The Peace Corps had a bigger impact in the 1960s partly because it was organized to recruit more young people straight from college who then considered graduate school afterward—influenced by their experience abroad. More recently, it has placed a greater emphasis on people who already had specific skill sets often obtained through graduate degrees or significant career experience.

17 David Szanton, ed., *The Politics of Knowledge: Area Studies and the Disciplines* (Berkeley: University of California Press, 2004), p. vii. See also two other collections responding to the 1990s crisis of area studies: Ali Mirsepanni, Amrita Basu, and Frederick Weaver, eds., *Localizing Knowledge in a Global World* (Syracuse: Syracuse University Press, 2003) and Masao Miyoshi and H. D. Harootunian, eds., *Learning Places: The Afterlives of Area Studies* (Durham, NC: Duke University Press, 2002). See also Jane Guyer's helpful account, *African Studies in the United States* (Atlanta: African Studies Association Press, 1996).

18 Even "Big Science" developed largely outside the core Arts and Science teaching departments; see Peter Galison and Bruce Hevly, eds., *Big Science: The Growth of Large-Scale Research* (Stanford, CA: Stanford University Press, 1992).

19 See Guilhot, op cit.; also Robert Vitalis, "Birth of a Discipline," pp. 159–82 in D. Long and B. C. Schmidt, eds., *Imperialism and Internationalism in the Discipline of International Relations* (Albany, NY: SUNY Press, 2005).

20 Thomas Bender, ed., *Rethinking American History in a Global Age* (Berkeley: University of California Press, 2002).

21 See Elizabeth Shakman Hurd, *The Politics of Secularism in International Relations* (Princeton, NJ: Princeton University Press, 2007) and Mark Jurgensmeyer, Craig Calhoun, and Jonathan VanAntwerpen, *Rethinking Secularism* (Oxford: Oxford University Press, forthcoming). The Luce Foundation has recently launched a major program supporting efforts of APSIA schools to integrate the study of religion into their research and curricula given its manifest importance in contemporary international relations. See Timothy S. Shah, Alfred C.

Stepan, and Monica Duffy Toft, *Religion and International Affairs* (New York: Oxford University Press, forthcoming).

22 Keohane, "The Globalization of Informal Violence, Theories of World Politics, and 'The Liberalism of Fear," pp. 77–92 in C. Calhoun, P. Price, and A. Timmer, eds., *Understanding September 11* (New York: New Press 2002), p. 72. See also Elizabeth Shakman Hurd, *The Politics of Secularism in International Relations* (Princeton, NJ: Princeton University Press, 2007).

23 Craig Calhoun, "The Public Mission of the Research University," in C. Calhoun and D. Rhoten, eds., *Knowledge Matters* (New York: Columbia University Press, 2010) and R. L. Geiger, *Knowledge and Money* (Stanford, CA: Stanford University Press, 2004).

24 Craig Calhoun, "The Class Consciousness of Frequent Travelers: Toward a Critique of Actually Existing Cosmopolitanism," *South Atlantic Quarterly*, vol. 101 no. 4 (2003), pp. 869–97.

25 See discussion of Project Minerva at http://essays.ssrc.org/minerva/.

PART 5

Global
Competitiveness

Title VI and Global Competitiveness: Building International Business Education for the Twenty-First Century

Melissa H. Birch

Introduction

The past fifty years have seen a dramatic change in the international environment for U.S. business. Highly regulated trade has given way to more open markets, and the volume of world trade has increased tremendously. Currently, about 25 percent of world production is sold outside the country in which it was produced, up from 7 percent in 1950. U.S. imports as a share of gross national product, a measure of openness, have grown from only about 5 percent in the 1960s to more than 17 percent in 2007.[1] Although U.S. firms had originally found their major competitors in Europe and then in Japan, increasingly firms from myriad other countries, including many emerging markets, are competing directly with U.S. firms at home and abroad. Whereas U.S. assets abroad were only about half the value of U.S. gross domestic product (GDP) in the 1970s, by 2004, they had grown in value to a sum almost twice as large as the U.S. GDP (Federal Reserve Bank of Dallas 2008).

Federal policy in the United States has recognized the growing importance of international trade and investment. In higher education, this recognition led to the expansion of the mandate of National Resource Centers (NRCs). Established in the 1950s to create a cadre of international experts able to work effectively in parts of the world that were seen as strategically important to the United States in terms

257

of military and diplomatic security, by 1972 the NRC mission was broadened to include reaching out to professional schools on campus to help internationalize the training of business graduates. This growing understanding that national security and international economic competitiveness were intertwined was demonstrated again in 1980 when the Title VI legislation was incorporated into the Higher Education Act of 1965; one of the new programs created during reauthorization was the Business and International Education (BIE) program, which provided matching funds for two-year grants to strengthen the international dimension of business education while assisting firms doing business overseas. A few years later, the Centers for International Business Education (CIBEs) were created under the Omnibus Trade and Competitiveness Act of 1988, again, with matching funds, "to strengthen the international dimensions of business education and serve as regional and national resources to the business and education communities, providing programs that help U.S. business succeed in global markets."[2] The CIBE legislation made it clear that Congress understood the increasing need to respond to growing competition from companies in foreign countries, particularly those in Europe and Japan. In its statement of Findings and Purposes, the legislation noted that the future economic welfare of the United States will depend on increasing the international skills of businesspeople.

This chapter will discuss the significant and continuing need for Title VI and the CIBE program in the preparation of the next generation of business leaders. Although the need for business professionals with international expertise is long-standing and undeniable, the response of business schools to this demand has been slow. The CIBE program has played a key role in filling the resulting gap and providing thought leadership in the internationalization of business curricula. Recent events underscore the way in which national economies increasingly are intertwined, highlighting the growing need in business for international specialists in the most traditional sense of Title VI.

From Globalization to Globality

By the end of the twentieth century, globalization was the term widely used to capture the growing integration of individual country markets and the contacts across cultures that were growing exponentially in terms of both frequency and extent. The Commission on Globalization defined the phenomenon as a

> [t]rend toward a single borderless global economy in which goods, services and capital can flow in response to market forces with minimal government interference. . . .
> The processes of globalization are viewed as the result of inevitable and irreversible forces driving a powerful engine of technological innovation and economic growth.[3]

Globalization was widely viewed as the culmination of a process of deregulation begun in the 1980s that opened economies domestically and internationally. The free-market economic systems adopted by many countries and foisted on many others opened countries to foreign trade and investment, sometimes in sectors previously off-limits to private investment, either foreign or domestic. Technology also played a key role in globalization, enabling many more players to take advantage of these newly available opportunities. Information technology provided valuable new tools for finding and pursuing economic opportunities while reducing the cost of doing so. The combination of deregulation and technology was particularly powerful in financial markets, facilitating transactions and collaboration that could be global in scope.

A somewhat less charitable view of globalization was presented by Sirkin, Hemerling, and Bhattacharya, who describe globalization as "a cavalcade that traveled from West to East—big multinational companies centered in Europe, Japan, and the United States marching out from their corporate fortresses to foreign lands in search of low-cost manufacturing and low-end markets" (2008: 1). In their view, however, this era has ended and is replaced by a new approach to international business, which they have called "globality." Originating outside the United States and Europe, new competitors that start with different cultural, political, and social assumptions are changing the dynamics of global trade. Sirkin et al. describe globality as "Western business orthodoxy entwined with eastern business philosophy, creating a whole new mind-set that embraces profit and competition as well as sustainability and collaboration" (2008: 2).

Heralding this shift from globalization to globality is the rise of the new multinational enterprises (MNEs). Variously referred to as third-world multinationals, latecomer firms, challengers, and emerging multinationals in the business literature, these firms come from the rapidly emerging Asian economies and the old Asian Tigers, the oil-rich countries in the Middle East and Africa, and, perhaps more surprisingly, middle-income countries such as Spain.[4] Unlike the traditional MNEs, these new players are not expanding slowly in stages beginning with the countries nearest to them. They are not exploiting advantages in technology or brand recognition. Instead, these new MNEs are expanding rapidly all over the globe, exploiting capabilities acquired in their home markets where they garnered size and financial resources along with a high tolerance for instability and uncertainty. Unlike their traditional counterparts, these firms are acquiring technology and building brand recognition through expansion (Guillen and Garcia-Canal 2008). Their presence in international markets changes the competitive dynamics and, in the parlance of globality, the result is "everyone competing everywhere for everything" (Sirkin et al. 2008: 1).

Globalization, Globality, and Global Competence

Whereas globalization highlights the opportunity of new international markets and global reach for established first-world players, globality emphasizes the increased competition that will exist in these markets and the new modalities for rivalry arising from the presence of the new entrants. Both academics and practitioners would agree with William Hunter (2004) that "globalization has made the world a tougher place to do business, unless of course, you are globally competent." For hypercompetitive globality, the skill set required might be even more sophisticated and more focused on cultures and countries with which Americans are historically less familiar. In a world of greater international competition, with new players from less familiar countries, the Title VI focus on building expertise in the languages and cultures of countries of strategic interest to the United States is increasingly relevant for business students, business scholars, and those currently engaged in business.

A recent survey of 180 human resource managers on six continents found that global competence was critical to the success of international managers and necessary for professional development. It also found that demand for training outstripped supply and that more programs were needed to provide the appropriate training for managers to achieve global competency.[5] Given a positive correlation between formal international business training and the international competitiveness of firms (Beamish 1989), providing some kind of education and training for global competence would seem to be in the strategic interest of both the United States and its companies. But what exactly would such global competence be? Using phrases such as "global competence," "global mindset," "cultural intelligence," "global perspective," and many others, academics have tried to explain the attributes individual managers will need to succeed in the increasingly global marketplace.[6] This chapter will focus on global competence because it is a somewhat more encompassing term and has been used widely by those seeking to identify the educational and training components required for its achievement.

There is a vast literature on global competence and its implications for university training. One widely accepted definition would be that a "globally competent individual has a knowledge of current events, can empathize with others, demonstrates approval (maintains a positive attitude), and has an unspecified level of foreign language competence that allows them to perform tasks in a foreign language and understand the value of something foreign" (Lambert 1996). William Brustein (2007), a former NRC director and now a senior university administrator, defines global competence as the ability to communicate effectively across cultural and linguistic boundaries and to focus on issues that transcend cultures and continents. He includes the ability to work effectively in different international settings, an awareness of the major currents of global change and the issues arising from such changes, knowledge of global organizations and business activities, the capacity for effective communication across cultural and linguistic boundaries, and personal adaptability to diverse cultures. Even though there are many definitions of global competence, they share a common focus on an ability to communicate effectively across language and culture in ways that are appropriate both culturally and professionally. Put more practically for the business world by the Swiss Consulting Group, globally competent managers can "parachute into any country and get the job done while respecting cultural pathways."[7] This set of skills would seem most likely to be developed through a combination of business, foreign language, and area studies.

Global Competence and the Needs of U.S. Business

Over the past thirty years, business educators have been surveying business leaders to ascertain the set of international skills that employers would find attractive when hiring personnel for international assignments. The surveys are not strictly comparable, as they vary in terms of who was surveyed and what exactly was asked. In some cases surveys were sent to the firms' chief executive officer (CEO), whereas in other cases, they were directed to the executive specifically responsible for international activities. In some cases, respondents were asked to evaluate international business courses and business curricula, whereas in others they were asked about their own educational and career backgrounds or about hiring and promotion decisions within their firms. Some surveys were clearly focused on preparation for expatriate assignments, whereas others asked about the training desirable for all employees. The surveys are summarized in Table 12-1 but require careful interpretation in view of the variability.

One of the first surveys of executives was conducted in 1977 by Lee Nehrt for the American Council on Education (ACE) as part of a larger survey about internationalizing business education. Nehrt asked the CEOs of Fortune 500 firms about their own preparation for international work and their recommendations for appropriate international business training. He found that few of the executives had had any international coursework in their degree program, whether graduates of business or liberal arts programs. Because business schools had not yet begun to internationalize their curricula, it is not surprising that only 7 percent of those who had had international postings felt that their university courses had prepared them for the assignment. In fact, these results highlighted the growing need for a national program to address this gap in business coursework and to provide working managers with access to international training. Most executives Nehrt surveyed had to rely on their own work experience abroad, or that of others, to acquire international

Table 12-1. Summary of Business Surveys

Author	Survey Title	Who Was Surveyed	Focus of the Survey	Main Conclusions
Nehrt (1977)	Business in international education	Presidents and CEOs from Fortune 500 companies; $n = 73$	Profile of CEOs with respect to experience and educational background related to international business	Only 7 percent of those who had international assignments felt that their university courses helped them prepare for them. Strong emphasis on learning from work experience abroad.
Ricks and Czinkota (1979)	International business [IB]: an examination of the corporate viewpoint	IB executives from Ohio businesses; $n = 28$	IB execs' views on IB teaching and research and identification of main IB issues faced	International business growing in importance and should be emphasized more in business curricula. Cross-cultural communication most important issue identified. Operations issues in international environments were also important. IB research not helpful in solving international challenges faced by the firms.
Kobrin (1984)	International expertise in American business	Junior and senior managers with international staff responsibilities in large American companies (Fortune 500), $n = 98$ for interviews, $n = 125$ for questionnaires	Kinds of international expertise managers need, how acquired, and how important managers perceive international expertise to be	People skills and functional knowledge (e.g., marketing, finance) are most important factors for an effective international manager, whereas country and technical knowledge were the least important. Business customs and economic systems identified as the most important international knowledge for success. All else constant, managers with good country knowledge are usually more successful. Virtually all respondents agreed on the importance of language, but also agreed that personnel were unlikely to be hired or promoted based on language ability alone. For most managers

Table 12-1. Summary of Business Surveys (*continued*)

Author	Survey Title	Who Was Surveyed	Focus of the Survey	Main Conclusions
				interviewed, international expertise was acquired through experience and/or travel.
Kohers (1985)	Corporate employment needs and their implications for an international business curriculum	Businesses in southeastern United States with international activity; *n* = 68	Desirability of various traditional, IB, and language courses as part of new hires' background	A business major with IB orientation and proficiency in a foreign language identified as most desirable preparation, followed by a foreign language major with completed courses in business topics and area studies. International business, international marketing, and international finance are the most desirable IB courses. Spanish is the most desirable foreign language, followed by German, Japanese, and French. International relations and international law are desirable political science courses.
Reynolds and Rice (1988)	American education for international business	IB managers of companies engaged in IB and listed in Uniworld business directory; *n* = 127	Areas of knowledge most valued for international assignments and adequacy of university, executive development, and in-house training for the acquisition of such knowledge	International marketing and international finance are the areas of knowledge most valued for international managers. University studies important in acquisition of those areas of knowledge, but overseas experience most important means of acquiring knowledge in international marketing. Executive development programs are the most important means of acquiring knowledge of international business finance; university studies least important for all areas except international accounting. Authors inferred from "open questions" that "American managers are not overly concerned with cultural problems in international business."

(*continued*)

Table 12-1. Summary of Business Surveys (*continued*)

Author	Survey Title	Who Was Surveyed	Focus of the Survey	Main Conclusions
Ball and McCulloch Jr. (1993)	Views on international business education for prospective employees	CEOs of U.S. MNEs; *n* = 76	All business graduates, not just international positions	IB course should be required for all graduates; knowledge of international dimensions of business important for hiring and promotion.
Moxon (1997)	Changing U.S. business needs for international expertise	Largely IB executives; *n* = 129	Training requirements for international business positions	Companies need more managers with global awareness and cultural sensitivity even if not sent abroad. Limited demand/value for language and country-specific expertise unless combined with management skills; then highly valued.
Kedia and Daniel (2003)	U.S. business needs for employees with international expertise	Top managers at large and small firms; *n* = 111	Professional staff and line management, emphasis on international positions	Companies believe business would increase if more international expertise was available on staff. Appreciation for cross-cultural differences was the most valued international skill. IB skills were more important at management level than at entry level.

acumen. This "learning by doing" attitude seems to permeate many of the surveys done in the 1970s, 1980s, and even into the 1990s.

At the same time, the respondents to the Nehrt survey were much in favor of adding international content to the business curriculum. Foreign languages and area studies were clearly identified as useful components of undergraduate preparation for business. From a list of possible international business courses, about two-thirds of the respondents felt that international accounting and international law were better learned during university studies, whereas two other subjects were clearly identified as better learned through overseas experience: international labor relations and international marketing.[8] Overwhelmingly, the respondents in the 1970s believed the demand for foreign language skills, area studies knowledge, and international business skills would be increasing in the future. Respondents also expected that the need for expatriate managers would be steady to increasing.

In a combination of interviews and surveys, Kobrin (1984) asked international business executives in large U.S. firms about the importance of international expertise in their careers and how such expertise was acquired. Again, only 7 percent responded that university courses had provided them with appropriate preparation, and most agreed that international expertise was acquired on the job, usually through expatriate assignments. With such international assignments for U.S. managers now becoming much less common, Kobrin discussed with the executives how appropriate skills for managing international business could be acquired. In a highly nuanced discussion, Kobrin concluded that given the growing importance in the 1980s of international business to major U.S. multinational firms, when combined with specific business skills, the knowledge and attributes derived from foreign language and area studies could be quite valuable.[9]

Ball and McCulloch Jr. (1993) surveyed the CEOs of a sample of leading American multinationals regarding the perceived importance of international business education for *all* business graduates, not just those aspiring to careers in international operations. Reflecting the greater importance of international transactions to American firms, 79 percent of all respondents believed that an "Introduction to International Business" course should be required of all business majors. Respondents also believed that international expertise (no matter how acquired) was an important characteristics in the hiring of college graduates. When asked "Does your firm consider the international qualifications of people when making hiring, promotion, or transfer decisions for people with responsibilities in international markets?" 90 percent responded "always" or "sometimes," whereas only 10 percent answered "never." When interpreted in conjunction with previous surveys, it seems clear that by the 1990s international skills combined with other attributes, usually business preparation, are important for a growing number of positions at the companies surveyed.

Moxon (1997) surveyed 129 businesses across the United States in both manufacturing and services and found that international sales accounted for an average of approximately 36 percent of total sales and were expected to increase significantly in the near future.[10] Moxon found that more small firms and more service sector companies were engaging in international business. Reflecting the rise of what were coming to be called emerging and transitional economies, managers surveyed reported that they expected markets in Asia, Latin America, Eastern Europe, and the former Soviet Union to be of particular importance and that U.S. managers would need in the near future a better knowledge of these regions, their languages and cultures.

While acknowledging the decline in the frequency of expatriate assignments, respondents to Moxon's survey identified a growing need for managers—even those working in the United States—to have a global awareness and cultural sensitivity. "Local nationals will run our overseas offices, but everyone at home needs global sensitivity" (1997: 14). As in previous surveys, respondents placed value on foreign language ability and country-specific expertise when combined with job-specific, management, and interpersonal skills. Interestingly, small firms tended to place more value on foreign language expertise than large ones. When asked about business curriculum, business executives in the Moxon study noted that "real international business experience," identified as foreign study and internships, not international business coursework delivered in the United States, was most valuable. Experiential learning, such as student projects with companies, was considered particularly beneficial.

In the most recent survey, Kedia and Daniel (2003) found that international business continued to be seen as an important and growing part of company sales. In fact, some 80 percent of respondents believed that international sales would increase if their staff had more international expertise. This survey distinguished between line jobs and management/staff positions in its questions and found that although companies believed that international business skills and knowledge were more important for professional staff, they expected to be placing a greater emphasis on international skills for *all* employees in the next ten years. Appreciation for cross-cultural differences was the most important international skill sought by companies surveyed, for both professional staff and line management employees, followed by a global perspective and the understanding of local markets and business practices. In terms of hiring, reassignment and/or promotion decisions, international skills were identified as more important at the management level than at the entry level. Some 77 percent of respondents attributed some or great importance to mandatory foreign language training. This result is surprisingly consistent with the responses obtained by Ball and McCullough in 1993 and the findings of the American Council on Education when surveying the general public. It seems to substantiate Moxon's view that foreign language skills could be very important for certain jobs or positions and perhaps reflects growing recognition that knowledge of a foreign language improves cultural sensitivity.

Finally, the Kedia and Daniel survey revealed that companies expected to place a greater emphasis on international capabilities among management and employees in the next ten years. Reflecting this growing demand for employees with international competencies, companies surveyed recommended that business schools provide a stronger international emphasis in business school curricula and place more emphasis on learning about other world areas and countries. In the meantime, to fill the gap, companies planned to turn to consulting firms or create in-house training programs to develop international competence among their employees.

In each of these surveys, conducted over more than thirty years, international business proved to be an important and growing part of corporate activity. In each case, companies valued knowledge of foreign cultures and countries when it was combined with managerial experience or job-specific skills. Although foreign language fluency is not always required of all hires, there is substantial support (more than 70 percent) for requiring foreign language study for business school graduates. Although international skills and knowledge are more important for staff and management positions, companies anticipate that a global mindset will be needed by an ever broader set of employees, including those who may never travel abroad as part of their job. Most respondents to these surveys felt that business schools had not yet become a good source of international business training and they often turned to consulting firms or developed their own in-house training programs.

The growing chorus of managers that identify a need for international business knowledge tracks quite closely with the growth of international trade in the United States and the shifting geographic focus of foreign investment. At the same time, as will be discussed later, the creation of the CIBEs at major universities across the country, and their growing role in providing outreach to businesses and other business schools, attempts to meet the growing demand for international business training, not only for students as they graduate but also for practicing professionals who now serve in more senior positions. Congressional leadership in expanding the focus of Title VI to include business needs, and skillful administration by the U.S. Department of Education, has resulted in programs that fill a clearly articulated need in the American business landscape.

International Business Education: Our "Local" in the "Global"

In response to the growing importance of international business to U.S. firms, business schools in the United States began to respond. In the mid-1980s, the Association to Advance Collegiate Schools of Business (AACSB) International commissioned a landmark study of international business education. The authors reported that "it is our impression from our extensive interviewing that business schools, collectively, have not yet become serious about the international dimensions of management" (Porter and McKibben 1988). A few years later, in 1994, a study by Kwok, Arpan, and Folks revealed that 62 percent of undergraduate business students, 57 percent of MBA students, and 59 percent of doctoral business students had received minimal or no international business training. Clearly, the creation of the CIBE program was well timed and the need was clear.

Over time, U.S. business schools increased both the breadth and depth of the international dimension of business education by adding international cases to the curriculum and international students to the classroom, establishing study abroad and international exchange programs, and developing international joint ventures to deliver programs or joint degrees, often with the help of CIBE or Title VI Business and International Education (BIE) funding. By 2002, Kwok and Arpan found that just more than half of business schools responding to a survey of accredited institutions were members of a consortium for international business activity, 27 percent required study abroad for some of their degree programs, and 22 percent offered degree programs in another country. Still, Kwok and Arpan noted, "Globalization . . . increased even faster than the internationalization of business schools' curricula and faculty—hence business schools continued to lag behind business needs and developments" (2002: 579). Fortunately, the number of CIBEs had grown over the previous twelve years, enabling the scope of their activities to increase so that their impact would soon begin to be felt.

The keynote speaker at the AACSB annual meeting in 2008 sought to explain the inertia of business schools in the face of rapid globalization of business. Describing the issues in historical and institutional context, he identified a combination of problems at the top and in the middle of the business school hierarchy, as well as some issues with the underlying knowledge base. According to Ghemawat (2008), at the top, deans and other academic administrators respond in large measure to national accreditation standards, whereas professors, in the middle, respond to the reward system embedded in academic hiring and promotion practices. At the base, the organization of business schools and the placement of international subject matter in that organization and the broader university have created further obstacles to internationalization.

AACSB, the premier organization that accredits business schools, was founded in 1916 and began setting standards for business education in 1960. The vernacular of business accreditation is a foreign language to many, but to deans and other business school administrators it provides direction and establishes priorities. It was not until 1974 that the standards included any reference to international dimensions of business, and then only a cursory one (Voris 1997). Not until the 1990s, nearly twenty years after the Nehrt survey identified the need, did AACSB adopt language that required accredited business schools to teach about the "domestic *and global* environments of business."[11] Interestingly, this sudden attention to internationalization coincided with the establishment of the first CIBEs (see Table 12-2).

A 2002 report by the AACSB's Management Education Task Force found that "many business schools had at least partially adapted their curricula to train students for markets and operations that span the globe" (2002: 9). The report identified some 400 programs that provided students with the opportunity to

Table 12-2. Title VI Centers for International Business Education Funding History since Inception of the Program[i]

Fiscal Year	Total Funding (U.S. dollars)	Number of CIBEs
1989	$741,000	5
1990	4,778,000	16
1991	5,036,000	16
1992	6,157,000	23
1993	6,478,000	25
1994	6,834,000	25
1995	6,851,000	27
1996	6,779,000	26
1997	7,026,000	26
1998	7,026,000	25
1999	7,917,358	28
2000	8,100,000	28
2001	8,760,000	28
2002	10,266,000	30
2003	11,100,000	30
2004	10,700,000	30
2005	10,700,000	30
2006	10,650,000	31
2007	10,650,000	31
2008	10,960,000	31
2009	11,527,300	31
Total	$192,226,300	

SOURCE: Miriam A. Kazanjian, Coalition for International Education, 2009

[i] According to the legislation, the federal share of a CIBE may be no more than 50 percent of the budget. As a result, all federal awards are matched on a 1:1 basis by the university grantees.

concentrate in international business—an increase, it noted, of 100 percent from a decade earlier (ibid.). According to the task force, the global scope of business was not adequately reflected in the business curriculum because, in part, "faculty themselves lack global exposure and training in global business strategy and practices. In addition, cases and curricula have not kept up with the rapid developments in the way business is developed, transacted, and consumed in real time across national boundaries" (ibid.: 20). The report highlighted the need for the kind of faculty development programs that CIBEs provide, as well as signaling the need for ongoing support for curriculum development initiatives with an international focus.

The 2003 accreditation standards and subsequent revisions have gradually and consistently given greater emphasis to the international dimension of business education. As of July 2009, AACSB standards require business curricula at accredited schools to include "learning experiences in such general knowledge and skill areas as the dynamics of the global economy" (2008: 71). In order to be judged "both current and relevant," undergraduate business degree programs "will prepare graduates to operate in a business environment that is global in scope. Graduates should be prepared to interact with persons from other cultures and to manage in circumstances where business practices and social conventions are different than the graduate's native country" (ibid.: 70). Master's graduates must have "capacity to understand management issues from a global perspective" (ibid.: 74). Even though there have been no specific international standards for doctoral education, in the 2009 revisions, business schools will be required to document for *all* programs, undergraduate, masters, and doctoral, "how the curriculum across the dimensions outlined in the standard demonstrate a global perspective" (ibid.: 77). In the parlance of AACSB, these changes are significant and will result in greater emphasis on international dimensions of business education.

In the middle, among faculty at business schools, international business teaching and research encounter significant obstacles. Ghemawat notes that faculty facing a six-year horizon to produce high-quality research in sufficient quantity for tenure will find that the difficulties associated with international research constitute a significant barrier. International data are notoriously difficult and expensive to obtain, and often of poorer quality compared to the large data sets widely available for research on domestic business activity in the United States. Financial support from CIBEs for international business research can be important for the acquisition of foreign data and the research assistance needed to improve the quality of data available. Still, even though high-quality international research may be more difficult to accomplish, it is not yet likely to be more highly valued or more easily published. Ghemawat calculates that between 2002 and 2006 only 5 percent of all articles in top management journals had explicit cross-border content, down from 6 percent in the period 1996 to 2000. His tally includes articles from the *Journal of International Business*, the top journal in international business. Although this result is surprising, Ghemawat speculated that the "gravitational pull" of large domestic markets may be strong on editorial boards at major journals that are dominated by U.S. nationals.

In addition to these issues within the business school, one might point out that most U.S. business schools find themselves embedded in a larger university organization and that many of the skills needed for international business are taught in language departments and area studies centers outside the business school. As a result, business schools have little ability to influence the practices or curricula of foreign language and international or area studies departments. In spite of the growing national interest in international dimensions of higher education, and consistent survey results that suggest growing demand for international expertise, there are few data to suggest that business undergraduates are acquiring cross-cultural skills or global competence at an increasing pace. The interdisciplinary mandate of the CIBE legislation, which requires collaboration among language departments, area studies programs, and business schools, is an important tool for bridging the institutional silos and creating international curriculum for professional students.

In the 1960s, 16 percent of all U.S. college students studied a foreign language. By 2000, only 8 percent of the same population studied a foreign language, reflecting the fact that a foreign language requirement had been dropped by many university programs. If we think about the languages that might be of future interest to U.S. business, the results are not encouraging. Of those studying a foreign language, only 6 percent studied Asian languages, and fewer than 1 percent studied Arabic. Fortunately, the availability of instruction in Asian languages is growing and Mandarin is now the seventh most studied foreign language in U.S. postsecondary schools.[12] But even though enrollment in languages like Arabic, Korean, and Chinese is growing rapidly, the base is small. The Modern Language Association (MLA) reports that there are only about 100 students studying Pashto and Tamil in the United States and fewer than 250 studying Farsi.

Nationally, only about 3 percent of all undergraduates study abroad, but between 1985 and 1997 the number of students spending more than a semester abroad fell from 18 percent to 10 percent.[13] There has been some concern about the popularity of study abroad for increasingly shorter periods.[14] While an encouraging 17 percent of U.S. students studying outside the United States in 1999–2000 were business students, the 10- to 15-day "study tour" has become popular as a study abroad experience for graduate business students.[15] Although short-term study abroad programs cannot offer all the cultural immersion, and particularly foreign language instruction, of a longer program, these short-term programs often provide the only firsthand international experience a student in a professional degree program will have before entering the workforce. In addition, there is growing interest among university students, including MBA students, to study abroad outside the traditional European venues. Although study abroad in the Middle East is down, presumably due to security concerns, study abroad in Africa, Asia, and Latin America is growing as a proportion of all study-abroad destinations (see Table 12-3).

Table 12-3. Host Regions of U.S. Students Studying Abroad: 1998/99–2007/08

Host Region	Percentage of U.S. Students Studying Abroad									
	1998/99	1999/00	2000/01	2001/02	2002/03	2003/04	2004/05	2005/06	2006/07	2007/08
Africa	2.8	2.8	2.9	2.9	2.8	3.0	3.5	3.8	4.2	4.5
Asia	6.0	6.2	6.0	6.8	5.6	6.9	8.0	9.3	10.3	11.1
Europe*	62.7	62.4	63.1	62.6	62.9	60.9	60.3	58.3	57.4	56.3
Latin America	15.0	14.0	14.5	14.5	15.3	15.2	14.4	15.2	15.0	15.3
Middle East	2.8	2.9	1.1	0.8	0.4	0.5	1.0	1.2	1.1	1.3
North America	0.7	0.9	0.7	0.8	0.7	0.6	0.5	0.5	0.6	0.4
Oceania	4.9	5.0	6.0	6.8	7.3	7.4	6.7	6.3	5.7	5.3
Antarctica	0.0	0.0	0.0	0.0	0.0	0.0	0.0	0.0	0.0	0.0
Multiple Destinations	5.2	5.8	5.6	4.9	5.1	5.5	5.6	5.5	5.6	5.7
Total	129,770	143,590	154,168	160,920	174,629	191,321	205,983	223,534	241,791	262,416

* Cyprus and Turkey were previously classified in the Middle East category but were moved to the Europe category in 2004/05.

SOURCE: Open Doors, *Report on International Educational Exchange*, 2008.

The Title VI Response

Given the obstacles to internationalization that U.S. business schools and universities face, the need for a national program of Centers of International Business Education and Research (CIBER) is clear. As stated in the 1988 authorizing legislation for CIBEs, "few linkages presently exist between the manpower and information needs of United States business and the international education, language training and research capacities of institutions of higher education in the United States." Despite overwhelming evidence of the increasing importance of international transactions to U.S. business, the academy acting alone seems unable to organize itself quickly enough to keep up with the need. "[C]oncerted efforts are necessary to engage business schools, language and area study programs, public and private sector organizations, and United States business" because "the future economic welfare of the United States will depend substantially on increasing international skills in the business community." This language, written in 1988, amended Title VI to include support for centers that would be "national resources in teaching improved techniques, strategies, and methodologies in international business, instruction in critical foreign languages, and other fields to better understand U.S. trading partners and to conduct research and training in international aspects of trade and commerce" (Scarfo 1998: 25).

CIBEs have responded with courses that strengthen the international business curriculum and programs that build linkages with foreign language and area studies courses. Addressing the need identified in the 2002 AACSB report for more business faculty with international experience, CIBEs design and deliver faculty development opportunities to enrich and expand the international competence of talented business faculty and provide financial support to faculty to enable their participation. Given the difficulty noted earlier for the conduct of international business research, CIBE support for international business research on various university campuses helps to make international research more feasible. Finally, outreach seminars and noncredit programming for small businesses and practicing managers enable those currently engaged in international business to share their experiences and learn about best practices.

Beginning in 1989 with only five awards and growing steadily in succeeding competitions to the present thirty-one CIBEs in twenty-two states, the Title VI CIBE program began by internationalizing graduate and undergraduate curriculum at the receiving school and creating executive education programs that would provide international business training to practicing managers who might not have had such an opportunity when they were students and now find themselves in positions with international responsibilities. Such CIBE initiatives addressed the needs identified in the surveys cited previously for both more international business courses and enhanced training opportunities for current managers. Soon, CIBE schools began creating international linkages with universities overseas to develop joint teaching and research programs that would expand opportunities for students and professors, at the same time strengthening the process of internationalization at the U.S. business schools.

Reflecting the growing importance that the Department of Education placed on outreach to proximately located institutions of higher education, CIBEs soon created professional development opportunities for faculty at other institutions, so a greater number of business schools could begin to internationalize their teaching and research activities. Over time, CIBEs developed such programs for faculty at community colleges as well as those at historically black colleges and universities.[16] The latter program was developed in collaboration with the Institute for International Public Policy. These outreach programs play a critical role in leveraging federal resources to reach the largest number of students at large and small universities across the country.

To address the needs of those currently working in international business, CIBEs host numerous programs in their respective geographical areas and work collaboratively with other organizations that promote international business, including district export councils and state offices for international trade development. These programs offer timely information on promising international markets, the latest developments in trade regulation, and "how-to" seminars on financing international transactions. Recently, fourteen CIBEs have assisted in the development of the NASBITE International Certified Global Business Professional credential, an international trade specialist credential that is acquiring growing recognition in the field. It is used for training professionals by the U.S. Chamber of Commerce, among others.

Over the years, CIBEs have developed a broad portfolio of activities that serve students, faculty, future business faculty, and business people. Whereas some target a local audience, others reach out to a national audience. CIBERweb, hosted by the Michigan State University CIBE (www.CIBERweb.msu.edu), provides easy online access to the set of CIBE offerings, including research conferences, faculty development opportunities for language and business faculty, study abroad opportunities, and outreach events for businesspeople. In addition, CIBERweb provides full-text copies of reports, including "Securing our Nation's Future through International Business Education: 15 years of CIBERs, 1989–2004" and "Engaging the World: U.S. Global Competence in the 21st Century," completed in honor of the 50th anniversary of Title VI. The impact of CIBE programs can be seen, in part, in the numbers in Tables 12-4 and 12-5. Almost 1.7 million students have been enrolled in CIBE-sponsored courses and more than 100,000 have studied abroad on CIBE programs. Some 200,000 students have acquired professional foreign language skills and more than 9,000 business or professional foreign language courses have been taught. Perhaps most important, with the help of CIBE funding, 7,500 international business research projects have been conducted and nearly 122,000 business professors have had international professional development experiences that will influence the course of their teaching and research well into the future. For doctoral students—those who will most likely be the business professors of tomorrow—CIBE has sponsored more than 1,000 international business education programs serving approximately 25,000 doctoral students. This investment in faculty capabilities, present and future, is estimated to have an impact on more than 14 million business students.

Table 12-4. Impact of CIBE-Sponsored Curricular Activities: 1989–2007

CIBE-Sponsored Curricular Activities	Undergraduate	Graduate
IB courses taught	18,687	28,015
Students enrolled in IB courses	1,043,450	608,489
Newly created IB courses	6,251	
Students experiencing overseas learning	97,998	
Business language courses taught	4,065	5,004
Students enrolled in business language courses	155,362	47,654

SOURCE: CIBER, Annual CIBER Statistical Study, 2008.

Table 12-5. Impact of CIBE-Sponsored Faculty Development Activities: 1989–2007

CIBE-Sponsored Faculty Development Activities	Programs	Participants
Faculty language programs	744	32,968
Faculty IB development programs	2,365	96,067
IB faculty/PhD research projects supported	6,644	

SOURCE: CIBER, Annual CIBER Statistical Study, 2008.

To meet the needs of current managers as identified in many of the surveys cited above, CIBEs have developed more than 5,000 executive programs, specialized conferences, workshops, or seminars with international business content, serving nearly 750,000 practicing managers. Often in collaboration with local international trade promotion groups, CIBEs offer seminars on topics such as trade finance, international marketing techniques, regulatory compliance, and international business ethics. Other programs, such as the Asia/Pacific Business Outlook conference, focus on recent developments in particular countries or regions. This conference provides business executives and entrepreneurs with the latest trade and investment opportunities in fifteen Asia–Pacific economies. The conference facilitates international business networking and helps arrange one-on-one meetings with senior commercial officers from American embassies in the Asia–Pacific region. Recently, CIBEs have offered conferences that focus on contemporary topics such as sustainable business practices, biotech, and the trading of services. These conferences bring a mix of academic and business perspectives to bear on some of the biggest challenges of global competitiveness and would not be possible without the organizational capabilities and funding of CIBEs located across the country.

The Next 50 Years

As the Title VI program turns fifty, globalization may be turning into something like "globality" with its new competitive reality rooted in non-Western cultures and emerging market economies. Over the past fifty years, international business has grown from transactions focused primarily on the triad of the United States, Europe, and Japan to include transactions initiated in the triad but involving the emerging economies. Most recently, the new MNEs have emerged, initiating global business transactions from a home base in emerging markets. Add to these the "born global" firms, those that have not followed the traditional path of MNE expansion, instead, have engaged in substantial international activity very early in their existence, and the recent international business literature identifies a growing number of firms that do not conform to the traditional view of internationalization.

275

The presence of these new firms in global markets, and the core competencies that they deploy in multiple markets, are changing the scope of competition on a global scale. Globality highlights the need for more knowledge and better skills in cross-cultural management, as well as a better understanding of foreign business environments, global financial markets, and international marketing, especially as they relate to emerging markets in Asia, Africa, Eastern Europe, Latin America, and the Middle East. The phenomenon of globalization pushed business students to study abroad in Europe, whereas globality will drive them to enroll in a ten-day study tour to India. Although students have been studying Spanish sixteen times more frequently than Mandarin, the availability of courses in Mandarin is rising along with enrollment. Eleven business language courses are taught at Brigham Young University, including Business Arabic, Business Korean, and Business Russian, and its CIBE hosts an annual case competition for students, who must analyze an international business problem and present their recommendations, working entirely in either Spanish or Portuguese. The CIBE at the University of Texas–Austin has developed video materials based on interviews with foreign executives who discuss in their own languages various aspects of conducting business in their countries.

Many believe that globality will require of business students the kind of competencies that can be gained from activities such as study abroad in Africa, internships with microfinance organizations in Latin America, and/or consulting projects in China, conducted mostly in Mandarin, for U.S. companies large and small. Whereas business school accreditation standards may evolve slowly, CIBEs are taking the lead by designing special programs and projects to increase the acquisition and use of strategic languages and to develop global competence among business graduates. For example, pooling MBA students from several universities, CIBEs have constructed cross-functional teams with capability in the relevant foreign language, matched them with real business projects abroad, and created consulting projects for the MBA students who work in virtual teams before doing in-country field work in emerging markets. These projects sharpen students' international business and foreign language skills as they apply what they have been learning. At the same time, the team provides usable results for American firms doing business abroad.

In another collaborative effort, a CIBE consortium provides resources for multi-year surveys on offshoring, creating an important new database and opportunities for doctoral students and faculty to conduct important research on the implications of offshoring for business processes. An annual CIBE research conference provides a forum for sharing incipient research on cutting edge topics such as diaspora investors,[17] resource nationalism,[18] trade and security, corruption and terrorism, and the role of business in stabilizing failed states.[19] To address the need for multilingual business executives, CIBEs work with colleagues in the language departments to promote the development of new pedagogies for teaching foreign languages to business professionals. An annual conference for foreign language faculty interested in teaching applied language courses facilitates the sharing of best practices and disseminates successful course design to other academic institutions.

Conclusion

Over the past fifty years, with the support of Title VI programs and funding, U.S. universities have been preparing generations of students for globalization, and over the past twenty years there has been an explicit commitment to developing the international expertise appropriate for business. Over a similar period, studies reveal, international business has been growing in importance, additional growth has been consistently anticipated by business practitioners, and qualified candidates for international positions have been difficult to find. With some notable exceptions, business schools have been slow to respond to the growing importance of international transactions in the activities of U.S. business. Without the impetus of Title VI, it seems quite likely that the capacity of business schools to help U.S. business succeed in global markets would have lagged even further. The consistent focus of Title VI programs on bringing the specialized international resources of universities to bear on the staffing needs of the nation has served thousands of students, faculty, and companies.

The next fifty years will require a different focus for those efforts as American firms and the American workforce transition from globalization to globality. The new competitive landscape represents a challenge for the incumbent firms and for U.S. business schools. Foreign language skills and area studies knowledge are likely to be even more valuable in this new competitive landscape. As U.S. firms prepare to compete against a growing number of talented, agile, and driven-to-succeed competitors from emerging markets, the Title VI mandate pushes universities to work more collaboratively across disciplinary divides and encourages business schools to develop the academic programs that surveys consistently demonstrate will meet the demands of U.S. business in an increasingly competitive global market.

Notes

1 Daniels, Radebaugh, and Sullivan 2007, p. 8.
2 CIBEs became CIBERs when the word "research" was added to the name of the centers, reflecting language in the original legislation and facilitating the creation of an easily pronounced acronym.
3 www.worldforum.org/commission/challenge.html (accessed March 3, 2009).

4 Boston Consulting Group identified 100 firms from countries such as Argentina, Egypt, Hungary, Malaysia, Thailand, Turkey, and, of course, the BRIC—Brazil, Russia, India, and China—that it believes are poised to succeed. Called the BCG Challenger 100, these firms compete across the globe in aerospace, petrochemicals, telecom, dry goods, food and beverages, and appliances. CEPAL (United Nations Economic Commission on Latin America and the Caribbean also known as ECLAC) has coined the term "trans-Latinas" for Latin American firms making multiple investments in other Latin American countries. Van Agtmael has identified a set of twenty-five firms he characterizes as the "World-Class Emerging Multinationals." There are other lists that appear periodically in the popular press.

5 Cendant Mobility 2002, as cited in Hunter 2004.

6 For a useful review of the literature on global mindset, see Levy et al. 2007. Lambert (1996) provides a thorough discussion of approaches to global competency and Ang and van Dyne (2007) provide a handbook on cultural intelligence. Kedia and Mukherji use the phrasing "global perspective."

7 Swiss Consulting Group, Global Competency Report 2002, cited in Hunter 2004.

8 Reynolds and Rice 1988, summarized in Table 12-1, also found that executives distinguished certain international business topics as better suited for academic study.

9 The results of a Canadian study (Beamish and Colof 1989) conducted five years later reinforced some of the same conclusions. Kohers (1985), summarized in Table 12-1, also surveyed firms in the southeastern United States about the desirability of particular courses at this time.

10 In 109 cases, the responding manger was responsible for some international aspect of the company's activity.

11 In 2003, this language was broadened to "domestic and global economic environments of organizations."

12 Language Log, 2009.

13 ACEnet.edu (American Council on Education), October 19, 2001.

14 The Council on International Education Exchange has associated global competence with "exchange programs [of at least three months duration] to universities abroad where U.S. citizens are not the majority population and where English is not the dominant language" (Council on International Educational Exchange 1988).

15 AACSB 2002, p. 9. According to the AACSB report, whereas some 24,411 U.S. business students studied abroad in 1999–2000, some 106,043 foreign students were enrolled in business programs in the United States in 2000–2001.

16 Michigan State University CIBER leads the consortium of CIBEs that provide a program for community college faculty and additional information about the program can be found at http://global.broad.msu.edu/ibi/. The program for HBCU faculty is led by the University of Memphis CIBER and is more fully explained at https://umdrive.memphis.edu/g-wangcenter/www/pages/hbcus1.htm.

17 Diaspora investors are those from immigrant communities that remit investment capital to their homelands through transnational entrepreneurship, foreign direct investment, and portfolio investment.

18 Resource nationalism is the growing trend in developing countries toward greater state control or ownership of natural resources, especially energy. Although foreign investment is not excluded, it is more tightly regulated or circumscribed.

19 Although business is sometimes blamed for sustaining conflict—for example, through producing or trafficking in "conflict diamonds"—there is increasing interest in the potentially powerful role of business in preventing conflict and in contributing to sustainable peace as it provides investment and employment that can lead to long-term improvements in living standards and security. CIBEs at the University of Kansas and George Washington University have done work in this area.

REFERENCES

AACSB International. 2008. Eligibility Procedures and Accreditation Standards for Business Accreditation. Tampa, FL: AACSB.

AACSB International. 2006. A World of Good: Business, Business Schools, and Peace. Tampa, FL: AACSB. Retrieved February 20, 2009 from www.aacsb.edu/Resource_Centers/Peace/Final-Peace-Report.pdf.

AACSB International. 2002. *Management Education at Risk: Report of the Management Education Task Force to the AACSB International Board of Directors.* Tampa, FL: AACSB.

Ang, S. and L. Van Dyne. 2007. Conceptualization of Cultural Intelligence: Definition, Distinctiveness, and Nomological Network, pp. 3–15 in S. Ang and L. Van Dyne, eds., *Handbook of Cultural Intelligence: Theory, Measurement, and Applications.* New York: M. E. Sharpe.

Ball, D.A. and W. H. McCulloch Jr. 1993. The Views of American Multinational CEOs on International Business Education for Prospective Employees. *Journal of International Business Studies*, 24(2):383–391.

Beamish, Paul W. and J. L. Calof. 1989. International Education: A Corporate View. *Journal of International Business Studies*, 20(3):553–64.

Black, J. S., A. J. Morrison, and H.B. Gregersen. 1999. *Global Explorers: The Next Generation of Leaders*. New York: Routledge.

Brustein, W. I. 2007. *Paths to Global Competence: Preparing American College Students*. Retrieved July 26, 2009 from www.iienetwork.org/page/84657.

Charting the Global Mindset, BizEd, Jan/Feb 2006, p. 50.

CIBER. 2009. Annual CIBER Statistical Summary, prepared by the Center for International Business Education and Research, McCombs School of Business, The University of Texas at Austin.

Cummings, W. 2001. *Current Challenges of International Education*. Washington D.C.: ERIC Clearinghouse on Higher Education.

Daniel, S. 1998. The Changing Demand for International Expertise in Business. In Hawkins, J. N., C. M. Haro, M. A. Kazanjian, G.W. Merx, and D. Wiley (eds.). *International Education in the New Global Era: Proceedings of a National Policy Conference on the Higher Education Act, Title VI, and Fulbright Hays Programs*. Los Angeles: University of California, International Studies and Programs, pp. 148–150.

Davis, T. M. (ed.). 1997. *Open Doors 1996/97: Report on International Educational Exchange*. New York: Institute on International Education.

De Sam, M., B. Dougan, J. Gordon, J. Puaschunder, and C. St. Clair. 2008. Building a Globally Competent Citizenry in the United States. Report for the U.S. Department of Education, Office of Postsecondary Education. Washington, D.C.: International Educational Programs Service.

Edwards, J. D., A. L. Lenker, and D. Kahn. 2008. National Language Policies: Pragmatism, Process, and Products. Joint National Committee for Languages. National Council for Languages and International Studies. *NECTFL Review*, no. 63, Fall/Winter 2008/2009: 2–42.

Globalization and Monetary Policy Institute Annual Report 2008. Federal Reserve Bank of Dallas. Dallas: U.S. Federal Reserve.

Ghemawat, P. 2008. The Globalization of Business Education: Through the Lens of Semiglobalization. *Journal of Management Development*, 27(4): 391–414.

Guillen, M. F. and E. Garcia-Canal. 2009. The American Model of the Multinational Firm and the "New" Multinationals from Emerging Economies. *Academy of Management Perspectives*, May 2009: 23–35.

Hayward, F. 2000. *Internationalization of U.S. Higher Education: Preliminary Status Report*. Washington, D.C.: American Council on Education.

Hunter, W. D. 2004. Got Global Competency? *International Educator*, Spring 2004: 6–12.

Hunter, B., G. P. White, and G. C. Godbey. 2006. What Does It Mean to be Globally Competent? *Journal of Studies in International Education*, 10:267–285.

International Education Programs Service. 2005. The History of Title VI and Fulbright-Hays: An Impressive International Timeline. Retrieved April 6, 2008 from www.ed.gov/print/about/offices/list/ope/iegs/history.html.

Kedia, B. L. and S. Daniel. 2003. U.S. Business Needs for Employees with International Expertise. Paper presented at the 2003 Needs for Global Challenges Conference, Duke University. Retrieved July 2009 from http://ducis.jhfc.duke.edu/archives/globalchallenges/pdf/kedia_daniel.pdf.

Kedia, B. L. and A. Mukherji. 1999. Global Managers: Developing a Mindset for Global competitiveness. *Journal of World Business*, 34(2):230–251.

Kets de Vries, M. F. R. 2004. *The Global Executive Leadership Inventory: Facilitator's Guide.* San Francisco: Pfeiffer.

Kobrin, S. 1984. *International Expertise in American Business: How to Learn to Play with the Kids on the Street.* New York: Institute of International Education.

Kwok, C. Y. and J. S. Arpan. 2002. Internationalizing the Business School: A Global Survey in 2000. *Journal of International Business Studies*, 33(3):571–581.

Kwok, C. Y., J. Arpan, and W. R. Folks Jr. 1994. A Global Survey of International Business Education in the 1990s. *Journal of International Business Studies*, 25(3):605–623.

Lambert, R. D. (1994), "Parsing the concept of global competence", in Lambert, R.D. (Eds), *Educational Exchange and Global Competence*, Council on International Educational Exchange, New York, NY, pp.11–24.

Lambert, R. 1996. Parsing the Concept of Global Competence, in *Educational Exchange and Global Competence*. New York: Council on International Educational Exchange.

Levy, O., S. Beechler, S. Taylor, and N. A. Boyacigiller. 2007. What We Talk about When We Talk about "Global Mindset": Managerial Cognition in Multinational Corporations. *Journal of International Business Studies*, 38:231–258.

Moxon, R., E. O'Shea, M. Brown, and C. Escher. 1997. *Changing U.S. Business Needs for International Expertise.* Center for International Business Education and Research (CIBER). Seattle: University of Washington Business School.

Nehrt, L. 1977. *Business and International Education.* Washington, D.C.: American Council on Education.

Oppenheimer, A. 2009. Time to Send More U.S. College Students Abroad. *Miami Herald*, March 1.

Porter, L. W. and L. E. McKibben. 1988. *Management Education and Development: Drift or Thrust into the 21st Century.* New York: McGraw-Hill.

Reimers, F. 2009. "Global Competency" Is Imperative for Global Success. *Chronicle of Higher Education*, 55(21):A29.

Reynolds, J. and G. H. Rice. 1988. American Education for International Business. *Management International Review*, 28(3):48–57.

Ricks, D.A. and M. Czinkota. 1979. International Business: An Examination of the Corporate Viewpoint. *Journal of International Business Studies*, Vol 10 No 2 Fall, 1979: 97–100.

Scarfo, R. D. 1998. The History of Title VI and Fulbright-Hays. In Hawkins, J. N., C. M. Haro, M. A. Kazanjian, G. W. Merkx, and D. Wiley (eds.) *International Education in the New*

Global Era: Proceedings of a National Policy Conference on the Higher Education Act, Title VI, and Fulbright-Hayes Programs. Los Angeles: UCLA International Studies and Overseas Programs, pp. 23–25.

Schiffer, M. 2009. The U.S. and Rising Powers. *2009 Great Decisions Briefing Book.* The Stanley Foundation, Muscatine, Iowa, pp. 5–16.

Sirkin, H. L., J. W. Hemerling, and A. K. Bhattacharya. 2008. *Globality: Competing with Everyone from Everywhere for Everything.* Boston: Boston Consulting Group.

Van Agtmael, A. 2007. *The Emerging Markets Century.* New York: Free Press.

Vietor, R.H.K. 2007. *How Countries Compete: Strategy, Structure, and Government in the Global Economy.* Boston: Harvard Business School Press.

Voris, W. 1997. A Retrospective of International Business Education in the United States over the Past Fifty Years. *The International Executive*, 39(2):271–282.

Welles, E. B. 2004. Foreign Language Enrollments in United States Institutions of Higher Education, Fall 2002. *ADFL Bulletin*, 35:7–26.

Zachrisson, C. U. 2001. New Study Abroad Destinations: Trends and Emerging Opportunities, pp. 28–30 in M. Tillman (ed.), *Study Abroad: A Twenty-First Century Perspective. Volume II: The Changing Landscape.* Stamford, CT: American Institute for Foreign Language.

CHAPTER 13

Title VI and the Global Competitiveness of U.S. Firms

Michael A. Hitt

Introduction

In his most recent book, Thomas Friedman (2008) cited a Daimler advertising slogan used to promote its Smart "Fourfor" compact car. The slogan reads as follows: "German engineering, Swiss innovation, American nothing." This slogan implies that the automobile advertised is superior because it is the product of German engineering and Swiss innovation and has no input from designers or manufacturers in the United States. On the one hand, this particular slogan describes the unfortunately weak competitive position of and low esteem in which U.S. automobile manufacturers are held throughout the world. On the other hand, it suggests a weak or ineffective understanding of cross-cultural dynamics and the capabilities that are held by U.S. firms. Thus, it likely explains one of the major reasons that Daimler's acquisition of Chrysler failed so miserably. Although this acquisition had the potential for creating considerable synergy between the two companies because each had some valuable capabilities that were complementary to each other (Hitt et al. 2001), the merger failed. It failed partly because Daimler dominated the American manufacturing operations after acquiring Chrysler and lost many of the most qualified and capable managers and engineers in the Chrysler organization. Further, it failed to effectively integrate the two businesses. As a result, it eventually had to sell off the Chrysler assets at a considerable loss from its original purchase price.

283

In the current global competitive landscape, it is absolutely essential that businesses, regardless of their home base, have an effective understanding of different cultures and different countries' institutional environments. Without this understanding, they are unlikely to be competitive in international markets and even unlikely to be successful in their home domestic market competing against multinational firms with home bases in other countries (Hitt et al. 1998; Hitt et al. 2009). Globalization has led to a penetration of many domestic markets by foreign firms, making these markets much more competitive than in previous times. As such, Hitt and He (2008) suggest that we can no longer discuss globalization in the future tense.

Firms now must operate in a highly dynamic and rivalrous global competitive landscape. In our current environment, major country stock exchanges across the world are interrelated, with each affected by the others. Currencies' values fluctuate regularly and sometimes significantly. For reasons noted above and more, the economic crisis in the later part of the first decade of the twenty-first century is global, rather than domestic. To help prepare U.S. citizens, U.S. businesses, and U.S. society in general to better operate in this dynamic and complex environment, there has been a series of legislation, regulations, and programs developed by the U.S. federal government that speak to these concerns. In this chapter, I review briefly the history of the relevant legislation and programs, with special focus in this chapter on their effects on business education and the competitiveness of U.S. firms.

On the front of the Norlin Library at the University of Colorado, there is a statement chiseled into the stone facing stating, "Who knows only his own generation remains always a child." Thus, it is important to understand history to better understand the present and the opportunities for the future. The following sections examine the history of Title VI and U.S. business competitiveness.

History—Title VI and Global Competitiveness

The 1950s–1960s

The history of important legislation begins with the passage of Title VI of the National Defense Education Act of 1958 (NDEA). Although U.S. concern for international education to support growing foreign relations had begun in the 1930s and strongly increased after the establishment of the United Nations, the NDEA itself was precipitated by the launch of the Sputnik satellite by the Soviet Union in 1957, which produced widespread alarm in the United States; Congress responded with the passage of the NDEA, including Title VI. The original beneficiaries of Title VI were intended to be individuals entering the teaching profession or entering public service.

The second important piece of legislation is the Mutual Educational and Cultural Exchange Act of 1961, referred to as the Fulbright-Hays Act. This act was aimed at promoting foreign exchange programs, in the hope of better coordinating the visits of foreigners to the United States and also improving the flow of Americans going abroad. The hope was that these outcomes would increase Americans' knowledge of different cultures and country environments. The act was particularly designed to enhance the knowledge of teachers and prospective teachers.

Over time, the Title VI program evolved from a response to a national emergency to a focus on the use of national resources to enhance the understanding and ability to manage trade, security, and other international issues. In fact, some of the original emphases on improving language skills continue today; however, there has been a gradual shift to emphasize the nation's economic competitiveness. Several other pieces of legislation were passed in the 1960s and early 1970s. The most important for our purposes was the Higher Education Act of 1965. Title VI was then placed under the U.S. Department of Education; it provides the framework for the development and implementation of the Business and International Education (BIE) and Centers for International Business Education (CIBE) programs, both of which are administered by the U.S. Department of Education, as described later.

In the 1950s and 1960s, U.S. firms began their international expansion activities in earnest. For example, in the 1950s, U.S. firms engaged in slightly more than $20 billion of foreign direct investment (FDI). During the 1960s, the FDI more than doubled to more than $42 billion by U.S. firms. Some of the early international expansion efforts that received considerable public attention were by Coca-Cola and Pepsi Cola. Coca-Cola began expanding its operations by selling its products in China and Pepsi, as a response, entered the market in the Soviet Union in the 1950s. In the 1960s, U.S. firms exported more than $350 billion worth of goods to foreign markets, whereas imports during this decade were slightly more than $320 billion (see Figures 13-1 and 13-2 for more precise information). In fact, this was the last decade to date in which U.S. firms' exports exceeded the imports of foreign goods into the U.S. market.

The 1970s

U.S. firms continued their dominance in global markets, especially in the early 1970s, despite several political disruptions such as the Vietnam War, Watergate, the resignation of a U.S. president, and the Arab oil embargo. U.S. automobile companies were aggressive in their international expansion during this time; McDonald's international expansion began during this time as well, and its global reach extended considerably during the 1980s. Most of the U.S. companies moving into international markets used what is referred to as a global strategy, in which U.S. brands and styles were emphasized. Although there was some local adaptation of the products, these changes were minimal, as the U.S. firms at the time were selling superior technology and styling, along with the American culture, to foreign customers. Because of the assumed success in international markets and different

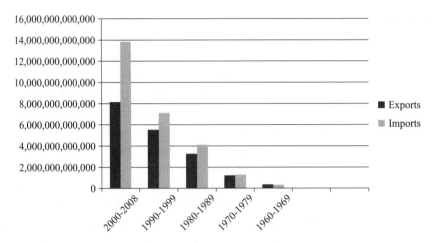

FIGURE 13-1

Comparison of U.S. Exports and Imports by Decade

Source: Bureau of Economic Analysis, Trade Stats Express, http://tse.export.gov/NTDMap.aspx? Unique URL=ybcieh451effjoj1avq1m1fl-2009-5, www.bea.gov/international/xls/table1.xls

administration philosophies, Title VI programs encountered a rather hostile funding environment during much of the 1970s.

However, concerns began to develop in the late 1970s about how the U.S. industry would fare in global markets in future years. This concern was partly due to the development of more capable foreign competitors. The concern was exemplified by the fact that during the 1970s, foreign imported goods in U.S. markets exceeded the exported goods into international markets by U.S. firms for the first time (Bureau of Economic Analysis 2009; see Figure 13-1). As a result, Congress passed

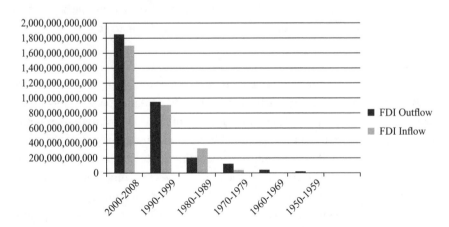

FIGURE 13-2

Comparison of FDI Outflow and Inflow by Decade.

Source: Bureau of Economic Analysis, Trade Stats Express, http://tse.export.gov/NTDMap.aspx? Unique URL=ybcieh451effjoj1avq1m1fl-2009-5, www.bea.gov/international/xls/table1.xls

major trade legislation in 1979, which translated into the development of a new section for Title VI with the goal of promoting activities that "contributed to the ability of the United States business to prosper in an international economy" (Slater 2007). The House Committee on Education and Labor suggested that the world's economy was becoming more interdependent and the United States was vulnerable if its citizens and businesses did not develop a greater appreciation for and knowledge of different cultures and languages of other countries (Slater 2007).

The BIE program was created in 1980 and added to Title VI, receiving its first funding in 1983. This program had several goals. First, it had the objective of internationalizing the business school curriculum. Another intent was to develop specialized educational materials that could be used by faculty and for students in the classroom and for learning more generally. Additionally, the program was established to provide student and faculty fellowships—in particular, to facilitate foreign travel to help gain the knowledge and appreciation of other cultures and other countries' institutional environments. This program, which has been continuously funded since its inception, awards about forty grants each year, at a total annual cost of approximately $4.5 million. The grantees are required to match the federal funds.

The 1980s

Certainly, U.S. businesses' foreign investments and expansion in international markets continued during the 1980s. However, international competition began to erode the competitive advantage enjoyed by U.S. businesses during the 1980s. Although companies such as McDonald's enjoyed significant and successful international expansion during the 1980s, a number of highly capable foreign companies developed into significant competitors even in the U.S. domestic market. This is probably best exemplified by Japanese auto manufacturers and the electronics manufacturers from Asia, particularly Japan. In addition, during the 1980s, for the first time since the 1950s, FDI by foreign companies into the United States was considerably higher than the FDI in other countries by U.S. businesses. Additionally, the imports from foreign companies into the United States grew at a substantial pace in the 1980s and far outstripped the exports of U.S. firms (these results are reflected in Figures 13-1 and 13-2).

In response to concerns about the competitiveness of U.S. firms, Congress passed new legislation, referred to as the Omnibus Trade and Competitiveness Act of 1988. This legislation implemented a number of statutory regulations to improve U.S. trade and competitiveness, and was signed by President Reagan in 1988. One component of the legislation authorized the CIBE program, which was transferred to Title VI of the Higher Education Act, for administration by the U.S. Department of Education. According to Easton (2009), this CIBE legislation was proposed and passed by Congress because of an assessment that the welfare of U.S. firms depended on increasing the international business skills available and used in their operations. As a result, there was a perceived need to engage business schools to internationalize their curricula, increase faculty research capabilities on global business concepts, and engage their students in language and area study programs. In particular, there was a desire to increase the linkages between colleges and public and private organizations in the United States. The CIBE program, also commonly known as the CIBER program because research was included in the legislation, is intended to support international education and research and language training to serve the human capital and knowledge requirements of U.S. businesses. Moreover, the intent was to enhance cultural understanding and knowledge of different countries' institutional environments as well as their effects on business activities in domestic and global markets.

Specifically, the program authorized the use of resources at the national level for the teaching of international business, foreign languages, and other international area fields. In addition, the financial resources provided were intended to support training and research on international trade, commerce, and related areas. The expenditures authorized were for support of faculty and staff travel related to the noted objectives and for curriculum planning and development. These resources also could be used to support visiting scholars and faculty and for training to increase the knowledge and skills of faculty and staff related to the goals noted above. The program required interdisciplinary subprograms, intensive language programs, collaborative efforts among different disciplines within universities, and research on international business education and U.S. competitiveness. CIBEs have been established in a number of major universities throughout the United States and have had a substantial impact over time. The outcomes became especially apparent in the 1990s.

The 1990s

The CIBE program greatly increased (in both the number of centers and in the breadth and depth of the education and research activities that the CIBEs developed and supported) during the 1990s. In fact, this program, along with a renewed emphasis on developing new capabilities and skills to enhance U.S. firms' competitiveness, helped U.S. businesses regain competitive advantages in several markets. For example, U.S. firms obtained new knowledge stocks from foreign competitors, using these and other unique knowledge stocks developed internally to cultivate new capabilities and enhance their competitiveness in domestic and international markets. Graduates of business schools with new emphases on international business education added to U.S. firms' knowledge and capabilities to compete in international markets and compete more effectively with foreign competitors in the U.S. domestic markets.

The global economic and competitive environment also began to change. For example, the interdependence of economic activity across country borders was growing, partly because of free trade pacts such as the North American Free Trade Agreement (NAFTA) and the increased amount of FDI made by multinational firms from all over the world. Increased technology development, such as enhancement and implementation of the Internet, facilitated economic trade across country borders. As noted earlier, the internationalization of U.S. businesses, to include even smaller and newer firms in the United States, started increasing dramatically during the 1990s (Hitt et al. 2006). Firms obviously were seeking larger markets but also increased returns by entering and competing in international markets. In addition, firms found that they could gain quicker and higher returns on innovation by increasing the size of the general market for their goods through entry into foreign markets. Finally, they also found that they could learn new capabilities by moving into new international markets where different skill sets were in existence (Hitt et al. 1997; Zahra et al. 2000). Of course, all these activities also enhanced global competition. The increasing global competition in many domestic and foreign markets highlighted the need for greater skills for managing operations and developing and implementing more sophisticated strategies in these markets. To do so required enhanced language skills, enriched knowledge of different cultures, and a better understanding of the institutional environments in regions and specific countries, as well as their effects on the types of strategies that could be most successful in those geographic and cultural markets.

In particular, we began to learn the importance of culture and cultural legacies. In his popular book, Gladwell (2008) argued that cultural legacies have an impact on twenty-first-century intellectual tasks. For example, he suggested that if we had a math Olympics and each country sent its thousand brightest students to compete, the five countries with the top performers would be (in order): China, Hong Kong, Japan, Singapore, and South Korea (Boe et al. 2004).

Each of these countries has cultures shaped by long, hard, and meaningful work. In particular, they demonstrate substantial persistence at a task until it is done. This is, perhaps, best exemplified by an old Asian saying, "No one who can rise before dawn 360 days a year fails to make his family rich" (Blinco 1991).

During the 1990s, U.S. firms regained the lead in amount of FDI made by U.S. businesses relative to the amount of FDI into the U.S. markets by foreign companies. Whereas exports of U.S. products grew to more than $5.5 trillion, however, imports of foreign goods into the U.S. increased to $7.1 trillion during the 1990s (see Figures 13-1 and 13-2).

The 2000s

The twenty-first century started with great expectations, and there has been much change evidenced since it began. In fact, the U.S. environment has been dynamic and might be characterized as chaotic. It began with an economic recession greatly exacerbated by the terrorist attacks on September 11, 2001. These events led to the "war on terror" and two simultaneous wars in Afghanistan and Iraq. The chaotic nature was fueled by an environment characterized by laissez-faire regulatory enforcement and exceptionally high oil prices. These events, coupled with administration actions since the early 1980s, led to a major domestic economic recession, which then precipitated the global economic recession. These events reflected the global and interconnected nature of economies that had been developing for some time. In addition, the U.S. institutional environment changed during the early 2000s, largely owing to new policies enacted during the war on terror and general administration philosophies.

Furthermore, global competition has become fierce with the growing competitive capabilities of many firms throughout the world, especially multinational firms based in major emerging economies such as China and India. There has been a significant increase in the number of functions and activities outsourced, especially by U.S. firms (Lei and Hitt 1995; Lewin 2005a; Holcomb and Hitt 2007). Much of the outsourcing occurred in order to enrich the U.S. firms' competitiveness in global markets. In particular, functional activities (such as manufacturing and information technology work) could be performed often at a much lower cost and with equal quality. These potential outcomes motivated firms to outsource noncore capabilities to businesses in foreign countries, many of them emerging economy countries.

There have also been an increased number of cross-border mergers and acquisitions (Hitt et al. 2009; Zhu et al. 2009). For example, cross-border merger and acquisition (M&A) transactions reached a record of $4.5 trillion in 2007, representing a 24 percent increase over the record set one year earlier (Thomson Financial 2007). Much of the cross-border acquisition activity has been targeted toward helping firms enter major markets, along with the intent to acquire new capabilities that allow a firm to increase its competitiveness in global markets. Most recently, a number of acquisitions have been made by major firms, particularly Chinese firms, from large emerging markets. Chinese foreign direct investments were more than $50 billion in 2008 and were estimated to reach almost $60 billion in 2009 (Roberts and Balfour 2009).

Therefore, there has been an increased amount of strategic activity of developed economy firms, such as those from the United States, entering major and economically growing emerging-economy countries, and increased strategic activity in global markets by major firms based in these emerging markets as well. Firms from the largest and critically important emerging markets of Brazil, Russia, India, and China (known as the BRIC countries), have been especially active. These BRIC countries have become major players in the global economy. China has been growing economically at a rate of 9 to 10 percent per year for the past decade and its firms have been building their capabilities. Similarly, India has been developing its economy at a fast pace and especially building its capabilities in the services industries, particularly information technology. Brazil is noted for its substantial natural resources and Russia also has been taking advantage of its natural resources, especially petroleum. As a result, there have been a number of economic projections related to changes in the global economy over the next several decades. For example, China has been projected to become the world's largest economy by 2040–2042. India has been projected to become the third largest economy in the world by 2050. Brazil has been projected to become the fifth largest economy and Russia the ninth largest economy, both by 2050 (Hitt and He, 2008).

All these strategic activities and changes that have occurred in the twenty-first century suggest the substantial need to learn about international markets if firms are to be competitive (Li and Hitt 2006; Hitt, Tihanyi et al. 2006) and to understand institutional environments. The CIBE program has played a major role in helping U.S. firms enrich their knowledge of foreign countries and markets. A report issued in 2005 on the first fifteen years of the program, 1989–2004, presented some important facts that depict the impact of the CIBE program. During the period of 1989–2004, more than 900,000 students took more than 28,000 courses with an international business emphasis in CIBE-funded universities. Almost 800 new degree programs, majors, and concentrations in international business were created or expanded. These programs included more than 4,000 new or upgraded international courses. During this period, CIBE universities have graduated more than 155,000 students, many with concentrations in international business. Of these, 73,000 are MBAs with international business expertise. Additionally, CIBE universities had more than 11,000 master's degree graduates in one academic year (circa 1993–1994) with international business expertise. They projected that by 2009, 92,000 graduates during the fifteen years would be working in positions with international content and tasks (Folks 2005). Supportive of these programs are commercial language courses and international language workshops. During these fifteen years, CIBEs supported 7,300 commercial language courses, and more than 2.4 million students benefited from foreign language instruction in U.S. universities (Sacco 2005)

Likewise, CIBEs have supported a significant amount of research, all of which has increased our knowledge of how businesses can enhance their competitiveness 291 in global markets. For example, CIBEs have supported more than 5,200 faculty members conducting international business research. More than 3,200 working papers from this research have been published, and the research results have been presented by faculty at more than 1,000 international conferences with CIBE support (Lewin 2005b). Many long-term research projects have resulted in articles in refereed journals, textbooks, and other scholarly publications.

One essential component of the CIBE program is the legislative requirement to disseminate the knowledge gained at the CIBE universities to a wider audience, and for this purpose the thirty-one currently funded CIBEs support CIBERweb, at http://ciberweb.msu.edu. Another form of educational outreach is the faculty development programs that have trained 148,000 professors and 30,000 PhD students since 1989 across the United States. Cumulatively, these programs have influenced almost two million students at non-CIBE institutions nationwide. Since 1989, workshops have been held for 40,000 language professors, affecting two million students studying foreign languages in a business context.

Outreach to the business community includes executive training programs with an international component, which reported the attendance of about 265,000 business executives. In addition, conferences, workshops, and seminars have been held for the business community, affecting about 600,000 businesspersons since 1989 (CIBER, 2009).

The Title VI BIE program, referenced earlier, along with the National Resource Centers, also supported under Title VI of the Higher Education Act, provide similar services for the business community as part of their outreach mandate.

Since 2000, U.S. firms have almost doubled the amount of their FDI and there have been continuing increases in FDI made in the U.S. domestic market by foreign firms. Additionally, U.S. firms' exports have continued to grow, to more than $8 trillion, but imports into the U.S. market from foreign firms reached approximately $13.8 trillion during the period 2000–2008 (see Figures 13-1 and 13-2).

Institutional Environments

Because of the importance of institutional environments for international business activities, an increasing amount of research has been conducted on them, and particularly their effect on multinational firms' strategies, in recent years. The institutional environment consists of formal and informal institutions that form the basis for behavior in a society (North 1991). As such, countries' institutional environments establish the "rules of the game" for the way organizations should behave within each country's context (Meyer and Rowan 1977; North 1990). As such, institutions influence economic exchange, laws and regulations, and direct economic transactions (North 1990). In fact, according to Scott (1995, 2005), the three bases of formal and informal institutions are rules (regulative), norms (normative), and culture (cognitive). Some of the norms—and, in particular, national culture—largely compose the informal institutions. The formal institutions largely consist of regulatory, economic, and political institutions; some scholars also include the physical infrastructure (Boddewyn 1988; Burdekin and Weidenmier 2001; Matten and Crane 2005; Khanna and Palepu 1997, 1999).

In previous years, most international business scholars focused on a single dimension of the institutional environment, such as political institutions (e.g., Henisz 2000) and economic institutions (Ghemawat 2001). Specifically, Hitt et al. (2009) developed a dataset measuring the institutional environments of fifty countries, which includes data on their regulatory, economic, and political institutions and their physical infrastructure. Their data show that these countries cluster into five different types of institutional environments and that countries' institutional environments can change or evolve over time. For example, their data suggest that the U.S. institutional environment changed in the early 2000s (perhaps partly the result of the events of September 11, 2001) and that the institutional environments in China, Russia, and India also evolved during the 1990s and early 2000s.

The variance in firm strategies around the world arises in part from the influences of these institutional forces. Previous research has shown that these institutional forces have both direct and indirect effects on firm strategies (Dunning 1988; Porter 1990; Ghemawat 2001; Hitt et al. 2004; Ahlstrom et al. 2009). For example, research has shown that countries' institutional environments (culture and formal institutions) have an effect on the amount of FDI made in those countries by foreign firms (e.g., Hitt et al. 2009). Furthermore, countries' institutional environments have been found to affect which countries firms choose to enter in order to compete (e.g., Arregle et al. 2009). Arregle et al. (2009) found that multinational firms direct their foreign investments to regions of the world and then make their investments in assets in selected countries within the region. In doing so, they use the institutional profile of the regions in the selection process and direct their investments into countries with the most favorable institutional investments within the region.

Additionally, countries' institutional environments have been found to affect the outcomes of major international strategies, such as the performance of cross-border M&A (Zhu et al. 2009) and innovation (Miller and Hitt 2009). Zhu et al. (2009) found that host country economic institutions have a strong positive relationship with value creation in cross-border acquisitions up to some point, but the effects actually become negative in very high levels of economic institutions. Alternatively, the effects of regulatory and political institutions are more complex. In   293 fact, they have a two-way interaction effect on value creation for such acquisitions. Interestingly, Zhu et al. (2009) found that more centralized political institutions with stronger regulatory institutions facilitated greater value creation in cross-border acquisitions. They suggested that this type of environment reduces the uncertainty that is often high in such strategic moves. Thus, foreign firms take fewer risks making acquisitions in countries with that institutional environment.

The two studies described here suggest that it is essential for top executives in firms to understand both the formal and informal institutions of countries around the world if they wish to compete in global markets. Further, because the effects of institutional environments are quite complex, involving both formal and informal institutions and multiple types of formal institutions, the knowledge held by executives must be fine-grained and systemic. The results explained above also suggest the need for more fine-grained research on the interaction of country institutions, multinational firms' strategies, and firm performance in host countries where they have made major investments in subsidiary operations. Thus, business students and executives alike must learn as much as possible about cultures and formal institutions in order to develop effective strategies and to enhance the performance of firms they serve.

Conclusions

We cannot expect the United States or U.S. businesses to compete and lead in a world that we and they do not adequately understand. Therefore, knowledge about international cultures and international environments is absolutely essential. Such knowledge is critical for firms trying to compete in global markets to gain and sustain a competitive advantage (Hitt et al. 2009). Such understanding is necessary to develop and implement the corporate strategies needed to compete effectively. A critical component of this understanding among U.S. businesses is the CIBE program administered by the U.S. Department of Education. In fact, the welfare of U.S. businesses and the nation as a whole depend on building effective international business skills.

The centers in schools of business supported by the CIBE program provide several essential services. First, they help to link the human capital and information needs of U.S. businesses to international business education, language training, and the research capabilities of major universities in the United States. Second, the centers serve as regional and national resources to businesses as well as to faculty members, students, and business schools in supporting their larger curriculum projects and major research programs. Third, the collaborative network of centers and individual contributions combine to enhance the competitiveness of U.S. firms, thereby helping them to succeed in global markets and providing a strong impetus for the U.S. economy. Since 1989, the federal investment in the CIBE program has been almost $200 million, and because the institutions are required to match the federal grants in cash or in kind, nearly $400 million has been expended to meet the legislative mandate. The CIBE program provides up to $1.4 million over a four-year term to each of thirty-one centers, selected in a rigorous application and peer-review process. The resources provided, along with a careful governance process including regular evaluation of programs, has made this a highly successful program since its inception twenty years ago (Easton 2009).

In recent times, it has been determined that firms must emphasize innovation to be leaders in global markets. In fact, the U.S. Council on Competitiveness issued a report in 2005 that argued that U.S. firms must be highly innovative if they are to remain leaders in the global marketplace (Council on Competitiveness 2005). Shortly thereafter, the Chinese government called for a national emphasis on innovation. To be a leader in innovation in global markets requires a substantial knowledge advantage, particularly in multicultural knowledge. In support of this argument, it has been shown that many U.S. firms are establishing regional research and development centers throughout the world in order to gain knowledge idiosyncratic to those countries and regions that can then be integrated into the development of products that make them more competitive in global markets. As a result, many major multinational firms have established important regional research and development centers in China. Originally, these research centers were developed largely to design products that would be attractive in the Chinese market. However, with greater knowledge of China and access to the engineering capabilities of Chinese engineers and scientists, these firms have learned that products can be developed and designed in these centers that are highly attractive in global markets (Li and Hitt 2006).

In a recent report, the Kauffman Foundation noted the importance of highly skilled immigrants for building the competitive advantage of U.S. businesses in both domestic and global markets, especially in the high-technology sector. In recent years, many U.S. businesses have declared a shortage of highly skilled professionals, especially engineers and scientists, and, thus, need more such immigrant experts from abroad. Having knowledge of different cultures and different international environments increases the appreciation for immigrants and their backgrounds and, thus, enhances the attraction for highly skilled and knowledgeable people to immigrate to the United States. Additionally, research has shown that the 50 percent of immigrants who return to their home country start new businesses and contribute to their local economies (Akee et al. 2009). Thus, it is important to attract immigrants as well as to keep the best among them in the United States contributing to the betterment of U.S. firms and U.S. society. Recent research has shown that U.S. entrepreneurs have institutional and perhaps other advantages

295

over entrepreneurs in a number of other countries, particularly in some of those emerging economies among the BRIC countries. As such, entrepreneurs in the U.S. achieve more success via higher performance relative to many entrepreneurs in these other countries (Batjargal et al. 2009).

Therefore, we need not only to have comprehensive knowledge of cultures and global institutional environments, but also to use the intellectual capital existing throughout the world for U.S. businesses to remain leaders in the global competitive landscape. Public and private organization leaders must develop a global mindset (Javidan et al. 2007) to avoid the end-game scenario described by Panzer (2009) as potentially the end of an America's leadership in the world. With the proper education and research, along with the use of the knowledge created and learned, America and U.S. firms will remain global leaders for many years to come, and the CIBEs play a key role in the development and dissemination of knowledge on global enterprise. As Friedman has said, "the future is our choice, not our fate. . . . [T]here is nothing in the universe as powerful as six billion minds wrapping around one problem. . . . We have exactly enough time—starting now" (2008: 412).

REFERENCES

Ahlstrom, D., E. Levitas, M. A. Hitt, M. T. Dacin, and H. Zhu. 2009. The three faces of China: Strategic alliance partner selection in greater China. Working paper. Hong Kong: Chinese University of Hong Kong.

Akee, R., D. A. Jaeger, and K. Tatsiramos. 2009. The persistence of self employment across borders: New evidence on legal immigrants to the United States. Working paper. http://ssm.com/1136412. Social Science Research Network.

Arregle, J.-L., T. L. Miller, M. A. Hitt, and P. W. Beamish. 2009. Institutional environment and MNEs' strategic foreign investment location decisions: A semi-globalization approach. Paper presented at the Academy of Management Conference, Chicago, August.

Batjargal, B., A. S. Tsui, M. A. Hitt, J. L. Arregle, J. Webb, and T. L. Miller. 2009. How relationship matters: Women and men entrepreneurs: Social networks and new venture success across cultures. Paper presented at the Academy of Management Conference, Chicago, August.

Blinco, P. N. 1991. "Task Persistence in Japanese Elementary Schools." In *Windows on Japanese Education*, ed. E. R. Beauchamp. New York: Greenwood Press, pp. 51–75.

Boddewyn, J. J. 1988. "Political Aspects of MNE Theory." *Journal of International Business Studies* 19:341–363.

Boe, E. E., H. May, G. Barkanic, and R. F. Boruch. 2004. "Predictors of National Differences in Mathematics and Science Achievement of 8th-grade Students: Data from TIMSS." In *The Six Nation Education Research Project: Learning through Collaborative Research*, ed. F. McGinn. Oxford, UK: Blackwell Publishing, pp. 21–52.

Burdekin, R. C. K. and M. D. Weidenmier. 2001. "Inflation Is Always and Everywhere a Monetary Phenomenon: Richmond vs. Houston in 1864." *American Economic Review* 91:1621–1630.

Center for International Business Education and Research. 2009. *Annual CIBER Statistical Summary.* Prepared by the Center for International Business Education and Research. Austin, TX: McCombs School of Business, The University of Texas at Austin.

Council on Competitiveness. 2005. *Innovate America: National Innovation Initiative Summit and Report.* Washington, D.C.: The Council on Competitiveness.

Dunning, J. H. 1988. "The Eclectic Paradigm of International Production: A Restatement and Some Possible Extensions." *Journal of International Business Studies* 19:1–31.

Easton, S. 2009. "Center for International Business Education and Research." Paper presented at the International Education Programs and Service Technical Assistance Workshop, February 2.

Folks, R. 2005. "Curriculum Development." In *Securing Our Nation's Future through International Business Education: Fifteen Years of CIBER, 1989–2004.* Washington, D.C.: U.S. Department of Education.

Friedman, T. L. 2008. *Hot, Flat, and Crowded: Why We Need a Green Revolution—And How We Can Renew America.* New York: Farrar, Straus and Giroux.

Ghemawat, P. 2001. "Distance Still Matters: The Hard Reality of Global Expansion." *Harvard Business Review* 79(8):137–147.

Gladwell, M. 2008. *Outliers: The Story of Success.* New York: Little, Brown.

Henisz, W. J. 2000. "The institutional environment for multinational investment." *Journal of Law, Economics and Organization* 16:334–364.

Hitt, M. A. and X. He. 2008. "Firm Strategies in a Changing Global Competitive Landscape." *Business Horizons* 51(5):363–369.

———., D. Ahlstrom, M. T. Dacin, E. Levitas, and L. Svobodina. 2004. "The Institutional Effects on Strategic Alliance Partner Selection in Transition Economies: China versus Russia." *Organization Science* 15:173–185.

———., L. Bierman, K. Uhlenbruck, and K. Shimizu. 2006. "The Importance of Resources in the Internationalization of Professional Service Firms: The Good, the Bad and the Ugly." *Academy of Management Journal* 49:1137–1157.

———. J. S. Harrison, and R. D. Ireland. 2001. *Mergers and Acquisitions: A Guide to Creating Value for Stakeholders.* New York: Oxford University Press.

———., R. M. Holmes, T. Miller, and M. P. Salmador. 2009. Modeling Country Institutional Environments, Working paper. College Station, TX: Texas A&M University.

———., R. E. Hoskisson, and H. Kim. 1997. "International Diversification: Effects on Innovation and Firm Performance in Product Diversified Firms." *Academy of Management Journal,* 40:767–798.

———., R. D. Ireland, and R. E. Hoskisson. 2009. *Strategic Management: Competitiveness and Globalization.* Mason, OH: South-Western Cengage Learning.

———., B. W. Keats, and S. DeMarie. 1998. "Navigating in the New Competitive Landscape: Building Strategic Flexibility and Competitive Advantage in the 21st Century." *Academy of Management Executive* 12(4):22–42.

———., L. Tihanyi, T. Miller, and B. Connelly. 2006. "International Diversification: Antecedents: Outcomes and Moderators." *Journal of Management*, 32:831–867.

Holcomb, T. R. and M. A. Hitt. 2007. "Toward a Model of Strategic Outsourcing." *Journal of Operations Management* 25:464–481.

Javidan, M., R. M. Steers, and M. A. Hitt, eds. 2007. *The Global Mindset; Advances in International Management, Volume 19.* Amsterdam: Elsevier.

Khanna, T. 1997. "Why Focused Strategies May Be Wrong for Emerging Markets." *Harvard Business Review* 75(4):41–51.

———. and Palepu, K. 1999. "Policy Shocks, Market Intermediaries, and Corporate Strategy: Evidence from Chile and India." *Journal of Economics and Management Strategy* 2:271–310.

Lei, D. and M.A. Hitt. 1995. "Strategic Restructuring and Outsourcing: The Effect of Mergers and Acquisitions and LBOs on Building Firm Skills and Capabilities." *Journal of Management* 21:835–859.

Lewin, A. 2005a. "Duke University: Offshoring Research Initiative." In *Securing Our Nation's Future through International Business Education: Fifteen Years of CIBER, 1989–2004.* Washington, D.C.: U.S. Department of Education, 19.

Lewin, A. 2005b. "Research." In *Securing Our Nation's Future through International Business Education: Fifteen Years of CIBER, 1989–2004*, Washington, D.C.: U.S. Department of Education, 19.

Li, H. and M.A. Hitt. 2006. "Growth of New Technology Ventures in China: An Introduction." In *Growth of New Technology Ventures in China's Emerging Market*, edited by H. Li. Northampton, M.A.: Edward Elgar Publishing Ltd., pp. 3–10.

Matten, D. and A. Crane. 2005. "Corporate Citizenship: Toward an Extended Theoretical Conceptualization." *Academy of Management Review* 30:166–179.

Meyer, J. W. and B. Rowan. 1977. "Institutionalized Organizations: Formal Structure as Myth and Ceremony." *American Journal of Sociology* 83:340–360.

Miller, T. L. and M. A. Hitt. 2009. "Search in a Distant Land: An Organizational Learning Perspective of Internationalization and Exploratory Knowledge Search." Paper presented at the Strategic Management Society Conference, Washington, D.C., October.

North, D. C. 1990. *Institutions, Institutional Change and Economic Performance.* Cambridge, UK: Cambridge University Press.

———. 1991. "Institutions." *Journal of Economic Perspectives* 5(1):97–112.

Panzer, M. J. 2009. *When Giants Fall: An Economic Roadmap for the End of the American Era.* Hoboken, NJ: John Wiley and Sons.

Porter, N. E. 1998. *Competitive Advantage of Nations.* New York: Free Press.

Roberts, D. and F. Balfour. 1999. "China's shopping spree." *BusinessWeek* July 27, 40–43.

Sacco, S. 2005. "Language Programs." In *Securing Our Nation's Future through International Business Education: Fifteen Years of CIBER, 1989–2004,* Washington, D.C. U.S. Department of Education, pp, 25–27.

Scott, W. R. 1995. *Institutions and Organizations.* Thousand Oaks, CA: Sage.

———. 2005. "Institutional Theory: Contributing to a Theoretical Research Program." In *Great Minds in Management: The Process of Theory Development,* ed. K.G. Smith and M.A. Hitt. Oxford, UK: Oxford University Press, pp. 460–484.

Slater, J. "Legislative History." In *International Education and Foreign Languages: Keys to Securing America's Future,* eds. M. P. O'Connell and J. L. Norwood. Washington, D.C.: The National Academies Press, pp. 267–284.

Thomson Financial. 2007. *Mergers and Acquisitions Review.* www.thomson.com. 2007.

Zahra S. A., D. R. Ireland, and M. A. Hitt. 2000. "International Expansion by New Venture Firms: International Diversity, Mode of Market Entry, Technological Learning, and Performance." *Academy of Management Journal* 43:925–950.

Zhu, H., M. A. Hitt, L. Eden, and L. Tihanyi. 2009. "Host Country Institutions and the Performance of Cross-Border M&As." Paper presented at the Academy of Management Conference, Chicago, August.

PART 6

Accessing, Benchmarking, and Assessing Title VI

CHAPTER 14

Beyond Accountability: A Balanced Approach to Assessment and Benchmarking

Carl Falsgraf

Developing a national capacity of proficient language users is a central purpose of Title VI. The need was urgent in 1959, and is felt even more so today. In these fifty years, however, there has been no systematic measurement of language outcomes from Title VI programs. Title VI programs do indeed produce proficient speakers of a wide variety of languages, and the means to document these outcomes are generally available. Why, then, have National Resource Centers (NRCs) been unable or unwilling to assess students' language abilities?

Conversations with colleagues reveal a variety of reasons:

- No language test could possibly capture the richness and depth of language and culture, much less students' intellectual development, in a liberal arts curriculum.
- Forcing standardized bubble tests on campuses like some postsecondary version of No Child Left Behind would undermine academic freedom.
- We are still waiting for a reliable test that quickly and inexpensively measures everything a student knows.
- Every minute and every dollar given to testing is a minute and dollar taken from learning.

These arguments are all quite reasonable at face value, but are based on an outdated paradigm of language testing that equates assessment with measurement, 303 usually in the form of a single, high-stress, timed event with a purpose to sort out winners from losers. I will argue in this chapter that the future of benchmarking and assessment in Title VI can and should move from the hegemony of measurement to an era of balanced assessment, in which multiple measures of linguistic and academic progress create a rich portrait of student ability consistent with individual student goals and local educational context. Performed correctly, this approach can not only keep political dogs at bay but also enhance students' motivation, help us advocate for our programs, and guide curricular and instructional decisions. This conceptual shift provides us with a more productive and practical way to look at assessment in Title VI and in language and culture education in general.

The Measurement Paradigm

The measurement paradigm has been so ubiquitous that we scarcely recognize it as a simple construct we can choose to change. The central tenet of the measurement paradigm is that a fairly stable body of knowledge and abilities exists in a learner's brain that scientific techniques of elicitation and mathematical models of analysis can objectively and quantitatively measure. The SAT, GRE, and TOEFL are common examples of this technology. The degree to which various instruments actually measure that body of knowledge and abilities is the subject of highly technical and impassioned arguments within the testing field. For the sake of argument, let us assume here that these instruments are generally reliable and valid.

Even if we had instruments that measure knowledge and ability perfectly, do we not care about other educational outcomes, such as the application of knowledge, critical thinking, cultural insight, and creativity? Is our sole purpose for assessment the generation of a number summarizing a learner's knowledge base? Certainly, a liberal or professional education should provide students with a body of knowledge and abilities, but to ignore more complex outcomes simply because they cannot be quantitatively measured in a timed test and reduced to a number sells ourselves and our students short. Assessment should be an opportunity to demonstrate excellence, not just an exercise in sorting students from "best" to "worst." We are politically and educationally foolish not to document the most important product of an international education: a global outlook allowing students to gather, analyze, and think critically about new information in a cultural context.

The search for a magic bullet, the one big test that will tell us everything we need to know, should end. I say this as the director of a U.S. Department of Education-designated Language Resource Center (LRC) with test development at the core of its mission. Although tests have their place, we must not limit ourselves to

measuring the relatively small subset of outcomes amenable to elicitation by standardized testing. The alternative to exclusive reliance on testing is not subjective evaluation but a contextualized portrait of student learning, a mosaic of quantitative and qualitative evidence.

Balanced Assessment Systems: The Educational Imperative

Following Stiggins (2008), I will refer to this orientation as "balanced assessment." The purpose of balanced assessment is not primarily to audit learning, but to improve it by helping teachers and administrators make better instructional decisions and by directly improving student performance by clarifying goals and progress toward those goals. A balanced assessment approach recognizes that language is never free of content: One always must talk about *something*. Surely that *something* will be different for a pre-med student at UCLA, a philosophy major at Amherst College, or a PhD candidate in literature at Yale. The evidence that these diverse learners can talk about something, therefore, must be individually and locally controlled. Students in all these contexts are presumably producing evidence every day in the form of class assignments, papers, group discussions, and presentations. The information is largely there; the challenge is to systematize the collection and catalogue the evidence so that others (graduate admissions committees, Title VI administrators, accreditation agencies, and so forth) can interpret it.

A central tenet of this new assessment paradigm is that purpose and context are imperative. If the purpose of a program is to give students a global perspective, then a standardized test is not an appropriate tool. A paper researched and written in English, which by definition limits students to perspectives of the English-speaking world, is equally inappropriate. A class project collecting and analyzing stories from immigrants in their native language (if you are in San Francisco), Mexico (if you are in El Paso), or Southeast Asia (if you are in Minneapolis) almost certainly would constitute evidence that students are making progress toward the goal of acquiring a global perspective. All programs share this goal, but local curriculum and culture determine the specific methods of collection and evaluation. If we claim that students in our program will develop global perspectives, then we are obligated to collect evidence that this actually occurs. Most often that evidence should be a natural by-product of instruction. Collecting immigrant stories is a reasonable assignment in a foreign language class or even a geography or anthropology class. If these types of assignments are not given, perhaps our curriculum is not aligned with its stated goal.

Capturing the exhaust of the instructional system in this way prevents assessment from becoming a disembodied activity that steals time and resources from the curriculum. This approach does not occur without effort, however. We must look beyond traditional departments and disciplines and take a program-level view of international education, something Title VI centers are well positioned to facilitate. We must take seriously our role in the overall liberal education enterprise and not allow ourselves to be consigned only to providing language skills as a service to other departments. Faculty in other disciplines must re-examine attitudes and beliefs about language teaching and learning. Requiring students to take language classes and then not providing them an opportunity to use those language skills in other classes sends the implicit message that language class is a hoop to jump through, not a foundational part of one's education.

Balanced Assessment Systems: The Political Imperative

Institutional and cultural barriers notwithstanding, the imperative for making languages central to international education and making assessment central to language learning is clear. Norris (2006) describes a current environment in which accreditation agencies, funders such as Title VI, and political bodies demand evidence of student learning, whereas the academic culture conflates measurement with assessment. Such an environment creates a "crisis" that threatens to further marginalize language programs. Ignoring this milieu and hoping it will go away allows others to define the agenda and impose accountability measures that may or may not fit our programs, which is essentially what happened in the K-12 system, where test preparation in math and English now takes precedence over almost all other goals.

As a community, we cannot afford to allow others to define us. Rather, we must define ourselves as essential to the national interest and to a liberal and professional education. Expressing this definition in terms of student outcomes makes a clear statement to internal and external stakeholders. Establishing the parameters of an assessment system that will improve our programs and student learning requires a fundamental shift in orientation from seeing assessment as a necessary evil and equating it with testing to a more holistic vision. High-quality assessment can help us think more consciously about general and specific program goals and constantly review a program's quality based on progress toward those goals.

A Familiar Balanced Assessment System: Back to the Future

Such a fundamental shift in our attitudes about assessment and evaluation may seem idealistic and perhaps naïve. A shining example of this "new" paradigm, however, has been with us for centuries, and anyone with a graduate degree is familiar with it. Graduate education in this country is based on a rich and rigorous balanced assessment system that relies on multiple measures of competence (e.g., course grades, comprehensive examination results, PhD guidance and dissertation committees, a dissertation), resulting in a rich portrait of student abilities that is locally controlled and individualized to student goals. That portrait eventually takes the form of a curriculum vitae that knowledgeable outsiders can evaluate when making decisions regarding employment, academic honors, and tenure. Although this system is imperfect, it ensures the academic quality of programs and individuals to internal and external stakeholders in a manner that protects local academic freedom without trivializing the intellectual complexities of a graduate education. The future of language assessment I will sketch here looks much more like our system for evaluating graduate students than it does the final examination of a second-year French course you may have suffered through decades ago.

Enabling Conditions for Balanced Assessment Systems

Today, we are capable of developing a practical system of multiple measures for assessing language proficiency because of advances in standards, technology-mediated testing, and electronic portfolios.

Standards

Since the 1950s, the U.S. government has relied on the Interagency Language Roundtable (ILR) scale of proficiency. The American Council on the Teaching of Foreign Languages (ACTFL) Proficiency Guidelines adjusted them in the 1980s to meet the needs of U.S. academic institutions. At last count, forty-seven of the fifty states have tied state K-12 language standards to the ACTFL guidelines. Despite their ubiquity, proficiency standards have a host of detractors. The main complaints are as follows:

- The guidelines are based on the construct of an "educated native speaker," which has not been rigorously defined and is not an appropriate metric for measuring lower-level second language development.
- The guidelines are Eurocentric and do not apply to non-Western languages and cultures.
- Reading and listening guidelines, in particular, lack empirical verification.
- The guidelines conflate linguistic and cognitive development.

This list is not comprehensive, but it highlights some concerns with the construct. One might well ask why such a maligned set of guidelines has been so durable. The most charitable interpretation is that the guidelines do express an underlying, near-universal path from zero to high-level proficiency, and future research will bear this out. At the very least, the guidelines are like the "qwerty" keyboard: perhaps an accident of history but of great practical use and too entrenched to be seriously challenged. Whether a blessing or a curse, the language field does have a universally understood set of descriptors serving as a common reference point for language assessment.

The Council of Europe made a significant advance in language and culture standards with the publication of the Common European Framework of Reference (CEFR; 2001). Beginning from empirical work on learner development, the CEFR provides a comprehensive set of scales in the form of specific "CanDo" statements such as "I can read a simple news article" or "I can converse on professional topics." The standards can be customized by selecting those relevant to particular programs or even individuals. For example, one of the scales relates to note taking in lectures. A program in which academic content is taught in the target language might have note taking as a central skill around which many assessment activities are focused. A traditional language and literature model, on the other hand, may not find this criterion relevant at all. Picking and choosing scales in this manner makes comparisons among students more difficult, but in the balanced assessment paradigm, ranking students is of secondary importance to describing performance. The advantage is that the description of student abilities aligns with program and curriculum goals.

Technology-Mediated Assessment
Technology-mediated assessment covers approaches ranging from online testing, to e-portfolios, to authoring tools allowing local programs to develop customized assessments. Technology-mediated assessment makes large-scale assessment practical, enhances the quality of information gathered, and facilitates the manipulation of data for reporting and program evaluation. A large cohort of students can take an assessment and have the results automatically graded, saving valuable teacher time. The quality of traditional approaches to assessment, such as the ubiquitous multiple-choice test, can be made "smart" through computer-adaptive testing, which constructs tests as learners respond. Finally, data can be aggregated and disaggregated so teachers and administrators can see snapshots of individual, class, program, or national performance.

Electronic Portfolios
Electronic portfolios represent the real conceptual leap from a focus on auditing student performance through timed, high-stakes tests to a future in which every language learner constructs a rich portrait of his or her abilities with supporting evidence from multiple assessment measures, including papers, projects, interviews,

readings—and, yes, test scores. An e-portfolio is not an assessment per se, but a means of organizing assessment data from a variety of sources. Visually oriented fields, such as architecture, studio art, and design, have long traditions of gathering evidence for evaluation in portfolios. Now, multimedia technologies make possible portfolios for the auditory-oriented field of language learning.

Assessment Tools from Language Resource Centers

Title VI LRCs have been at the forefront of research and development of twenty-first-century assessment tools. They range from online tests, to authoring tools, to e-portfolios. Taken as a whole, they provide the kinds of resources NRCs and others need to develop a locally relevant and balanced assessment system.

Computer-Mediated Tests

Testing still has an important place in a balanced assessment system. Two key differences distinguish traditional language testing from the current approach taken by several LRCs. Modern tests are proficiency-oriented and computer-mediated. Proficiency-oriented means that these instruments measure students' ability to communicate meaningful content in realistic contexts rather than abstract knowledge of grammar and vocabulary. Multimedia computer-mediated tests facilitate the presentation of visual and audio material that places test items in culturally realistic contexts.

These examples from the Center for Advanced Research in Language Acquisition (CARLA) at the University of Minnesota show how proficiency tests can elicit students' communicative abilities through contextualized items.

Notice that the text in Figure 14-1 is authentic (i.e., written by a native speaker for a native speaker) and requires the student to use general literacy skills such as skimming and scanning, not just translating isolated words or sentences. This item is set in a realistic visual and cultural context, ensuring that we are measuring students' communicative abilities, not just the mastery of abstract linguistic knowledge. Finally, because computers deliver the item, it can be automatically and instantaneously scored and reported.

Online testing has the additional advantage of gathering, analyzing, and displaying student performance data to appropriate stakeholders. The following reports from the Standards-based Measurement of Proficiency (STAMP) developed by the Center for Applied Second Language Studies (CASLS) at the University of Oregon demonstrate how data can be easily aggregated and disaggregated for various audiences, including students, teachers, administrators, and policy makers (see Figures 14-2 and 14-3).

309

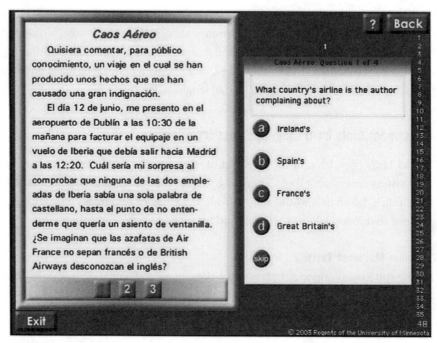

FIGURE 14-1

Sample Spanish Reading Comprehension Question

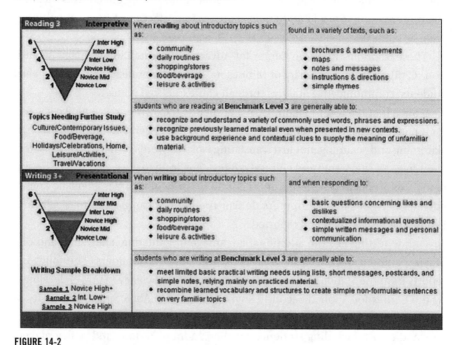

FIGURE 14-2

Sample of Standards for Reading and Writing Benchmark Levels

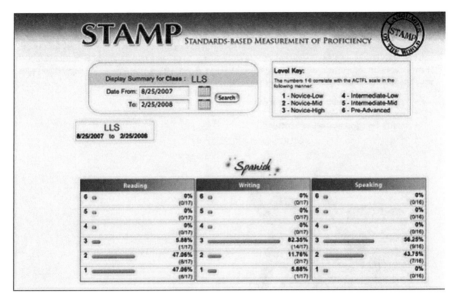

FIGURE 14-3
Sample STAMP Report for a Spanish Class

Because computers are so adept at managing data, aggregating data by class or program is easy, providing teachers and administrators with useful information for reflecting on program goals and providing other stakeholders with standardized performance data expressed according to common standards.

Collecting student data online also allows students and teachers to look at written and spoken production in detail, which facilitates individualized feedback. In Figure 14-4, for example, this student of Japanese repeated one simple grammatical pattern three times and made a mistake on a locative particle. Providing detailed feedback in this way allows a summative test to also serve formative purposes.

E-Portfolios

The true conceptual leap in balanced assessment, however, springs not from better testing, but from different ways of evaluating student performance outside the traditional test. Several LRCs are innovating in alternative approaches to assessment that go beyond auditing to learning to actually enhancing learning.

The Center for Advanced Language Proficiency and Research (CALPER) at Penn State has pioneered an approach called *dynamic assessment*, which not only shows the learners' current state of competence but also predicts future areas of development. Traditional, static assessments measure only what learners can produce in isolation at a particular point in time. Dynamic assessment intervenes with support to elicit information on developing, but still latent, abilities. In language, this   311

STAMP STANDARDS-BASED MEASUREMENTS OF PROFICIENCY

Your host family in Toyota, Japan wants to make sure you have a good time during your stay with them and has asked for you to share some of your favorite things to do. Before your arrival in Toyota, write them an email in Japanese in which you describe **at least 4 activities** that you would enjoy doing with your host family. You might include such things as:

- recreational & leisure activities you enjoy
- places you would like to visit
- events that you would like to attend
- etc.

日本で、おいしいりょうりをたべたいです。にほんのがらんをいきたいです。まだ、日本のだいかくへいきたいです。

Ratable?	TT/NRR	Comprehensibility	Language Control	
Yes	Simple Sentences	(S) Easily comprehended by a sympathetic reader, occasional influence of L1 on L2	(S) Errors in grammar, spelling, word order or punctuation, while present, do not interfere with overall meaning.	1_68305

FIGURE 14-4
Sample Student's Online Assignment

may be what is on "the tip of the tongue" and only requires a prompt or hint to surface. Departing from the measurement model of assessment, the purpose of dynamic assessment is not to rank students or catalog past development, but to develop a nuanced portrait of student performance predicting future development. Tools to help teachers develop their own dynamic assessment protocols are available from CALPER at http://calper.la.psu.edu/.

In the same spirit of assessment as a means of improving learning, CASLS has created an e-portfolio called LinguaFolio Online in collaboration with the National Council of State Supervisors for Languages (NCSSFL) and the National Foreign Language Center (NFLC). A set of CanDo statements derived from the CEFR describing functional language ability, such as "I can ask simple questions," "I can write business letters," or "I can understand news broadcasts," is at the heart of LinguaFolio Online. Students self-assess on each statement, checking either "This is a goal," "I can do this with help," or "I can do this." They can support these claims by attaching evidence to each statement. For example, if a student claims to be able to write a business letter, he or she can attach a Word or PDF document written for a class or perhaps during an internship.

The critical point is that students are in control of their own LinguaFolio Online account. In this way, it is similar to the graduate education model previously discussed. Just as a job applicant makes claims on a curriculum vitae and has evidence in the form of transcripts, papers, and recommendations, a student self-evaluates and organizes evidence to substantiate that claim. In the measurement paradigm, information from self-assessment is meaningless because students could cheat. This is possible, of course, just as it is possible for someone to lie on a resume or buy a term paper online. Self-assessment alone should not be used for high-stakes decisions. The granularity of detail and the richness of the evidence in a portfolio, however, demonstrates learning beyond a timed testing environment. Furthermore, the evidence in a portfolio is customized to a particular program and particular student's goals. Figure 14-5 illustrates the LinguaFolio Online self-assessment grid, showing how learners can track, document, and display their developing abilities in the language.

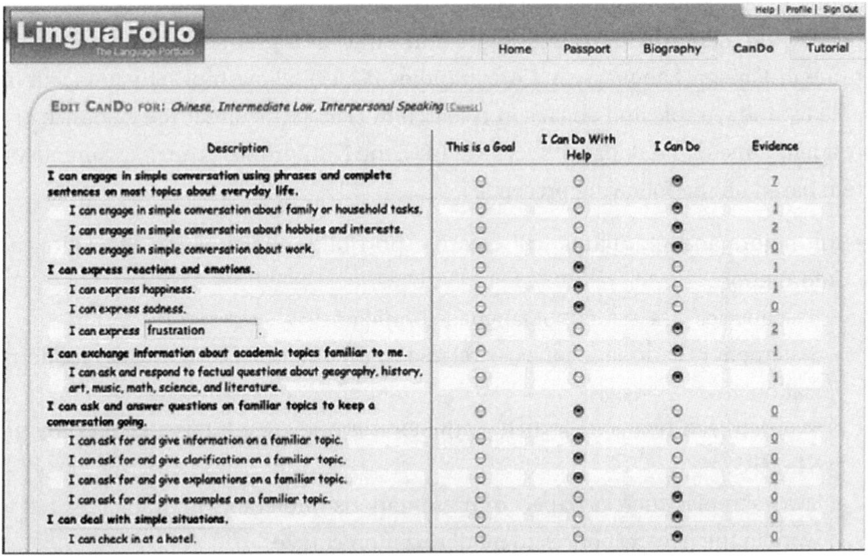

FIGURE 14-5
Sample LinguaFolio Online Self-Assessment Grid

A Comprehensive Title VI Assessment System

How could these tools and conceptual frameworks be applied to the specific, complex needs of Title VI centers? In addition to measuring pure linguistic abilities, we need to document students' ability to talk about meaningful content. Furthermore, the constituency for these data is multifaceted. The federal government, which provides funding, obviously needs evidence that taxpayer money is wisely spent. Internally, our institutions need to see the evidence of learning in our programs, and we need to communicate this convincingly. We ourselves need information on student performance to evaluate, modify, and improve our programs. Students, perhaps the most important constituency, are often forgotten. The traditional paradigm of assessment in which the primary purpose is to sort sheep from goats encouraged students to focus exclusively on "How did I do?," not "What did I do?," "How well did I do it?," and "Where do I need to go next?" Research (e.g., Black and Wiliam 1998) has shown that good formative assessment improves student learning. Used properly, a language assessment does more than reports results; it improves them.

Here is a scenario of a Title VI NRC and how it might develop a local system that also allows common reporting. This hypothetical NRC actually is a composite of a number of centers.

In developing its 2009 proposal, the NRC steering committee determines that it will focus on responses to modernization in the Arabic-speaking world. Building on strong offerings in Arabic language and Middle East sociology, anthropology, and history, the center will expand course offerings and graduate student support through Foreign Language and Area Studies (FLAS) fellowships. Students will be able to study Arabic and engage in research in Damascus under the guidance of a resident director. Working with its local LRC, the NRC proposes an assessment system based on the following precepts:

- All majors and graduates will create e-portfolios that include the following information:
  - Baseline self-assessment of language proficiency
  - Statement of academic purpose related to the theme of responses to modernization
  - Standardized test scores such as the Oral Proficiency Interview (OPI) or the STAMP
  - Work samples such as papers or presentations (preferably in Arabic) related to work in the new responses to modernization courses
  - Multiple work samples tied to the statement of academic purpose from Arabic language classes

- All study abroad students will create e-portfolios and include the following information:
  - A statement of purpose for the study abroad experience
  - Pre-, during-, and post-experience self-assessments
  - Dynamic assessment administered before departure
  - Work samples from Arabic language classes
  - Work samples (preferably in Arabic) from undergraduate content classes and graduate research projects
  - Before-and-after standardized test scores
- All majors and graduate students will take OPIs and STAMP tests before graduation.
- All study abroad students will take tests before and after the experience.

This scenario places minimal burden on faculty, because information is gathered primarily through online testing and student-managed e-portfolios, with evidence collected through common classroom and extracurricular activities. Different aspects of the portfolios can be highlighted for different audiences. For example, the Department of Education may be most interested in the summative scores from standardized tests to demonstrate program effectiveness. Social science faculty will be most interested in the work samples from classes and overseas research. Language faculty will want to look in a more fine-grained manner at the self-evaluations and dynamic assessment results to evaluate the evidence in greater detail.

The future of language assessment in Title VI centers and programs sketched here differs significantly from traditional paradigms that equate assessment with externally-imposed standardized testing events. Advances in technology allow a system of multiple measures serving different purposes, needs, and audiences to be feasible. Gathering, organizing, and disseminating assessment results becomes easy and efficient. The ability to localize assessment systems protects academic freedom and ensures that the information we collect is relevant to the purposes and goals of our diverse programs.

REFERENCES

Black, P. and D. Wiliam. 1998. "Assessment and Classroom Learning. Assessment in Education: Principles," *Policy & Practice* 5.1:7–32.

Giordano, G. 2005. *How Testing Came to Dominate American Schools: The History of Educational Assessment.* New York: Peter Lang Publishing.

Norris, J. 2006. "The Why (and How) of Assessing Student Learning Outcomes in College Foreign Language Programs." *Modern Language Journal* 90(4):576–582.

Stiggins, R. 2008. *Assessment Manifesto: A Call for Balanced Assessment.* Portland, OR: ETS Assessment Training Institute.

CHAPTER 15

Accessing and Assessing Title VI International Education Programs: The View from Black Colleges

LaNitra Berger

In 2005, the National Association for Equal Opportunity in Higher Education (NAFEO) received Title VI funding to complete a survey of foreign languages, international studies, and study abroad at historically black colleges and universities (HBCUs) and predominantly black institutions (PBIs).[1] This chapter is based on the results of that study (NAFEO 2009: 17), focusing on an assessment of the role of international education on black college campuses, the level of minority student participation in international education, and the presence of minority-serving institutions (MSIs) in Title VI programs. It argues that better and more frequent assessment will help federal agencies, nonprofits, study-abroad providers, and higher education institutions understand how to increase the number of minority students who are reached by international education programs. Although HBCUs have participated in various Title VI programs for several decades, it is crucial to Title VI's diversity goals that it increase participation among these institutions.[2] This NAFEO study is one example of how Title VI funds can be used to assess black colleges' internationalization efforts.

NAFEO and Its Role International Education

NAFEO is the umbrella organization of the nation's historically and predominantly black colleges and universities. Founded in 1969 by a group of presidents of HBCUs, NAFEO is "the voice for blacks in higher education." The association represents the presidents and chancellors of all the nation's black colleges and universities: public, private, land-grant, two-year, four-year, graduate, and professional, and historically and predominantly black colleges and universities.

NAFEO was founded to provide an international voice for the nation's HBCUs; to place and maintain the issue of equal opportunity in higher education on the national agenda; to advocate policies, programs, and practices designed to preserve and enhance HBCUs; and to increase the active participation of blacks at every level in the formulation and implementation of policies and programs in American higher education. As such, internationalizing black college campuses has been a priority for the organization since its inception. This commitment has manifested itself in different ways over the years, including creating exchange opportunities with college campuses around the world, establishing consortia of institutions to complete international development projects, and encouraging students to apply for federal fellowships such as the Gilman, Fulbright-Hays, and Truman fellowships. In 2009, NAFEO created the Division of Leadership and International Programs, signaling its commitment to building international education programs on its member campuses and to promoting international education among minority student populations.

In the past thirty years, NAFEO institutions have received a number of Title VI international education grants. These grants have supported international research, foreign language training, research abroad, and internationalization of business education, among many other programs. Howard University, for example, was home to a Title VI National Resource Center (NRC) in African Language and Area Studies, and Clark Atlanta University has organized several Fulbright-Hays Group Projects Abroad to countries in Africa and Latin America. Various HBCUs have received Title VI Undergraduate International Studies and Foreign Language (UISFL) grants for increasing international education capacity for their students and faculty.[3] As a method of increasing capacity in international education on black college campuses, these programs have had a tremendous impact, which is why it is vital that more institutions participate.

Some Title VI programs focus specifically on minority students; these programs have brought black institutions further into the Title VI sphere of influence. The Institute for International Public Policy (IIPP), a Title VI program, targets MSIs and minority students who are interested in international public service. Currently, IIPP is the only Title VI program specifically designed to assist HBCUs and to increase minority student participation in international study. In the past decade, the Title VI IIPP program has funded the United Negro College Fund Special Programs Corporation (UNCFSP) with a large single grant to establish an institute designed to increase the representation of minorities in international service, including private international voluntary organizations and the U.S. Foreign Service.[4] Each year, a cohort of twenty to thirty students begins a multiyear IIPP Fellows program designed to culminate in an international affairs career. The program is carried out in cooperation with the Woodrow Wilson National Fellowship Foundation, the Hispanic Association of Colleges and Universities, the American Indian Higher Education Consortium, and the Association of Professional Schools of International Affairs. This grant has funded summer policy institutes, junior year abroad experience, internships, language training, a master's degree program in international affairs, and grants to strengthen undergraduate international affairs programs at selected campuses.

After fourteen student cohorts, this program has made progress toward providing minority students with opportunities to study abroad, learn foreign languages, and to use these skills for public service. IIPP also provides black college students with access to other Title VI NRCs for research and foreign language study, valuable resources for internationalization. The program, however, needs to be expanded if we aim to see a more diverse workforce in international affairs.

The NAFEO Evaluation Survey

The NAFEO survey represented a tremendous opportunity to learn about capacity and access issues at HBCUs and PBIs. Because these institutions represent only 3 percent of all higher education institutions nationwide but educate more than 30 percent of all black undergraduates, NAFEO's survey would yield rich data about whether and how minority students, particularly African Americans, are participating in international education at their institutions.

As anticipated, the NAFEO survey did provide valuable information about what HBCUs and PBIs are doing to provide access to international education on their campuses. This survey and the resulting report provided a blueprint for organizing NAFEO for effective work on internationalization with member institutes and for NAFEO's future activities to internationalize HBCU and PBI campuses.[5]

In 2005, NAFEO received a Title VI International Research and Studies Program (IRSP) grant to survey its members about their capacity in foreign languages, international studies, and study abroad opportunities. The survey demonstrated the Department of Education's interest in collecting data and assessing the levels at which black colleges and their students were participating in international education. The structure of NAFEO's survey on international education at black colleges was based on a study of internationalization in higher education in 2000 by the American Council on Education (ACE). The ACE report was based on a survey of higher education institutions nationally, providing a brief, yet concise, overview of the assessment challenges relative to internationalization of higher education:

> International education at U.S. colleges and universities is a poorly documented phenomenon. Many of the data available for analysis are methodologically suspect, inappropriate for comparison, and/or too outdated to be of much contemporary value. When carefully scrutinized as a whole, however, a snapshot of the state of internationalization emerges. Unfortunately, this picture leaves much to be desired: Foreign language enrollments are low; international courses constitute only a small part of college and university curricula; study abroad, although increasingly available in a variety of contexts, remains an undervalued and underutilized means of instruction; internationalization as an institutional concept worthy of campus-wide integration is rare; and most graduates are ill-prepared to face the global marketplace of employment and ideas (Hayward 2000: 4).

Although the international education landscape has changed dramatically since 2000, many of the assessment challenges described above still exist. Accurate data for comparison are difficult to obtain, except in the area of study abroad. Student interest in international education has certainly increased since 2000, but capturing and assessing the ways in which this interest is measured is challenging, at best. NAFEO began its survey in the 2005 in this context.

NAFEO's survey was designed by George Ayers and Associates, an educational research and evaluation consulting firm. The survey design was based on the 2000 ACE internationalization study. The NAFEO staff shortened the Ayers survey slightly and added questions about less commonly taught languages (LCTLs), including Haitian Creole. The final survey included fifty-four questions.

Choosing which recipients to survey was a challenge. As the nation's only trade association representing black college presidents, NAFEO's general policy is to send the survey directly to the office of the president of each institution for distribution on campus to the appropriate office. Because of the short survey period, however, copies of each survey also were mailed directly to faculty, department chairs, and administrators who were responsible for the three survey areas.

The survey was mailed to NAFEO's 120 member institutions in October 2005, asking respondents to provide information from the previous 2004–2005 academic year. NAFEO staff completed three rounds of telephone and e-mail follow up, mailing or faxing the survey to institutions that needed another copy. At the end of the data collection period, NAFEO had collected a wealth of information about international education capacity as well as the role of assessment in international education.

Survey Results

Forty-four percent (53) of NAFEO's 120 member institutions responded to the survey. The survey results indicated that overall, the respondents were committed to internationalizing their campuses but that financial and human resources posed major barriers. Because many institutions serve predominantly low-income and first-generation students, a large portion of institutional resources are dedicated to financial aid and student retention. As a result, staffing in all three survey areas—foreign languages, international studies, and study abroad—prevented institutions from expanding capacity. Institutions also faced challenges in creating partnerships that would help them to leverage and share resources. Despite the barriers, however, many institutions found creative ways to build or enhance innovative international education programs on their campuses.

The data indicated that many institutions want to internationalize and that institutional leaders understand and are committed to the need to expose their students to the world beyond the borders of the United States. Of the responding institutions, 62 percent indicated that a commitment to internationalization was included in their mission statement (NAFEO 2009: 7).

For foreign language offerings, Spanish was the most popular language taught at NAFEO member institutions, followed by French and German (ibid.). Critical LCTLs such as Japanese, Arabic, and Chinese, also were offered, with 11 percent of reporting institutions noting that courses in at least one of these languages were taught on their campuses. These numbers are consistent with national trends in foreign language course offerings (Furman et al. 2006: 2). Several other LCTLs, such as Haitian Creole and Danish, were offered by one institution each (NAFEO 2009: 19). Even though few students at HBCUs enter college with foreign language preparation, 79 percent of responding institutions required foreign language coursework for graduation. Unfortunately, the length of the survey did not allow us to ask more detailed information about the number of courses or the level of language instruction, particularly for critical languages, but this topic is robust enough to justify its own survey in the future.

In international studies and study abroad, institutions also described an interesting variety of courses, programs, and study-abroad options for their students. The interdisciplinary nature of international studies allows flexibility and breadth in the types of courses available, but it also poses a challenge in accurately accounting for each institution's offerings. Although the survey results indicated that a majority of institutions were committed to internationalization as evidenced through their mission statements, few had the capacity they needed to realize their internationalization goals. Only 28 percent of institutions, for example, reported receiving grants or other outside funding to support their international, area, or ethnic studies programs. African studies had the largest aggregate enrollment of all area studies programs, with 591 undergraduate students on the fifty-three responding campuses. Respondents noted that courses taught in international studies and area studies were decentralized, often coordinated by a faculty member in a specific academic department. Examples of these courses included Foreign Policy Studies at Johnson C. Smith University in North Carolina, Puerto Rican Studies at York College, and an African Diaspora and the World program at Spelman College.

Black colleges noted a number of challenges in their efforts to internationalize their campuses. Staffing was one of the most frequently cited challenges. The study abroad results indicated that 25 percent of the institutions (13) do have full-time staff working on study-abroad issues. When asked if they planned to hire a full-time coordinator by the 2007–2008 academic year, 82 percent said they did not (NAFEO 2009: 29). At many smaller higher education institutions, and at both majority- and minority-serving institutions, the study-abroad coordinator has multiple roles on campus, either as faculty or administration. Although this situation is preferable to having no study abroad coordinator at all, time and financial constraints lead to staff turnover and limited outreach to students with the greatest needs. In these situations, priority given to program outreach and execution outweighs that of responding to assessments, such as NAFEO's survey, and data collection, such as that of the Open Doors annual survey by the Institute for International Education (IIE).

During the 2004–2005 academic year, responding NAFEO member institutions sent 844 students abroad to countries around the world. Although two-thirds (66 percent) of the students went on short-term programs (defined as less than one academic quarter or semester), 7 percent of the students studied abroad for an entire academic year. This percentage is higher than the 6 percent of all U.S. students who studied abroad for a full academic year, according to IIE's Open Doors report (Chow 2006). Additionally, the diversity in study-abroad destinations also suggested that students were pursuing a wide variety of opportunities related to their academic interests. Students studied in programs in, for example, Australia, China, Spain, Ghana, Denmark, and the Dominican Republic, among many other countries.

Lessons Learned

In this project, NAFEO learned several important lessons about assessment of international education on black college campuses. First, the decentralized nature of international education on most campuses made it difficult to locate individuals on campuses who could provide accurate information for the survey. Second, the very definition of international education—even when divided on the survey into foreign languages, international studies, and study abroad—was still too vague to capture the information needed to assess what other international studies activity occurred across campuses. Third, a substantial amount of internationally focused activities are occurring on campuses that fall outside the traditional definitions of international education.

This study revealed that collecting accurate data on international education is difficult.

When institutions that do have international education activities fail to respond to surveys, however, they give the appearance to agencies and other funders that black colleges either do not offer international education at all or are not interested in international education. In fact, they are interested, as was indicated in the NAFEO study. Since 2008, NAFEO has worked with IIE to increase HBCU response rates for the Open Doors survey by sending a follow-up letter to each institution explaining the survey's importance and requesting participation. As a result of NAFEO's effort, the HBCU response rate for the 2008 survey increased 40 percent over the previous year. Emphasizing the important connections among assessment, funding, and policy encourages administrators to give more priority to assessment.

Discussion

Black college participation in Title VI programs is crucial in diversifying international education and in fulfilling our nation's twenty-first-century workforce needs. Currently, too few black colleges are applying for or are involved in Title VI programs, a crucial funding stream for internationalization.

To remedy this, Title VI program officers should strengthen their relationships with the White House Initiative on HBCUs to ensure that all HBCUs are aware of funding opportunities and programs. A number of HBCUs have received grants from the Title VI Business and International Education Program, whose purpose is "to improve the academic teaching of the business curriculum and to conduct outreach activities that expand the capacity of the business community to engage in international economic activities."[6] To alleviate some of these problems, the University of Memphis and Michigan State University partnered with a number of Centers for International Business and Education (CIBEs) in a program for globalizing business schools in HBCUs. During the four-year period ending in 2007, this program offered a grant workshop and CIBE consultations, business faculty development workshops, and faculty study seminars abroad on international business in Botswana and South Africa.[7] In 2009, twenty-eight HBCUs received grants through the Business and International Education (BIE) program, creating increased capacity for these institutions to internationalize their campuses.[8] Similar workshops for faculty at MSIs were offered in Asian, Southeast Asian, and Latin

American business studies by other Title VI centers.[9] In spite of the success of these collaborative programs, there still is not enough awareness of their potential effectiveness in the black college community. During a NAFEO conference panel discussion on opportunities in international education at the federal level, for example, few black college representatives reported knowing about the Title VI CIBE or BIE programs or how to apply for them.

The CIBE program is an example of successful institutional collaborations between HBCUs and Title VI grantees; black colleges should work with Title VI to achieve similar levels of representation in its other programs. Black colleges and black college students are underrepresented in Title VI programs such as Fulbright-Hays Faculty Research Abroad and Doctoral Dissertation Research Abroad grants, which are targeted principally for graduate research institutions, and Foreign Language and Area Studies (FLAS) fellowship grants, which are awarded only to insitutions with large international studies faculties, libraries, and expensive language and area studies instruction in the LCTLs. To improve future participation in the Title VI programs available to minority-serving institutions, it would be important to develop a method to assess why black colleges and their students are not participating and to disseminate information better about Title VI programs for which they are eligible and competitive, especially the BIE, UISFL, and Fulbright-Hays Group Projects Abroad programs.

To summarize, the following are recommendations on how we can use assessment to improve black college participation in Title VI programs.

1) Complete a fuller assessment of black college participation in Title VI programs, including which institutions are participating, and at what levels.

2) Strengthen Title VI program relationships with black college presidents, faculty, and administrators, either through the White House Initiative on HBCUs or through the establishment of a black college or MSI Title VI advisory panel. Several HBCUs are doing innovative work in the area of international education; these institutions could offer important advice and guidance to Title VI administrators and to other institutions.

3) Sponsor a summit conference of black college leaders to discuss their views on internationalization and determine how they can work with Title VI program administrators and directors of the NRCs, Language Resource Centers (LRCs), CIBEs, and the Council of American Overseas Research Centers to take advantage of Title VI programs.

4) Assess the role of international students on campuses in internationalizing these campuses. International students add intellectual diversity to classroom discussions, assist students in learning foreign languages, and inspire them

to travel and study abroad. Several black colleges have large percentages of international student enrollment and have successfully integrated these students into the campus life. Each year, for example, only a few international Fulbright scholars are placed on black college campuses. Although the 2005 NAFEO survey did not study international students on campus and the Title VI and Fulbright-Hays programs are forbidden by legislation from funding international students, the Fulbright-Hays Group Projects Abroad and the Title VI BIE and UISFL programs could make black colleges more attractive to prospective international students.

Other International Education Initiatives

Despite the fact that most HBCUs are not doctoral-granting or research institutions, there still should be full opportunity for them to participate in Title VI programs designed for two- and four-year colleges and universties. It is also important to reach out to institutions that have very few international programs or no previous participation in Title VI programs. The possibility also exists to enlarge the collaborations between MSIs and Title VI centers outside the Title VI grants.[10]

In addition, since receiving its Title VI grant, NAFEO has institutionalized international education reform as a core part of its mission. All NAFEO meetings and conferences, for example, now include an international education component. In 2007, NAFEO established a Collaborative for Diversity in Education Abroad (CDEA) initiative with two nonprofit organizations, the Phelps Stokes Fund and Bardoli Global, to promote awareness of policy issues that affect diversity in international education. Part of CDEA's goals are to encourage more minority students to consider careers in international affairs and international public policy by promoting awareness of the IIPP program on MSI campuses. In June 2007, CDEA organized an advocacy day in support of the congressional legislation for the Paul Simon Study Abroad Foundation to provide federal funds for study abroad scholarships. The event drew more than fifty students, congressional staff, researchers, and members of the diplomatic community in support of increasing minority student participation in study abroad. In 2008, NAFEO staff participated in a high-level dialogue with Nordic college and university presidents in Helsinki, Finland to establish exchange relationships between Nordic institutions and black colleges. In 2009, NAFEO began working with the American Institute for Foreign, Study (AIFS) to administer a scholarship program for black college students to study in AIFS programs around the world. The Title VI assessment grant made it possible for NAFEO to identify and fill the critical needs for improving international education on black college campuses.

Conclusion

This chapter is not intended to criticize the way in which Title VI has been administered in the past. Instead, its intent is to describe the real barriers that HBCUs face in trying to internationalize and ways in which Title VI programs can play a more active role on black college campuses. Title VI programs have the potential to transform international education on black college campuses. As we celebrate the fiftieth anniversary of Title VI programs, it is important to remember that the historical relationship between Title VI and black colleges is not as long as it is for other institutions. Because these Title VI international education programs—Fulbright-Hays, NRCs, LRCs, IIPP, and so on—have defined the relationship between international education and higher education in the United States, particularly in terms of bringing prestige to the field of international education, it is crucial that the diversity of America's college student population is reflected in Title VI programs.

The movement to internationalize the American higher education system is growing, and it is important that America's black colleges are at the center of this movement. As our nation becomes more diverse, we must ensure that minority students graduate with the skills to compete in the American economy. This includes preparing students for global citizenship. The face of America abroad should reflect the diversity of America at home and should become a public diplomacy priority. Assessment of black colleges and their needs can help both agencies and administrators achieve Title VI's "comprehensive approach to expanding international education in the United States" by assisting black colleges in developing globally competitive students (IEPS 2008).

Assessment in international education is a challenging task, but it is one that must be improved to clarify our understanding of the role Title VI programs can play in internationalizing college campuses in the next ten years. As we develop better tools and better ways to use them, we will begin to find ways to expand even further the collaboration and partnerships of Title VI NRCs and CIBEs with black colleges and other MSIs. As a result of the Title VI IRSP grant to NAFEO, the organization has been able to serve its members by assessing international education across institutions and to use this information to develop programs that will assist institutions in building international capacity. The relationships and partnerships developed through this assessment work have proved to be invaluable in sharing international education knowledge and resources within the black college community. The capacity of Title VI programs to fund the NAFEO study—as well as more programs such as the IIPP, IRSP, BIE, UISFL, and, now the newly authorized undergraduate FLAS fellowships—are promising signs that this fifty-year-old program will contribute measurably to expanding international education on black college campuses.

Notes

1 PBIs were first created as a category of higher education institutions in 2007 through the College Cost and Reduction Act. Institutions must apply to receive the PBI designation and must meet the following criteria: (1) undergraduate enrollment of no less than 40 percent black students, (2) total undergraduate student enrollment of 1,000 students or more, and (3) At least 50 percent of enrolled students are low-income or first-generation college students.

2 Title VI has made an explicit commitment to increasing diversity in its programs. See www2.ed.gov/about/offices/list/ope/iegps/toward-diversity.html.

3 See www.ed.gov/programs/iegpsugisf/awards.html for awardees 2001–2009.

4 See www.ed.gov/programs/iegpsiipp/index.html.

5 NAFEO is grateful to the International Education Programs Service for funding its research survey. Program officers Ed McDermott and Amy Wilson were extremely supportive of this project.

6 See www.ed.gov/programs/iegpsbie/index.html.

7 This Globalizing Business Schools pilot program leveraged the resources and expertise of Title VI National Resource and CIBE centers with the interests and expertise of participating HBCUs, which included sixteen HBCUs such as: Albany State University, Dillard University, Morgan State University, Norfolk State University, Prairie View A&M University, Southern University A&M, Tennessee State University, and Tuskegee University. Participation costs of nearly $650,000 over the four years were underwritten by Title VI-funded institutions.

8 For more information about the CIBE program and its HBCU partnerships, see http://ciberweb.msu.edu/.

9 See www.ed.gov/about/offices/list/ope/iegps/toward-diversity.html for details.

10 One such non-Title VI collaboration is that of the IIPP, the University of Wisconsin-Madison Language Resource Center, and Howard University in the Language Flagship partnership in African languages funded by the DOD Defense Intelligence Agency through the National Security Education Program.

REFERENCES

Chow, Patricia. 2006. *Open Doors 2006*. New York: Institute for International Education.

Furman, Nelly, David Goldberg, and Natalia Lusin. 2006. Enrollments in Languages Other Than English in United States Institutions of Higher Education—Fall 2006. MLA web publication, www.mla.org/pdf/06enrollmentsurvey_final.pdf.

Hayward, Fred M. 2000. Internationalization of US Higher Education: Preliminary Status Report. American Council on Education, www.acenet.edu/bookstore/pdf/2000-intl-report.pdf.

IEPS, International Education Programs Service. 2008. Expanding Title VI's Reach. www.ed. gov/about/offices/list/ope/iegps/title-six.html.

NAFEO, The National Association for Equal Opportunity in Higher Education. 2009. Survey on Foreign Languages, International Studies, and Study Abroad Opportunities on Historically and Predominantly Black College Campuses.

PART 7

Future Directions for Title VI and Fulbright-Hays Programs

CHAPTER 16

Preparing for the Future: Title VI and Its Challenges

Patrick O'Meara

Occasions such as this fiftieth anniversary are times to remind ourselves of the roots and aspirations of the transformative legislation that we refer to as Title VI. The funding that began as a result of the National Defense Education Act (NDEA) in the 1950s has made a significant contribution to scholarship and to national security as it became Title VI of the Higher Education Act of 1965 and operated in tandem with the Fulbright-Hays programs. At the same time, there have been challenges to the very existence of the funding. My approach in reviewing this historic period is based to a large extent on my own experiences as a student and professor of political science and public affairs, as an African Studies director, and as a dean and vice president for international affairs.

For some, national security is a basic one-dimensional phenomenon or, at best, a somewhat simplistic concept with a blurred connection between national defense and foreign policy. I believe that in the international context there are layers of complexity that have too often been ignored. For a long time, national security and geography were one and the same. Separated by oceans, with travel across them so much slower than today, the United States had no need either for a large standing army or for a national security plan that could be invoked at a moment's notice. World War II, the Cold War, and Sputnik changed all this.

The origin of support for U.S. international competence and authority began after World War II in the early days of the Cold War, when the Ford and Rockefeller foundations along with the Carnegie Corporation, funded university initiatives in area and language studies in the face of perceived threats from the Soviet Union, China, and newly emerging nations around the world. The Soviet Union's successful launch of the Sputnik satellite brought Congress into the educational effort, one part of which was to ensure that the U.S. educational system would prepare future academic and government leaders with international skills. The U.S. Congress passed the NDEA in August 1958, and President Dwight D. Eisenhower signed it into law on September 2, 1958.

The implementation of Title VI legislation became a mission of the Department of Education, not the Department of Defense. This original paradigm established core educational precepts—language proficiency and multicultural understanding—as a basis for national security and the nation's international presence. At the same time, the implementation provided freedom for students and scholars to explore topics without intellectual or disciplinary constraints. Some of the resulting research and scholarship was indeed of narrow, if not rarefied, significance. Other research directly addressed major issues and set out strategic dimensions that still underlie U.S. foreign policy. In retrospect, even what might have appeared "rarefied" has sprung into relevance. Social, cultural, and linguistic studies in Afghanistan might have appeared an indulgence forty years ago, but they are guiding major diplomatic and military actions now. The Title VI paradigm has stood the test of time. The programs that exist because of fifty years of federal funding for Title VI have taught generations of U.S. citizens how to be effective educators and public officials and how to adapt their skills in a changing world.

When I reflect on the preparation of Title VI applications of the 1960s and 1970s, I realize how deeply and dynamically the scope of Title VI has changed. In the early days, the lines were clear. Title VI was focused on a few fixed objectives—to sustain, enhance, and consolidate the study of the world's languages and cultures. Applicants were not asked to consider outreach to the community or the involvement of professional schools in the international issues of the day. As the number of players on the world stage grew and as the variety of issues recognized to have a global impact increased, however, so Title VI programs extended their original mission to new constituencies and new kinds of issues.

In the reauthorization in 1980, a new Part B of Title VI was instituted for matching grants for business and international education programs. In 1988, legislation amended Part B to included Centers for International Business Education and Research (CIBER). The establishment of the CIBER program was prescient. Many at the time questioned whether support for the needs of international business belonged with the U.S. Department of Education, whether this was an appropriate use of scarce federal funds. Today's interdependent global economic environment demands that U.S. schools of business develop courses with international content, ensure that faculty members are sensitive to the global context, provide overseas experiences for graduate and undergraduate students, and reach out to meet the needs and demands of the business community. This is not only in the strategic national interest, but also essential for universities to maintain their credibility and their stature when reaccredited or reviewed.

Still, the core mission of international engagement runs steadfastly through fifty years of Title VI legislation. There have been amplifications and additions, rather than a fundamental redirection. Centers began to devote attention to issues of the environment and technology and to pursue global connections in business. Indiana University has been privileged to be part of this program from its inception—first, with the Russian and East European Studies program and then with African Studies and others. Our rich resources in these fields, and generations of faculty and students, have resulted from this funding and are reflected in the hundreds of books and journal articles and of students who have gone into government, business, and academic positions over the past fifty years. Our graduates, and those of other Title VI centers, serve in key U.S. government positions in all agencies involved in international relations and foreign affairs, in positions both military and civilian. Many others are employed by state and local government.

Title VI has been successful in large part because the Congress authorized a program that enabled scholars and students to pursue a wide range of academic interests without constraints on their areas of research. Shifting priorities within different universities and lean budgets might have led to the abandonment of research and teaching of such languages as Persian, Pashto, Somali, and Uyghur. Some within the university questioned their importance and wondered whether they were peripheral to the university's mission. Although it might have been difficult in the past to justify their validity or their application to national security, no one today would deny their importance. These languages and the study of what might have been considered esoteric cultural studies thrived because of Title VI support. Had universities followed the dictates of budget and economy, the United States would have faced the leadership challenges of the new millennium with a knowledge vacuum in regard to countries, languages, and cultures that are now at the core of strategic national interest.

Issues of security have followed a similar course. A generation ago, "national security" meant watching out for the Soviets and the Eastern bloc and avoiding anything that might lead to nuclear war. World politics no longer coalesces around rival political ideologies, however. Now, terrorism, scarcity of resources, environmental disaster, and failure to ensure basic human rights confront us. The things that threaten global security in the twenty-first century cannot be contained by ideology or geography; they are without borders. With its promotion of a broad definition of cultural knowledge, Title VI programs, especially as they were expanded in the 1980s, have prepared scholars and experts to look beyond traditional disciplines and traditional boundaries.

Title VI programs have not been immune to criticism and challenges. The very existence of Title VI was threatened during the budget-cutting era of the Nixon administration. When Title VI was first established, $3.5 million was appropriated for academic year 1959–1960 and increased every year thereafter. In the 1970s, the Nixon administration sought to reduce funding, and ultimately to eliminate the program, based on the belief that there was no longer the urgency to produce specialists. Because the national need for specialists had been met, universities could take on the burden of funding. The Title VI initiative survived the Nixon years as a result of active grassroots support from university faculty, center directors, administrators, and students, as well as from national organizations.

During the first Bush presidency, the National Security Education Program (NSEP) was born with staff and funding through the Defense Intelligence Agency. Like Title VI, it stressed the importance of language mastery and established nationwide competition for scholarships and fellowships for undergraduate and graduate students to undertake extensive study of a language and culture. In addition, it set a government service requirement for recipients after they completed their studies. NSEP placed its program under a board chaired by the secretary of defense.

Under Title VI, university centers were free to establish the priorities of their activities. Under NSEP, those priorities are set by the central board. Some scholars, centers, and national associations feared that their credibility at home and abroad or the research access of their students would be compromised by priorities set externally by NSEP or by the commitment to work for the government.[1] Response at the government level questioned the need for Title VI, when NSEP might have been a "better model." The fundamental issue was whether the building of international competence should be continued as it was originally conceived—as an educational project—or whether it should be treated instead as a purely strategic initiative. Although that debate was never formally resolved, federal funding continued for both programs. Congress evidently felt that both projects had merit and served national interests.

During the past several decades, Title VI has faced ideological challenges. The accusation was made that Title VI funding for some Middle East studies and language centers had been used for pro-Palestinian activities or for support of anti-American academics, outreach materials, or publications.[2] Some government units were concerned that the academic work and foci of Title VI centers were growing increasingly out of sync with federal priorities. Critics accused the centers of failing to produce the level of language competence the nation needed because of their insistence on addressing cultural issues broadly.[3] Kenneth D. Whitehead, a Department of Education administrator who was in charge of Title VI in the Reagan era, supported the establishment of an oversight board to ensure that Congress, not universities, set the priorities of Title VI centers:

> We were not getting a good value for our dollar. Many of those who studied "hard" languages (e.g., Arabic, Persian, and Chinese) in Title VI-supported programs turned out to be less proficient than they needed to be to work effectively in diplomacy, intelligence, aid-related work, and even international business. It was a common assumption in my day that the graduates of the government-operated Foreign Service Institute and Defense Language Institute were more proficient in "hard" languages than their university-trained colleagues.[4]

In 2007, the federal government contracted with the National Research Council (NRC) of the National Academy of Sciences (NAS) to review the success of Department of Education's Title VI and Fulbright-Hays programs. The congressional mandate did not limit the review to language acquisition alone, but rather specified eight areas of concern—from developing an effective infrastructure that would support expanded language instruction at all academic levels to meeting business needs and using technology to support international studies. The NRC–NAS report, "International Education and Foreign Languages: Keys to Securing America's Future," noted the difficulty of making a completely reliable assessment at all these levels because of "the paucity of rigorous, reliable information on program performance." Still, the conclusions note the varied ways that Title VI centers have contributed to global competency. The Title VI and Fulbright-Hays programs have been "a catalyst for language or area studies initiatives." They have provided important support for less commonly taught languages. They have been the impetus for universities' own investment in area studies and have produced instructional materials for students of all ages.[5] Thus, both Congress and the council recognized that global competence certainly demands language fluency, but requires more as well. The report concludes that Title VI has "served as a foundation for internationalization in higher education."

As part of the debate regarding the strategic relevance of Title VI centers, universities were accused of resting on a false sense of entitlement. Middle East author and academic, Martin Kramer, for example, asserts that by the 1980s, Title VI "pretty much stabilized as a semi-entitlement" for the centers it funded.[6] I have been much engaged in Title VI activities for many years, however, and a sense of entitlement has never been a part of the way Indiana University's centers operated. Indeed, there were years when some of our centers were not funded at all. The three-year cycle with a rigorous national peer-review process in selecting National Resource, Language Resource, and International Business Centers made us regularly reflect on past successes and future needs. We had to justify activities and effectiveness, prove their value, and indicate evaluation processes to verify accomplishments. The cycle created an atmosphere very different from a sense of entitlement. It required us to look for innovative solutions. The preservation of the status quo was never the result of such reflection.

An example of our attempt to be in the forefront of language and culture instruction is Indiana University's well-known course in Uzbek. The program is one of the university's most innovative. Students studying at a distance via videoconferencing regularly consult on course issues and practice the language with the instructor via web cameras. Audio files and video materials are posted to the web for all students. Classes have regularly scheduled chat room sessions. Instructors point students to online news services as well as to YouTube, so they can experience Uzbekistan in ways that used to be possible only by going to the country. Students use online Uzbek dictionaries, and a scholar at Indiana University is working on a major project to provide an audio- and video-enhanced online dictionary of Uzbek dialects. Technological innovations are not confined to Uzbek. News of such experiments travels quickly on the campus, and language instructors in other areas now have these kinds of resources for their students.

Finally, Title VI centers and the area and international studies programs they represent have been caught in an intellectual challenge by those who assign diminished theoretical importance to world areas, countries, and cultures, who would focus instead on behavior and game theory and on comparative data on a macro level. When Title VI programs began, we were in the heyday of traditional area studies. One had to learn a new culture just as one learned a new language—the expectation was that the differences were what mattered and that successful cross-cultural communication could occur only by recognizing those differences. However, much scholarship of the late twentieth century involved "the search for universal, value-neutral models in the study of social and human life," note Mitchell Stevens and Cynthia Miller-Idriss in their report on "Academic Internationalism" for the Social Science Research Council.[7] Rational choice theory made transnational studies attractive. Scholars sought the common elements of economic and political development in divergent cultures. If human behavior could be explained outside its national context, then the scholarship that prized the differences in nations could be seen as obsolete. There is now an increasing recognition that both approaches can be productive, and there is resurgence in language and area studies.

Another part of the intellectual debate challenges conventional definitions of nations and regions. Stevens and Miller-Idriss explain:

> The end of the Cold War led many scholars to question the extent to which U.S. global political interests had defined world areas as academics had come to know them. At the same time intellectual developments in the humanities, especially, called into question the notion that cultures, nations, or world regions could appropriately be conceived as coherent units.

The extent to which current scholarship will undermine the ability to define nations and cultures remains to be seen. I believe that global competence requires us to maintain a double vision of similarities and differences, that the answer lies in embracing them both, and that area studies of the future will grapple with ways to do that. Indeed, the study of such issues as climate, population, joint security, and many other pressing global issues demands the analytical framework of transnational theories, but effective solutions to these problems also must take into account important national and cultural differences.

Conclusion

The world after September 11, 2001 changed our perception of national security forever. The government's immediate need for experts in languages it might have neglected was met in large part by the previous decades of work of Title VI centers. In addition, policy makers began to realize that security issues had grown immensely more complex than anyone in the Cold War era could have imagined. Area studies scholars had developed exactly the tools that could begin to embrace this complexity. Many of the scholars in our centers were also acutely aware that new knowledge and theoretical approaches were being developed in different parts of the world and that a U.S.- or Euro-centered approach was no longer appropriate. By ignoring this development, we would not be serving our academic or strategic interests.

There are still concerns among scholars about the NSEP and the preservation of academic freedom. I feel that there is no such thing as too much language instruction, and no opportunity to promote it should be dismissed out of hand. Indeed, every language is really many languages. What is needed to learn to communicate successfully in the military context is not the same as language proficiency for discussions of policy or for academic research, or for what children in elementary and high school might learn in studying the language. Title VI must continue to respond to these different needs and to innovate in new pedagogical directions, just as NSEP must continue to serve its mission of assuring fluency in strategic languages for government agencies. In the post September 11, 2001 context, key questions need to be considered about the nature of U.S. interests. While respecting the positions of those who are opposed to NSEP, its relevance and importance to specific world areas should not be ignored.

Academic freedom permits scholarship concerning rarefied topics. Still, scholars and universities must reach out to policy makers, who are focused on outcomes. Scholars must find ways to render their research and their knowledge in ways that policy makers can understand and can use. Through their writings, testifying to legislators and consultations, they are an invaluable strategic resource. Just as scholars have to find ways to convey knowledge and insights to students, so they must find innovative ways to share their expertise with policy makers. This is demanding, but not constraining.

From the first period of the Sputnik era and its aftermath, there were challenges and redefinitions. Ideological considerations became part of the debate on Title VI, and there is no question that Title VI operates in an ideologically charged environment. Still, as we look to the future, "Dramatic post-cold War changes in the world's geopolitical and economic landscapes are creating needs for American expertise and knowledge about a greater diversity of less commonly taught foreign languages and nations of the world."[8] Title VI is helping to lead the way in assessing and evaluating the effectiveness of international education.

The security, stability, and economic vitality of the United States in a complex global era depend upon American experts in and citizen's knowledge about world regions, foreign languages, and international affairs, as well as upon a strong research base in these areas. Title VI has provided these things for half a century. Furthermore, it has had the capacity to evolve and adapt to the strategic needs of a changing world. However "strategic" and "national interest" are defined, Title VI has served this country well.

In looking toward the future, is it possible to speculate on strategic national interests for the next several years of the twenty-first century? There are some clues. Although it has become a cliché to speak of a world that is "flat," in many ways this is indeed the case. Communications, banking, academic research, and teaching have all been fundamentally changed by the possibilities of a virtual, unified, electronic world. But differences in meaning, context, language, history, and interpersonal relationships cannot be ignored even if we are meeting face to face through ever more proficient technological advancements.

At the same time, we are also living in a world of continuing, if not increasing, religious, political, social, and economic divisions—a world that is not always "flat." Small-scale wars, hijackings, terrorism, and profound religious and political differences are now a central part of the international reality.

What does this mean to the mission of Title VI? All its programs and accomplishments become more sharply etched and point the way to new needs.

Languages, modes of interaction, the understanding of ethnicity, economics, and so many other forms of scholarship are now essential to understanding who is an "enemy" or who is a "friend" in conflicts. But we must not confine "strategic" to the realm of conflict. New alliances with clear terms of reference are now vital to deal with urgent environmental issues, renewable resources, trade, and the day-to-day processes of engagement. Our faculty will do more research with colleagues in what were once "remote" places. Our students will navigate easily and successfully in an interconnected and interdependent world and will use their skills as public servants, military personnel, or teachers.

But they will need resources and opportunities. International research, teaching, and service function differently from the way they did in 1958. Advances in technology have changed the nature of libraries and increased access to materials and collections. The walls of the classroom and of pedagogy are disappearing as interactive connections and tools transform the delivery of instructional materials. Conferences, workshops, and seminars still benefit from face-to-face interaction, but there are now exciting and immediate ways of engaging in academic conversations. As a university administrator and as a faculty member, I am acutely aware of these changes. Universities are addressing them, and it is essential for the future of Title VI that it too should address them by assuring support for innovations now and to come.

The core elements of Title VI have the dynamic capacity to respond to shifting demands. The scope and range of Title VI centers have proven their ability to adapt, and they must be given the support to enable them to continue to evolve and to be ready to serve new strategic concerns.

Acknowledgment

I would like to thank Lynn Schoch, Director of Communications and Information Resources for International Affairs at Indiana University, for his assistance with this article.

Notes

1 See, for example, Price, David H., "Cold War Anthropology: Collaborators and Victims of the National Security State," *Identities* Vol. 4, Issue 3–4 (June 1998): 416.

2 See, for example, Kramer, Martin, "Congress Probes Middle Eastern Studies," *Sandstorm Blog*, June 23, 2003, www.geocities.com/martinkramerorg/2003_06_23.htm.

3 See, for example, Kurtz, Stanley, "Taking Sides on Title VI: Middle East Studies Reform Goes Partisan," *National Review Online* (December 12, 2007).

4 Whitehead, Kenneth D., "Learning the Language," *National Review Online* (January 14, 2004). www.nationalreview.com/comment/whitehead200401140823.asp.

5 O'Connell, Mary Ellen and Janet Lippe Norwood, eds. *International Education and Foreign Languages: Keys to Securing America's Future* (Washington, D.C.: National Academies Press, 2007), 3.

6 Kramer, Martin, "Can Congress Fix Middle Eastern Studies?" *Sandstorm Blog*, November 2003. www.geocities.com/martinkramerorg/HR3077.htm.

7 Stevens, Mitchell L. and Cynthia Miller-Idriss, "Academic Internationalism: U.S. Universities in Transition: a Report on Consultations convened at the Social Science Research Council, New York City, 14 and 17 October 2008" (March 2009), 17.

8 "The History of Title VI and Fulbright-Hays: An Impressive International Timeline," International Education Programs Service, Office of Postsecondary Education Department of Education, www.ed.gov/about/offices/list/ope/iegps/history.html.

CHAPTER 17

Future Directions for Title VI and Fulbright-Hays Programs: Creativity and Competence for Facing Global Challenges

William I. Brustein

For the past fifty years the U.S. Department of Education's Title VI and Fulbright-Hays programs (Title VI/FH) have played a highly significant and successful role in preparing generations of graduates from U.S. institutions of higher education to confront our nation's economic, political, and security realities and challenges. In this chapter, I focus principally on new challenges and opportunities and propose direction for Title VI and Fulbright-Hays in addressing these new challenges and opportunities, thereby ensuring the survival and growth of these programs during the next fifty years.

My principal thesis is that the future of Title VI/FH depends largely on the ability of these programs to respond creatively to new challenges and opportunities emanating from Washington and from our university campuses. The list of challenges I present is in no way exhaustive, but simply reflects my views as shaped by my experiences as a professor, former director of a Title VI National Resource Center, and the senior international officer at two major public research universities with active Title VI and Fulbright-Hays programs.

Key Challenges

The key challenges before the Title VI/FH community are (1) the persistent characterization of area studies as a "dying" field of study; (2) the continuing allegations   341 by critics that Title VI/FH has underperformed in equipping our graduates with foreign language expertise, indepth knowledge, and understanding of non-U.S. societies, familiarity with critical global issues (e.g., international conflict, global health, sustainable development, global economic competitiveness) as well as in placing our graduates in careers addressing our national security interests; (3) the difficulty of the Title VI/FH programs in carving out a definable market niche within the pantheon of (competitive) federal international programs oriented toward national security interests (e.g., the National Security Education Program's [NSEP] ROTC Language and Culture Project); (4) the increasing demand for foreign language proficiency for students in disciplines outside the foreign languages and literatures; (5) not confronting the erroneous perception that the primary objective and value of Title VI/FH should be the rapid production of linguists and interpreters fluent in critical foreign languages, while neglecting the fact that the distinct advantage of Title VI/FH is the ability to *combine* foreign language acquisition with critical thinking skills and indepth knowledge of world regions; (6) the ability to operate in a fiscally constrained environment in which colleges and universities have limited resources to hire traditional area studies scholars, inadequate resources to maintain separate campus library area studies collections and area studies librarians, and in which many colleges and universities can no longer support foreign language courses with single-digit enrollments; and (7) the task of convincing our university and college administrators and faculty that the Title VI/FH programs add significant value to the overall missions of teaching, research, and engagement, especially in light of campuswide budget rescissions and low overhead (8 percent) allowed for Title VI NRC grants.

Responding to the Challenges

To address these challenges, I propose that Title VI/FH programs embrace as a new central mission the education of globally competent students—that is, students possessing a combination of critical thinking skills, technical expertise, and global awareness. This combination will allow them not only to contribute to knowledge but also to comprehend, analyze, and evaluate its meaning in the context of an increasingly globalized world, so they are well prepared to seek and implement solutions to the challenges of global significance (e.g., social, cultural, economic, technological, political, and environmental challenges).[1] To this end, the Title VI/FH programs should focus on the cultivation, for both students and faculty, of globally competent foundational skills, such as the ability to work effectively in international settings; the awareness of and adaptability to diverse cultures, perceptions, and approaches; a familiarity with the major currents of global change and the issues they raise; the capacity for effective communication across cultural and linguistic boundaries; and a comprehension of the international dimensions of one's field of study.

I propose that the ideal loci for and drivers of a globally competent citizenry should be the Title VI/FH programs. If these programs are to succeed, they will need to rethink the manner in which they interact with the various constituencies on and off our campuses. For the purposes of this chapter, I will concentrate on the challenges and opportunities arising on our college and university campuses.

Adding Value to Campus Constituencies

The future of Title VI/FH will depend largely on the ability of the program to make a convincing case that it demonstrates relevance and adds value to our campuses' core missions of teaching, research, and engagement. Particularly in times of campus budget declines and rescissions, voices are raised at colleges and universities about the return on investment (ROI) of Title VI centers in light of the dollar amount required for an informal but expected institutional match, the low overhead from these grants, and the perception among many campus leaders and faculty that these programs do not directly benefit students and faculty outside the humanities and social sciences. Title VI National Resource Center (NRC) grants include an overhead of only 8 percent, whereas grants from federal agencies such as NIH and NSF produce facilities and administrative (F&A) indirect cost rates of 50 to 60 percent, and some Title VI NRC directors report exclusively to an administrator within arts and sciences instead of to a central campus administrator. These factors make it all the more imperative that we demonstrate the ways by which Title VI/FH funding enriches teaching, research, and engagement not solely for faculty and students in the arts, humanities, and social sciences but equally for those in the professional schools.

How might Title VI/FH programs cast a wider campus net while maintaining the U.S. Department of Education's International Education Programs Service (IEPS) mission of meeting the national needs for expertise and competence in foreign languages and area or international studies as well as the nation's interests in national security and global competitiveness? All college units seek to equip their students with skills to enhance their marketability and to provide their faculty with the knowledge and resources to enable them to improve their teaching and research productivity. Title VI/FH programs have great potential to assist college units in meeting these goals. For instance, engineers and businesspeople find themselves increasingly engaged in multinational projects in which an appreciation and understanding of diverse cultures, perceptions, and approaches are critical to the success of the team. Moreover, they benefit greatly from an indepth understanding of   343 local cultures in the design, marketing, and application of their projects. Stories abound of U.S.-sponsored engineering projects abroad that, by neglecting local religious and social customs, resulted in local protests and projects that failed to attain local support. A recent issue of *SAISPHERE* focusing on water scarcity highlighted the indispensable value of village-level understanding—including knowledge of local politics, economic incentives, and use patterns—in addressing water-related problems such as improving the accessibility of clean water in the rural areas surrounding Cochabama, Bolivia. Without knowledge of the local customs and dialects, engineers would likely have encountered unimaginable obstacles.[2] We should not forget, furthermore, how many business transactions collapsed due to inadequate cross-cultural training of U.S. employees. The Committee for Economic Development's 2006 report cites the highly embarrassing incidents of the worldwide dissemination of Microsoft Windows 95 that placed the Indian province of Kashmir outside India's geographical boundaries, and the distribution in Arab countries of a video game in which Arabic chanting of the Koran accompanied violent scenes.[3]

What concrete steps might the Title VI/FH programs take to speak to the needs of our campus units as they struggle to position their students and faculty for the challenges of the twenty-first century? Title VI/FH programs should lead campuswide efforts to ground the study of challenges of global significance within world regions. Both our understanding of these global challenges and our ability to develop solutions will benefit immensely by examining global issues at a regional or country level. There is no better way to respond to critics who opine that the field of area studies is dead than by pointing to the value of such studies in examining how phenomena at a macro or global level reveal themselves at the local and regional levels. Knowledge provided from a local or regional examination of global issues has a huge potential to enrich the understanding of our scholars and policy makers of the critical global problems facing the nation and the world. Our Title VI NRC area studies programs, given their mission of cultivating expertise in critical foreign languages and world regions, are well suited to this task and will strengthen the case for their unique worth to the academic enterprise. For instance, scholars and policy makers will never successfully comprehend and furnish viable options for resolution to the seemingly intractable conflicts between Pakistan and India without an indepth analysis of the contrasting conceptions of the national project (dating back to the end of British India) in those two countries today. It is only through this contextual knowledge and deep historical understanding that conflict resolution can begin.

There are some excellent examples of Title VI centers contributing to the grounding of important global issues within world regions. First, consider the Joint Area Centers Symposium (JACS) initiative at the University of Illinois at Urbana-Champaign, launched as a combined effort of the eight Title VI programs. The most recent JACS initiative focused on "A New Green Revolution? Meeting Global Food and Energy Demands." The two-day symposium organized by the centers brought together experts dealing with food and energy at the global level and experts focusing on these issues at the regional/local levels, to examine the extant theories for the purpose of revision and propose new models to deal with these challenges. In particular, the conference addressed the current state of agriculture around the world, the shifting demand for food and energy, biofuel development and its effects on agriculture, and the role of agribusiness in meeting global demands.

Second, a successful model of joining generalists with area studies specialists in the study of critical global concerns is the University of Pittsburgh's Global Studies Program (GSP), which builds on Pitt's highly respected area studies programs. In designing the GSP, the Title VI NRCs selected six cutting-edge teaching and research themes reflecting both key global challenges and the university's academic strengths (sustainable development, global health, international conflict and conflict resolution, changing identities in a globalizing world, global governance and economy, and global communications). Within the GSP, Pitt faculty and students concentrate on developing real-world solutions to global problems—from providing disaster relief to erasing health inequities among poor population—creating coursework based on their study. By bringing indepth area studies expertise to the study of critical global issues (e.g., global migration, sustainable development, poverty, conflicts and conflict resolution) programs such as those at Illinois and Pittsburgh enhance the prospects that Title VI/FH programs will be perceived as providing greater impact in addressing real-world challenges, which will enhance their value on our campuses, in our communities, and in Washington.

Similarly, our Title VI area studies centers will profit from greater emphasis on comparative studies. Comparative case studies can emanate from within world regions or across regions. The value of comparative case studies is similar to that of combining the global and the regional—that is, it provides a means to test our theories and to revise our understanding of significant global issues. Also, by placing a greater emphasis on the value of the comparative approach, the likelihood of convincing colleges and departments to hire faculty who can contribute to our area and international studies programs may increase. During my years as a senior international administrator, I have found that when our annual area studies faculty requests included the hiring of regional specialists as well as comparative case specialists (e.g., sustainable development in Brazil and Angola) my negotiations with deans and department chairs were more likely to succeed.

Title VI centers should serve as a locus for and drivers of the effort to comprehensively internationalize the curriculum on our campuses. I propose that our Title VI   345 centers focus on the internationalization of each major with the ultimate objective of producing a curriculum delivering the globally competent foundational skills previously mentioned. If the training of globally competent graduates is accepted as one of the chief goals of our system of higher education, our curricula will have to be redesigned to ensure that outcome. Most of our institutions address the need for global competence by adding a diversity or international course(s) require-ment—hardly sufficient to instill global competence in our students—or by offer-ing degrees, minors, or certificates in area or international studies. However, there are serious shortcomings in the way many area and international studies' curricula are generally carried out. Many area studies programs tend to be highly descriptive and often display an apparent abhorrence toward theorizing or practical applica-tion. The curriculum frequently resembles a cafeteria-style menu: one selection or course from this shelf, followed by selections from various other shelves. Somehow students are expected miraculously to pull together the disparate pieces into some coherent whole. Area studies frequently fail to take advantage of opportunities to generalize from their rich contextual findings to the broader world. International studies programs (particularly when they fall under the rubric of international rela-tions) frequently manifest a lack of appreciation for the importance of the local and regional cultural contexts. There are few, if any, attempts at applying the theoreti-cal approaches to the empirical context of the regions. As a result, American students often complete these programs without any competency in a foreign language or any specific grounding in the culture of a society outside of the United States.

Additionally, our area and international studies programs often fail to give appropriate attention to such crucial steps as (1) integrating relevant learning-abroad opportunities into the degree, minor, or certificate; (2) incorporating criti-cal thinking skills of knowledge, comprehension, analysis, synthesis, explanation, evaluation, and extrapolation into the learning experience;[4] (3) assessing or evalu-ating global competence as an outcome; and (4) aligning the area or international studies concentration to a disciplinary major (e.g., biology, anthropology, history, or engineering).

We must continually ask ourselves whether we are doing a disservice to our undergraduate students by encouraging them to spend their undergraduate years pursuing stand-alone degrees in area or international studies. I often meet with heads of multinational corporations, government offices, and nongovernmental organizations (NGOs). When I ask these leaders to describe to me what they look for when making hiring decisions, they invariably begin by reminding me that they hire engineers, chemists, economists—in other words, graduates with technical expertise. They proceed, however, to inform me of the enormous added value they see in graduates who combine a technical expertise with area and international studies knowledge, foreign language, and learning-abroad experience. In particular, they highlight the benefits of global awareness, cultural sensitivity, and foreign language competency.

I proffer an additional criticism of stand-alone undergraduate degrees in area and international studies: If we are to achieve global competence, we are obliged to internationalize the educational experience regardless of the discipline. If we require students to select either a stand-alone major in area or international studies or a traditional disciplinary degree, students most likely will opt for the latter and we will be left with a situation in which only a small number of students will have exposure to an international studies concentration. Global competence cannot be the preserve of only a few students. It is incumbent on us as international educators to gain buy-in and participation in designing undergraduate programs that will let our students earn area studies certificates or minors truly linked and relevant to their disciplines, or carefully thought-out disciplinary or international and area studies majors in which both disciplinary expertise and area or international studies are fully integrated. The answer is not area studies *or* disciplines—it is developing a comprehensive and coherent curriculum that will train our students to become globally competent critical thinkers.

The University of Pittsburgh's Global Studies certificate provides a useful model of creating an international curriculum component that is available to all students. The Pitt Global Studies certificate provides undergraduates and graduate students with an opportunity for interdisciplinary training concurrent with academic or professional degrees in any major field. In consultation with an academic advisor, students design an individualized program of study requiring no fewer than eighteen credits. Global Studies students choose one of the six global concentrations (sustainable development; globalized economy and global governance; changing identities in a global world; communication, technology, and society; global health; and conflict and conflict resolution) and unite it with the study of a particular region and a language of that region. In so doing, the program effectively integrates the study of major global issues with the study of their application in different regions and cultures, ensuring both the global relevance of area studies and the empirical grounding of globalization studies. The six Global Studies concentrations are thus designed to promote holistic learning while creating new and specialized forums for discussion and learning that break across disciplinary boundaries in order to better address the causes, consequences, and search for solutions arising from globalization. Each student must complete a capstone research project as part of the coursework on a topic relating to chosen global and regional concentrations, ultimately receiving a certificate in Global Studies.

The Title VI area and international centers at Michigan State University have brought this global perspective to the undergraduate curriculum, offering a Global and Area Studies B.A. major, additional major (especially for students in professional fields), or a second degree. Instead of traditional majors in African or Asian studies, separate concentrations in the global major focus on Africa, Asia, Europe, Latin America and the Caribbean, and Russian and Eurasian studies, as well as two tracks in International Development and Gender and Global Change. Globally focused courses give attention to global trade, environment and sustainable resource management, democratization and human rights, global and local culture and identities, as well as issues of education, health, poverty, development, and gender. Area courses bring those issues into the context of each world region.

The University of Pittsburgh's Global Studies certificate and the MSU Global and Area Studies major are significant steps forward in providing students with a relevant international curriculum component open to all students. However, these fall short of a fully integrated internationalized curriculum because they are add-ons. To ensure a globally competent curriculum, our colleges and universities need to rethink the contents of each academic department's major in an effort to infuse the international into each course required for the major and into the major's capstone experiences. Georgia Tech has made tremendous strides in this direction through its International Plan (IP), in which international studies, language acquisition, and an overseas experience are integrated into the traditional bachelor of science degree for the various disciplines. Furthermore, upon completion of the undergraduate degree in the student's major and the IP requirements, the student's transcript and diploma state that the degree is a "Bachelor of Science with International Plan." The next step for schools such as Georgia Tech should be to seek ways to internationalize every course within the major. The point here is that Title VI centers whose faculty affiliates include experts in international comparative case studies, area studies, and global studies are best suited to work with departments to design and implement a truly internationalized major.

A truly internationalized major for all students will require rethinking how we develop foreign language proficiency for our students. As stated in the 2007 Modern Language Association (MLA) report, deep cultural knowledge and linguistic competence are equally necessary if one wishes to understand people and their communities.[5] Among the challenges we face is the lack of adequate foreign language preparation for our students. Enrollment in foreign language courses in U.S. universities and colleges has fallen from 16.5 percent (language course enrollments per 100 total student enrollments) in 1965 to less than 9 percent today; between 1965 and 1995 the share of four-year institutions with language degree requirements for some students fell from roughly 90 percent to 67 percent, and in 2001 only 27 percent of four-year institutions of higher education required foreign language for all students. Most disconcerting is that among the foreign languages taught in U.S. institutions of higher education, the percentage of students taught such critical languages as Chinese (3.3 percent), Russian (1.6 percent), and Arabic (1.5 percent) are wholly insufficient when compared with Spanish (52.2 percent), French (13.1 percent), German (6 percent), Italian (5 percent), and American Sign Language (5 percent).[6]

Foreign language proficiency is a necessary component of global competence. If our institutions are to produce globally competent students, foreign language preparation must extend beyond students matriculating in our departments of foreign languages and literature. The multicultural character of our societies and the globalizing trend of the workplace require foreign language competency for graduates in the social and natural sciences and in our professional schools. Too frequently at our institutions the primary responsibility for foreign language preparation falls on faculty in language and literature departments who have few resources and limited interest to teach foreign languages to students including both majors and nonmajors. In most research universities, promotion and tenure for faculty in language and literature departments are more dependent on publishing articles and books in literature and producing marketable PhD students in literature than on teaching foreign language courses to nonmajors. Complicating matters further, foreign language departments have resisted efforts to allocate tenure-track positions to language teaching specialists, as the national reputation of a language and literature department correlates strongly with research publications in the field of literature rather than the teaching of foreign languages. Moreover, nonmajors in literature and language often find the content of foreign language courses boring and irrelevant to their disciplinary interests. Our challenge is to create a comprehensive and effective plan for foreign language preparation that has as a primary objective the attainment of at least conversational proficiency in a second language for all our students.

The 2007 MLA report recommends the replacement "of the two-tiered language-literature structure with a broader and more coherent curriculum in which language, culture, and literature are taught as a continuous whole, supported by alliances with other departments and expressed through interdisciplinary courses."[7] Although I do not disagree with the MLA recommendation, I propose, however, that this more coherent curriculum include content courses such as economics, engineering, mathematics, and history in addition to language, culture, and literature. It is crucial that sociologists, engineers, health professionals, and business students become conversant in foreign languages relevant to their fields of study. Ultimately, this will equip our students with a set of skills to enable them 349 to communicate effectively with native speakers in the target language, and equally be able to comprehend relevant written materials in the target language to achieve their academic objectives and to be able "to reflect on the world and themselves through the lens of another language and culture."[8]

Accordingly, our campuses should strive to facilitate foreign language training for *all* faculty members—which, among other things, would spur the creation of new programs for languages across the curriculum.[9] How do we produce content-based foreign language expertise? I recommend that Title VI/FH launch an initiative to train language faculty in content-based language skills and nonlanguage discipline-based faculty to incorporate language learning relevant to their disciplines. Fulbright-Hays, in particular, should sponsor summer programs abroad for faculty members with the goal of improving the foreign language teaching skills of nonlanguage and literature content-based faculty. The Monterey Institute of International Studies may provide a useful model for intensive training for both language and literature and nonlanguage and literature faculty interested in developing foreign-language content-based courses. Furthermore, we are not doing an adequate job of drawing on our international students and members of our heritage communities who have received training in the teaching of second languages to assist us in the foreign language preparation of our students. Also, institutions of primary, secondary, and tertiary education must work together to improve the foreign language preparation of students especially in regard to proficiency in critical languages such as Mandarin, Japanese, Korean, Arabic, Russian, and Farsi, so when students arrive on our campuses they have a solid footing on the way to advance foreign language learning. These goals are totally consistent with the aims of the U.S. Department of Education's Title VI/FH programs for international and area studies. Our Title VI centers should spearhead the effort of foreign language proficiency for every student and faculty member on our campuses.

Up to this point, this chapter has discussed how Title VI/FH programs can enhance their value to campus constituencies by taking the lead in grounding the study of challenges of global significance within world regions by guiding the efforts on our campuses to comprehensively internationalize the curriculum and drive the initiative toward foreign language proficiency for all students. The final challenge and opportunity I want to address is the role of Title VI area centers in promoting models of campus efficiency, flexibility, and financial entrepreneurship. Campus administrators facing budget constraints expect that units will seek greater efficiencies through shared services, distance education, and collaborations, as well as seeking new sources of external revenue. Title VI centers can contribute to the quest for greater efficiencies through several means. Perpetually bothersome to senior administrators is subsidizing courses that consistently draw low enrollments. Many of our less commonly taught language (LCTL) courses fall into this category. Efforts led by our Title VI centers to partner with other Title VI centers and/or language faculty on other campuses to link low enrollment courses through distance education are much welcomed by administrators. One such model is CourseShare, organized under the auspices of the Committee on Institutional Cooperation (CIC), consisting of the Big Ten universities plus the University of Chicago. CourseShare allows students interested in specialized courses such as the LCTLs to enroll in courses offered at other CIC institutions from a distance, primarily via videoconferencing, without having to temporarily relocate.

Along a similar vein, the ever-rising costs of purchasing new monographs and journals and the costs associated with hiring additional area studies librarians are taking a toll on the budgets of our campus libraries. In my years as a senior international educator I have been dismayed by the apparent inflexibility and lack of sensitivity on the part of some area studies faculty to the difficulty facing our library administrators toward reconciling the needs of our Title VI centers to remain competitive for grants while under the challenge of tightening library budgets. Title VI centers will certainly be able to enhance their value among campus administrators by working with our librarians to develop more cost-efficient models for our area studies library collections. In this digital age, there is obviously more than one way to organize a collection to address the Title VI requirements of maintaining library holdings, including basic reference works, journals, and works in translation. Creating efficiencies within our libraries in the long run may strengthen our area studies collections.

Another irritant to senior administrators, especially deans, are requests by Title VI directors for faculty hires in specific fields in specific years (e.g., a historian of eighteenth-century China in year two of the grant). Deans appreciate flexibility; the more that Title VI directors are willing to compromise with regard to which year in the four-year cycle the hire occurs, and in which department (e.g., willingness to accept an Africanist hired in the disciplines of anthropology, political science, history, or sociology), the greater the likelihood of success. Similarly, in light of tight budgets, deans are more likely to agree to area and international studies hiring requests that do not bind them to long-term commitments (e.g., lecturers, instructors, and visiting personnel). Consequently, requests targeting three-year renewable faculty, particularly in languages, are more likely to gain the approval of deans. Another means to ensure that faculty with international experience and perspectives are hired that does not require the creation of new faculty lines is a program by which the university offers incentives for departments to include global experiences as a preference in its hiring. Here, for example, a department could agree to include in its advertisement for a faculty search a preference for an economist with   351 teaching and research expertise relevant to Africa. If the department hired such an individual it would receive extra funds to be used in the start-up package for the new hire or to be used as it sees fit to address other departmental needs.

We are all aware that obtaining and retaining Title VI NRC/FLAS funding requires an exemplary effort on the part of many individuals on our campuses, and that winning Title VI NRC/FLAS funding is one of the clearest markers of campus success at comprehensive internationalization. But how often do we attempt to leverage our success at winning Title VI NRC/FLAS funding for additional internal and external funding? My experience is that few Title VI directors and faculty invest sufficient energy in promoting the honor and benefits to our campus and community of having won these prestigious grants. In most cases, the award of a Title VI NRC demonstrates that the campus is peer-review ranked among the top ten to twenty colleges and universities within the United States in expertise in the study of a particular world region. I cannot think of a campus leader who would not try to take advantage of having his or her program ranked among the top U.S. programs listed annually in *U.S. News & World Report*. We should treat Title VI awards similarly. Again, my observations and experiences convince me that openings to funding opportunities at foundations, corporations, other government agencies and to individuals will become more readily available for requests to internationalize our campuses by promoting our competitive success at winning Title VI NRC/FLAS funding. The more success we have at obtaining additional external funding, the greater the likelihood of garnering additional internal funds and, most importantly, increasing the perception of the return on investment of Title VI/FH among the various campus constituencies.

In conclusion, during the past fifty years, Title VI/FH programs have accomplished much to enhance our understanding of foreign nations, their cultures, and their languages. These achievements have served the nation well. Today, we are confronted with new global challenges, and the survival of Title VI/FH will depend largely on its ability to respond effectively to these new challenges by producing globally competent student graduates. I am not advocating that Title VI/FH abandon its core missions of meeting the national needs for expertise and competence in foreign languages and area and international studies. However, I do propose that we look at these missions as not only ends in themselves but also as necessary means to the goal of tackling the global challenges before us. By spearheading efforts to examine significant global issues from a regional perspective, by taking the lead in the drive to comprehensively internationalize the curriculum, and by promoting the effort toward foreign language proficiency for all students and faculty, Title VI/FH programs are well positioned nationally and on their campuses to become the principal loci and drivers of global competence. I am confident that success on this front will fortify the perception of the value of Title VI/FH on our campuses, in our communities, and in Washington, ultimately ensuring the future of Title VI/FH for the next fifty years.

Notes

1 The definition employed here for global competence derives from the report *A Call to Leadership: The Presidential Role in Internationalizing the University* (Washington, D.C.: National Association of State Universities and Land Grant Colleges, 2004), which I helped to craft.

2 "Water: The New Reality." *SAISPHERE*, Paul H. Nitze School of Advanced International Studies of Johns Hopkins University, 2008.

3 *Education for U.S. Economic and National Security.* Washington, D.C.: Committee for Economic Development, 2006.

4 Caldwell, Agnes (ed.), *Critical Thinking in the Sociology Classroom.* Washington, D.C.: The American Sociological Association, 2004.

5 "Foreign Languages and Higher Education: New Structures for a Changed World," *Modern Language Association*, 2007.

6 Welles, E.B. Foreign language enrollments in United States institutions of higher education, Fall 2002. *ADFL Bulletin*, 32(2–3): 7–24; J. Howard. "Enrollments in foreign-language courses continue to rise, MLA survey finds." *The Chronicle of Higher Education* 54(13) (2007, November 23): A13.

7 "Foreign Languages and Higher Education: New Structures for a Changed World," *Modern Language Association,* (2007).

8 Ibid.

9 Schneider, Ann I. "Internationalizing Teacher Education: What Can Be Done?" (unpublished paper), 2007.

Title VI and Fulbright-Hays Programs of the U.S. Department of Education

This appendix briefly describes each of the Title VI and Fulbright-Hays programs. These fourteen international education programs are managed by the U.S. Department of Education's International Education Programs Service (IEPS), located in the Office of Postsecondary Education. Ten of the programs are authorized under Title VI of the Higher Education Act of 1965, as amended, and as reauthorized by The Higher Education Opportunity Act of 2008. Four of these programs are authorized under the Mutual Educational and Cultural Exchange Act (Fulbright-Hays Act) of 1961.

The web site of IEPS provides official information about each program; see www.ed.gov/about/offices/list/ope/iegps/index.html and www.ed.gov/about/offices/list/ope/iegps/title-six.html. (Some text for this section is taken from descriptions on these sites.) A searchable database of grants made by the IEPS-administered programs is at www.ieps-iris.org/iris/ieps/irishome.cfm. Other web sites specific to various programs are listed below.

Title VI Programs

1) National Resource Centers (NRC)
2) Foreign Language and Area Studies Fellowships (FLAS)
3) International Research and Studies Program (IRS)

4) Language Resource Centers (LRC)

5) American Overseas Research Centers (AORC)

6) Undergraduate International Studies and Foreign Language Program (UISFL)

7) Technological Innovation and Cooperation for Foreign Information Access Program(TICFIA)

8) Centers for International Business Education (CIBE)

9) Business and International Education Program (BIE)

10) Institute for International Public Policy (IIPP)

Fulbright-Hays Programs

1) Doctoral Dissertation Research Abroad (DDRA)

2) Faculty Research Abroad (FRA)

3) Group Projects Abroad (GPA)

4) Seminars Abroad (SA)

The Core Programs of Foreign Language and Area/International Studies Training

National Resource Centers (NRCs) focus on both area (or international) studies and the study of modern languages, particularly less commonly taught languages (LCTLs). The NRCs, located at single universities or consortia of higher education institutions, form the backbone of U.S. language and area expertise. NRCs are funded in a variety of world areas defined by the applicants, including Africa, Asia, Southeast Asia, Middle East, Russia and Eastern Europe, and Latin America. "International" NRCs also cover a variety of topics and languages, from international relations and international development to transnational or "global" studies. NRCs are required to include a strong component of outreach to elementary and secondary (K-12) teachers, and a number have strong outreach programs to higher education institutions, the media, business, government, and the general public. Many cooperate with and provide service to a variety of professional schools, including law and criminal justice, education, agriculture, medicine, and communications. Further information can be found at www2.ed.gov/programs/iegpsnrc/ and at a dedicated web site about the National Resource Centers at: www.nrcweb.org.

    Foreign Language and Area Studies (FLAS) fellowships support graduate training at most NRCs and a few non-NRC institutions. They provide opportunities for intensive study of LCTLs and world areas both in the United States and abroad during either summer or the academic year. FLAS fellowships are allocated to NRCs so eligible students may compete for opportunities to pursue advanced language and area studies at those institutions with nationally recognized training programs. In 2009, Congress expanded the FLAS program to include undergraduate students. Learn more at www2.ed.gov/programs/iegpsflasf/.

The **International Research and Studies Program (IRS)** provides funds to develop and publish foreign language and other area studies curricular materials designed to improve and strengthen foreign language and area and related studies in the U.S. education system. It also supports surveys, studies, research, and evaluations of various types:

- Studies and surveys to determine needs for increased or improved instruction in modern foreign languages, area studies, or other international fields, including the demand for foreign language, area, and other international specialists in government, education, and the private sector.
- Research on more effective methods of providing instruction and achieving competency in foreign languages, area studies, or other international fields.
- Research on applying performance tests and standards across all areas of foreign language instruction and classroom use.
- Studies and surveys of the use of technologies in foreign language, area studies, and international studies programs.
- Studies and surveys to assess the use of graduates of programs supported under Title VI of the Higher Education Act by governmental, educational, and private-sector organizations and other studies assessing the outcomes and effectiveness of supported programs.
- Comparative studies of the effectiveness of strategies to provide international capabilities at institutions of higher education.
- Evaluations of the extent to which programs assisted under Title VI of the Higher Education Act that address national needs would not otherwise be offered.
- Studies and evaluations of effective practices in the dissemination of international information, materials, research, teaching strategies, and testing techniques throughout the educational community, including elementary and secondary schools.
- Evaluation of the extent to which programs assisted under Title VI reflect diverse views and generate debate on world regions and international affairs.
- Systematic collection, analysis, and dissemination of data that contribute to achieving the purposes of this program.
- Programs or activities to make data collected, analyzed, or disseminated under this section publicly available and easy to understand.

See further details on IRS at http://www2.ed.gov/programs/iegpsirs/.

Developing Critical Language and Area Expertise

The **Language Resource Centers (LRCs)** are a small number of national language resource and training centers (numbering fifteen in 2009) working to improve U.S. capacity to teach and learn foreign languages effectively. LRCs sponsor research, training, and creating and disseminating materials about teaching methods and strategies, performance testing, educational technology, and materials development at the K-12 and postsecondary levels. A number of LRCs operate intensive summer language institutes designed for either of two purposes: (1) to train in-service and future language teachers in using new pedagogical strategies and developing curricular materials; or (2) to provide advanced foreign language training in LCTLs to students, many of whom receive FLAS fellowships to support their studies. In response to needs identified by area studies specialists, the number of LRCs has expanded to include several with area-specific responsibilities. For further information, see www2.ed.gov/programs/iegpslrc/ or the dedicated LRC joint web site at http://nflrc.msu.edu/index-1.php.

The **American Overseas Research Centers (AORCs)** program provides grants to consortia of U.S. institutions of higher education to establish or operate overseas research centers that promote research, exchanges, and area studies among U.S. faculty and researchers. These centers sponsor scholarly conferences, publications, symposia, and travel grants and provide library and archives support that enable post-doctoral researchers and faculty to pursue independent research important for expanding their knowledge of foreign nations and cultures. They are located in diverse countries throughout the world, including Senegal, Tunisia and Morocco, Egypt, Pakistan, Sri Lanka, and others. Information about these centers can be found at www.caorc.org and www2.ed.gov/programs/iegpsaorc.

Strengthening International Studies and Foreign Language Teaching and Research

The UISFL and TICFIA facilitate the development of foreign language, area, and international studies programs, courses, teaching materials and strategies, and also support the use of new technologies to provide access to research materials in these areas.

The **Undergraduate International Studies and Foreign Language Program (UISFL)** provides funds to institutions of higher education, to consortia of such institutions, or to partnerships between nonprofit organizations and institutions of higher education to plan, develop, and implement programs that strengthen and improve undergraduate instruction in international studies and foreign languages.

Grant awards normally are made for two years; organizations, associations, and institutional consortia are eligible for three years of support.

Funded programs must primarily enhance the international academic program of the institution. Eligible activities may include but are not limited to:

- Development of a global or international studies program that is interdisciplinary in design;
- Development of a program that focuses on issues or topics, such as international business or international health;
- Development of an area studies program and programs in corresponding foreign languages;
- Creation of innovative curricula that combine the teaching of international studies with professional and preprofessional studies, such as engineering;
- Research for and development of specialized teaching materials, including language instruction (e.g., business French);
- Establishment of internship opportunities for faculty and students in domestic and overseas settings; and
- Development of study abroad programs.

Learn more about UISFL at www2.ed.gov/programs/iegpsugisf/.

The Technological Innovation and Cooperation for Foreign Information Access Program (TICFIA) provides grants to develop innovative techniques for using technologies to access, collect, organize, and preserve information obtained outside the United States and disseminate this information about world regions and countries via the Internet. TICFIA grants, which require a one-third cost match by the grantees, may be used to:

- Facilitate access to or preserve foreign information resources in print or electronic forms;
- Develop new means of immediate, full-text document delivery for information and scholarship from abroad;
- Develop new means of shared electronic access to international data;
- Support collaborative projects for indexing, cataloging, and providing other means of bibliographic access for scholars to important research materials published or distributed outside the United States;
- Develop methods for the wide dissemination of resources written in non-Roman alphabets;
- Assist teachers of less commonly taught languages in acquiring, via electronic and other means, materials suitable for classroom use; and
- Promote collaborative technology-based projects in foreign languages, area studies, and international studies among grant recipients under Title VI of the HEA.

Learn more about the TICFIA program at http://www2.ed.gov/programs/iegpsticfia.

Addressing the Global Economy

Centers for International Business Education (CIBEs) were created under the Omnibus Trade and Competitiveness Act of 1988 to increase and promote the nation's capacity for international understanding and economic enterprise. As of 2009, thirty universities have designated centers that serve as regional and national resources to business, students, and academics, forming a network focused on improving American competitiveness and providing comprehensive services and programs that help U.S. businesses succeed in global markets. The CIBE network links the manpower and information needs of U.S. business with the international education, language training, and research capacities of universities across the United States. CIBEs work collaboratively with each other, with other departments and disciplines within their universities, other colleges and universities regionally and nationally, government and trade councils, professional associations, and business.

Building on the strengths of their faculty and staff, each CIBE organizes a variety of activities to advance the study and teaching of international business and to support applied research on U.S. competitiveness in the global marketplace. Examples of such activities are:

- Internationalizing the business curriculum by dramatically increasing the number of interdisciplinary courses, existing courses with international content, study abroad, and other international exchange opportunities for students;
- Creating faculty development and enrichment programs for business faculty from colleges and universities around the nation, such as low-cost study trips to Africa, Asia, Latin America, Western and Eastern Europe, and intensive two-to-three-week workshops at host universities;
- Collaborating with modern foreign language departments to develop business language courses for students and to provide intensive language training programs for businesspersons;
- Providing support to small and medium-size business firms seeking to develop overseas markets, such as educational programs about export training, market information, management reviews, and response strategies to increased international competition; and
- Funding research projects, events, and publications on issues of strategic national interest, such as international competitiveness issues.

More information about the CIBEs can be found at their dedicated web site, http://ciberweb.msu.edu and at www2.ed.gov/programs/iegpscibe/index.html.

The **Business and International Education Program (BIE)** provides funds to institutions of higher education that enter into agreements with trade associations and/or businesses for two purposes: to improve the academic teaching of the business curriculum and to conduct outreach activities that expand the capacity of the business community to engage in international economic activities. Whereas CIBEs tend to be located at major universities, BIE funds usually enhance internationalization of business education and area businesses at smaller four-year institutions and community and two-year colleges. Both CIBEs and BIEs promote education and training that will contribute to the ability of U.S. businesses to prosper in an international economy. Learn more at www2.ed.gov/programs/iegpsbie.

Toward Diversity in International Service Professions

The 1992 reauthorization of the Higher Education Act expanded Title VI to include the **Institute for International Public Policy (IIPP)**, a program to train minority students for international careers. Administered since 1994 by the United Negro College Fund, it concentrates its internationalization efforts on two levels, individual and institutional. At the individual level, IIPP's centerpiece is its Fellows Program, which provides underrepresented minority students from across the United States with an integrated program that allows them to develop solid international education credentials, including language competence, overseas study, analytical skills and practical internship experience. At the institutional level, IIPP works to develop the international education infrastructure of historically black colleges and universities and Hispanic-serving institutions by providing support for strategic planning assistance, library materials, faculty and staff development, and curriculum projects. More information about IIPP can be found at www2.ed.gov/programs/iegpsiipp and at www.uncfsp.org/iipp.

Three new related programs were authorized by the Higher Education Opportunity Act of 2008 and have been funded in 2009–2010 for promoting postbaccalaureate opportunities for Hispanic Americans and for master's degree programs at historically black colleges and universities and predominantly black institutions.

Fulbright-Hays Programs

Three years after Congress authorized federal funding to establish foreign language and area studies programs at U.S. universities, it enacted the Mutual Educational and Cultural Exchange (Fulbright-Hays) Act of 1961 to enable scholars to obtain the critical overseas educational experiences necessary for developing high levels of language and area expertise.

The **Fulbright-Hays programs**, administered by the U.S. Department of Education, are distinct from the Fulbright programs administered by the U.S. Department of State, primarily through the Council for the International Exchange of
Scholars (CIES) and the Institute of International Education (IIE). Although both
sets of programs serve international education and national security interests, their
specific goals and emphases differ. State Department programs focus on exchange
for mutual understanding by bringing overseas scholars and professionals to the
United States and sending U.S. citizens (often with no prior international experience) abroad.

In contrast, the four Fulbright-Hays programs administered by the U.S. Department of Education serve a domestic agenda. Authorized under Section 102(b)(6) of
the Fulbright-Hays Act, they support the internationalization of the nation's educational infrastructure by strengthening area and foreign language expertise among
current and prospective U.S. educators by (1) providing critical, advanced overseas
study and research opportunities for area and language experts and faculty-in-
training; and (2) offering experiences and resources enabling educators to
strengthen their international teaching.

These Fulbright-Hays Programs send U.S. citizens abroad, but they do not provide reciprocal opportunities for international scholars to visit the United States.
Further, Fulbright-Hays programs are targeted *primarily* (though not exclusively) at
educators and future educators.

The Doctoral Dissertation Research Abroad and Faculty Research Abroad programs allow participants who have already acquired a level of expertise in an area
or language to deepen and expand this knowledge, thereby creating a larger pool of
highly qualified experts.

Doctoral Dissertation Research Abroad (DDRA) grants allow doctoral students
to conduct overseas research in modern foreign languages and area studies for periods of six to twelve months. Projects deepen research knowledge on and help the
nation develop capability in world regions not generally included in U.S. curricula.
Proposals focused on Western Europe are not eligible. Grantees must possess sufficient language and area knowledge to conduct research in a foreign language of the
area on which they will focus. Faculty apply for these awards through their college
of university. Learn more at www2.ed.gov/programs/iegpsddrap/.

Faculty Research Abroad (FRA) grants enable faculty to develop, maintain, or
improve their skills in modern foreign languages and area studies by conducting
research abroad. This program is used most often by junior faculty conducting significant research to strengthen their tenure cases, but also is open to participants
at any stage in their faculty careers. Individuals receiving FRA funding must have
been engaged in teaching relevant to their language or area specialization for two

years preceding the award. Program details can be found at www2.ed.gov/programs/iegpsfra.

Group Projects Abroad and Seminars Abroad provide indepth, overseas study experiences to current and prospective educators who are becoming specialists in foreign languages and cultures. Both programs help to expand and strengthen international teaching across the American educational spectrum.

Group Projects Abroad (GPA) fund U.S. colleges and universities, state departments of education, and private non-profit educational organizations to design and offer intensive international learning experiences for both students and education professionals—short-term seminars (5–6 weeks), curriculum development teams, group research projects (3–12 months), or advanced intensive language institutes. Emphasis is placed on humanities, social sciences, and languages outside of West Europe. GPA allows participants to obtain valuable overseas experience while developing new curricula focused on international topics of regional and national priority for use in their U.S. classrooms. See details of this program at www2.ed.gov/programs/iegpsgpa/.

Seminars Abroad (SA) enables approximately 160 educators each year in the humanities, social sciences, and languages to experience non-West European countries and form cross-cultural partnerships while engaging in curriculum development projects. Eligible participants include elementary and secondary (K-12) teachers, as well as postsecondary faculty and administrators from two- and four-year colleges, librarians, museum educators, and media or resource specialists. Unlike the other Fulbright-Hays programs, individuals apply directly to the U.S. Department of Education. See more on these seminars at www2.ed.gov/programs/iegpssap.

Assembled by Christine E. Root
and David S. Wiley
February 2010

U.S. Department of Education Title VI National Resource Centers, Language Resource Centers, Centers for International Business Education, American Overseas Resource Centers, and the Institute for International Public Policy, 2006–2010

Source: www.ed.gov/about/offices/list/ope/iegps/
nrcflasgrantees2006–09.pdf

International Education Programs Service, U.S. Department of Education, Office of Postsecondary Education Web site for all programs: www.ed.gov/about/offices/list/ope/iegps/index.html

National Resource Centers for Foreign Language and International Studies

Host University Name	Name of Center	Title VI Center Web Page
Africa		
Boston University	African Studies Center	www.bu.edu/africa
Columbia University	Institute of African Studies	www.sipa.columbia.edu/ias
Indiana University	African Studies Program	www.indiana.edu/~afrist
Michigan State University	African Studies Center	http://africa.msu.edu
Ohio University	African Studies Program	www.african.ohio.edu
University of Florida	Center for African Studies	www.africa.ufl.edu
University of Illinois	Center for African Studies	www.afrst.illinois.edu
University of Kansas	African Studies Center	www.kasc.ku.edu

University of North Carolina	African Studies Center	www.unc.edu/depts/africa
University of Pennsylvania / Bryn Mawr College / Haverford College / Swarthmore College	African Studies Consortium: African Studies Center / Africana Studies / Aficana and African Studies / Black Studies Program	www.africa.upenn.ed/; www.brynmawr.edu/ africana/; www.haverford. edu/african/; www. swarthmore.edu/x10452.xml
University of Wisconsin – Madison	African Studies Program	http://africa.wisc.edu
Yale University	Council on African Studies	www.yale.edu/macmillan/ african
University of California, Berkeley / Stanford University (FLAS only)	Center for African Studies / Center for African Studies	africa.berkeley.edu/; http://africanstudies. stanford.edu

Asia

Michigan State University	Asian Studies Center	http://asianstudies.msu.edu
University of Minnesota	Consortium for the Study of the Asias	www.all.umn.edu
University of Colorado	Center for Asian Studies	www.colorado.edu/CAS

East Asia

Columbia University	Weatherhead East Asian Insitute	www.columbia.edu/cu/weai/ index.html
Cornell University	East Asia Program	www.einaudi.cornell.edu/ eastasia
Duke University	Asian / Pacific Studies Institute	http://web.duke.edu/apsi
Harvard University	Asia Center	www.fas.harvard.edu/ ~asiactr
Ohio State University	East Asian Studies Center	http://easc.osu.edu
University of California, Berkeley	Institute of East Asian Studies	http://ieas.berkeley.edu
University of California, Los Angeles / University of Southern California	Asia Studies Institute / East Asian Studies Center	http://international.ucla.edu/ asia; http://college.usc.edu/ east_asian_studies/home/ index.cfm
University of Chicago	Center for East Asian Studies	http://ceas.uchicago.edu
University of Hawaii	East Asia Studies	http://manoa.hawaii.edu/ eastasia
University of Illinois / Indiana University	Center for East Asian / Pacific Studies / East Asian Studies Center	www.eaps.illinois.edu; www.indiana.edu/ ~easc/about/consortium. shtml
University of Kansas	Center for East Asian Studies	www.ceas.ku.edu
University of Michigan	Center for Chinese Studies, Center for Japanese Studies, Center for Korean Studies	www.ii.umich.edu/ ccs; www.ii.umich.edu/ cjs; www.ii.umich.edu/cks

University of Pennsylvania	Center for East Asian Studies	www.ceas.sas.upenn.edu
University of Pittsburgh	Asian Studies Center	www.ucis.pitt.edu/asc
University of Washington	East Asia Center	http://jsis.washington.edu/eacenter
University of Wisconsin	Center for East Asian Studies	http://eastasia.wisc.edu
Yale University	Council on East Asian Studies	http://research.yale.edu/eastasianstudies
George Washington University (FLAS only)	Sigur Center for Asian Studies	www.gwu.edu/~sigur/
Stanford University (FLAS only)	Center for East Asian Studies	http://ceas.stanford.edu
University of California, Santa Barbara (FLAS only)	East Asia Center	www.eac.ucsb.edu
University of Oregon *(FLAS only)	Center for Asian and Pacific Studies	http://caps.uoregon.edu

Inner Asia

Indiana University	Inner Asian and Uralic National Resource Center	www.indiana.edu/~iaunrc/

South Asia

Columbia University	South Asia Institute	http://sipa.columbia.edu/regional/sai/index.html
Cornell University / Syracuse University	South Asia Program / South Asia Center	www.einaudi.cornell.edu/southasia; www.maxwell.syr.edu/moynihan/programs/sac/
Duke University / North Carolina State University / University of North Carolina	North Carolina Center for South Asia Studies	www.jhfc.duke.edu/csas/index.php
University of California, Berkeley	Center for South Asia Studies	http://southasia.berkeley.edu
University of Chicago	South Asia Language and Area Center	http://southasia.uchicago.edu
University of Pennsylvania	South Asia Studies	www.southasia.upenn.edu
University of Texas	South Asia Institute	www.utexas.edu/cola/insts/southasia/?path%5b0%5d=southasia
University of Washington	South Asia Center	http://jsis.washington.edu/soasia
University of Wisconsin – Madison	Center for South Asia	www.southasia.wisc.edu
University of Michigan (FLAS only)	Center for South Asian Studies	www.ii.umich.edu/csas

Southeast Asia

Cornell University	Southeast Asia Program	www.einaudi.cornell.edu/SoutheastAsia
Northern Illinois University	Center for Southeast Asian Studies	www.seasite.niu.edu

Ohio University	Southeast Asian Studies	www.seas.ohio.edu/index.html
University of California, Berkeley / University of California, Los Angeles	Center for Southeast Asia Studies / Center for Southeast Asian Studies	http://cseas.berkeley.edu/; http://www.international.ucla.edu/cseas
University of Hawaii	Center for Southeast Asian Studies	www.hawaii.edu/cseas
University of Michigan	Center for Southeast Asian Studies	www.ii.umich.edu/cseas/resources/nationalres
University of Washington	Southeast Asia Center	http://jsis.washington.edu/seac
University of Wisconsin – Madison	Center for Southeast Asian Studies	http://seasia.wisc.edu

Pacific Islands

University of Hawaii	Center for Pacific Islands Studies	www.hawaii.edu/cpis

Latin America and Caribbean

Brown University	Center for Latin American and Caribbean Studies	www.watsoninstitute.org/clacs
Columbia University / New York University	Institute of Latin American Studies / Center for Latin American Caribbean Studies	http://ilas.columbia.edu; http://clacs.as.nyu.edu/page/home
Duke University / University of North Carolina	The Consortium in Latin American and Caribbean Studies: Center for Latin American and Caribbean Studies / Institute for the Study of the Americas	www.duke.edu/web/carolinadukeconsortium/index.html; http://clacs.aas.duke.edu/; http://isa.unc.edu/about/about.asp
Georgetown University	Center for Latin American Studies	http://clas.georgetown.edu
Harvard University	David Rockefeller Center for Latin American Studies	www.drclas.harvard.edu
Indiana University	Center for Latin American and Caribbean Studies	www.indiana.edu/~clacs
San Diego State University / University of California, San Diego	Center for Latin American Studies / Center for Iberian and Latin American Studies	www-rohan.sdsu.edu/~latamweb/; http://cilas.ucsd.edu
Tulane University	Stone Center for Latin American Studies	http://stonecenter.tulane.edu
University of California, Berkeley	Center for Latin American Studies	http://clas.berkeley.edu
University of California, Los Angeles	Latin American Institute	www.international.ucla.edu/lai

University of Florida / Florida International University	Center for Latin American Studies / Latin American and Caribbean Center	www.latam.ufl.edu/; http://lacc.fiu.edu
University of Illinois / University of Chicago	Center for Latin American and Caribbean Studies / Center for Latin American Studies	www.clacs.illinois.edu/; http://clas.uchicago.edu
University of Michigan	Latin American and Caribbean Studies	www.ii.umich.edu/lacs
University of Pittsburgh	Center for Latin American Studies	www.ucis.pitt.edu/clas
University of Texas	Teresa Lozano Long Institute of Latin American Studies	www.utexas.edu/cola/insts/llilas
University of Wisconsin – Madison / University of Wisconsin, Milwaukee	Latin American, Caribbean, and Iberian Studies / Center for Latin American and Caribbean Studies	www.lacis.wisc.edu/; http://www4.uwm.edu/clacs
Vanderbilt University	Center for Latin American Studies	www.vanderbilt.edu/clas
Yale University	Council on Latin American and Iberian Studies	www.yale.edu/macmillan/lais

Middle East

Columbia University	Middle East Institute	www.sipa.columbia.edu/REGIONAL/mei
Georgetown University	Center for Contemporary Arab Studies	http://ccas.georgetown.edu
Harvard University	Center for Middle Eastern Studies	http://cmes.hmdc.harvard.edu
New York University	The Hagop Kevorkian Center	www.nyu.edu/gsas/program/neareast
Ohio State University	Middle East Studies Center	http://mesc.osu.edu
Princeton University	Program in Near Eastern Studies	www.princeton.edu/nep
University of Arizona	Center for Middle Eastern Studies	www.cmes.arizona.edu
University of California, Berkeley	Center for Middle Eastern Studies	http://cmes.berkeley.edu
University of California, Los Angeles	Center for Near Eastern Studies	www.international.ucla.edu/cnes
University of Chicago	Center for Middle Esatern Studies	www.cmes.uchicago.edu
University of Illinois	Center for South Asian and Middle Eastern Studies	www.csames.illinois.edu
University of Michigan	Center for Middle Eastern and North African Studies	www.ii.umich.edu/cmenas
University of Pennsylvania	Middle East Center	http://mec.sas.upenn.edu

University of Texas	Middle Eastern Studies	www.utexas.edu/cola/depts/mes
University of Utah	Middle East Center	www.mec.utah.edu
University of Washington	The Middle East Center	http://jsis.washington.edu/mideast
Yale University	Council on Middle East Studies	www.yale.edu/macmillan/cmes

Europe and Russia

Cornell University / Syracuse University	Institute for European Studies / Center for European Studies	www.einaudi.cornell.edu/Europe; www.maxwell.syr.edu/moynihan/Programs/euc
University of California, Los Angeles	Center for European and Eurasian Studies	http://international.ucla.edu/euro/
Yale University	The European Studies Council	www.yale.edu/macmillan/europeanstudies

Russia and East Europe

Columbia University	East Central European Center	www.sipa.columbia.edu/ece
Duke University / University of North Carolina	Center for Slavic, Eurasian, and East European Studies / Center for Slavic, Eurasian, and East European Studies	www.duke.edu/web/CSEEES/; http://www.unc.edu/depts/slavic/
Georgetown University	Center for Eurasian, Russian, and East European Studies	www1.georgetown.edu/sfs/ceres
Harvard University	Davis Center for Russian and Eurasian Studies	http://daviscenter.fas.harvard.edu/index.html
Indiana University	Russian and East European Institute	www.indiana.edu/~reeiweb
Ohio State University	Center for Slavic and East European Studies	http://slaviccenter.osu.edu
Stanford University	Center for Russia, East European, and Eurasian Studies	www.stanford.edu/dept/CREES/
University of California, Berkeley	Institute of Slavic, East European, and Eurasian Studies	http://iseees.berkeley.edu
University of Chicago	Center for East European and Russian/Eurasian Studies	http://ceeres.uchicago.edu
University of Illinois	Russian, East European, and Eurasian Center	www.reec.illinois.edu
University of Kansas	Center for Russian, East European, and Eurasian Studies	www.crees.ku.edu
University of Michigan	Center for Russian and East European Studies	www.ii.umich.edu/crees
University of Pittsburgh	Russian and East European Studies	www.ucis.pitt.edu/crees

University of Texas	Center for Russian, East European, and Eurasian Studies	www.utexas.edu/cola/centers/creees
University of Washington	Ellison Center for Russian, East European, and Central Asian Studies	http://jsis.washington.edu/ellison
University of Wisconsin – Madison	Center for Russia, East Europe, and Central Asia	www.creeca.wisc.edu

Western Europe / Europe

Indiana University	West European Studies	www.indiana.edu/~west
New York University / Columbia University	Center for European and Mediterranean Studies / Institute for the Study of Europe	http://cems.as.nyu.edu/page/home; www.ei.columbia.edu/main.html
University of California, Berkeley	Institute of European Studies	http://ies.berkeley.edu
University of Florida	Center for European Studies	www.ces.ufl.edu/index.shtml
University of Illinois	European Union Center	http://euc.illinois.edu
University of Minnesota	European Studies Consortium	www.esc.umn.edu
University of North Carolina	Center for European Studies	www.unc.edu/depts/europe
University of Pittsburgh	European Studies Center	www.ucis.pitt.edu/euce/euce.html
University of Washington	Center for West European Studies	http://jsis.washington.edu/cwes
University of Wisconsin – Madison	Center for European Studies	http://uw-madison-ces.org/

International

Duke University	Center for International Studies	http://ducis.jhfc.duke.edu
Indiana University	Center for the Study of Global Change	www.indiana.edu/~global
Michigan State University	Center for Advanced Study of International Development – Women and International Development	www.casid.msu.edu
University of Chicago	Center for International Studies	http://internationalstudies.uchicago.edu
University of Illinois		http://cgs.illinois.edu
University of Minnesota	Institute for Global Studies	http://igs.cla.umn.edu
University of North Carolina	Center for Global Initiatives	http://cgi.unc.edu
University of Washington	Center for Global Studies	http://jsis.washington.edu/isp/index.shtml
University of Wisconsin – Madison	Global Studies	http://global.wisc.edu

Language Resource Centers   www.ed.gov/programs/
                                                                 iegpslrc/lrcabstracts2006.pdf

University of Hawaii	National Foreign Language Resource Center (NFLRC)	www.nflrc.hawaii.edu
Pennsylvania State University	Center for Advanced Language Proficiency Education and Research (CALPER)	http://calper.la.psu.edu
University of Wisconsin – Madison	National African Language Resource Center (NALRC)	http://lang.nalrc.wisc.edu/ nalrc/home.html
University of Oregon	Center for Applied Second Language Studies (CASLS)	http://casls.uoregon.edu
University of Minnesota	Center for Advanced Research on Language Acquisition (CARLA)	www.carla.umn.edu
University of California, Los Angeles	National Language Resource Center for Heritage Language Education (NLRC-HLE)	www.international.ucla.edu/ languages/nhlrc
University of Chicago	South Asia Language Resource Center (SALRC)	http://salrc.uchicago.edu
Michigan State University	Center for Language Education and Research (CLEAR)	http://clear.msu.edu/clear
Iowa State University	National K-12 Foreign Language Resource Center (NK-12LRC)	www.nflrc.iastate.edu
San Diego State University	Language Acquisition Resource Center (LARC)	http://larc.sdsu.edu
Ohio State University	National East Asian Languages Resource Center (NEALRC)	http://nealrc.osu.edu
Brigham Young University	National Middle East Language Resource Center (NMELRC)	http://nmelrc.org
Georgetown University	National Capital Language Resource Center (NCLRC)	http://nclrc.org
Indiana University	Center for Languages of the Central Asian Region (CeLCAR)	www.indiana.edu/~celcar
University of Arizona	Center for Educational Resources in Culture, Language and Literacy (CERCLL)	http://cercll.arizona.edu

Centers for International Business Education   www.ed.gov/programs/
                                                                 iegpscibe/cibegrantees
                                                                 2006–10.pdf AND
                                                                 http://ciberweb.msu.
                                                                 edu/cibers.asp

Brigham Young University	Global Management Center, Marriott School of Management	www.marriottschool.byu.edu/gmc
Columbia University	CIBER, Columbia Graduate School of Business	www7.gsb.columbia.edu/ciber
Duke University	CIBER, Fuqua School of Business	http://faculty.fuqua.duke.edu/ciber/index.html
Florida International University	CIBER, College of Business Administration	www.fiu.edu/%7Eciber
The George Washington University	CIBER, College of Business Administration	www.gwu.edu/%7Ebusiness/CIBER
Georgia Institute of Technology	CIBER, College of Management	www.ciber.gatech.edu
Indiana University	CIBER, Kelley School of Business	www.kelley.iu.edu/CIBER
Michigan State University	CIBER, Eli Broad Graduate School of Management	http://ciber.msu.edu
The Ohio State University	CIBER, Fisher College of Business	http://fisher.osu.edu/international
Purdue University	CIBER, Krannert Graduate School of Management	www.mgmt.purdue.edu/centers/CIBER
San Diego State University	CIBER, College of Business Administration	www.sdsu.edu/ciber
Temple University	CIBER, Fox School of Business	www.fox.temple.edu/ciber
Texas A&M University	Center for International Business, Mays Business School	http://cibs.tamu.edu
University of California, Los Angeles	CIBER, The Anderson School at UCLA	www.anderson.ucla.edu/research/ciber
University of Colorado, Denver	CIBER, Institute for International Business	www.cudenver.edu/International/CIBER/default.htm
University of Connecticut	CIBER, International Business Programs	www.business.uconn.edu/ciber
University of Florida	CIBER, Warrington College of Business Administration	http://bear.cba.ufl.edu/centers/ciber
University of Hawaii, Manoa	CIBER, College of Business Administration	www.pami.hawaii.edu/ciber
University of Illinois	CIBER, College of Commerce and Business Administration	www.ciber.uiuc.edu
University of Kansas	CIBER, KU School of Business	www.business.ku.edu/KUCIBER
University of Maryland	CIBER, Robert H. Smith School of Business	www.rhsmith.umd.edu/ciber/
University of Memphis	CIBER, Wang Center for International Business Education and Research	www.memphis.edu/wangctr

University of Michigan	CIBER, University of Michigan Business School	www.umich.edu/%7Ecibe
University of North Carolina at Chapel Hill	CIBER, Kenan-Flagler Business School	www.ciber.unc.edu
University of Pennsylvania	Penn Lauder CIBER, The Wharton School	http://lauder.wharton.upenn.edu/ciber/default.asp
University of Pittsburgh	International Business Center, Joseph M. Katz Graduate School of Business	http://ibc.katz.pitt.edu
University of South Carolina	CIBER, Moore School of Business	http://mooreschool.sc.edu/moore/ciber
University of Southern California	CIBER, Marshall School of Business	www.marshall.usc.edu/ciber
Univeristy of Texas, Austin	CIBER, McCombs School of Business	www.mccombs.utexas.edu/ciber
University of Washington	CIBER, Foster School of Business	http://depts.washington.edu/ciberweb/
University of Wisconsin – Madison	CIBER, School of Business	www.bus.wisc.edu/ciber

American Overseas Research Centers

	www.caorc.org/centers/index.html
American Academy in Rome (AAR)	www.caorc.org/centers/aar.htm
American Center for Mongolian Studies (ACMS)	www.caorc.org/centers/acms.htm
American Center of Oriental Research (ACOR)	www.caorc.org/centers/acor.htm
W.F. Albright Institute of Archaeological Research (AIAR)	www.caorc.org/centers/aiar.htm
American Institute of Afghanistan Studies (AIAS)	www.caorc.org/centers/aias.htm
American Institute of Bangladesh Studies (AIBS)	www.caorc.org/centers/aibs.htm
American Institute of Iranian Studies (AIIrS)	www.caorc.org/centers/aiirs.htm
American Institute of Indian Studies (AIIS)	www.caorc.org/centers/aiis.htm
American Institute for Maghrib Studies (AIMS)	www.caorc.org/centers/aims.htm
American Institute of Pakistan Studies (AIPS)	www.caorc.org/centers/aips.htm
American Institute of Sri Lankan Studies (AISLS)	www.caorc.org/centers/aisls.htm
American Institute for Yemeni Studies (AIYS)	www.caorc.org/centers/aiys.htm
American Research Center in Egypt (ARCE)	www.caorc.org/centers/arce.htm
American Research Center in Sofia (ARCS)	www.caorc.org/centers/arcs.htm
American Research Institute in Turkey (ARIT)	www.caorc.org/centers/arit.htm
American School of Classical Studies at Athens (ASCSA)	www.caorc.org/centers/ascsa.htm
Cyprus American Archaeological Research Institute (CAARI)	www.caorc.org/centers/caari.htm
Center for Khmer Studies (CKS)	www.caorc.org/centers/cks.htm
Center for South Asia Libraries (CSAL)	www.caorc.org/centers/csal.htm
Mexico-North Research Network (MNRN)	www.caorc.org/centers/mnrn.htm
Palestinian American Research Center (PARC)	www.caorc.org/centers/parc.htm
The American Academic Research Institute in Iraq (TAARII)	www.caorc.org/centers/taarii.htm
West African Research Association (WARA)	www.caorc.org/centers/wara.htm

Institute for International Public Policy

The College Fund/UNCFSP (in cooperation with the Woodrow Wilson National Fellowship Foundation, the Hispanic Association of Colleges and Universities, the American Indian Higher Education Consortium, and the Association of Professional Schools of International Affairs)   www.uncf.org/

Other Title VI and Fulbright-Hays Programs of the U.S. Department of Education

Business and International Education   www.ed.gov/programs/iegpsbie

Foreign Language and Area Studies Fellowships   www.ed.gov/programs/iegpsflasf

Fulbright-Hays Training Grants—Doctoral Dissertation Research Abroad   www.ed.gov/programs/iegpsddrap

Fulbright-Hays Training Grants—Faculty Research Abroad   www.ed.gov/programs/iegpsfra

Fulbright-Hays Training Grants—Group Projects Abroad   www.ed.gov/programs/iegpsgpa

Fulbright-Hays Seminars Abroad—Bilateral Projects   www.ed.gov/programs/iegpssap

International Research and Studies   www.ed.gov/programs/iegpsirs

Technological Innovation and Cooperation for Foreign Information Access   www.ed.gov/programs/iegpsticfia

Summary of Discussions from Plenary Panels, Title VI 50th Anniversary Conference

Plenary I: Panel on Current Issues and Future Directions for International Education

Panel: Chair – Craig Calhoun, President, Social Science Research Council; University
Professor of the Social Sciences, New York University

Members: Gene Block, Chancellor, University of California, Los Angeles
Mark Gearan, President, Hobart and William Smith Colleges
Kim Wilcox, Provost and Vice President for Academic Affairs, Michigan
State University

Date: Thursday, March 19, 2009

- "We must produce a new wave of workers and informed leaders who can address global demands. Title VI can do this by strengthening performance in global education and enabling all students to understand foreign cultures and languages."
- Internationalization occurs on campuses not only through study abroad programs but also through international university partnerships, as well as undergraduate student engagement with faculty, graduate students, and immigrant diaspora populations near our campuses.
- Undergraduates are looking for an education that includes service learning, community building, and international experience. These endeavors need to be well

funded for both the students traveling abroad and the foreign students coming to the United States to study.

- Study abroad is key to language study; however, the experience can be deepened by the addition of preparatory foreign area and language studies, as well as re-entry education on returning from abroad.
- In the current economic climate, universities and colleges need to embed activities within their budgets, look to private and philanthropic donors, work with alumni who have benefited from international experience as a source of donations, and form new collaborations to ensure funding.
- Title VI funding transforms existent programs and creates new programs, but the Title VI community needs to heighten awareness on campus and in our communities about the needs for and benefits of this unique funding. Even though internationalization might not be measured correctly on reporting forms, the experiences are invaluable for the individual as well as the country.

Plenary II: Panel on Advancing the Internationalization of Higher Education

Panel: Chair – Jeffrey Riedinger, Dean, International Studies and Programs; Professor, Department of Community, Agriculture, Recreation, and Resource Studies Michigan State University

Members: Robert Berdhal, President, Association of American Universities
Maureen Budetti, Director of Student Aid Policy, National Association of Independent Colleges and Universities
Constantine Curris, President, American Association of State Colleges and Universities
Madeleine Green, Vice President, International Initiatives, American Council on Education
Peter McPherson, President, Association of Public and Land-Grant Universities

Date: Friday, March 20, 2009

- "The definition of being well-educated in the United States also must include being *internationally educated.*"
- Accountability to an "international mission" must occur at the highest administrative levels of a higher education institution.
- Study abroad programs need not apply only to U.S. undergraduates. Institutions that are internationalizing need to create more opportunities to send more of their faculty members abroad, as well as to bring more foreign students to the U.S. institutions.

- Institutions, particularly community colleges, need to find ways to integrate international education pedagogy into the curriculum for students who cannot travel abroad, as well as to find creative study abroad programs that fit the needs, schedules, and budgets of working students.
- Institutions of higher education need to find methods and resources to make study abroad affordable for both the students based in the United States and foreign students already studying in the United States. We also must assist those foreign students to secure visas.
- In this economic climate, institutions need to be more vocal to members of Congress about the products and outcomes that Title VI and Fulbright-Hays funding produces on campus and in the states.

Assembled by Marita Eibl, Michigan State University
March 19–20, 2009

Papers Presented at the Title VI 50th Anniversary Conference March 19–21, 2009, Washington, D.C.

Early in the planning stage of this conference, a public call for papers was disseminated to allow diverse description and commentary by many authors about the Title VI and Fulbright-Hays programs of the past fifty years. The archived call for paper submissions for the program of the conference can be viewed at http://titlevi50th.msu.edu/submission/index.html.

In addition to proceedings in this volume, all authors were invited to submit their presentations to create Online Conference Proceedings. Papers below with a bullet (■) are available online at http://titlevi50th.msu.edu/agenda/.

Thursday, March 19, 2009—Session I: 8:30 AM–9:50 AM

SESSION I-A: TITLE VI AND NATIONAL AND GLOBAL SECURITY

History and Impacts of Title VI (with focus on area studies)
　　　Patrick O'Meara, Indiana University
History and Impacts of Title VI (with focus on Less Commonly Taught Languages)
　　　David Wiley, Michigan State University

SESSION I-B: BUSINESS LANGUAGE ASSESSMENT AND CULTURAL COMPETENCE

■ Fifteen Years on the Pathways to Advanced Skills
　　　Gala Walker and Minru Li, The Ohio State University

- Assessing Student Learning in International Environments
    Bradley Farnsworth, University of Michigan
- European Language Portfolios and Global Language Portfolios
    Patricia Cummins, Virginia Commonwealth University

SESSION I-C: U.S. POLICY IN ASIA: THE INTERSECTION OF AREA STUDIES AND THE DISCIPLINES

U.S. Policy in Asia: The Intersection of Area Studies and the Disciplines
    Richard J. Ellings, The National Bureau of Asian Research and Robert Hathaway, Woodrow Wilson International Center for Scholars Asia Program
China's Rise
    Robert Sutter, Georgetown University
Japan's Resurgence
    Bill Heinrich, U.S. Department of State

SESSION I-D: DIGITAL RESOURCES AND TECHNOLOGY

- Digital Resources in Title VI: Planning the Next fifty Years
    Doug Cooper, Center for Research in Computational Linguistics
The Collaborative global-e http://global-ejournal.org/
    Niklaus Steiner, University of North Carolina, Chapel Hill and Steve Witt, University of Illinois, Urbana-Champaign
Internationalizing the University of North Carolina at Chapel Hill through Multi and Mixed Media Sharing
    Tripp Tuttle, University of North Carolina, Chapel Hill

SESSION I-E: INNOVATIVE APPROACHES TO INTERDISCIPLINARY RESEARCH AND GRADUATE TRAINING IN LATIN AMERICAN STUDIES

Panel Chair
    Carmen Diana Deere, University of Florida
A Graduate Education Framework for Tropical Conservation and Development
    Jon Dain, University of Florida
Interdisciplinary Graduate Training in Latin American Business
    Mary Risner, University of Florida
Finding Solutions to Crime, Law, and Governance in the Americas
    Tim Clark, University of Florida

SESSION I-F: TITLE VI AND COMMUNITY COLLEGES: LESSONS OF THE PAST AND DIRECTIONS FOR THE FUTURE

Internationalizing the Curriculum: Lessons of the Past and Directions for the Future
    Theo Sypris, Midwest Institute for International / Intercultural Education

- Fulbrights: A Medium for Transformational Change and Professional Engagement
    Joanna Sabo, Monroe County Community College
  Study Abroad: Lessons of the Past and Directions for the Future
    Cindy Epperson, St. Louis Community College
- Overseas Projects: Vehicles for Positive and Meaningful Change
    Robert Keener, Sinclair Community College
  International Students: A Promising Direction for Community Colleges
    Annouska Remmert, Lorain Community College

SESSION I-G: PROGRAMS IN INTERNATIONAL EDUCATIONAL RESOURCES
(PIER): THE MACMILLAN CENTER'S INTEGRATED OUTREACH PROGRAM

PIER: Its Rationale and K-12 Professional Development
    Maxwell Amoh, Yale University
PIER: Programs for K-12 Students
    Elena Serapiglia, Yale University
PIER: Community and Business Outreach
    Molly Moran, Yale University

SESSION I-H: AREA STUDIES AND THE DISCIPLINES

- Area Studies Course Coverage: Then and Now
    Ann Imlah Schneider, Independent International Education Consultant
- Global Realignments and the Geopolitics of Transatlantic Studies
    Abril Trigo, The Ohio State University
  The Contribution of Area Studies to Political Science: Reassessing the Controversy
    Stephen E. Hanson, University of Washington

Thursday, March 19, 2009—Session II: 10:20 AM–11:40 AM

SESSION II-A: INTERNATIONALIZING HIGHER EDUCATION

History and Impacts of Title VI
    Gilbert Merkx, Duke University
Current Status and New Directions
    Sandra Russo, University of Florida

SESSION II-B: LEARNING IN THE K-12 COMMUNITY

Mapping and Enhancing Language Learning in Washington State
    Tamara Leonard, University of Washington
- World Language Teaching in U.S. Schools: Results of a National Survey
    Nancy Rhodes and Ingrid Pufahl, Center for Applied Linguistics

- K-12 Gateway to the Less-Commonly-Taught Languages
    Thomas Hinnebusch and Barbara Blankenship, University of California,
    Los Angeles

SESSION II-C: EXTENDING GLOBAL SECURITY TO HUMAN SECURITY: PEDA-GOGICAL CHALLENGES AND OPPORTUNITIES

- Studies in Human Security
    Sara R. Curran, University of Washington
- Studies in Religion and Human Security
    James Wellman, University of Washington
  Human Rights and Security
    Angelina Godoy, University of Washington
- Environmental Security
    Patrick Christie, University of Washington

SESSION II-D: MIDDLE EAST LANGUAGE LEARNING IN U.S. HIGHER EDUCATION

- Overview of Middle East Language Learning in U.S. Higher Education
    R. Kirk Belnap, Brigham Young University
  Unfortunate Implications of Unhappy Language Teachers
    Mahmoud Al-Batal, University of Texas
  Increasing Access to Quality Intensive Study
    Shmuel Bolozky, University of Massachusetts
  Measuring Success in Language Learning
    Erika Gilson, Princeton University
  Extending our Reach into K-12 and further out into Higher Education Campuses
    Maggie Nassif, Brigham Young University

SESSION II-E: PEACE STUDIES AND INTERNATIONAL EDUCATION

  Building Capacity in Teaching about Global Peace and Security in U.S. Higher
  Education
    David Smith, U.S. Institute of Peace
  Finding a Common Ground: A Dialogue between Military, Non-Profit, Academia,
  and Muslim Organizations in the Delaware Valley
    Zeynab Turan, University of Pennsylvania
  Toward a Meaningful Understanding of "Diverse Perspectives" in Middle East
  Educational Outreach
    Zeina Azzam Seikaly, Georgetown University
- Creating Peace: Creating Effective Teachers of Arabic at SDSU and Bahrain Teach-
  ers' College
    Hanada Taha-Thomure, San Diego State University

SESSION II-F: TECHNOLOGY AND LANGUAGE STUDIES

- Innovative Technology-Based Pedagogies for the Foreign Language Classroom
    Linda R. Waugh and Beatrice Dupuy, University of Arizona

- Creating Learner Corpora from the Computer Assisted Screening Tool for Advanced Level Proficiency (CAST)
    Michael Trevor Shanklin, San Diego State University
  Mongolian Language Learning in a Virtual Classroom
    Curt Madison, University of Alaska, Fairbanks and Brian White, American Center for Mongolian Studies

- Language-Learning in Cyberspace: Hindi-Urdu on the Web
    Afroz Taj, University of North Carolina, Chapel Hill

SESSION II-G: TITLE VI AND RESEARCH PROGRESS IN THE DISCIPLINES: AFRICAN HISTORY, AFRICAN POLITICS, AND AFRICAN LANGUAGES AND LITERATURE AT WISCONSIN

Regionalism and Progress in the Disciplines
    James Delehanty, University of Wisconsin–Madison
Title VI and Research on African History at Wisconsin
    Thomas Spear, University of Wisconsin–Madison
Title VI and Research on African Politics at Wisconsin
    Crawford Young, University of Wisconsin–Madison
Title VI and Research on African Languages and Literature at Wisconsin
    Edris Makward, University of Wisconsin–Madison

SESSION II-H: INTERNATIONALIZING HIGHER EDUCATION: THE NEGLECTED LINK BETWEEN AREA STUDIES AND STUDY ABROAD

- Study Abroad, Area Studies, and Cultural Learning: The Conceptual Map
    Richard Michael Paige, University of Minnesota
  Study Abroad, Area Studies, and Cultural Learning: A Meta Synthesis of University of Oregon and University of Minnesota Title VI Programs
    Gerald Fry, University of Minnesota

Thursday, March 19, 2009: 1:10 PM–3:00 PM

Plenary Panel I: Current Issues and Future Directions for International Education
    Craig Calhoun—Social Science Research Council, Moderator
    Gene Block—University of California, Los Angeles
    Mark Gearan—Hobart and William Smith Colleges
    Kim Wilcox—Michigan State University

Thursday, March 19, 2009—Session III: 3:30 PM–4:50 PM

SESSION III-A: AREA STUDIES AND THE DISCIPLINES

History and Impacts of Title VI
    Michael D. Kennedy, University of Michigan
Current Status and New Directions
    Craig Calhoun, Social Science Research Council and New York University

SESSION III-B: INTERNATIONAL BUSINESS, U.S. COMPETIVENESS, AND GLOBAL SECURITY

No Man is an Island: Title VI, the CIBERs and National/Global Security
    Rochelle A. McArthur, University of Hawai'i, Manoa
The Global Business Project Course: An Innovative Multi-school, Multilanguage Approach to Promoting Global Competitive Students and Corporations"
    M. Lynne Gerber, University of North Carolina, Chapel Hill
Public-Private Partnerships to Develop Programs to Promote the Competitiveness of U.S. Business: The Case of Hawai'i
    Shirley J. Daniel, University of Hawai'i, Manoa
■ Defining Global Competence and the Metrics of Global Leadership Group Process
    Kim Cahill, Arvind V. Phatak, and Julie Fesenmaier, Temple University

SESSION III-C: BUILDING LANGUAGE COMPETENCE, PROGRAMMING, AND ASSESSMENT

Critical Language Competence through Immersion and Outreach to Secondary Education
    Hui Wu, University of Central Arkansas
Building a Khmer Language Program with Title VI Funding
    Frank Smith, University of California, Berkeley
Investment in Assessment: The South Asian Example
    Steven M. Poulos, University of Chicago

SESSION III-D: WHO IN THE WORLD IS COMING TO NATIONAL COUNCIL FOR THE SOCIAL STUDIES (NCSS)?: FUTURE DIRECTIONS FOR TITLE VI OUTREACH

NCSS and its Outreach Potential for International NRC Partners
    Susan Griffin, National Council for the Social Studies
■ Canada is Coming to NCSS! A Model for Conference Outreach and Beyond
    Tina Storer, Western Washington University
Complementary On-Site Outreach at the Annual NCSS Conference
    Amy Sotherden, State University of New York, Plattsburgh
NCSS Conference and Surrounding Area Outreach
    Betsy Arntzen, University of Maine

SESSION III-E: TEACHER TRAINING AND LANGUAGE COMPETENCY

■ Meeting the Need for Critical Language Teachers
> Johanna Watzinger-Tharp, University of Utah

  Methods Preparation for Instructors of Less Commonly Taught Languages
> Dianna L. Murphy and Antonia Schleicher, University of Wisconsin–Madison

  Examining Approaches to Advanced-Level Foreign Language Competence in Less Commonly Taught Languages
> Kimi Kondo-Brown, University of Hawai'i, Manoa

  The Impact of Undergraduate Language Requirements on Less-Commonly-Taught Language Enrollment and Instruction: The Cornell Story
> Sydney van Morgan, Cornell University

SESSION III-F: ASSESSING THE IMPACTS OF TITLE VI PROGRAMS

■ Competing Views of Assessment and Accountability in Higher Education: The New Public Management Versus National Resource Centers as "Public Goods"
> Davydd J. Greenwood, Cornell University

■ Impact of Title VI on the U.S. Higher Education System: Lessons from the First Thirty Years
> Nancy L. Ruther, Yale University

  The Value of National Resource Centers for Enrollments in Critical Languages
> Elizabeth Welles, Council of American Overseas Research Centers

SESSION III-G: INTERNATIONAL EDUCATION AND RESEARCH IN THE DIGITAL AGE: A CRITICAL LOOK AT PROMISES, CHALLENGES, AND FUTURE OF TECHNOLOGICAL INNOVATION AND COOPERATION FOR FOREIGN INFORMATION ACCESS (TICFIA)

■ The Digital Revolution and TICFIA
> David Wiley and Mark Kornbluh, Michigan State University

  TICFIA: South Asia: Overseas Resources for Understanding the Subcontinent
> James Nye, University of Chicago

  The Tibetan and Himalayan Library
> David Germano, University of Virginia

  The African Digital Library Projects
> Stephen Backman, Michigan State University

  TICFIA: The View from Washington
> Susanna Easton, U.S. Department of Education

SESSION III-H: ON THE FUTURE OF OUTREACH: APPROACHES FOR MORE EFFECTIVE PROGRAMS

■ Professionalization of Outreach: A Continuing Challenge for Title VI Centers
> Valerie McGinley Marshall, Tulane University

387

Is This Covered in the Standards? Outreach in the Era of Standardized Testing
>Christopher Rose, University of Texas, Austin

Title VI and Fulbright-Hays: Toward a Closer Partnership and Enhanced Resources
>Natalie Arsenault, University of Texas, Austin

On the Air
>Randi Hacker, University of Kansas

Outreach and K-12 Teachers: A View from the Classroom
>Lorelei Clark, Thurgood Marshall High School

Keynote Dinner and Keynote Address by The Honorable Madeleine K. Albright, 7:00 PM

Friday, March 20, 2009—Session IV: 8:30 AM–9:50 AM

SESSION IV-A: CROSSING BOUNDARIES

History and Impacts of Title VI
>Anne Betteridge, University of Arizona

Current Status and New Directions
>Anand A. Yang, University of Washington

SESSION IV-B: ONLINE RESOURCES FOR INTERNATIONAL BUSINESS

On the globalEDGE
>Irem Kiyak, Michigan State University

- Online International Business Modules: A Title VI Project
>Sarah Singer, Michigan State University

Toward the Creation of an International Business Measurement Repository
>Gangaram Singh, San Diego State University

- Building Entrepreneurial Skills in Niger: Expanding Community Service Learning Abroad
>Lauren Eder and Sigfredo Hernandez, Rider University

SESSION IV-C: THE NRC WEB PORTAL

The Role of the NRCs in the Operation of the Web Portal
>Edna Andrews, Duke University

Format and Capabilities of the NRC Web Portal
>Mark Garbrick, Duke University

SESSION IV-D: LATIN AMERICAN LANGUAGE AND OUTREACH INNOVATIONS

- Report on the First Biennial Symposium on Teaching Indigenous Languages of Latin America (STILLA)
>Serafin Coronel-Molina and Daniel Suslak, Indiana University

Student Advances in Spanish and Intercultural Proficiency through a Title VI Interdisciplinary Study Abroad Course

> Isabel Moreno-Lopez and Tami Kopischke, Goucher College

Technology as the Essential Basis for LAC/LSP

> Nina Garrett, Yale University

SESSION IV-H: REALIZING TITLE VI GOALS FOR INTERNATIONAL EDUCATION THROUGH QUALITY STUDY ABROAD PROGRAMS

- Historical Overview of NRCs and Undergraduate Study Abroad Programming
  > John Metzler, Michigan State University
- Promoting International Competency Through Study Abroad Programming: Case Study MSU's Programming in Africa
  > Cindy Chalou, Michigan State University

Promoting International Competency Through Study Abroad Programming: Case Study of University of Minnesota's Programming in Africa and Asia

> Martha Johnson and Nanette Hanks, University of Minnesota

Friday, March 20, 2009—Session V: 10:20 AM–11:40 AM

SESSION V-A: GLOBAL COMPETITIVENESS

- History and Impacts of Title VI
  > Michael Hitt, Texas A&M University

Current Status and New Directions

> Melissa H. Birch, University of Kansas

SESSION V-B: TECHNOLOGY AND CHINESE LANGUAGE STUDIES

- Evaluating Reading Proficiency Gain and Reading Program Effectiveness: A Three-Tiered Web-Based Assessment Approach
  > Helen Shen and Chen-Hui Tsai, The University of Iowa

The Virtues of Virtual Chinese

> Xiaoliang Li, Georgia Institute of Technology

Infusing New Technologies in Elementary English as a Foreign Language (EFL) Instruction in China: Design of a Blended E-Learning Curriculum TALENT

> Guofang Li, Michigan State University

Innovative Approaches to Chinese Language Teaching and Learning in America

> Christy Lao, San Francisco State University

SESSION V-C: HERITAGE LANGUAGE EDUCATION: THE INTERSECTION OF LINGUISTICS, DEMOGRAPHY, LANGUAGE POLICY, AND PEDAGOGY

The National Survey of Heritage Language Learners: From Survey Data to Pedagogical Implications

    Olga E. Kagan, University of California, Los Angeles

What do Heritage Speakers Know and How Can They (Re-)learn?

    Maria Polinsky, Harvard University

More Speakers, More Places: Heritage Language Vitality Across Suburban Networks

    Gerda de Klerk and Terrence Wiley, Arizona State University

A Task Force for the Preservation of Heritage Language Skills: Findings and Observations

    Catherine W. Ingold, University of Maryland

SESSION V-D: SOCIAL SCIENCE RESEARCH COUNCIL – THE PRODUCTION OF KNOWLEDGE ON WORLD REGIONS

Panel Chair

    Holly Danzeisen, Social Science Research Council

A Reluctant Internationalism: Area Studies and the Social Sciences at U.S. Universities

    Mitchell Stevens, Stanford University and Cynthia Miller-Idriss, New York University

■ Trends in Arabic Language Learning on U.S. Campuses: Needs and Challenges

    Elizabeth A. Anderson, American University, and Jeremy Browne, State University of New York

Middle East Studies—Exploring the Factors Shaping Post September 11, 2001 Knowledge Production

    Jennifer Olmsted, Drew University

Discussant

    Seteney Shami, Social Science Research Council

SESSION V-E: BUILDING PROFESSIONAL, LOCAL AND NATIONAL PARTNERSHIPS: CHALLENGES AND STRATEGIES ADOPTED IN OUTREACH TO NON-TRADITIONAL COMMUNITIES (AFRICA)

Engaging Media and Business Constituencies through Partnerships and Technology: Challenges and Successes

    Agnes Ngoma Leslie, University of Florida

Reflection or Information? Providing Professional Development to Biomedical and Public Health Constituencies

    Barbara S. Anderson, University of North Carolina, Chapel Hill

Working with Publishers: Challenges and Opportunities for Making Maximum Impact

    Barbara B. Brown, Boston University

Title VI Centers and Media Coverage of Crises
> Ali B. Dinar, University of Pennsylvania

SESSION V-F: CROSSING BOUNDARIES: NEW DIRECTIONS IN TITLE VI - INTERNATIONAL STUDIES FROM A CIRCUMPOLAR PERSPECTIVE

Circumpolar Studies
> Nadine C. Fabbi, University of Washington

The Indigenous World
> Daniel Hart, University of Washington

Circumpolar Cooperation
> Duane Smith, Inuit Circumpolar Council

Circumpolar Health
> Mark Oberle, University of Washington

SESSION V-G: COORDINATING STRATEGIC AND THEMATIC DIRECTIONS FOR INTERNATIONAL EDUCATION AT U.S. UNIVERSITIES: THE ROLE OF THE INTERNATIONAL NATIONAL RESOURCE CENTER

The Center for Advanced Study of International Development, Michigan State University
> Robert S. Glew, Michigan State University

The Women and International Development Program, Michigan State University
> Anne Ferguson, Michigan State University

■ Global Studies, University of Wisconsin–Madison
> Amy Stambach, University of Wisconsin–Madison

The Center for the Study of Global Change, Indiana University
> Brian Winchester, Indiana University

SESSION V-H: NATIONAL FOREIGN LANGUAGE CAPACITY AND LANGUAGE COMPETENCE

Collaboration and Innovation: Pathways to Increased Language Competence
> Gilles Bousquet, University of Wisconsin–Madison

■ The Need to Build National Foreign Language Capacity: A Comprehensive National Strategy
> Frederick Jackson, University of Maryland, and Margaret Malone, Center for Applied Linguistics

Future Federal Investments in Language: The Role of Title VI and Fulbright-Hays
> Richard Brecht, University of Maryland

Friday, March 20, 2009—Session VI: 1:10 PM–2:30 PM

SESSION VI-A: LANGUAGE COMPETENCE: PERFORMANCE, PROFICIENCY, AND CERTIFICATION

- History and Impacts of Title VI
    Elaine Tarone, University of Minnesota

- Current Status and New Directions
    Catherine Doughty, University of Maryland

SESSION VI-B: CENTERS FOR INTERNATIONAL BUSINESS EDUCATION (CIBES) AND INTERNATIONALIZING EDUCATION

Benchmarking International Business Education in U.S. Community Colleges
    Tomas Hult, Michigan State University, and William Motz, Lansing Community College
San Diego State University CIBER: Engaging Corporate Partners in the Development of a New Global Entrepreneurship MBA Program
    Mark J. Ballam, San Diego State University
Global Minds, Not Global Buildings: An Internationalization Agenda for 4,000 Business Students
    David Platt, University of Texas, Austin
Internationalizing Higher Education: Overseas Faculty Development in International Business (FDIB) Programs
    Michael Shealy, University of South Carolina

SESSION VI-C: AMERICAN OVERSEAS RESEARCH CENTERS (AORC) AND TITLE VI—SUPPORTING HIGHER EDUCATION INTERNATIONALLY

Panel Chair
    Mary Ellen Lane, Council of American Overseas Research Centers
Building from Title VI: The Experience of the American Center for Mongolian Studies
    Charles Krusekopf, Royal Roads University
- Collaborative Programs and Leveraging Funding: The Contribution of American Overseas Research Centers to International Education and Diplomacy
    Irene B. Romano, American School of Classical Studies, Athens
Increasing Diversity in Participation—A Case Study in Outreach
    Robin Presta, Council of American Overseas Research Centers
- Using New Technology to Increase Access to AORC and Other Host-Country Resources
    Maria Ellis, American Institute for Yemeni Studies
Study Abroad as an Entry Point to Global Issues and a Training Ground for Research
    Ousmane Sène, West African Research Center

SESSION VI-D: NRC CONTRIBUTIONS TO TEACHER EDUCATION PROGRAMS AND INTERNATIONAL OUTREACH

Bridging the Divide: Collaboration between Title VI Area Studies and Thematic Centers and the College of Education at Michigan State University
> Cheryl Bartz, Michigan State University

Preparing for a Global Future: Best Practices for Connecting NRCs to Teacher Education and Preparation
> Katharine Douglass, Michigan State University

■ International Outreach: Best Practices and Future Directions (Africa, Russia, Eurasia, East Asia, and Latin America)
> Tatyana Wilds and Jane Irungu, University of Kansas

International Education and Engagement
> Deborah Gonzales, University of Georgia

SESSION VI-E: TITLE VI GRANTS: LAYING THE GROUNDWORK FOR IMPROVED LANGUAGE SKILLS ASSESSMENT

The Past: A History of Title VI Funded Language Assessment Initiatives
> Elvira Swender, American Council on the Teaching of Foreign Languages

The Present: A National Look at Language Assessment Capabilities
> Helen Hamlyn, Language Testing International

The Research: A Review of Research Related to Title VI Funded Language Assessment Initiatives
> Eric Surface, SWA Consulting

The Future: Title VI Future Initiatives
> Ray T. Clifford, Brigham Young University

SESSION VI-F: INTERNATIONALIZING TEACHER EDUCATION AND THE UNDERGRADUATE CURRICULUM

NRC, Teacher Education Collaboration: Future Directions
> Margo Glew, Michigan State University

Title VI and Teacher Education: International Internships
> Stefanie Kendall, Michigan State University

Internationalizing European Studies: at Home and Abroad
> Philip Ross Shekleton, University of Washington

SESSION VI-G: HISTORICAL PERSPECTIVES ON THE DEVELOPMENT OF LATIN AMERICAN STUDIES PROGRAMS AT U.S. UNIVERSITIES

Panel Chair
> Hannah Covert, University of Florida

■ The Development of Latin American Studies at the University of Florida, 1930–2009
> Paul Losch, University of Florida

Looking Back, Looking Forward: 25 Years of Latin American Studies at the University of Notre Dame
>> Sharon Schierling, University of Notre Dame

■ From a Shared Border to Western Hemisphere Concerns: The History of Latin American Studies at the University of Texas at Austin
>> Carolyn Palaima, University of Texas, Austin

Latin American and Caribbean Studies at the University of Wisconsin
>> Alberto Vargas, University of Wisconsin–Madison

SESSION VI-H: CROSSING BOUNDARIES: MIDDLE EASTERN-AMERICAN INTERSECTIONS

Panel Chair
>> Jonathan Friedlander, University of California, Los Angeles

■ Crossing Boundaries in Action: The Middle East and Middle Eastern American Center
>> Mehdi Bozorgmehr, City University of New York

Linguistic Crossings: Teaching Persian as a Foreign and Heritage Language
>> Kathryn Paul, University of California, Los Angeles

The Politics of Language: Teaching Arabic and More in U.S. High Schools
>> Greta Scharnweber, New York University

Literature in the Classroom: Bridging Middle Eastern and American Cultures
>> Barbara Petzen, Middle East Policy Council, Education

Friday, March 20, 2009: 3:00 PM–4:50 PM

Plenary Panel II: Advancing the Internationalization of Higher Education
>> Jeffrey Riedinger—Michigan State University, Moderator
>> Robert Berdhal—Association of American Universities
>> Maureen Budetti—Director of Student Aid Policy, National Association of Independent Colleges and Universities
>> Constantine Curris—American Association of State Colleges and Universities
>> Madeleine Green—American Council on Education
>> Peter McPherson—Association of Public and Land-Grant Universities

Saturday, March 21, 2009—Session VII: 8:30 AM–9:50 AM

SESSION VII-A: BENCHMARKING AND ASSESSMENT
>> Current Status and New Directions
>>>> Carl Falsgraf, University of Oregon
>> Current Status and New Directions
>>>> LaNitra Walker Berger, National Association for Equal Opportunity in Higher Education

395

★ SESSION VII-B: ROUND TABLE DISCUSSION ON FULBRIGHT-HAYS GROUP
PROJECTS ABROAD: LESSONS LEARNED, INNOVATIVE APPROACHES AND
FUTURE DIRECTIONS
Panel Chairs
> Kristin Janka Millar, Michigan State University, and Michelle Guilfoil, U.S.
> Department of Education
Budget and Recruitment: Issues and Challenges
> Joseph Adjaye, University of Pittsburgh, and John Caldwell, Duke University
Beyond Tourism: Preparation and Planning
> Diane Ruonavaara, Michigan State University

SESSION VII-C: TITLE VI AND THE UNIVERSITY LIBRARY

- Panel Chair
> Lynne Rudasill, University of Illinois, Urbana-Champaign
- Strategic Approaches to Title VI Centers at the University Library
> Paula Kaufman, University of Illinois, Urbana-Champaign
- The Slavic Reference Service—Past and Future
> Helen F. Sullivan, University of Illinois, Urbana-Champaign
- Interdisciplinarity and Multi-Disciplinarity in the Global Studies Library - Chang-
ing Services and Outlook
> Paula Carns, University of Illinois, Urbana-Champaign

SESSION VII-D: TECHNOLOGY AND ARABIC LANGUAGE STUDIES

- The Marhaba! Curriculum and Strategies that Work
> Steven Berbeco, Charlestown High School
CultureTalk Islamic Worlds: Seeing the World through the Eyes of the Other
> Elizabeth Mazzocco, Five Colleges, Incorporated
Regarding TICFIA: International Collaborations and Technological Innovations
> Elizabeth Beaudin, Yale University

SESSION VII-E: FASHIONING GLOBAL COMPETITIVENESS: TITLE VI'S IMPACT
ON THE U.S. APPAREL INDUSTRY

- Apparel and Textile Education in the U.S.—Is it International Enough?
> Marsha Dickson, University of Delaware
- Going Global: Meeting the Demands of an International Industry
> Nate Herman, American Apparel & Footwear Association
- UD's FIBER Grant—A Title VI Grant in Action for the Industry
> Hye-Shin Kim, University of Delaware

SESSION VII-F: THE SOUTHEAST ASIAN STUDIES SUMMER INSTITUTE (SEASSI) AND SOUTH ASIA SUMMER LANGUAGE INSTITUTE (SASLI): NATIONAL SUMMER INTENSIVE LANGUAGE PROGRAMS FOR LESS COMMONLY TAUGHT LANGUAGES (LCTLS)

SEASSI's 25-Year Legacy: Building National Capacity for Research, Business, and International Cooperation with Southeast Asia

Mary Jo Wilson, University of Wisconsin–Madison

■ SASLI: Meeting the Critical National Need for South Asian Language Acquisition and Leading the Way in South Asian Language Assessment and Pedagogy

Laura Hammond, University of Wisconsin–Madison

Saturday, March 21, 2009—Session VIII: 10:10 AM–11:40 AM

SESSION VIII-A: TITLE VI AND NATIONAL AND GLOBAL SECURITY

Current Status and New Directions

Mark Tessler, University of Michigan

Future Directions for Title VI and Fulbright-Hays Programs

■ Current Status and New Directions

William Brustein, University of Illinois, Urbana-Champaign

★ SESSION VIII-B: ROUND TABLE DISCUSSION ON FULBRIGHT-HAYS GROUP PROJECTS ABROAD: LESSONS LEARNED, INNOVATIVE APPROACHES, AND FUTURE DIRECTIONS (CONTINUED)

Implementation and Follow-up

Rachel Weiss, University of Wisconsin–Madison, and Kate Mackay, University of Arizona

Fostering Collaboration with Colleges of Education

Elaine Linn, University of Pittsburgh

SESSION VIII-C: THE PARTNERSHIP FOR GLOBAL LEARNING

Excellence and Equity in International Education

Shari Albright, Asia Society

■ Teacher Preparation for the Global Age: The Imperative for Change

Betsy Devlin-Foltz, Longview Foundation

Going Global: Preparing Our Students for an Interconnected World

Vivien Stewart, Asia Society

The Growth of Chinese in K-12 Schools

Shuhan Wang, Asia Society

SESSION VIII-D: DIGITALIZING THE ARCHIVES

Highlights of Materials and Curriculum Development for Less Commonly Taught Critical Languages: The Evolution of the Digital Media Archive
>Mary Ann Lyman-Hagar, Christopher Brown, and John Vitaglione, San Diego State University

Title VI and Academic Library Support: Traditional Opportunities and the Potential Future
>Gayle A. Williams, Florida International University

Digital Library of the Caribbean: Crossing Borders to Improve International Research and Education
>Brooke Wooldridge, Florida International University

SESSION VIII-E: THE ART OF SUBTITLING: EXPANDING THE RANGE OF SOUTHEAST ASIAN FILM

The Art of Subtitling: Expanding the Range of Southeast Asian Film
>Paul Rausch and Rohayati Paseng, University of Hawai'i, Manoa

Less Commonly Taught Languages Offered in the Title VI National Resource Centers

To address the pressing national needs of U.S. students, faculty, businesses, media, and government for communicating in hundreds of diverse languages around the globe, fifty-three of the nation's leading research universities that receive Title VI National Resource Center (NRC) awards and Foreign Language and Area Studies (FLAS) fellowships taught 167 less commonly taught languages (LCTLs) in the 2006–2007 academic year. Over the longer period of 2000–2007, graduate students at these universities used FLAS fellowships to study more than 150 LCTLs. NRCs at these universities reported that they had the capacity to offer 191 LCTLs during the 2006–2010 NRC and FLAS grant period.

The long-lasting partnership between the Title VI and Fulbright-Hays programs of the U.S. Department of Education and U.S. research universities has created an unparalleled capacity to teach both foreign languages and "area studies" about societies around the world. Indeed, one study estimates that more than 80 percent of all instruction in these less commonly taught languages was at institutions with Title VI-supported centers (excluding the "commonly-taught" languages of French, Spanish, German, and Italian).[1]

This appendix brings together dispersed and complex data about LCTL training being supported by the Title VI NRC and FLAS programs, along with some comparative information about other selected federal language training programs.

In the tables that follow, we offer a summary of all world regions followed by detailed data for each of fourteen world areas designated by Title VI NRCs, including one "International Studies" group of NRCs. (A few universities that have FLAS fellowships but not NRC awards are included as well.) For each world area, we report the number and names of the languages these universities taught, the full list of languages they had available capacity to teach, the course enrollments in those languages, and the number of FLAS fellowships supporting study of the languages by graduate students. We also summarize the languages that are available from the two largest federal language teaching units, the Foreign Service Institute of the Department of State and the Defense Language Institute of the Department of Defense. (Data about some other government-funded programs are not included because they are not publicly available. For example, languages in which fellowships and scholarships have been awarded by the National Security Education Program [NSEP] are not available to the public, and information about National Security Agency [NSA] language instruction is not public.)

List of Tables

Data Sources and Their Interpretation and Limitations

The data for this report are from the International Resource Information System (IRIS) web site of the U.S. Department of Education (US/ED) International

Education Programs Service (IEPS) at www.ieps-iris.org. Here, universities that receive NRC and FLAS awards are required to report annually—to the U.S. Department of Education and the public—about their language offerings and enrollments and other grant activities for all the Title VI and Fulbright-Hays programs. The data that were analyzed were last accessed from this source on December 10, 2008 and January 15, 2010. The academic year 2006–2007 was the most recent academic year for which language enrollments and FLAS awards data were complete at that time. The languages available for instruction are reported in the NRC program abstracts in which each center reports the languages and the countries of that world region for which it has capacity and seeks to offer instruction and research.

Enrollments: The languages are ordered in the tables by their total enrollments, as reported by NRCs to IEPS. The enrollments are by semester; they can be divided by two to roughly estimate years of enrollment. All FLAS fellowship allocations by language are recorded which may include these more commonly taught languages at a more advanced level.

The data that are compiled here from reports by NRCs to the U.S. Department of Education are a uniquely rich source for understanding LCTL instruction at U.S. universities. The Modern Language Association regularly collects language enrollment data from the offices of the registrar at a larger number of U.S. universities. These reports often miss significant information about LCTLs that have low enrollments or are taught in individualized instruction and that often appear in registrars' data simply as "other languages". Mining the reports provided by individual NRCs, as we have done, yields much more detailed data about LCTLs. However, these data contain double-counting of enrollments in some languages. More than two dozen universities have two or more NRCs focused on different world regions, and more than one NRC may report enrollments for languages that are spoken in multiple regions. For example, the same university enrollments in a Portuguese course may be reported by both a Latin America and the Western Europe center; it is impossible to identify students in a single language class who may be studying different world areas.

The IRIS database contains very detailed enrollment data by university and level of language instruction. It was too time-consuming for us to correct for duplicate data and analyze instruction by different levels for all 135 LCTLs at fifty-three institutions included in this report. However, individuals who wish to analyze data about particular languages in greater detail can access all the available data on the IRIS website.

FLAS fellowships: FLAS fellowships for modern language and area study are awarded to individual graduate students by centers at their universities. The fellowships ordinarily are for an academic year of language and area studies or the an 401 academic year equivalent in summer intensive language study. (This differs from language course enrollment data, which are by semester.) Although most FLAS awards are used for language study at the student's own university, some study takes place by distance learning through courses at other universities with Title VI centers on other campuses or in intensive programs abroad in countries where the language is spoken. Also, NRCs focused on several world regions with a large number of LCTLs—including Southeast Asia, South Asia, Africa, and the Middle East—cooperate to offer intensive summer language institutes at one university each year where students can use FLAS fellowships for study, thus using public funds efficiently. The FLAS fellowships used by students at these summer institutes ordinarily are reported by the university from which student receives the FLAS fellowship, not by the NRC hosting the institute. The enrollments at these summer institutes are included in a narrative report by the hosting NRC, but these centers usually do not include these enrollments in the numerical data they enter in the IRIS database. Therefore, FLAS fellowships, but not enrollments, are counted in these important summer institutes.

Languages available to be offered: Languages identified in the tables as being "available" are those that Title VI NRCs state that they have the capacity to teach in their abstract for the 2006–2010 grant period (available on the IRIS website), or in which they report enrollments, or in languages for which FLAS fellowships were awarded. The capacity to offer languages ordinarily requires adequate instructional materials (texts, audio or video files, dictionaries, and target reference grammars) as well as a first-language tutor and a faculty linguist supervisor. Enrollments in languages during a particular time period depend on student demand and available funding. Included in the list of 191 LCTLs available at universities with NRCs are several historical languages that are ancient or extinct, according to Ethnologue (www.ethnologue.com) or are used only for reading ancient texts (e.g., Akkadian, Sumerian, Latin).

Languages that are available for instruction as reported by multiple NRCs focused on different world regions are counted only once in the "Total" row of each table. Thus, we have avoided double-counting of enrollments in languages available across universities for instruction in different area centers that utilize the same language courses. These multicenter languages include, notably, Arabic, Russian, Chinese, Japanese, Korean, and Portuguese.

Comparative data about languages available for instruction at the Foreign Service Institute (FSI) appear in the FSI 2008–2010 course catalog, http://fsitraining. state.gov/catalog/2008_SchCoursesCatalog.pdf (accessed January 12, 2010). The list of languages available at the Defense Language Institute (DLI) is taken from the DLI web site at www.dliflc.edu/academics/academics_index.html (accessed

January 12, 2010). (These 2010 data from DLI and FSI about languages offered are more recent than the information from NRCs.) Information from FSI and DLI about which languages were actually being taught and enrollments in those languages were not available for this report.

Future Data Reporting on the e-LCTL Initiative Web Site

These tables on LCTL capacity of the Title VI centers and any future revisions will be available on the website of the Michigan State University *e-LCTL Initiative* (www.elctl.msu.edu). Already available here are parallel data about LCTL offerings and enrollments during the period 2000–2005 and the essays from NRC and LRC directors of each world region on prioritizing the choice of languages for instruction on their campuses and in summer institutes. Data in this appendix were compiled by Stephen Backman, Joel Christian Reed, Christine E. Root, and David Wiley.

Table E-1. Languages Offered by US/ED Title VI National Resource Centers (NRC) and by the Defense Language and Foreign Service Institutes, 2000–2010[1]

World Area of National Resource Centers	Title VI NRC Languages Taught in 2006-2007	Title VI NRC Languages Available 2006–2007[1]	FSI[2] & DLI[3] Languages Available 2006–2010	All NRC Language Enrollments (semesters) 2006-2007	Title VI FLAS Awards 2006–2007	Title VI FLAS Awards 2000–2007	Percent Title VI FLAS Awards 2000–2007
Africa	25	44	8	4,455	188	1,326	9.3%
Asia	14	21	19	5,439	47	89	0.6
East Asia	17	19	10	33,830	294	1,853	13.1
Southeast Asia	11	12	8	3,678	133	875	6.2
Pacific Islands	4	13	0	537	6	32	0.2
South Asia	17	23	13	3,682	163	1,336	9.4
Inner Asia	15	15	13	428	35	187	1.3
Middle East	19	33	10	14,121	264	2,058	14.5
Russia & Eastern Europe	32	40	30	7,994	289	2,430	17.1
Europe & Russia	22	28	25	13,660	32	251	1.8
Western Europe	23	35	23	76,004	108	900	6.3
Canada	2	6	2	3,528	14	207	1.5
Latin America and Caribbean	14	25	6	87,232	289	1,838	13.0
International Studies	71	80	61	69,936	220	804	5.7
Total All Languages[4]	167 different languages	195 different languages	83 different languages	324,524 enrollments	2,082 awards	14,186 awards	100.0%
Total LCTLs[5]	164 different Languages	191 different languages	79 different languages	112,619 enrollments	1,894 awards	13,203 awards	

[1] Languages are those that Title VI NRCs list as available in their proposal abstracts or that are reported with enrollments or FLAS fellowships allocations in the US/ED IEPS-IRIS website at www.ieps-iris.org/iris/ieps/search.cfm?sort=Institution&type=ADV&tab=BRW&goFind=go&programs=13. Several languages are excluded from the table that are ancient or historic languages according to Ethnologue (www.ethnologue.com) and are used only for reading ancient texts. FLAS awards are not allowed for these languages.

[2] Foreign Service Institute (FSI) data on language offerings available are taken from the FSI 2008–2010 course catalog available on the FSI website at http://fsitraining.state.gov/catalog/2008_SchCoursesCatalog.pdf (last accessed on January 12, 2010). Language is denoted as "available" if either FSI or DLI list it.

[3] Defense Language Institute (DLI) data about languages available are taken from the DLI website at www.dliflc.edu/academics/academics_index.html (last accessed January 12, 2010).

[4] Includes Spanish, French, German, and Italian. The number of languages that overlap world regions are counted only once in the "Total" row; therefore, the total is not the sum of the data in the column. Historic languages are excluded.

[5] "Less Commonly Taught Languages" exclude French, German, Italian, and Spanish.

Table E-2. African Languages Offered, Enrollments, and FLAS Fellowships at 12 Universities with African Title VI NRCs or FLAS Fellowships, 2000–2007

■ – language taught at NRCs in 2006–2007   × – language available 2006–2007

African Language	Available 2006–2007 NRC	Available 2006–2007 FSI/DLI	Semester Enrollments[1] 2000–2007	African NRC FLAS[2] Fellows 2000–2007	FLAS Awards by NRCs in Other Areas 2000–2007[4]
Arabic	■	×	9,794	139	1,482[3]
Arabic, Egyptian	■	×	940	2	0
Arabic, Moroccan	■		398	12	0
Arabic, Sudanese	■		211	21	0
Aribic, Gulf	×		0	4	7
Swahili/kiSwahili	■	×	5,947	451	79
Lingala	■		979	16	1
Yoruba	■		860	61	2
Wolof	■		853	91	5
Zulu	■	×	775	95	6
Akan/Twi	■		686	101	8
Bambara/Bamana	■		593	52	2
Hausa	■	×	282	46	5
Amharic	×		179	34	1
Xhosa	■	×	134	39	0
Afrikaans	×	×	62	9	0
Igbo	■		59	4	0
Shona	■		47	20	6
Chewa/Nyanja	■		31	16	8
Nyanja (taught separately)	■		0	2	0
Fulfulde, Pulaar (Fula/Fulani)	■		26	22	6
Kikuyu/Gikuyu	×		23	7	0
Somali	■		18	17	0
Swati/Siswati	×		16	3	0
Tigrinya	■	×	13	8	0
Luo	×		11	1	0
Malagasy	■		9	7	0
Oromo	×		4	2	0
Tswana/seTswana	■		1	4	0
Mandinka/Mandingo	■		0	7	0
Kongo	■		0	6	0
Ewe	×		0	6	0
Luganda	×		0	4	0
Mbundu (Loanda)	×		0	3	0
Ruanda/Rwanda/Kinyarwanda	×		0	3	0
Dogon	■		0	2	0
Masaai	×		0	2	0
Abron	×		0	2	0

(continued)

Table E-2. African Languages Offered, Enrollments, and FLAS Fellowships at 12 Universities with African Title VI NRCs or FLAS Fellowships, 2000–2007 (*continued*)

■ – language taught at NRCs in 2006–2007   × – language available 2006–2007

African Language	Available 2006–2007		Semester Enrollments[1] 2000–2007	African NRC FLAS[2] Fellows 2000–2007	FLAS Awards by NRCs in Other Areas 2000–2007[4]
	NRC	FSI/DLI			
Sotho/seSotho	×		0	1	0
Dagbani	×		0	1	0
Acholi	×		0	0	0
Bemba	×		0	0	0
Temne	×		0	0	0
West African Krio	×		0	0	0
African LCTLs unspecified	×		178	3	0
Total Available and Enrollment	**44**	**8**	**23,129**	**1,326**	**1,618**

[1] Enrollments are in semesters; divide these numbers by two to obtain estimated academic years of enrollment.

[2] FLAS fellowships are for an academic year (two semesters/three quarters) or summer intensive study.

[3] Arabic enrollments in multiple world areas include Modern Standard, Egyptian, Algerian-Saharan, Sudanese, Gulf, Qur'anic, and Moroccan. African centers awarded 139 of the 1,621 total Arabic FLAS Fellowships. Middle East, International, and other centers awarded the balance of 1,482.

[4] FLAS fellowships for African languages may be offered by NRCs in other world areas or the International Studies category.

Table E-3. Asian Languages Offered, Enrollments, and FLAS Fellowships at Three Universities with Pan-Asia Title VI NRCs or FLAS Fellowships, 2000–2007

■ – language taught at NRCs in 2006–2007   x – language available 2006–2007

Asian Languages in Pan-Asia NRCs	Available 2006–2007		Semester Enrollments[1] 2000–2007	Asian NRC FLAS[2] Fellows 2000–2007	FLAS Awards by NRCs in Other Areas 2000–2007[3]
	NRC	FSI/DLI			
Japanese	■	x	1,920	20	640
Chinese (Mandarin)	■	x	1,468	26	825
Arabic, modern standard	■	x	837	9	1,520
Korean	■	x	390	2	384
Hindi	■	x	249	16	599
Hmong	■		00	1	17
Vietnamese	■	x	87	1	158
Arabic, Egyptian	■	x	22	0	19
Tagalog/Filipino	■	x	22	2	111
Thai	■	x	16	1	222
Japanese, Classical	x		20	0	0
Chinese, Classical	x		17	0	1
Nepali	■	x	7	1	70
Turkish	■	x	0	3	330
Urdu	■	x	0	4	207
Tibetan	■	x	0	2	175
Indonesian	x	x	0	1	247
Farsi, Eastern	x	x	0	0	0
Farsi, Western	x	x	0	0	4
Uzbek	x	x	0	0	140
Vietnamese	x	x	0	0	158
Total Available and Enrollment	**21**	**19**	**5,402**	**89**	**5,827**

[1] Enrollments are in semesters; divide these numbers by two to obtain estimated academic years of enrollment.

[2] FLAS fellowships are for an academic year (two semesters/three quarters) or summer intensive study.

[3] FLAS fellowships for Asian languages may be offered by NRCs in other world areas or the International Studies category.

Table E-4. East Asian Languages Offered, Enrollments, and FLAS Fellowships at 21 Universities with East Asian Studies Title VI NRCs or FLAS Fellowships, 2000–2007

■ - language taught at NRCs in 2006–2007   × - language available 2006–2007

East Asian Languages	Available 2006–2007		Semester Enrollments[1] 2000–2007	East Asian NRC FLAS[2] Fellows 2000–2007	FLAS Awards by NRCs in Other Areas 2000–2007[3]
	NRC	FSI/DLI			
Japanese	■	×	80,372	612	48
Chinese, Mandarin	■	×	70,105	779	72
Chinese, Cantonese Yue	■	×	1,271	6	0
Chinese, Classical	■		2,934	1	0
Chinese, Gan Minh (Taiwanese)	■		652	2	0
Chinese, Jinyu	■		0	1	0
Chinese, Min Bei	■		0	1	0
Taiwanese	■		31	0	0
Korean	■	×	22,626	371	15
Japanese, Classical	■		1,332	0	0
Tibetan	■	×	696	48	129
Vietnamese	■	×	276	6	153
Okinawan, Central	■		73	1	0
Tagalog (Pilipino)	■	×	65	0	113
Uyghur	■		57	13	28
Thai	■	×	43	2	220
Mongolian (Halh)	■	×	8	9	14
Nepali	×	×	0	1	68
Sanskrit	×		129	0	21
Total Available and Enrollment	**19**	**10**	**180,670**	**1,853**	**881**

[1] Enrollments are in semesters; divide these numbers by two to obtain estimated academic years of enrollment.

[2] FLAS fellowships are for an academic year (two semesters/three quarters) or summer intensive study.

[3] FLAS fellowships for East Asian languages may be offered by NRCs in other world areas or the International Studies category.

Table E-5. Southeast Asian Languages Offered, Enrollments, and FLAS Fellowships at Eight Universities with Southeast Asian Title VI NRCs or FLAS Fellowships, 2000–2007

■ – language taught at NRCs in 2006–2007   × – language available 2006–2007

Southeast Asian Language	Available 2006–2007		Semester Enrollments[1] 2000–2007	Southeast Asian NRC FLAS[2] Fellows 2000–2007	FLAS Awards by NRCs in Other Areas 2000–2007[3]
	NRC	FSI/DLI			
Japanese	■	×	1,920	20	640
Tagalog (Pilipino)	■	×	7,844	110	3
Vietnamese	■	×	6,351	146	7
Thai	■	×	3,462	218	5
Indonesian	■	×	2,753	239	8
Ilocano	■	×	2,567	0	0
Khmer, Central (Cambodia)	■		856	70	1
Burmese	■	×	682	47	0
Chinese, Mandarin	■	×	443	0	851
Hmong	■		239	16	2
Lao	■	×	82	21	0
Javanese	■		8	6	0
Other			6	2	0
Total Available and Enrollment	**11**	**8**	**25,293**	**875**	**877**

[1] Enrollments are in semesters; divide these numbers by two to obtain estimated academic years of enrollment.

[2] FLAS fellowships are for an academic year (two semesters/three quarters) or summer intensive study.

[3] FLAS fellowships for Southeast Asian languages may be offered by NRCs in other world areas or the International Studies category.

Table E-6. Pacific Island Languages Offered, Enrollments, and FLAS Fellowships at Three Universities with Pacific Island Title VI NRCs or FLAS Fellowships, 2000–2007

■ – language taught at NRCs in 2006–2007   × – language available 2006–2007

Pacific Island Languages	Available 2006–2007		Semester Enrollments[1] 2000–2007	Pacific Island NRC FLAS[2] Fellows 2000–2007	FLAS Awards by NRCs in Other Areas 2000–2007[3]
	NRC	FSI/DLI			
Japanese	■	×	1,920	20	640
Samoan	■		78	16	0
Tahitian	■		35	11	0
Tongan (Tonga)	×		30	0	2
Chamorro	×		28	0	0
Maori	■		20	3	1
Marshallese	■		0	2	0
Chamorro	×		0	0	0
Chuuk (Chuukese)	×		0	0	0
Fijian	×		0	0	0
Marquesan	×		0	0	0
Palauan	×		0	0	0
Polynesian	×		0	0	0
Tok Pisin	×		0	0	0
Total Available and Enrollment	**13**	**0**	**191**	**32**	**3**

[1] Enrollments are in semesters; divide these numbers by two to obtain estimated academic years of enrollment.

[2] FLAS fellowships are for an academic year (two semesters/three quarters) or summer intensive study.

[3] FLAS fellowships for Pacific Island languages may be offered by NRCs in other world areas or in the International Studies category.

Table E-7. South Asian Languages Offered, Enrollments, and FLAS Fellowships at 13 Universities with South Asian Title VI NRCs or FLAS Fellowships, 2000–2007

■ – language taught at NRCs in 2006–2007   × – language available 2006–2007

South Asian Languages	Available 2006–2007 NRC	FSI/DLI	Semester Enrollments[1] 2000–2007	South Asian NRC FLAS[2] Fellows 2000–2007	FLAS Awards by NRCs in Other Areas 2000–2007[3]
Hindi	■	×	1,436	562	53
Persian	■	×	566	26	313
Urdu	■	×	452	205	6
Sanskrit	■		360	21	1
Tamil	■	×	281	153	2
Bengali	■	×	95	74	3
Malayalam	■	×	74	23	0
Panjabi, Eastern	■	×	70	6	0
Panjabi, Western (Lahnda)	■		0	1	0
Tibetan	■	×	50	114	63
Gujarati	■	×	43	12	0
Marathi	■		31	18	0
Nepali	■	×	19	67	4
Pali	■		18	1	0
Telugu	■	×	17	12	0
Sinhala/Singhalese	■	×	9	20	0
Kannada	■		3	3	0
Pashto	×	×	0	6	4
Ngala (Bangala)	×		0	4	0
Kashmiri	×		0	1	0
Khmer, Central (Cambodian)	×		0	1	70
Newari	×		0	1	0
Oriya	×		0	1	0
Other			0	4	0
Total Available and Enrollment	**23**	**13**	**3,524**	**1,336**	**519**

[1] Enrollments are in semesters; divide these numbers by two to obtain estimated academic years of enrollment.
[2] FLAS fellowships are for an academic year (two semesters/three quarters) or summer intensive study.
[3] FLAS fellowships for South Asian languages may be offered by NRCs in other world areas or the International Studies category.

Table E-8. Inner Asia Languages Offered, Enrollments, and FLAS Fellowships at the One University with an Inner Asia Title VI NRC and FLAS Fellowships, 2000–2007

■ – language taught at NRCs in 2006–2007   × – language available 2006–2007

Inner Asia Languages	Available 2006–2007		Semester Enrollments[1] 2000–2007	Inner Asian NRC FLAS[2] Fellows 2000–2007	FLAS Awards by NRCs in Other Areas 2000–2007[3]
	NRC	FSI/DLI			
Persian	■	×	75	7	332
Turkish	■	×	57	8	347
Uzbek	■	×	53	42	98
Uyghur	■		44	19	22
Hungarian	■	×	36	15	58
Kazakh	■	×	33	26	20
Tibetan	■	×	28	13	164
Mongolian (Halh)	■	×	21	12	11
Finnish	■	×	17	4	11
Pashto	■	×	15	4	6
Tajiki (Persian)	■	×	14	16	16
Azeri/Azerbaijani	■	×	14	9	6
Estonian	■	×	11	6	12
Turkmen	■	×	10	6	0
Yakut	■		0	0	0
Total Available and Enrollment	**15**	**13**	**428**	**187**	**1,103**

[1] Enrollments are in semesters; divide these numbers by two to obtain estimated academic years of enrollment.

[2] FLAS fellowships are for an academic year (two semesters/three quarters) or summer intensive study.

[3] FLAS fellowships for Inner Asian languages may be offered by NRCs in other world areas or the International Studies category.

Table E-9. Middle Eastern Languages Offered, Enrollments, and FLAS Fellowships at 17 Universities Middle East Title VI NRCs or FLAS Fellowships, 2000–2007

■ – language taught at NRCs in 2006–2007   × – language available 2006–2007
+ – historic language

Middle Eastern Languages	Available 2006–2007 NRC	Available 2006–2007 FSI/DLI	Semester Enrollments[1] 2000–2007	Middle Eastern NRC FLAS[2] Fellows 2000–2007	FLAS Awards by NRCs in Other Areas 2000–2007[3]
Arabic, Modern Standard	■	×	7,391	1,323	345
Arabic, North Levantine	■	×	50	1	0
Arabic, Levantine Bedawi	■		43	8	0
Arabic, Egyptian	■	×	110	17	2
Arabic, Moroccan	×		0	16	1
Arabic, Gulf	×		0	7	0
Arabic, South Levantine	×		0	2	0
Arabic, Algerian	×		0	1	0
Arabic, Tunisian	×		0	1	0
Arabic, Iraqi Mesopotamian	■	×	23	0	0
Hebrew	■	×	2,379	108	3
Persian/Farsi	■	×	2,053	293	46
Farsi, Western	×		0	4	0
Turkish	■	×	865	240	115
Ancient Egyptian +			455	17	0
Hebrew, Biblical +			299	0	0
Urdu	■	×	220	2	209
Akkadian +			178	0	0
Bosnian	■	×	170	0	17
Armenian	×	×	168	7	12
Armenian, Eastern	×	×	247	0	0
Armenian, Western	×		61	0	0
Aramaic	×		136	0	0
Hindi	■	×	100	0	578
Uzbek	■	×	80	5	135
Hieratic +			75	0	0
Syriac	×		43	0	0
Ugaritic	×		43	0	0
Assyrian	×		35	0	0
Hittite +			35	0	0
Coptic	■		20	0	0
Slavic (Serbo-Croatian)	■	×	15	0	0
Sumerian +			15	0	0
Armenian, Classical +			5	0	0
Yiddish	■		3	0	38
Greek	■	×	2	0	31
Hazaragi	■		2	0	0

(continued)

Table E-9. Middle Eastern Languages Offered, Enrollments, and FLAS Fellowships at 17 Universities Middle East Title VI NRCs or FLAS Fellowships, 2000–2007 (*continued*)

■ – language taught at NRCs in 2006–2007   × – language available 2006–2007
+ – historic language

Middle Eastern Languages	Available 2006–2007		Semester Enrollments[1] 2000–2007	Middle Eastern NRC FLAS[2] Fellows 2000–2007	FLAS Awards by NRCs in Other Areas 2000–2007[3]
	NRC	FSI/DLI			
Tajiki (Tajik)	■	×	0	3	29
Berber	×		0	1	0
Uyghur (Uighur)	■		0	1	40
Other			0	1	0
Total Available and Enrollment	**33**	**16**	**15,361**	**2,058**	**1,601**

[1] Enrollments are in semesters; divide these numbers by two to obtain estimated academic years of enrollment.

[2] FLAS fellowships are for an academic year (two semesters/three quarters) or summer intensive study.

[3] FLAS fellowships for Middle Eastern languages may be offered by NRCs in other world areas or the International Studies category.

Table E-10. Russian and Eastern European Languages Offered, Enrollments, and FLAS Fellowships at 21 Universities with Russian and Eastern European Title VI NRCs or FLAS Fellowships, 2000–2007

■ – language taught at NRCs in 2006–2007 × – language available 2006–2007
+ – historic language

Russian and Eastern European Languages	Available 2006–2007 NRC	Available 2006–2007 FSI/DLI	Semester Enrollments[1] 2000–2007	Russian and Eastern European NRC FLAS[2] Fellows 2000–2007	FLAS Awards by NRCs in Other Areas 2000–2007[3]
Russian	■	×	4,401	1,082	115
Polish	■	×	664	261	42
Turkish	■	×	372	48	307
Persian	■	×	368	1	338
Serbo-Croatian (Serbian)	■	×	345	249	25
Croatian	■	×	5	50	4
Czech	■	×	304	213	20
Greek	■	×	200	6	25
Hungarian	■	×	164	50	23
Yiddish	■		114	21	17
Armenian	■		113	5	11
Romanian	■	×	110	51	9
Ukrainian	■	×	98	97	6
Uzbek	■	×	82	91	49
Bosnian	■	×	58	14	3
Uyghur	■		58	8	33
Bulgarian	■	×	34	27	0
Latvian	■	×	33	5	0
Georgian	■	×	29	25	3
Azeri/Azerbaijani	■	×	28	6	9
Slovak	■	×	28	14	0
Tajiki	■		27	11	21
Slavonic, Old Church +	×		26	0	0
Estonian	■	×	23	9	9
Lithuanian	■	×	22	16	2
Macedonian	■	×	19	15	0
Finnish	■	×	18	0	15
Kazakh	■	×	16	17	29
Turkmen	■	×	10	0	6
Mongolian (Halh)	■	×	8	1	22
Albanian	■	×	6	5	3
Kirghiz	■	×	1	6	0
Romani	×		0	8	0
Slovenian	×	×	0	9	0
Buriat	×		0	5	0

(*continued*)

Table E-10. Russian and Eastern European Languages Offered, Enrollments, and FLAS Fellowships at 21 Universities with Russian and Eastern European Title VI NRCs or FLAS Fellowships, 2000–2007 (*continued*)

■ – language taught at NRCs in 2006–2007   × – language available 2006–2007
+ – historic language

Russian and Eastern European Languages	Available 2006–2007		Semester Enrollments[1] 2000–2007	Russian and Eastern European NRC FLAS[2] Fellows 2000–2007	FLAS Awards by NRCs in Other Areas 2000–2007[3]
	NRC	FSI/DLI			
Belarusan	×	×	0	1	0
Chechen	×		0	1	0
Chinese (Mandarin)	×	×	0	1	850
Rejang	×		0	1	0
Total Available and Enrollment	**39**	**30**	**7,784**	**2,430**	**1,996**

[1] Enrollments are in semesters; divide these numbers by two to obtain estimated academic years of enrollment.

[2] FLAS fellowships are for an academic year (two semesters/three quarters) or summer intensive study.

[3] FLAS fellowships for Russian and Eastern European languages may be offered by NRCs in other world areas or the International Studies category.

Table E-11: European and Russian Languages Offered, Enrollments, and FLAS Fellowships at Three Universities with Europe and Russia Title VI NRCs or FLAS Fellowships, 2000–2007

■ – language taught at NRCs in 2006–2007   x – language available 2006–2007
+ – historic language

European and Russian Languages	Available 2006–2007 NRC	Available 2006–2007 FSI/DLI	Semester Enrollments[1] 2000–2007	Russian and Eastern European NRC FLAS[2] Fellows 2000–2007	FLAS Awards by NRCs in Other Areas 2000–2007[3]
Spanish	■	x	5,284	10	307
French	■	x	2,673	38	238
Italian	■	x	1,990	26	126
Russian	■	x	687	63	1,134
German	■	x	681	30	208
Armenian	■	x	300	4	12
Greek	■	x	134	0	31
Dutch/Flemish	■	x	82	12	70
Czech	■	x	73	3	230
Romanian	■	x	64	5	55
Polish	■	x	60	15	288
Swedish	■	x	55	2	50
Turkish	■	x	46	6	349
Serbo-Croatian (Serbian)	■	x	31	14	260
Yiddish	■		31	0	38
Catalan – Valencian – Balear	■		29	4	17
Portuguese	■	x	24	8	912
Hungarian	■	x	23	2	71
Latvian	■	x	9	0	5
Estonian	■	x	4	0	18
Slavic	■		2	0	0
Kazakh	x	x	0	2	44
Ukrainian	■	x	0	2	101
Bengali	x	x	0	1	76
Croatian	x	x	0	1	50
Finnish	x	x	0	1	14
Georgian	x	x	0	1	27
Tamil	x	x	0	1	154
Total Available and Enrollment	**28[4]**	**25**	**12,282[5]**	**251**	**4,885**

[1] Enrollments are in semesters; divide these numbers by two to obtain estimated academic years of enrollment. Centers may report no enrollments in a language for which they grant a FLAS Fellowship to a student for study in a summer intensive language institute or another institution.

[2] FLAS fellowships are for an academic year (two semesters/three quarters) or summer intensive study.

[3] FLAS fellowships for European and Russian languages may be offered by NRCs in other world areas or the International Studies category.

[4] Includes four commonly taught languages (French, German, Italian, Spanish).

[5] Includes 10,628 enrollments in commonly taught languages.

Table E-12. European Languages Offered, Enrollments, and FLAS Fellowships at 11 Universities with West European/European Title VI NRCs or FLAS Fellowships, 2000–2007

■ – language taught at NRCs in 2006–2007   × – language available 2006–2007
+ – historic language

European Languages	Available 2006–2007		Semester Enrollments[1] 2000–2007	European NRC FLAS[2] Fellows 2000–2007	FLAS Awards by NRCs in Other Areas 2000–2007[3]
	NRC	FSI/DLI			
Spanish	■	×	304,962	38	279
Italian	■	×	72,021	120	32
German	■	×	69,716	202	36
Portuguese	■	×	24,503	54	866
French	■	×	7,945	131	145
Greek	■	×	5,693	25	6
Swedish	■	×	4,451	50	2
Norwegian	■	×	3,527	23	0
Russian	■	×	3,322	21	1,176
Dutch/Flemish	■	×	2,472	64	18
Gaelic (Irish)	×		1,538	20	0
Gaelic (Scottish)	×			2	0
Danish	■	×	1,487	22	0
Finnish	■	×	1,295	10	5
Polish	■	×	1,238	18	285
Latin +	■		373	0	0
Czech	■	×	360	11	222
Serbo-Croatian	■	×	323	4	270
Turkish	■	×	320	12	343
Hungarian	×	×	249	1	72
Catalan–Valencian–Balear	■		247	17	4
Yiddish	■		170	16	22
Latvian	■	×	155	0	5
Icelandic	■	×	123	10	0
Lithuanian	■	×	75	2	16
Slovak	×	×	69	0	14
Estonian	■	×	53	0	18
Basque	×		0	6	1
Bosnian	×	×	0	2	15
Arabic, Modern Standard	×	×	0	11	3,457
Arabic, Moroccan	×		0	1	16
Welsh	×		0	3	0

Table E-12. European Languages Offered, Enrollments, and FLAS Fellowships at 11 Universities with West European/European Title VI NRCs or FLAS Fellowships, 2000–2007 (*continued*)

■ – language taught at NRCs in 2006–2007   × – language available 2006–2007
+ – historic language

European Languages	Available 2006–2007		Semester Enrollments[1] 2000–2007	European NRC FLAS[2] Fellows 2000–2007	FLAS Awards by NRCs in Other Areas 2000–2007[3]
	NRC	FSI/DLI			
Hebrew	×		0	2	109
Romanian	×		0	1	59
Faroese	×		0	1	0
Total Available and Enrollments	**35[4]**	**23**	**506,687[5]**	**900**	**7,493**

[1] Enrollments are in semesters; divide these numbers by two to obtain estimated academic years of enrollment. Centers may report no enrollments in a language for which they grant a FLAS Fellowship to a student for study in a summer intensive language institute or another institution.

[2] FLAS fellowships are for an academic year (two semesters/three quarters) or summer intensive study.

[3] FLAS fellowships for European languages may be offered by NRCs in other world areas or the International Studies category.

[4] Excludes one historic language (Latin).

[5] Includes 454,674 enrollments in commonly taught languages.

Table E-13. Canadian Languages Offered, Enrollments, and FLAS Fellowships at Two Universities with Canadian Title VI NRCs or FLAS Fellowships, 2000–2007

■ – language taught at NRCs in 2006–2007   x – language available 2006–2008

Canadian Languages	Available 2006–2007		Semester Enrollments[1] 2000–2007	Canadian NRC FLAS[2] Fellows 2000–2007	FLAS Awards by NRCs in Other Areas 2000–2007[3]
	NRC	FSI/DLI			
French	■	x	3,444	95	181
Mohawk	x		5	1	0
Inuktitut (Eskimo)	x		0	8	0
Japanese	x	x	0	2	658
Dan	x		0	1	0
Friulian	■		1	0	0
Total Available and Enrollment	**6**	**2**	**3,450**	**207**	**839**

[1] Title VI NRCs reported enrollments in semesters; therefore, these numbers need to be divided by two to obtain academic years of enrollment. Centers may report no enrollments in a language for which they grant a FLAS fellowship to a student for study in a summer intensive language insititute or another institution.

[2] NRCs reported FLAS fellow awards in two semester units or academic year units.

[3] FLAS fellowships for languages taught for Canada may be offered for use in other world areas by other NRCs.

Table E-15. Languages Offered, Enrollments, and FLAS Fellowships at Nine Universities with International Studies Title VI NRCs or FLAS Fellowships, 2000–2007

■ – language taught at NRCs in 2006–2007   × – language available 2006–2007

International Center Languages	Available 2006–2007 NRC	Available 2006–2007 FSI/DLI	Semester Enrollments[1] 2000–2007	International NRC FLAS[2] Fellows 2000–2007	FLAS Awards by NRCs in Other Areas 2000–2007[3]
Spanish	■	×	24,467	57	261
French	■	×	8,388	12	254
Italian	■	×	4,404	6	147
Japanese	■	×	4,354	26	25
German	■	×	4,033	6	231
Chinese (Mandarin)	■	×	3,925	45	782
Arabic (Standard)	■	×	2,456	186	1,372
Russian	■	×	1,991	31	1,088
Portuguese	■	×	1,554	88	828
Korean	■	×	1,080	13	178
Hebrew	■	×	1,000	1	100
Swahili	■	×	826	79	409
Hindi	■	×	823	37	513
Latin +	■		429	0	0
Swedish	■	×	395	0	52
Persian	■	×	393	12	313
Norwegian	■	×	323	0	23
Polish	■	×	310	9	261
Vietnamese	■	×	253	6	151
Turkish	■	×	234	38	311
Dutch/Flemish	■	×	213	6	77
Danish	■	×	165	0	36
Finnish	■	×	147	0	29
Greek	■	×	143	0	28
Tagalog/Filipino	■	×	140	1	115
Czech	■	×	104	6	199
Thai	■	×	87	2	276
Zulu	■	×	86	6	84
Lingala	■	×	68	1	13
Kazakh	■	×	64	1	42
Serbo-Croatian	■	×	55	7	248
Wolof	■		54	5	83
Slavic	■		53	0	0
Uyghur	■	×	51	0	37
Urdu	■	×	46	0	210
Uzbek	■	×	45	2	137
Romanian	■	×	44	3	48
Bosnian	■	×	39	1	16

Table E-14. Latin American and Caribbean Languages Offered, Enrollments, and FLAS Fellowships at 23 Universities with Latin American and Caribbean Title VI N or FLAS Fellowships, 2000–2007

■ – language taught at NRCs in 2006–2007   × – language available 2006–2007

Latin American and Caribbean Languages	Available 2006–2007 NRC	Available 2006–2007 FSI/DLI	Semester Enrollments[1] 2000–2007	Latin American and Caribbean NRC FLAS[2] Fellows 2000–2007	FLAS A by NR Other 2000
Spanish	■	×	776,702	212	
Portuguese[3]	■	×	37,771	770	
Haitian Creole French	■	×	1,753	93	
French	■	×	707	0	
Maya[4]	■		555	353	
Quechua (Ayacucho)	■		466	61	
Quechua (Quichua)	■		405	63	
Quechua (Cuzco)	■		342	62	
Quechua	■	×	186	55	
Nahuatl	×		150	44	
Mixtec	■		114	81	
Catalan–Valencian–Balear	×		114	0	
Tohono O'Odham	×		77	0	
Aymara	■	×	54	13	
Garifuna	×		35	2	
Zapotec	■		26	16	
Cakchiquel	■		14	0	
Inga	×		10	0	
Quichi (Maya Quichi)	■		10	0	
Waorani	×		1	0	
Guarani	×		0	7	
Cha'palaachi (Chachi)	×		0	1	
Chatino	×		0	3	
Iquito	×		0	1	
Miskitu (Miskito)	×		0	1	
Total Available and Enrollment	**25**	**6**	**819,492**	**1,838**	

[1] Enrollments are in semesters; divide these numbers by two to obtain estimated academic years of enrollment
[2] FLAS fellowships are for an academic year (two semesters/three quarters) or summer intensive study.
[3] NRC enrollment reports mix the data of Brazilian Portuguese and Iberian, African, or other Portuguese.
[4] Maya includes Maya, Maya, Mam 3 FLAS; Maya, Quiché (K'iche') 54 FLAS awards; Cakchiquel (Caqchikel) 13 FLAS; and Maya, Yucatec with 42 FLAS awards and an addition 130 uncategorized "Maya."
[5] FLAS fellowships for Latin American and Caribbean languages may be offered by NRCs in other world area Studies category.

Table E-15. Languages Offered, Enrollments, and FLAS Fellowships at Nine Universities with International Studies Title VI NRCs or FLAS Fellowships, 2000–2007 (*continued*)

■ – language taught at NRCs in 2006–2007   x – language available 2006–2007

International Center Languages	Available 2006–2007 NRC	Available 2006–2007 FSI/DLI	Semester Enrollments[1] 2000–2007	International NRC FLAS[2] Fellows 2000–2007	FLAS Awards by NRCs in Other Areas 2000–2007[3]
Akan/Twi	■		34	8	101
Catalan	■		34	0	35
Croatian	■	x	32	3	46
Yiddish	■		31	1	36
Tibetan	■	x	27	0	152
Latvian	■	x	23	0	5
Maya	■		22	3	354
Estonian	■	x	22	3	13
Ukrainian	■	x	20	4	93
Mongolian (Halh)	■	x	19	1	17
Hausa	■	x	19	5	41
Georgian	■	x	18	2	25
Bengali	■	x	17	2	72
Pashto	■	x	15	0	10
Azeri (Azerbaijani)	■	x	14	0	14
Tajiki	■		14	2	31
Haitian Creole French	■	x	13	4	93
Macedonian	■	x	13	0	12
Venda	■		13	0	0
Bulgarian	■	x	10	0	38
Kurdish	■	x	9	1	0
Chewa/Nyanja	■		8	8	16
Albanian	■	x	6	3	11
Icelandic	■	x	7	0	10
Nepali	■	x	6	2	63
Pali	■	x	4	0	1
Quechua	x	x	2	6	241
Yoruba	x		1	2	53
Indonesian	■	x	0	7	247
Fula / Pulaar	x		0	6	0
Shona	x		0	6	16
Hungarian	■	x	0	5	60
Arabic (Egyptian)	x	x	0	5	0
Arabic (Moroccan)	■		0	4	0
Arabic (Omani)	x		0	2	0
Bamana/Bambara	■		0	2	46
Sesotho	x		0	2	0

(*continued*)

Table E-15. Languages Offered, Enrollments, and FLAS Fellowships at Nine Universities with International Studies Title VI NRCs or FLAS Fellowships, 2000–2007 (*continued*)

■ – language taught at NRCs in 2006–2007   × – language available 2006–2007

International Center Languages	Available 2006–2007 NRC	Available 2006–2007 FSI/DLI	Semester Enrollments[1] 2000–2007	International NRC FLAS[2] Fellows 2000–2007	FLAS Awards by NRCs in Other Areas 2000–2007[3]
Tongan (Tonga)	×		0	2	0
Basque	×		0	1	8
Chinese (Xiang)			0	1	0
Amharic	×	×	0	1	30
Galician			0	1	0
Guarani	×	×	0	1	7
Hmong	■		0	1	16
Maori	×		0	1	3
Tamil	×	×	0	1	144
Armenian	■		0	0	3
Other			0	2	0
Total Available and Enrollments	**81**	**61**	**63,695[4]**	**804**	**11,140**

[1] Enrollments are in semesters; divide these numbers by two to obtain estimated academic years of enrollment.

[2] FLAS fellowships are for an academic year (two semesters/three quarters) or summer intensive study.

[3] FLAS fellowships for languages offered by International Studies centers may be offered by NRCs in all other world areas.

[4] Enrollments of 41,292 are reported in the more commonly taught languages of French, German, Italian, and Spanish.

Acknowledgment

Christine E. Root assisted with many aspects of the data analysis and preparation of this appendix.

Notes

1 Brecht, Richard D. and William P. Rivers. 2000. *Language and National Security in the 21st Century: The Role of Title VI/Fulbright-Hays in Supporting National Language Capacity.* Dubuque, IA: Kendall/Hunt Pub. Co.

About the Contributors

LaNitra Berger is Director of Leadership and International Programs at the National Association for Equal Opportunity in Higher Education.

Anne H. Betteridge is Director of the Center for Middle Eastern Studies and Associate Professor of Practice in the Department of Near Eastern Studies at the University of Arizona.

Melissa H. Birch is Associate Professor of Business and Director of the Center for International Business at the University of Kansas.

William I. Brustein is Vice Provost for Global Strategies and International Affairs at Ohio State University.

Craig Calhoun is President of the Social Science Research Council and University Professor of the Social Sciences and Director of the Institute for Public Knowledge at New York University.

Catherine J. Doughty is Senior Research Scientist and Area Director for Second Language Acquisition at the Center for Advanced Study of Language at the University of Maryland.

Carl Falsgraf is Director of the Center for Applied Second Language Studies and Director of the Oregon Chinese Flagship at the University of Oregon.

Robert S. Glew is director of the Center for Advanced Study of International Development and Associate Professor of Anthropology at Michigan State University.

Michael A. Hitt is Distinguished Professor of Management at Texas A&M University, where he holds the Joe B. Foster Chair in Business Leadership.

Michael D. Kennedy is Professor of Sociology and International Studies and the Howard R. Swearer Director of the Watson Institute for International Studies at Brown University.

Richard D. Lambert formerly was Professor of Sociology, Chairman of the South Asia Regional Studies Department, and Director of the Office of International Programs at the University of Pennsylvania. He also served as President of the American Academy of Political and Social Science.

Gilbert W. Merkx is Professor of the Practice of Sociology, Director of the Center for International Studies, and Vice Provost for International Affairs at Duke University.

Patrick O'Meara is Vice President for International Affairs, Professor of Political Science, and Professor in the School of Public and Environmental Affairs at Indiana University-Bloomington.

Nancy L. Ruther is Associate Director of the Whitney and Betty MacMillan Center for International and Area Studies at Yale University.

Elaine E. Tarone is the Director of the Center for Advanced Research on Language Acquisition, a USDE Title VI Language Resource Center housed in the Office of International Programs at the University of Minnesota. She is also Distinguished Teaching Professor in Second Language Studies at the University of Minnesota.

Mark Tessler is the Samuel J. Eldersveld Collegiate Professor of Political Science, Vice Provost for International Affairs, and Director of the International Institute at the University of Michigan.

David S. Wiley is Professor of Sociology and African Studies at Michigan State University. He was co-chair of the Council of National Resource Centers until 2008.

Index